THE TIME OF TEA

TRANSLATED BY
ROBIN BUSS
ALEXANDRA CAMPBELL
AND EMILY READ

EDITED BY ABIGAIL S. LANG

30, RUE DE CHARONNE
75011 PARIS

ISBN 2-84576-009-4

PRINTED & BOUND IN ITALY

THE TIME
OF
TEA

DOMINIQUE T. PASQUALINI
writing and layout

BRUNO SUET
photographs

VILO
PUBLISHING

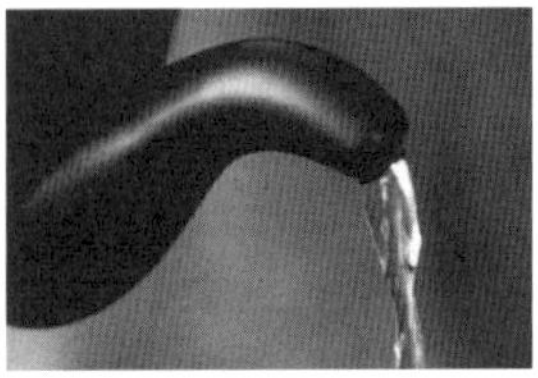

T

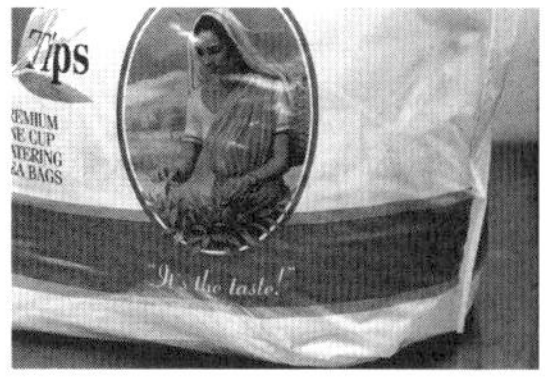

TEA?

End of Story

The thirtieth of June, nineteen ninety-eight. The event rated no more than a brief mention in a few quality newspapers, the sort of news item where the editor does not even take the trouble to alter the words supplied by the press agency. This was not news. It was a long time since business had been transacted at Mincing Lane; this was merely the formal closing down of the London Tea Market. And yet, the disappearance of this institution, passing unnoticed in this way a year and a half before the start of the third millennium, marked the final collapse of a three-hundred year history which, equally unheralded, had seen wars, drugs and even concentration camps. As it happens, this discreet withdrawal from the scene took place one year, to the day, after another ending, far better covered by the media, long anticipated with expectation and anxiety: the handing back of Hong Kong to China on June 30, 1997. And this territory, which had been conquered after the Opium Wars, was only one outcome of British economic imperialism, in which the most coveted and significant commodity was tea.

Final Tea Break

In 1679, on the upper floor of one of the coffeehouses that preceded the Stock Exchange, the East India Company held its first auction selling three barrels of *dust of thea* from China for twenty-three shillings. In 1798, the English company's quarterly sale catalog contained no less than 635 pages of offers, every chest of tea being inspected and sampled by experts. The first official sale of the free Tea Market took place in 1834 in the district previously reserved for wine and sugar, to dispose of the stocks of the East India Company. This concentration in one place for practical reasons had unfortunate consequences in May 1941, when a bomb destroyed a large part of the offices and many documents. Although, at the end of the 1970s, 15 percent of the world tea trade still passed through the London Market, both Hamburg in Europe and Colombo in Sri Lanka were beginning to control the trade. On June 29, 1998, the eve of the Market's closure, only 20,000 of the 2,600,000 tons of global production went through its hands. What the United Kingdom had started in Assam, in Ceylon, and in Darjeeling, and continued in Kenya, Zimbabwe, and Tanzania, had spread to some thirty countries. These now negotiate the sale of their commodities direct. The electronization of commerce—via the telephone, fax, and email—has made floor-based trading redundant. With the admission that "tea has become just like other commodities" (Tom Buerkle, *Herald Tribune*), there ended an interlude of three centuries in which tea had been wrested from the Middle Kingdom to become a sign of the British Empire. It was now abandoned to the intangible traffic of things. At this last sale, barely thirty buyers from the companies Tetley, Twining, and Brooke Bond took part in the auction; many lots, or breaks, of Darjeeling, Sri Lankan Hellbodde, and Chinese Keemun failed to find a buyer.

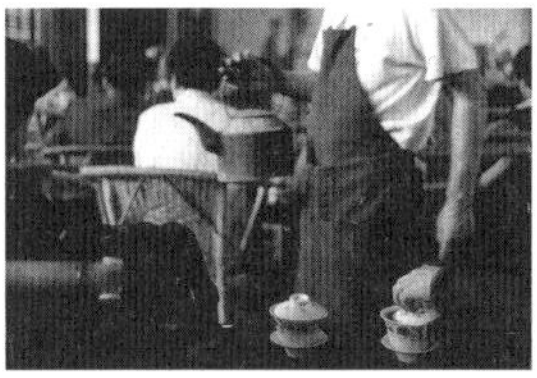

Another Story

On August 18, 1998, somewhere in Fujian, for the first time in its history the Chinese government put on sale the legendary Wulong tea "Red Robe," whose very limited production is strictly controlled, the few centenarian tea plants being kept secret in the mountains. The event, although unnoticed in the West, attracted the tea lovers and traders of Taiwan and Hong Kong. Presented in a small sealed box, under the strict surveillance of two uniformed guards, the precious tea was sold by a group of auctioneers before an audience of Chinese officials and professionals. The price obtained reflects the interest that tea is able to command in this part of the world: close to $900,000 a kilo. A few minutes after the hammer fell, the ministry official received a higher bid from Singapore: $1,350.000.
Three months earlier, in London, a historic record had been broken by a Hellbodde sold for charity at £555 a kilo. This was ten times more than the previous record at a London auction. This snip at the price, achieved, moreover, for the benefit of a charity, remains over a thousand times less than the price achieved at the Chinese auction. Clearly, as the sales director of R. Twining & Co. said, with more seriousness than he intended: "It's the end of an era."
And the beginning of another.

Time for Tea

These extremes of price so close in date have also occurred with the recent craze for Chinese and Japanese green teas, unappreciated outside their own regions since the nineteenth century. Green tea: in slimming diets, alcohol and tobacco detox regimes, treatments for diabetes and asthma; as a fighter of free radicals, and therefore anti-aging; with digestive properties, stimulating properties, calming properties; cosmetic, dietetic, marketable. In changing from black to green, tea has lost its poor image as a not innocuous herb tea, a diluted coffee, to find itself invested, in its reconquered color, with a vegetable vitality. Rather as wine and meat, being red, still keep their association with strength: the signature of things—*signatura rerum*—and magic thinking.
This green fashion in the West has its counterpart in the eastern predilection for red. Chinese wine production. Consumption of French *grands crus* by the Taiwanese and above all the Japanese. In 1995, the best sommelier in the world was a Japanese man, while Japanese women queued to enroll in wine schools and become experts in appellations, vines, and vintages. The continued interest in haute cuisine, reinforced by the reported health benefits of wine, and boosted by the Japanese tendency to follow a trend, led consumption to triple in eighteen months while, side by side with the traditional *sakayasan*, a new type of distribution chain opened: discount stores.
But if, at the end of the twentieth century, tea was back in its empire, in the civilization that invented it, this does not mean that its authenticity has been restored: the massive commercial development of slimming Tuo Tea, intended for export to

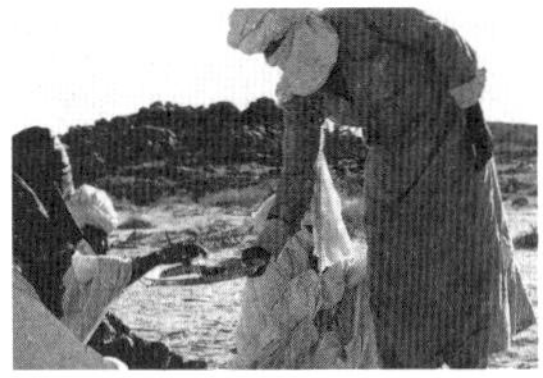

pharmacies, is now monopolized by a firm that makes it by an accelerated method. This guarantees only one thing: that the product has lost all the effects attributed to it in Chinese pharmacopoeia. Nevertheless, the renewed interest in Chinese tea could serve to support the cultivation of the plant—which bears resemblances with European viticulture. It is worth noting that China, which has more species of vine than anywhere else in the world, is developing wine production on a very large scale, at sale prices of less than fifteen cents a bottle.

Fluid

At the end of the twentieth century, tea remained the most consumed drink in the world—after water, but well ahead of beer, coffee, wine, and fizzy soft drinks. And this because of the force of the traditions that go with it, not because of the imperialism of advertising. Despite all the misfortunes that have, in less than a century, threatened its cultivation in China, and tried to reduce it to a standardized taste in India, tea maintains a tremendous—although little known—diversity of flavors, ecotypes, and social practices. Tea is a "fluid" that still circulates among people, without being a currency, a narcotic, or even a new type of cola. In China, people carry round their *gaibei*, their tea mug. In Britain, in 1942, Churchill declared tea to be more important than munitions for the country's soldiers; and the ritual of the tea break continues to be observed in the work place, while tea bars have become the latest trend. In Japan, while the tea ceremony is degraded for the sake of tourists (outward show: *omote*), this is the better to hide (inside: *ura*) what really underlies it, from Zen to samurai, from the art of pottery to that of the kimono or garden. So, as exemplified in Poe's *Purloined Letter*, the tritest of clichés can still contain the essence of a culture. In France, although people may be unaware that Marcel Proust's original title for *Du côté de chez Swann* was "Gardens in a cup of tea" (letter from Proust to Louis de Robert, at Grasset publishing house), many businesses invent out of nothing a "French art of tea." The most powerful lubricant on the planet thus remains an infusion of water, which, like the dollar in Cuba, could be called *El Verde*.

"Tea is Tea"

The paradox of tea is that it is the most consumed and at the same time the most unknown of drinks. The most unknown, of course, because it is the most consumed: whether in the West or in China, in the Middle East, Russia, or Japan, tea is drunk without regard to its provenance, and even less to the quality of its vintage. Having "a" cup of tea implies the expectation of "the" habitual, standard flavor: Georgian Tchaï, Gunpowder with fresh mint in Arab countries, broken "black" tea in Europe, Japanese Sencha, Chinese green tea. Only when crossing from one sphere to another is one likely to be surprised by a sudden bitterness, an unknown aroma, an unusual insipidity that runs counter to one's taste "of" tea.

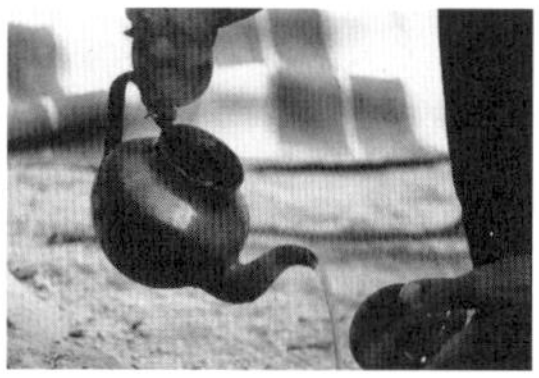

World of Tea

On one of the three hills of Paris, there is a tea house that opens up on a new world. For anyone familiar with the different ways of drinking tea in Japan, Europe, or the desert, it means another time, another place, another history. What could appear to be simply a new specialty, an extra sophistication, or a regional custom, imposes itself, from the "first visit," as the ultimate foundation or as a horizon previously unseen yet always there. What is thus being manifested is the apparition of an immensity, a duration and a world which one could never before have imagined or conceived.

Frankly, most of the books about tea available in the West or Japan are concerned exclusively, and often in third-hand versions, with the European discovery of tea or the Japanese "way of tea." The few contemporary works that mention "China tea" only repeat second-hand scraps of unread stories, list names of teas that have never been tasted and make generalizations so wide as to become self-contradicting.

Discovery of Tea

For a long time, it was impossible to taste great vintages of tea, and few people would have even dreamt that they existed. It is as if wine drinkers who had only ever known wine in a plastic box from the supermarket were suddenly given a Château Petrus 1949, a Chambertin-Clos de Bèze 1990, an Yquem—Lur Saluces 1921. In this improbable place, a world unknown to the West and little known in China itself, brutally opens up. Coming from lands more vast and diverse than those of Europe, the vintages of tea are greater in both number and variety than those of the grape: over 1500 named types of green tea and several thousands of tea altogether. There are teas from plants over a thousand years old, in other words planted under the legendary Song dynasty. Aged teas that have been maturing for decades, and sometimes more than a century. Teas with a world production seldom above three hundred kilos, and often with a harvest of only six kilos; or, as in the case of a famous Bai Hao in 1995—its aroma was the accidental result of an insect attack—, a scant fifty grams. Prize-winning teas from the sales and auctions of Taiwan or protected areas of China that have obtained, on their home ground, prices inconceivable in the West: a genuine Dong Ding, whose total production is not more than 210 kilos, will currently fetch some $13,500 a kilo. In 1998, an An Xi Tie Guan Yin went for $45,000 a kilo in China itself. Most high quality vintages range in price from $225 to $9,000. None of the upmarket tea rooms of Europe or America, whose ranges still include teas doused with synthetic essences, has access to teas of this kind, a far cry from the usual repertoire of industrially produced Indian and China teas.

In certain tucked-away tea houses, a few fortunate customers can meet a "professor" of tea (*chashi*). These are not the flashy or kitsch establishments to be found in Taipei or Hong Kong, but well-guarded backrooms or cellars, where the tiny but

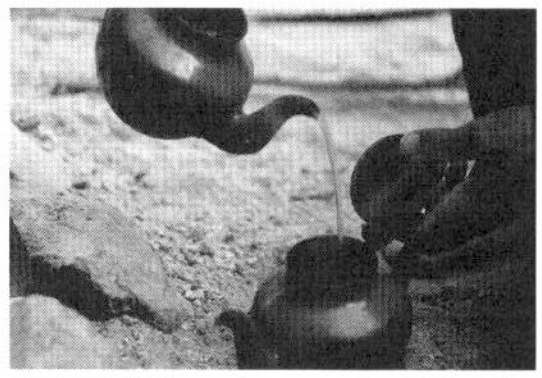

precious Yixing teapots are carefully unwrapped and used ceremoniously to prepare infusions that resemble rare liqueurs and where the arrivals of new leaves and teas produced only in very small quantities are tasted.
Hours are spent brewing and sampling all the plant nuances. In a single protected tea from the heights of Taiwan, one can catch scents of magnolia, lilac, orchid; and, in the cooled cup, one can smell papaya or pineapple, even a taste of fresh butter, followed by one of raw cane sugar. One lingers over the "smelling cup" for several long minutes, up to fifteen infusions being produced from the same measure of tea. Attention is paid to the rhythmic movement in the mouth and the circulation through the body.

Tea Lists

A few tea houses, notably in France, have tried to promote tea by inventing a tradition that never previously existed. This has mainly involved reintroducing a "flavor" to so-called "black" Anglo-Indian tea, which lost all its taste with standardization. Synthetic flavoring made this development possible in the mid-twentieth century. The ever-growing number of flavors (apple, cinnamon, caramel) has led to an ever-lengthening tea list. And this medley of tastes has been accompanied by a mushrooming of areas of provenance: teas from all over the world (India, China, Japan, but also Kenya, Ecuador, Georgia) are offered together, with nothing to indicate that all these plantations except the first three are cultivating the same Ceylon clone, and under conditions of production that will not allow the tea to improve.

Libertea, Equalitea, Fraternitea

It is only recently that *salons de thé* and cafés or bars in France have offered what is presented as a choice: the inevitable "Ceylon-Darjeeling-Ear Grey-Lapsang-Jasmin-China," or even a list of fruit teas. A few tea houses have admittedly appeared for the benefit of tea lovers and "drinkers of hot water," where sometimes overabundant choices of teas are offered for sale and where tea is prepared according to some "golden rules." The French spirit has in fact found its "art of tea" in this universalism which summous every country—or, at least, brings them all under the same banner, its own, bearing the slogan "Libertea, Equalitea, Fraternitea." In this way several French companies practice a philosophy of the Enlightenment in which there remain a few vestiges of the Old Régime, or even nostalgia for the colonial era, the eternal aura of which hangs over some European *salons de thé*.

Tea in Fashion

For some years now, there has been a marked trend towards green tea, the form most commonly drunk between India, Indonesia, and Japan, above all in China. This Asiatic manner, now fashionable in the West, has profited from faster forms of transport, not available to the tea carried by the East India Company, which suffered in transit; but it has also had to adapt to the tea-making methods of the West, which

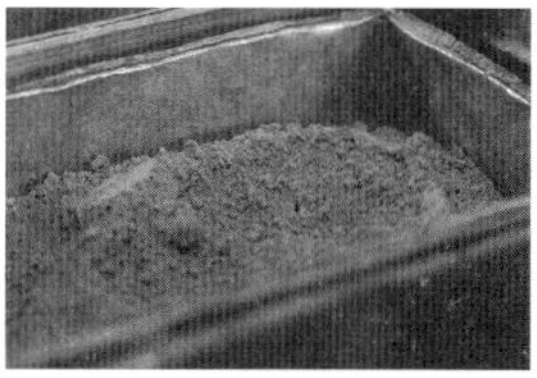

were established only at the end of the nineteenth century and do not suit unfermented tea. Green tea should be made not in a teapot but in a *zhong*—a cup with a curving rim, a lid but no handle, which prevents scalding the leaves, lets the tea release its most subtle aromas, and evenly distributes the flavors.

The "taste" for Anglo-Indian black tea, full-bodied but flavorless; the widespread "customs" of the tea bag, of iced tea (sometimes in cans or bottles); and the tendency to reduce the "aroma" of tea on one hand—with milk and sugar—while supplementing it on the other—with sprayed essences—do nothing to establish the ideal tradition for bringing out the qualities of the thousands of vintages of Chinese green tea, unknown even in their own country. The misadventures strewing the long history of West and East are echoed in the "famous" of the names marketed on an industrial scale: Yunnan, Gunpowder, and Tuo Cha are the names of teas with supposedly beneficial properties and a legendary provenance. When it comes to the packaging of the teas, whose quality, regardless of vintage, depends essentially on their plucking season and freshness, so little regard is paid to the rules of conservation that we end up with those astringent, drying infusions presumed characteristic of Chinese tea.

Colors of Tea

Few places offer tea in the rainbow of colors that can still be found in China, in remote areas outside state control. This is altogether different to the pseudo-diversity of a single broken tea covered in a litany of flavors or of the same Assam tea industrially produced by different countries as a unique export crop.

What differentiates a tea is firstly the "work" done to it—the various manipulations of its treatment after plucking—and its degree of fermentation: yellow, white, and green teas are fermented little or not at all; red teas are completely fermented, and black doubly so. As for Wulong, their completely unknown varieties—who has heard of three thousand vintages of blue-green Chinese tea?—are the result of differing degrees of fermentation.

Teas also vary according to their stock, which is another subject neglected in the West, where "scientific" taxonomy recognizes a single variety of *Camellia sinensis* instead of the few dozen or so identified in China: rather as if all types of vine were run together. A *chashi*, in the same way as an enologist or winegrower, will be able to select teas according to the variety of the trees. The Chinese tea culture has an exact if unexpected counterpart in the French vineyard with its tradition of "*cru*," "*sol*" and "*climat*" (vintage, soil, and climate). Indeed, while green, blue-green, and red teas should be consumed within the year, Chinese black teas can keep for thirty, sixty, even a hundred years, and Wulong and Pu Er come from plants that can be several hundred years old. When the number of Chinese vintages—no less than six thousand—is taken into account, the comparison with wine is no way far-fetched.

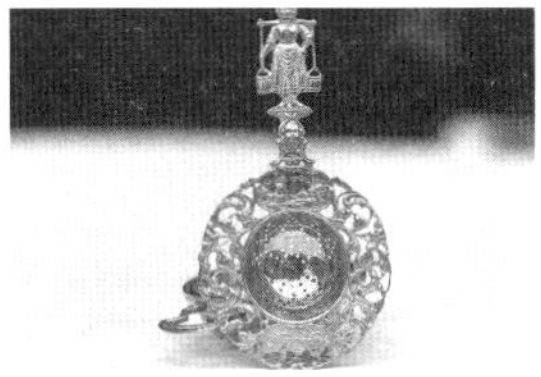

Wine & Tea

While Paris now offers exceptional access to the best tea, this is paradoxically in the absence of a French "art of tea" or tradition. The European countries that adopted tea at the end of the eighteenth century were, from England to Russia, including Holland, Germany, and Scandinavia, those where the climate, social customs, or religious prescriptions fostered heavy alcohol consumption, but where the vine could not be cultivated. By a sort of practical necessity—the Russian samovar—or under pressure of the forces of morality—the English mug—tea drinking became established, while in France it found no place at the side of wine, which with its lower alcohol strength and nutritional role had neither had the same destructive effects as spirits nor undergone the same fate as beer. Its culture was always sufficiently widespread in the many regions of France for it not to be reduced to a toxic substance completely cut off from its links with production and drinking tradition. Regions where tea, in its Anglo-Indian version, never became more than a generic tisane, tend to be those that have developed a gastronomy and maintained a relationship with the cultivated land. This concerns above all the countries of southern Europe, where sugar consumption has also never reached the levels of the north and particularly the British Isles. That black tea has never caught on in France is also because the Chinese product reached Europe only in a much-deteriorated state or in the very mediocre version of the new Indian plantations. These are a few elements in the paradox that has made Paris the venue for the very complex Chinese tradition of tea.

Enology & Gongfucha

Before addressing what links *gongfucha* to its particular world, at the risk, accepted but often unnoticed, of slipping into Oriental stereotypes, it is worth comparing the Chinese art of tea with the European, and specifically French, art of wine, in the hope of grasping a novel culture and reconsidering one's own. The two have common traits. First, both these "arts" or "techniques," because of the nature of their product, lie somewhere between agriculture, art, and gastronomy. Lie between them but embrace them also. In France, at least three terms refer to the science or practice of wine: viticulture, viniculture, and enology. The three words each emphasize an aspect of the art of wine, pointing to a different activity or specialty, but they operate in unison, often with the same person officiating in all three fields. Next, tea and wine bring similar skills into play and have a comparable relationship with nature: in their cultivation—the plant, soil, and climate—but also in their manufacture—the time of harvest, variation of treatment, and period of conservation—and in their consumption and appreciation—the tasting techniques, typology of flavors and smells, and discreet handing on of tradition. Lastly, wine and tea have equivalently defined roles in their different communities: both are integrated to the dominant religion, Judeo-Christianity in the West, and Buddhism–Confucianism–Taoism in the East; they play an important part in the trade and tax systems; and

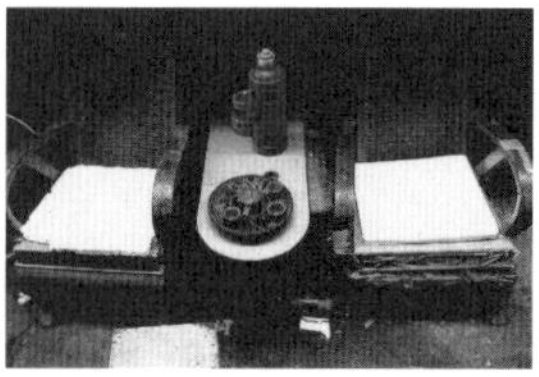

they promote the passage to culture, in its derived sense of art and poetry. "Black" Benedictine and "White" Cistercian monks invented viticulture in the West during the Middle Ages. From the first vineyard at Meursault to Côte-d'Or and then Kloster of Eberbach, the monks of the Order of St. Bernard in Burgundy were to develop a veritable laboratory of vines, soils, and climates, in a comparative study of the colors, body, and bouquets of wine. In China, it was also in the precincts of the monasteries that tea was first cultivated in a systematic manner. And the plant's introduction to Japan, precisely recorded, is attributed to three religious founders. Saichô (762-822), founder of the first great sect—*Tendaï*—of esoteric Buddhism, brought the first tea seeds, which were planted near Kyoto, at the foot of his monastery Enrakyu-ji. Eisai (1141-1215), the father of Zen Buddhism, published the *Kissa Yôjôki* in which he promoted tea drinking by the Japanese, "unhealthy and very thin people"; he brought back seeds of tea plants grown in Kyushu and Toganôô, and also the Chinese recipe for beaten powder tea—Macha. Finally, in 1654, the Chinese monk Ingen, with a group of learned men, established the last Zen sect to arrive from the continent at the Obakuji monastery; he introduced the fashion for infused tea, Sencha.

So tea and wine, a cup of green water and a glass of red liquid, drunk unceremoniously at any time or as the focus of a ritual, each the fluid of a civilization, find common ground within their differences, which may thus even appear more relevant. From the French and Dutch treatises of the seventeenth century to the professional bodies of today, even if tea is to be bracketed with coffee and cocoa on the ground of the parallel histories of their introduction to the West, yet it is only with wine that tea finds a proper measure of comparison.

Art & Technique

Gongfucha sounds another transcription of *kung fu*, whose esotericism is conveyed by the weightless choreography of Hong Kong films. Most of the masters and practitioners of *gongfucha* also engage in other arts—martial arts, calligraphy, music. Conversely, the practitioners of the traditional arts of the "fist" (*quan*) and paintbrush seek to control their *qi* through their knowledge of tea. In the slowness of *taijiquan*, movements that appear to flow naturally prove difficult for the novice to follow in sequence. In the strict sense, *gong fu* is an exercise, an activity pursued as a training, an apprenticeship, concentration directed at an accomplishment, a mastery of gesture and conduct. In this respect, *gongfucha* should be translated literally: not the "art of tea" but the "tea of art"—where, more than skill or aura, "time" and "technique" must be allowed infusion.

Tea of Art

To give the brief measure of this "tea of art," it is probably worth noting in the comparison with the art of wine how many practices coincide. While tea is no less

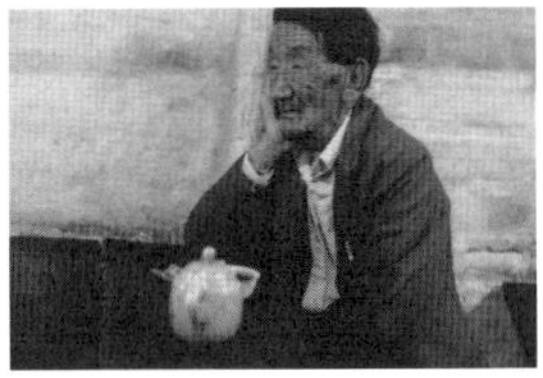

complex than wine as a product—either in its number of vintages, organoleptic properties or techniques of cultivation and production—a number of extra factors come into play, which Western history has either rejected or neglected. Thus a practitioner or *a fortiori* "master" of tea needs to consider all the therapeutic, climatic, and cardinal parameters: the immediate or prolonged effects on the body, according to the type of tea, the season, and the place of drinking; and, conversely, all the changes that affect the tea itself as it matures, hence the science that operates both over very short time spans—a tea can change completely in a few weeks—and very long ones—black teas keep like alcohol, although they are more fragile and need more care. Similarly, just as wine requires special attention at the point of drinking—decanting, bringing to room temperature, pouring—, the time and tools involved in the preparation of tea are enormously important: for a start, the implements are far more numerous, while the actions performed and the minutely calculated doses, temperatures, and timings can produce strongly contrasting effects. The question of ritual, central from the Japanese to the Tuaregs, is bound up with this technical aspect, which finds its most exact expression in Chinese *gongfucha*. If a *chashi*, a Chinese tea master, has authority, it is because he dominates this wide body of knowledge.

The Master's Tea

Here, the term "tea master," which contemporary literature on this unscrupulously misuse, is again justified. "Tea master" was originally the title of the host in Japanese Chadô, but is now applied in very different tea cultures, including those furthest removed from its history: people will speak of a Chinese, a Korean, even a French tea master—although in the last case the book of tea has become a comic genre. The descriptions "tea ceremony" or ritual have also been used in a variety of unconsidered ways: the Tuaregs, for example, are said to have a "ceremony" whenever they quench their thirst. And in Turkey a supposed coffee ceremony has been recently "rediscovered." In Korea, the only Asian country where the drink had almost disappeared, a tea ritual has lately been invented from nothing. Even in China, a similar line of thought seeks to attach a liturgy to *gongfucha*. The expression "tea ceremony" is, moreover, a decidedly unjustified adaptation of *chanoyu*, which literally and tritely translates—this is not irrelevant to the grasp of what is at stake—as "hot tea water," while "tea master" is the translation of *chajin*, meaning only a "tea person." To try to see *gongfucha* as a ritualized form is undoubtedly to overlook its complexity and above all its necessary function. All the same, more precisely than in its Japanese context, "tea master" translates the Chinese *chashi*: the latter is indeed the authority in his art, who develops its practice, and ensures its continuity. In the world of tea, which has experienced a brutal reversal since the nineteenth century in China and Europe, the plantations, places of consumption,

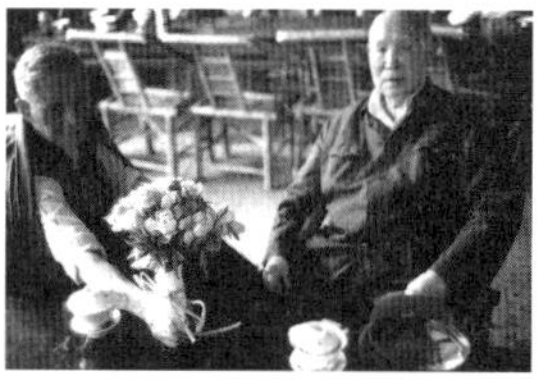

and wide-ranging technical expertise's have all suffered extensively. Only in recent years has there been a form of renaissance in the tea practices of Taiwan and China.

Round the World

A world tour planned around tea might lead to five places where the drink has a strong and still active tradition: England, China, Japan, Sikkim, and the Tuaregs in the Sahara. This necessary choice may seem limited and arbitrary. The implied equivalence in such a geographical constellation, both from a comparative viewpoint and as a programmatic itinerary, will inevitably call for a few adjustments. Should one focus only on the tea ritual, this will throw up the huge disproportion between the giant civilization still contained in a Chinese's worst cup of tea and the African style of tea with mint, which hardly goes back to the end of the nineteenth century. There is little to link the bowl of a Tibetan lama with the *chawan* of the Japanese tea master, although both observe a Buddhist rite. And while Chinese, Japanese, and English tea has a history that goes back for centuries, this is not true of Sikkim and the Tuaregs. Japan, England, and the Tuaregs have an established order of service for tea, while China and Sikkim have held back from this, although the latter has tea in its temples. While tea with mint or artemisia is essential to the survival of the Tuaregs, and tea with yak butter is part of a Tibetan meal, it does not in these regions have the symbolic force or the esthetic emphasis that attend it in Japan. So where ritual is concerned, some destinations are not worth attention, while others have little to contribute from the historical point of view; and when it comes to timings, places reserved for tea-taking, and the extension of practices linked to tea, parallels are difficult to draw.

Necessity

It remains the case that the traces of memory, recorded here, draw their force very much from the necessity—live, symbolic, or imaginary—that tea still represents in these parts of the world. And this need is probably satisfied best in places where tea has the shortest history. The small kingdom of Sikkim (near the famous tea region of Darjeeling), subject alternately to India and Tibet, and one of the rare places outside China where the plant existed before the English plantations, concentrates several complementary aspects of tea. The Tuaregs, nomadic people, near the Arab world and far from Asia, also reveal aspects that differ from the stronger and more closed traditions of China, Japan, and Great Britain. So these five places, distinct and of differing importance, display most of the essential motifs infused by tea. Chinese, Japanese, and Tuareg teas are unfermented green teas. Chinese and Japanese teas are the only ones taken without additions. Sikkim and English teas are mixed with milk. Tuareg and English teas are sweetened. Chinese and Tuareg teas are clear teas, while the three others are cloudy and opaque. English and Chinese teas are brewed. Japanese and Tibetan teas are beaten (whipped or

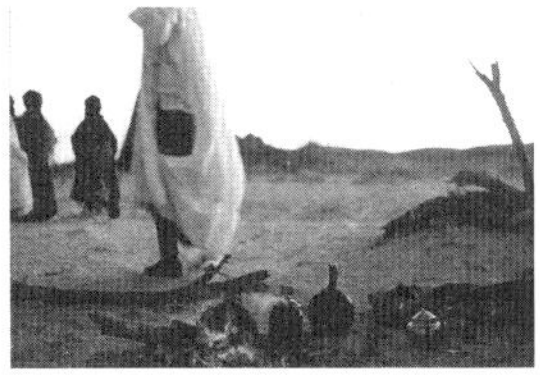

churned). Tuareg and Sikkim teas are boiled and reheated. Hardly surprisingly, not all these teas can be given an equal importance. The century of Tuareg tea cannot equate to nearly six thousand years of history in China; nor can the ceremonial complexity of a Japanese tea gathering be summed up in the same way as the etiquette of an English tea party, or the short service of Tibetan tea. Here our writing needs to break down the coherence, the interweaving, the melding—more of a parallel montage—of the photographs; it needs to bring out, instead, the distinctiveness of the different practices, regions, and traditions. The simple description of the beverage, separated from the circumstances in which it is drunk—whether reunion, liturgy, welcome, meal, or meditation—shows the great variety of combinations to which the five places give rise. In the interior of each of these regions, tea has an identity that has nothing in common with that of the other areas. The common point lies in the plant matter which is so differently treated that it is hard to identify from one area to the next: emerald-green purée or mousse, thick golden liquor, brown heterogeneous soup, murky gray beverage, crystalline aromatic liquid. "The" tea undergoing these metamorphoses is none the less always considered as a drink, and a drink drawn from the same leaf, of a tree that scientific classification—outside China!—resolutely classes as virtually a single species. Here again, within each of these areas, tea is broadly determined by customs or rites. The Japanese Macha is the strictest in form, taste, and accompanying gestures. Tuareg and Tibetan teas are also prepared in a prescribed way, centered on the communal teapot; but the time of year, difficulties of supply, and wealth of the consumer can lead to variation of some ingredients: a fistful of the hardier artemisia will replace mint, which grows only around the oasis; mare's milk is an alternative to yak butter, and spices can differ from region to region. English tea is made to suit the taste (or diet) of the individual: milk, sugar, and lemon are added only in each person's cup. As for Chinese tea, it will never be of a type: there are six main colors (corresponding to types of fermentation), over six thousand vintages, and at least three methods of brewing (*zhong*, Yixing teapot, large teapot), not to forget the place or circumstances in which it is imbibed, as an everyday comfort drink or a tasting for adepts.

The Tea Resistance

"The jealousy of the Chinese government, in former times, prevented foreigners from visiting any of the districts where tea is cultivated, and the information derived from the Chinese merchants, even scanty as it was, was not to be depended upon." (Robert Fortune, *Three Years Wanderings in the Northern Provinces of China*, 1847) In fact, China maintained an exclusive hold over all tea production—as it had done for silk and porcelain—until the mid-nineteenth century; Japan, the only other country that could have come to the rescue of the West, was locked in its end

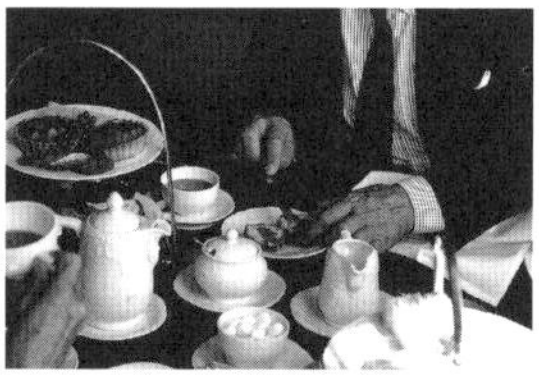

of history, until the black ships threatened its port. "This art has until recent times been a secret that the Chinese religiously avoided revealing to foreigners. For some years now, people have managed, in a few countries, such as Java and Brazil, to create tea plantations, and make the bush bear the same quantity of fine leaves as in China; but this was the limit of the success of these ventures; the real method used in the Celestial Empire had remained an impenetrable secret. All the Europeans who visited China in the past two centuries returned as ignorant in this matter as they had been when they left." (J.-G. Houssaye) Despite all the smuggling, the unequal treatises, the play of influences that went with the business of the East India Company in its various forms, tea remained in a unique position: the object of continual search, like spices, coffee, and cocoa, it resisted all the transfers, transplantation, and migrations that those three commodities must have undergone: the slave trade, alienation, and gradual transformation from cult substance to consumer good. Tobacco, because its plants adapted to temperate lands, was successfully acclimatized. Coffee and cocoa, on the other hand, underwent an extraordinary continental exchange. Mocha declined as a port long ago, and Africa has left to South America the bulk of coffee production. In exchange, although great vintages of *criollo* still grow in a few high valleys in Venezuela, the African countries have taken over the large-scale production of cocoa. The resistance of tea, while it may be attributable in part to the difficulty of acclimatizing the plant—cocoa and coffee trees have the same problem—must also have been reinforced by the sort of ritual that has always accompanied tea-drinking, and ultimately by the policies of the Chinese authorities who, despite the endless succession of regimes, remained consistent on one front in the face of the "barbarian": neither the silkworm nor kaolin nor the seed of the tea plant—not to mention the technical knowledge to go with them—were to cross the frontiers of the Middle Kingdom. The consequences would be considerable, with the peregrinations of the silk worm larvae smuggled in the bamboo sticks of fake pilgrims, and the adventures of the botanist Robert Fortune who sought the tea plant disguised as a Manchu; but also with the reinvention and emulation to which the Europeans were spurred (Lyonnaise silk, Palissy enamels). The persisting protectionism fostered, on the Chinese side, what could be called a xeno-industry: to maintain this trade and a monopoly of production, as early as the fourth century goods were specifically designed and made for foreign countries near and far. One still finds, buried in the Iranian desert, Chinese celadon ware from before the year 1000. Many motifs and designs done in Europe were used as stencils or pouncing in order to adapt to foreign tastes, but a stereotyped production also promoted a distinct exotic image: China always was the first producer of *chinoiseries*, as Japan was later to be of "Japaneseries." And this, well before the nineteenth century when, like Egyptomania, they became dominant. It

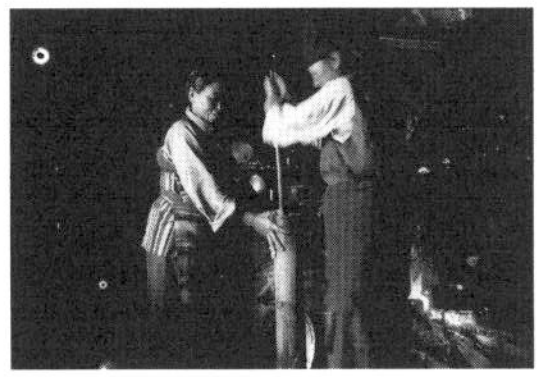

took until the twentieth century for the West to recognize that the great Chinese ceramics (Song, Tang, Ming) existed in another form than "blue and white," an effect that Delft and Meissen put their ingenious best into reproducing. As for the drink, while green tea was fairly soon recognized to be the local beverage, it is perhaps not yet understood that the teas seen by the West as having a "Chinese taste"—smoked black, Lapsang Souchong, Yunnan—are simply unknown in China. Purely kept for export, they are said to owe their existence only to the carelessness of a grower in the late eighteenth century and the poor assessment of an English merchant. Beyond these many misunderstandings, Chinese protectionism provoked competition on the part of the Europeans: traffic, particularly maritime, a trade in the more exact sense of the word than that conducted with the other "Indies." Africa, the New World, and India itself were only sporadically able to muster the forces to establish a relationship of exchange of merchandise, rather than endure slavery, genocide and colonization. Finally, the restriction of production to the Chinese region opened, between East and West, the routes of silk, porcelain, and tea, in other words that axis, maintained by the succeeding Byzantine, Mongol, and Ottoman empires, which was to be the first passage of communication on a world scale. Its fixed infrastructure was made up of stopping posts in central Asia, its vehicles were caravans, the mobile goods were ceramics, brocades, and bricks of compressed tea. Thus tea resisted transplantation until the nineteenth century, by a combination of strategy—like silk and porcelain—and geographical necessity (climate and soils)—like coffee and cocoa. An interlocking of economy and ecology.

Triads

In modern China, teas are difficult to find: the famous names (Bi Lo Chun, Long Jing, Yin Zhen) give rise to traffic, overvaluation, and adulteration on a grand scale; the triads are involved; the regulation and control of production by the central government administration imposes norms and excessive mechanization; businesses serve tea that bears no relation to the loose product: the horribly chlorinated water, which tears the throat, prevents any real appreciation of what might be of good quality; tea houses offer either one tea or a choice of up to three. This is the situation in Shanghai where the only tea house, serving the working classes on the ground floor and the new bourgeoisie or the former Party élite on the first floor, has an inauthentic, tourist atmosphere.

Nameless Tea

The botanist Joseph Banks suggested as early as 1788, that tea should be grown in India, followed by Robert Bruce, who had found tea growing wild there. But the idea was taken up only in 1833, when the English East India Company created the Tea Committee and sent G. J. Gordon to China to obtain seeds, technical knowledge,

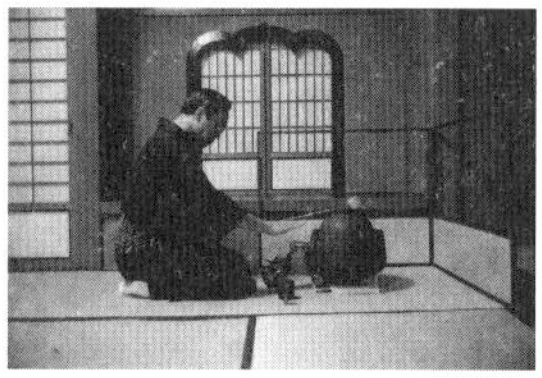

and workmen. Charles Bruce, Robert's brother, was to succeed in the first attempts at cultivation. Tea was thus planted outside the Far East in the mid-nineteenth century (Assam, Darjeeling, Ceylon), and again in the mid-twentieth (Kenya, Brazil, Tanzania), but only in an exogenous variant. The variety cloned all over the world for factory-made "black" tea—Ceylonese Assam—and its method of treatment—CTC (Crushing, Tearing, Curling)—produce something even less like China tea than white sugar is to molasses. It is worth noting that the biggest brand of tea, now owned by a giant holding company of detergents, long ago stopped featuring the word tea with any prominence on the packet: tea is mentioned only in the small print in the mandatory list of ingredients. The historic label and disquieting banner "yellow quality" have blotted out the name of the thing itself. In contrast, the names "Fun Tea," "Ice Tea," and "Nestea" appear on cans of soft drinks that contain tea only as synthetic flavoring or a minimal quantity of extract, swamped by carbon dioxide, caramel coloring, and caffeine: the ingredients of cola. While tea in China has tended to extend and diversify colors, tastes, and smells, as if playing on the infinite divisibility of its characteristics, the West, in reverse seems to have done its best to reduce the gamut of its tea, already a stunted variety: what is English tea-with-milk if not an atrophied coffee? Thomas Lipton moreover described the thing that made his fortune as "hot, wet and black."

Adopted Tea

The teas that were drunk in the European courts in the days when Europe traded through the exploitative agency of what was in effect a multi-national—the various East India Companies—were probably still recognizable, although they were those reserved by the Chinese for export—rare greens and probably a type of Wulong—which had had to suffer the unsatisfactory conditions of holds where they did not keep. In an English coffeehouse, tea was the most expensive of the three black drinks, followed by chocolate and lastly coffee. Owing to its economic and ecological resistance, tea would probably have remained a luxury product until the revolution in transport, had England, from the end of the eighteenth century, not needed it for the Industrial Revolution—and adopted it. The forces of morality, which had until that point condemned the drink, now poured it out during "tea moralities" in an attempt to mobilize a work force too heavily diverted and ravaged by gin, ale, and beer, distilled or brewed in working class kitchens.

Effects of Tea

At this period, England had almost a monopoly of tea importation and trade, in order to meet its internal needs, but also in a situation where the Dutch, French, and Scandinavians were gradually abandoning their trading posts. So the British Empire found itself strategically placed to remove the monopoly of tea manufacture from the Middle Kingdom: as ceramics and silk had been reinvented in the West, it

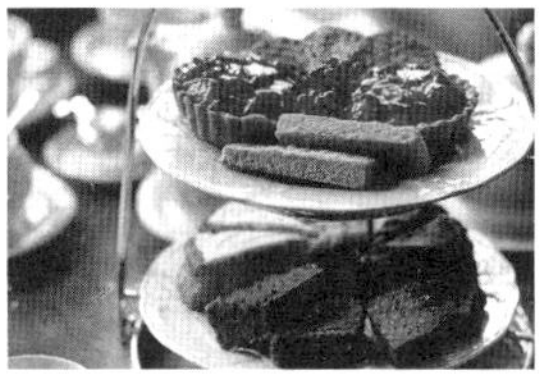

was now the turn of tea. In this enterprise, there was not a corner of the world that would not be overturned: *I.* The first detonator of the American War of Independence was the Boston Tea Party, where colonists disguised as Red Indians threw into the sea the tea chests of three English ships. The English did not want to let the inhabitants of the New World get their supplies direct from China and imposed a heavy additional tax. North America can be said to have begun with these renegades, who put on native dress, and wanted to drink tea free of tribute; *II.* In China, before the English stole the tea plants, the Company exchanged tea for opium from Indian plantations: Chinese drug use was a deliberate policy by Europe. The ensuing wars (Opium War, Boxer Rising, and so on) were in effect armed intimidation by a State racket. When opium dens were forbidden by the Chinese authorities, the poppy fields in India were replaced by tea gardens. Only the Indian and later the Ceylonese climate provided the conditions for British tea. That famous "Indian tea" did not exist before the 1830s: only a few tribes in Assam must have chewed the leaves; *III.* As for the Arab countries, from Morocco to Egypt, they became the recipients of surplus green tea from China. Here again, a whole tradition was to be invented, between the end of the nineteenth and beginning of the twentieth centuries. While a few cakes of black tea must have arrived before then among the riches imported from the Far East, they only rarely appeared in the decoctions of mint or artemisia that the people used to drink.

Rite, Custom, Art

In this new way of partitioning the world, a prelude to all those that would take place after wars to come, there is one constant: tea, for so long tied to its native land, now gave rise, in the different countries where it was drunk, to a custom, a technique, a very formalized art: a rite. Without it being possible to identify a proper sequence of its development from culture to culture, or the law of its integration or absorption. Churned Tibetan tea; the Russian samovar; sweetened and reheated Arab tea with mint; brewed tea with added milk, in the English style; Japanese powdered green tea, whipped to a froth; Chinese tea in a *zhong*; Taiwanese *gongfucha*, and so on. Teatime, *chanoyu*, *gongfucha*, tea-in-a-tent, the lama's tea.

French Tea

Tea is still the most consumed beverage in the world, water apart. A third of the world population drinks tea—one and a half billion cups per day. In France, who got its tea before England did, through the Dutch Company, the drink never gave rise to an art or a culture. The tradition of tea is at its weakest there, and the tea served in the average Paris café one of the worst. It is no more than a sachet of dust left in water full of nitrates, defying the description *salon de thé*—always bracketed with "café," "brasserie" or "*bar-tabac*"—which still carries echoes of the court and its pomp, where tea was for a long time restricted. In the land of the Revolution,

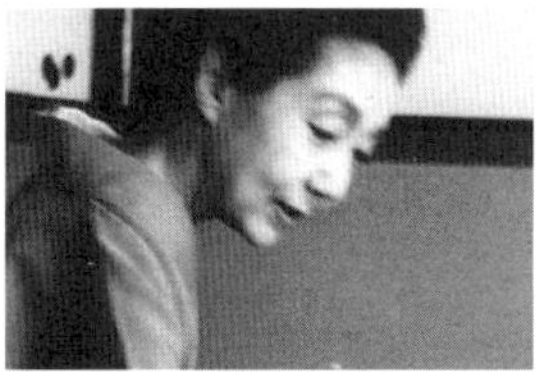

the main invention related to tea is in fact the *salon de thé*, which, strangely, has survived and exported itself. Chinese tea houses, except for a few gardens in Chengdu, all disappeared half a century ago. In London, tearooms have been relegated to the entrance hall of a few grand hotels. The tea pavilion, although still the central stage of the Japanese ceremony, is now a rare luxury found only in the dwellings of a privileged few. It is meanwhile impossible to order a green tea in a *kissaten*, the Japanese "café" that translates as tea bar, but where only international black tea is served. The poverty of the local tradition has paradoxically made France a place where, for the past fifteen years or so, it has been possible to get a global perspective of tea. A number of companies, maisons and counters serve a great choice of teas not to be found elsewhere, whether in Germany, the United States, or Taiwan. The inventor of the flavored or scented teas that gave a fresh impetus to tea drinking (and extended tea lists more or less happily) in post-Sixties Europe is a Frenchman: Jumeau-Lafond of Dammann. The first establishment to offer a choice of teas imported from all over the world is also French: Mariage Frères. And it is in Paris that the Maison des Trois Thés has opened, the first Taiwanese tea house in the West to practice the *gongfucha* tradition and serve the finest vintages of tea. Next to wine, which has been put into the French Paradox capsule, we shall have to accept the New French Paradox, which puts tea in the place where it has been least known, precisely for that reason.

Records of Rites

It is against this background—surely no coincidence—that Bruno Suet, nine years ago, made his plan to visit and photograph the different places observing a tea ritual. When I met him, he was passing through Japan, and we went together to broach the difficult entry to the *chanoyu*. The *nijiriguchi*, the very low, narrow entrance to the "tea hut" that obliges one to kneel to get inside, was a tangible emblem of how the Japanese way of tea, while highly reputed, can be very deceptive. Bruno and I had to return several times to get shots that, without unmasking the ceremony, captured its intensity. This is the spirit in which he has traveled the world to photograph a cup or a bowl of tea from all angles. In five destinations, where tea certainly does not have the same social function, but where it always occasions a definite ritual, the test being that the tradition could not be taken away without loss to the people who practice it; *I.* Tea poured during prayers in lamaseries of Tibetan obedience; *II.* Tea made as a needed, energizing refreshment when the camel driver stops to rest; *III.* A tea gathering in a pavilion, organized weeks ahead and following a rigidly prescribed code; *IV.* A miniature banquet and upper class entertainment, where etiquette rules the pleasure; *V.* A reflex action that punctuates the day with a few leaves at the bottom of any covered receptacle. That is, and in this order, Sikkim, the desert of the Tuaregs, Japan, England, and China. These photographs,

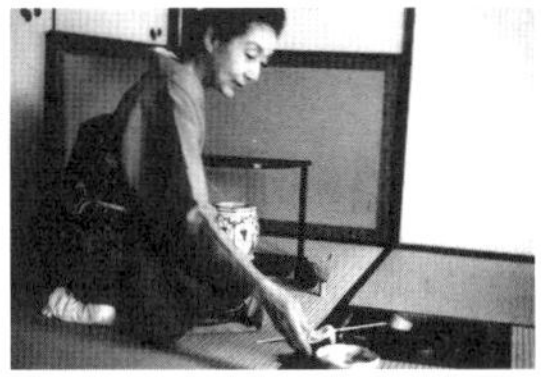

selected, reframed and ordered, show the necessity that underpins the tea cultures, and all the more strongly because they seem called to disappear in their present forms. The images display their archaeology and emotion: they are records of rites.

TEA, ETC.

Thirst

"Buying things in America today is just unbelievable. Let's say you're thirsty. Do you want Coke, Diet Coke, Tab, Caffeine-Free Coke, Caffeine-Free Diet Coke, Caffeine-Free Tab, New Improved Tab, Pepsi, Diet Pepsi, Pepsi Light, Pepsi Free, Root Beer, Royal Crown Cola, C&C Cola, Diet Royal Crown Cola, Caffeine-Free Pepsi, Caffeine-Free Diet Pepsi, Caffeine-Free Royal Crown Cola, Like, Dr. Pepper, Sugar-Free Dr. Pepper, Fresca, Mr. Pibb, Seven-Up, Diet Seven-Up, orange, grape, apple, Orelia, Perrier, Poland, Ginger Ale, tonic, selzer, Yoo-Hoo or cream soda? Do you want pineapple, papaya, guava, peach, coconut, apple, orange, strawberry, grapefruit, pink grapefruit, cherry-apple, apple-strawberry, grape, pina colada, sparkling apple, or Juicy Juice? Do you want one of the fifty varieties of malteds, the twenty kinds of frozen fruit shakes, the fifteen kinds of coffee or the thirty kinds of tea?" (Andy Warhol). In the beginning was thirst. Then came choice, and fizzy drinks, juices, thirty teas. From now on there will be doubt.

"Three are the species born between earth and sky: those endowed with wings that fly, those covered in hair that walk, and those with a large mouth that speak. To live, all species need to eat and drink. But the circumstances of drinking have hidden motives! To quench thirst one drinks water, to ease melancholy one drinks wine, to drive away sluggishness and sleep one drinks tea." (Lu Yu, *Chajing*, III, 6, "Drinking the tea")

According to a recent study, "even if the human organism remains disturbed by a prolonged shortage of water, the desire for liquid is quickly satisfied as the brain is capable of calculating the quantity that the person must absorb to appease his thirst. The brain bases its calculation on the sensations emanating from the mouth, on the movements of the pharynx in relation to the quantity of water swallowed and on messages indicating the degree of dilation of the stomach. None of these elements alone is enough to slake the thirst." This research adds to theories about the evolution of consciousness. The recent hypotheses of Nobel Gerald Maurice Edelman that it emerged in the ability to unite different sensations into a single "scene" would therefore extend to include the initial trigger of "primary emotional states"—the need for air, hunger, thirst. Rapid quenching of thirst is explained by factors linked to the demands of evolution. Derek Denton and Peter Fox have defined thirst as a phenomenon essential to survival, which drives an animal to go to the spring, where

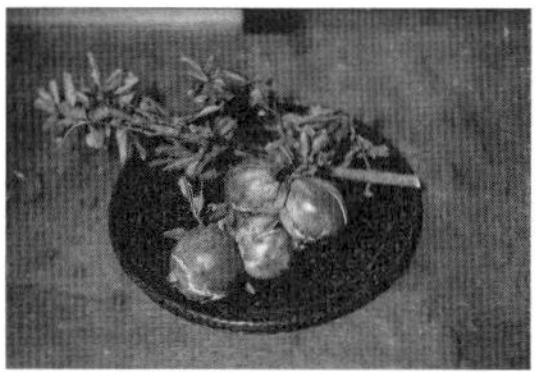

it quickly swallows a few pints before running to avoid predators. Consciousness would thus be designed as a system of choice and anticipation of the threat of death, over and above the needs formulated by primitive cerebral regions, such as thirst.

Object without History

"The modern eater literally no longer knows what he eats. His most basic signposts and criteria are confused, muddied, twisted... Between the eater-consumer and his diet, there is no longer any link of common origin, not even that which attaches eater and eaten to an ecological corner, to the same territory. A food, to be specific, has become an object with no known history, an artifact floating in an almost sidereal void, between past and future, at once menacing and fascinating." (Claude Fischler). The diet is guilty. Guilt is dietary. What can a gastro-nomy be? Bulimia, anorexia, drug addiction, alcoholism, diets, compulsions.

Civilization of the Toxic

The perfection of nicotine: at once a stimulant and relaxant; the quickest of all poisons in its effects. The perfection of the packaging, made apotropaic, and condemned to be sublime by the "danger to health" warning, regardless of name or brand. The perfection of the white tube, which signs as much the finish of the industry as the elegance of a paper consumed virgin.
"Three cigarettes in the evening, when the game bores you, are a divine way of killing time." (Alfred de Musset). "Ash, smoke and fire / Some smoke it fast / Others savor it." (Manuel Machado). "All the soul expressed / When we slowly exhale it / In a few wreaths of smoke." (Stéphane Mallarmé) Before it became, at the end of the twentieth century, the subject of battle between leagues and lobbies, tobacco emblematically laid out, in the extent of its empire and its different forms, the progressive civilizing of poison. It contains three main alkaloids (nicotine, nornicotine, anabasine) and more than 4800 other toxins, without counting the tar, carbon dioxide, and carbon monoxide associated with combustion. Tobacco has been classed as food, an emetic or a poison. It has been reduced to powder and snorted as snuff, alone or in company, swallowed as powder, steeped and drunk, chewed, licked as sticky syrup thickened by boiling then evaporation, and, finally, inhaled. Smoked in a pipe, a cigar, or a cigarette. The first machines for making the latter were called "cigarettotypes," a pointer to the fact that each cigarette coming out of the press or informed, immediately calls for another just like it to follow. The climax of consumption of an additive substance, which finds its counterpart in the numerical logic of the industry that controls it. Life is a cigarette—but the latter is the inflexible unit of the countdown of the former.

Time of Fermentation

Gen. 9:20-22: "And Noah began to be an husbandman, and he planted a vineyard: And he drank of the wine, and was drunken; and he was uncovered within his tent. And Ham, the father of Canaan, saw the nakedness of his father, and told his two

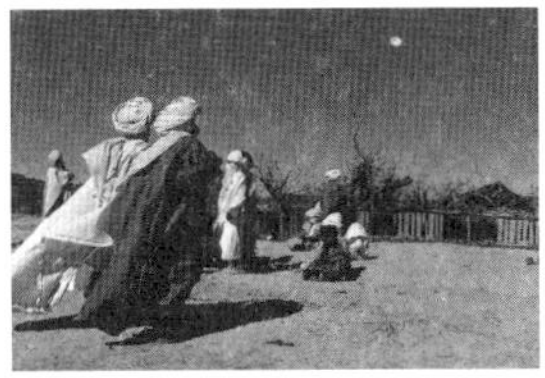

brethren without." This very first planting has its mystery: although the olive branch borne by the dove managed to survive the Flood, there was no mention of plants on the Ark. Drunkenness of Noah, the new fall of Adam. The grape after the apple. The difference is a difference of time—the time of fermentation. From its earliest traces (6000 BC) at the Indo-European heart, near the Persian shore of the Caspian Sea—although the divining bones of the Chinese Bronze Age also mention it: *li*, *chang* or *chiu*—wine was part of all Western civilization, from Egypt to Palestine, Mesopotamia to Greece, Rome to Islam, the Mongols to the Christians. It belonged to all empires and all wars, the wars of the Gauls, the Hundred Years War, the Inquisition, the Religious Wars, the *Reconquista*, the discovery of the New World, the Seven Years War, Prohibition. Its history is one of religious and magic proscriptions (Dionysian or Bacchic cults, Jewish and Islamic prohibitions, monastic secrets) and of laws to regulate its cultivation, production, harvest, sale, taxation, soil, and vines up to the introduction of *appellation d'origine contrôlée* (AOC). Its history is also that of a constant attempt to regulate trade: customs laws, tax collection, tithes, tolls, allowances, and privileges—"wine polices." Wine, milk, and honey are the delights of the Judeo-Christian paradise. Wine, bread, and oil are the signs of Mediterranean civilization. According to Ovid, the three daughters of Anius had the power to turn all they touched into cereal (*Spermô*), wine (*Oinô*), and oil (*Elaïs*). These were civilized, manufactured, denatured foods (in contrast to meat).

Crazy for Tea & Crazy for Wine

Tea, wine, and spirits are defined by the precision of a vintage, a soil, and a climate. In China, connoisseur drinkers embrace all three of these liquids. The famous poets Li Po, Tu Fu, and Tu Lung were "immortal drinkers," wine-crazy as much as tea-crazy. Their works may surprise those who have never attended a long tea-drinking session and do not know the deep and singular intoxication of the Chinese leaf—extraordinary because it has nothing noxious or tiring about it—but modern initiates will confirm that the effects of wine and tea are comparable. Like wine, the mixing of teas, the successive tasting of different vintages often produce intense effects. Wulong and Dan Cong teas—plucked from a single tree many centuries old—induce euphoria, the mark of which is a fixed grin and a mixture of lucidity and jubilation: the vertigo has none of the unsteadiness and heaviness that go with alcohol, and the sharpened sensibility is without the tension and letdown of cocaine. The secondary effects consist of an increased sensual perception that can, in an urban context, break down a person's defenses, and of a hunger that, having been suppressed as it is with coca or qat, can open a vast emptiness in the belly.

Wine & Cigarettes

Alcohol and cigarettes know few exceptions to their worldwide empire. The poetry of Zen Buddhism and the Arab mystics shows how the proscription on fermented

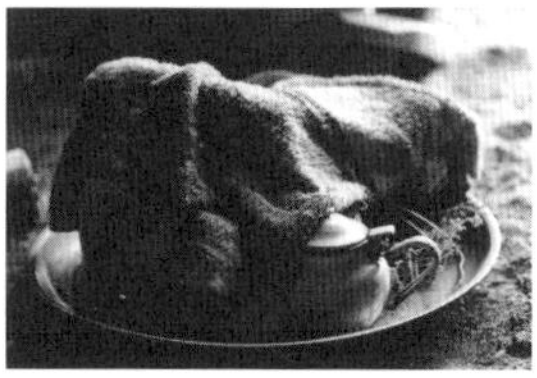

drink was ignored at the heart of religion itself. Tobacco—arrived later from the New World—, suffered less than alcohol from prohibition: it is quicker to list the communities that refuse to smoke—Parsis, Sikhs, Tunguses, Korean monks, Abyssinian Christians—than the abstainers. No doubt this general dominance, which on the one hand lumps together very different drinks (from the lightest beer to the most lethal spirit), and on the other reduces the ways of using tobacco (smoking is the virtually exclusive method and the cigarette far outstrips the pipe and cigar), prevents a clear view of their importance other than on the world market, or of their effect elsewhere than the statistics of the World Health Organization. No doubt too, this generalization only becomes apparent in the partitioning of spaces into zones where one may and may not smoke—drawing a new line between the private and the public—and of moments when one may and may not drink—distinguishing times of leisure from those involving work, safety, or control of machines. No doubt again, this vast extension allows one to assess, by the thresholds of tolerance, the moral climate of the age and the "advanced" countries: the United States, with its ever-increasing restrictions on smoking in public, northern Europe, with its limits on drinking hours and the sale of alcohol.

Without Urbanity

The capsules of French Paradox (concentrates of flavonols) and antiseptic alcohol (90 percent proof) are the only extreme manifestations of the therapeutic value of wine—for a long time medicine's sole weapon other than simples—while its central role in nutrition, shared with beer soup, in northern and southern Europe, has completely dissolved into the "drink" it has become. And in these post-industrial times, when, Aids notwithstanding, cancer remains the metaphor-disease of the age, it may seem an aberration that tobacco was for a long time a resort of pharmacopeia. As for the accompanying rites—antique libations and medieval drinking contests to the point of alcoholic blackout or death; divinatory or propitiatory smoking ceremonies—these have given way to a cliché of "conviviality" without urbanity, a reflex gesture whose sole value subsists in the fact it is blacklisted.

Removal of Taste

The highly varied forms taken by tea divide its image in contiguous representations: an everyday stimulant and a work of art to be tasted and a therapeutic drink. "It has not the arrogance of wine, the self-consciousness of coffee, nor the simpering innocence of cocoa." (Okakura Kakuzo) But in the depleted state to which it has been reduced in the course of this century, tea is so lacking in taste and effect that its very meaning is left in the air.

Tea, Coffee, Cocoa

Tea, coffee, cocoa. From the first writings about tea in the West, in particular that of Philippe Sylvestre Dufour, to the economic and dietary classifications that now

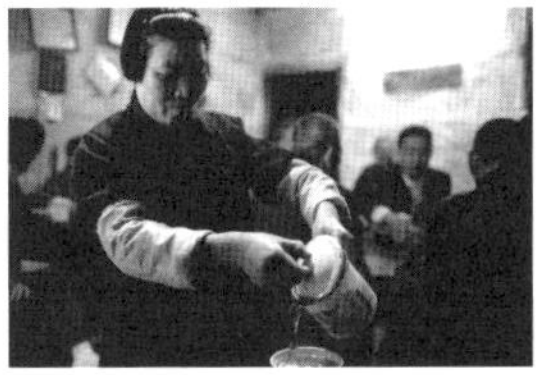

define "the structures of everyday life" (Fernand Braudel), tea is ranked in the grand trio of exotic beverages. On its native ground, China, Japan, and Taiwan, this trinity is just meaningless. Clearly many other groupings are possible, according to where one is: Qat-Coffee (Yemen-Ethiopia); Coca-Maté-Cocoa (America); Tea-Maté-Qat-Betel-Coca (green leaf); Qat-Coca-Betel-Kola-Tobacco-Kava (chewed stimulant); Tobacco-Hashish-Opium (smoked stimulant); Tea-Maté-Coffee-Tisane (infused stimulant); Tea-Coffee-Kola-Maté-Guarana-Cocoa (plant with caffeine); Cocoa-Coffee-Kola (fruit and not leaf); Coffee-Chocolate-Cigar (the three Cs to end a French meal); Coffee-Tea-Tobacco (Iranian treaty of Ahmad al-Motabbet al-Hoseyni, 1617); Sarsaparilla-Tea-Coffee (treaty of Qâzhi b. Kâsef al-din Mohamad Yazdi, 1642); Coffee-Tea (product and house of consumption); Alcohol-Tobacco (duty free); Coca-Cola (marketing).

Stimulating, Fermented, Non-Alcoholic

Tea has been adopted. Like others. Like the three stimulating, fermented, non-alcoholic drinks: Asian tea, American cocoa, African coffee; all borrowed, enjoyed, and transformed by the West. Many other plants were not: six stimulants from Asia and the South Sea Islands, America, and Africa respectively: betel (*piper chavica betle*) and kava (*piper methysticum*), maté (*ilex paraguayensis*) and coca (*erythroxylon coca*), the kola nut (*sterculia acuminata*) and qat (*catha edulis*). Each is a stimulant chewed either by itself or with an accompaniment, as the betel leaf is with the almond of a palm tree (*areca catechu*) and lime. However extensive their use—qat in Yemen and Ethiopia, coca in Peru, Colombia, and Bolivia, maté in Argentina, Paraguay, Chile and Brazil, betel in a great part of Asia—Europe did not adopt them. The poppy, cannabis, and coca were not to be adopted until the industrial age, and then solely in a prepared, extracted, or refined form (morphine, hashish, cocaine), and by the so-called underworld.

The Three Beverages

Tea, coffee, and chocolate are kin: at meals and breaks we choose between them; they are the three black beverages, stimulating and sweet; the West went very far to get them. Tea, coffee, and chocolate are consumed at the same times and in the same venues: from the first coffee houses of Oxford and London to the first (French) writings concerning them and to today's financial papers, the three drinks have always been associated. In fact, all three contain alkaloids, or xanthines, closely akin but in different assemblies (theophylline, theobromine, caffeine), whose effects, perhaps because of differences of treatment (fermentation, roasting, drying), are hard to compare: the exciting coffee, the relaxing chocolate, the stimulant tea.

Each finds itself isolated against the others: *I.* Tea and coffee share the stimulus of caffeine, or theine, while chocolate plays more on the aphrodisiac in theobromine;

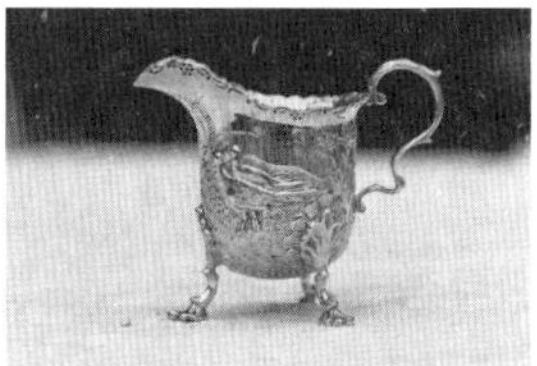

II. Chocolate and tea have certain connotations of leisure (old ladies in a teashop), in contrast to the coffee break where the worker regains strength, as he might do with a glass of red wine. Wine, a metaphor of blood, would, however, be the prop of the manual worker, whereas coffee reinvigorates the stressed employee. This division makes coffee the drink of the service industries, the little helper of a society of back-up troops, the purposeful ally of work. From this perspective, in the countries where it is drunk, wine loses ground in the face of constant technological advances, which create more service and fewer manual jobs, while at the same time drunkenness is outlawed as a danger when in control of machines (road safety); *III.* Coffee and chocolate both have the opacity of particles in suspension, while tea, without milk, displays the transparency of an infusion; with the notable exception of the tea in a Japanese ceremony, which is a powder beaten to a froth, looks like a thick green coffee, and is maybe similar to the sacrificial *cacahualt* of Montezuma.
Western agriculture, industry, and botany have divided each of the three plants into three species or varieties of astonishing similarity. Coffee thus occurs as *arabica* (with its varieties *mocha, bourbon, maragogipe*), *robusta* (*palembang, mandheling, kouilou, canephora, niaouli, nana, excelsa, liberic*a) and *arabusta*. The many varieties of cocoa (*cundeamor, amarillo, colorado*) are regrouped as *criollo, forastero*, and *trinitario*. The varieties of tea are condensed into *sinensis, assamica*, and *indonesia*. In each case the first type (*arabica, criollo, sinensis*), which is the oldest in cultivation and provenance (Abyssinia, Venezuela, China), is acknowledged to produce the subtlest vintages. The second type (*robusta, forastero, assamica*) is found in a wild state but was brought into cultivation late and on a massive scale by Westerners (Spanish Jesuits in Brazil, the Dutch in Indonesia and Java, the English in India and Ceylon), producing a mediocre quality. The third type *(arabusta, trinitario, indonesia*) is either a hybrid of the first two or a variety with intermediary qualities—the aromatic qualities of the first and the robustness of the second.

A Less Blurred Definition

Cocoa does not have a clear and fixed identity like tea and coffee, which, although used as aromatic essences in all sorts of preparations, are first and foremost hot, stimulating drinks. Cocoa is broken down in its transformation into cocoa powder and cocoa butter, which, with sugar, constitute the three ingredients of chocolate. Chocolate is eaten, sucked, and drunk: it belongs with soft drinks, cakes, and confectionery. In its appellation, manufacture, and use, cocoa / chocolate has a complex identity; as does wine, with its climates, soils, and additives; coffee is a drink, a flavor, and, in France, a place of consumption (café). Tea, particularly in its "narrow" Japanese or "restricted" English versions, but even in its wider Chinese manifestations and however diverse its vintages, remains an infusion of a leaf, thus retaining a less blurred definition.

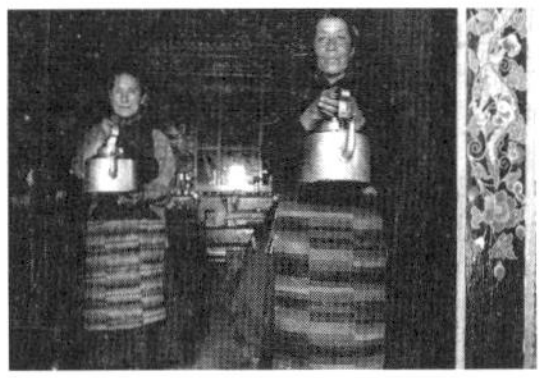

A General Inversion

Like King Sugar, the three Magi tea, coffee, and cocoa have been driven to the epiphany of Christendom: the "alienation" (deportation, transplantation, and exploitation), in the very precise sense humans, plants, and an entire culture have been self-estranged. "I do not know if coffee and sugar are necessary to the happiness of Europe, but I know with certainty that the two plants have been the unhappiness of two parts of the world. America has been depopulated to clear land for plants; Africa has been depopulated to get a people to cultivate them." (Bernardin de Saint-Pierre, 1773). In tandem with the vast traffic in humans, reduced to slavery for sugar, the three black drinks were swept into an extraordinary global cycle. A general inversion: *I.* Coffee, native to Africa, was henceforth cultivated in America; *II.* Cocoa, inversely, moved from America to Africa; *III.* Tea was spirited out of China to be planted in India.

These movements were of course more complex, granted that coffee was produced by the Arabs and Persians, and that the Spanish and Portuguese replanted it in the New World. While the Spanish, after the Mayas and the Aztecs, cultivated cocoa in Central America, which in the seventeenth century included Jamaica, Santo Domingo, the Philippines, Martinique, and Ecuador. But in 1824, the Portuguese transplanted cocoa to Africa, on the island of Sao Tome, one of the chief exporters of the end of that century; and after 1850, to Ghana, Nigeria, the Ivory Coast, Cameroon, Java, Sumatra, New Guinea, and Samoa. Ever since, Africa has been the chief world producer of cocoa. As for tea, this was wrested from the Middle Kingdom by the English in the nineteenth century to be cultivated in a colonized India, something that would be repeated, after Indian Independence, in the 1960s in Kenya, thenceforth one of the main tea exporters. These movements are further complicated by the fact that in Ceylon tea took the place of coffee, because of its resistance to the parasite that entirely destroyed the latter. Meanwhile in Taiwan, until very recently the largest sugar cane exporter in the world, with an annual production of over a million tons, priority has been given to tea. The very ancient Chinese tea tradition and the art of *gong fu* have thus been reinvented on that island where the British had helped develop an "Oriental Beauty" to their liking, and where the Japanese had extended the cultivated ground, thanks to their agronomic techniques.

Again one sees the dance of commodities—speculative and not subsistence crops—that are called basic although they are non-essential foods in their current forms, that find new lands, to become products reserved exclusively for export: sugar, coffee, cocoa, but also palm oil, jute, and rubber.

Seasoning, Drink, Fooddrogue

In our world, all materials that contribute to nutrition are foods. These are divided into drinks, seasonings, and foods in the narrow sense of the word. Tea is at once a seasoning, a drink, and a food (in northern and eastern China, nomads got their

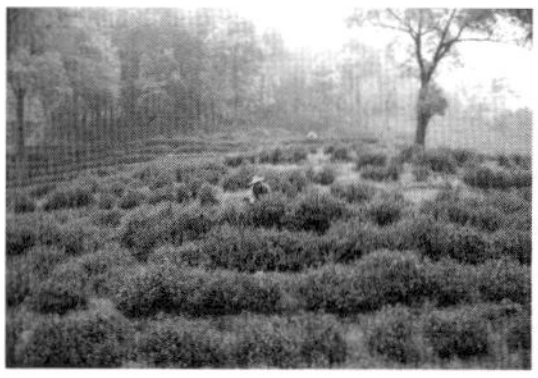

minerals, vitamins, and fiber from tea soup, which the Tibetan "butter tea" can give an idea of). It was not as a food, however, that Europe first discovered tea. The weekly *Mercurius Politicus*, in its issue of September 23-30, 1658, published the first advertisement of the beneficial effects of the drink and its endorsement by doctors, at a stage when the word "tea" itself seemed to be undecided: "That excellent, and by all Physitians approved, *China* drink, called by the *Chineans*, *Tcha*, by other Nations, *Tay alias Tee*, is sold at the *Sultaness*-head, a *Copheehouse*, in *Sweetings* Rents by the Royal Exchange, *London*." In the oldest written text on the subject in Japan—*Kissa Yôjôki*, "Drink tea for good health"—the Chinese plant was also recommended in this capacity to islanders by one of the great fathers of Buddhism, Myôan Eisai (1141-1215), said to have brought tea powder from the continent: "In these times, tea is an excellent elixir for the health, which has the ability to prolong human life. It grows in the mountains and valleys, where the spirit of the gods retreats. We humans take it and lengthen our lives."

Drug

Before providing for their necessities, men first domesticated the superfluous (spices, drugs, domestic pets) for magic, medical, and esthetic purposes. "Tea began as a medicine and grew into a beverage. In China, in the eighth century, it entered the realm of poetry as one of the polite amusements. The fifteenth century saw Japan ennoble it into a religion of estheticism—Teaism." (Okakura Kakuzo) "These countries have given us such an abundance of sugar, that all our kitchens are full of it, and we now devour too much from greed, whereas before sugar could only be got from the apothecaries, who kept it only for the sick, which is to say that what once served as a medicine now serves as a food." (A. Ortelius, 1572) In the seventeenth and eighteenth centuries, tea, like coffee and chocolate, was a medicine; and in the same category, surprising as it may now seem, were spices, pepper, and even salt and sugar (*saccharum officinarum*). They were first adopted in the royal court, then apothecaries took over the use of them. Holland and its doctors—Jacob Pontius, Nicolas Tulp, Cornelius Bontekoe, author of *Tractaat van het excellente ruyde Thee*—produced countless theses on the effects of tea, generating much controversy, as did France, where Dr. Spon, alias Philippe Sylvestre Dufour, published a treatise on *Caphé, thé et chocolate* in Lyons.

Pharmacy

Panacea or poison: the ambiguity is there in the words themselves, from the Greek *pharmakon* to the Latin *venenum* to the word drug itself: the health-giving and the toxic ever hand in hand; the list of counter-indications as proof of the potency of the remedy. Or again, against pain and for intoxication: antiseptic and analgesic alcohol—without moderation. But Africa, the East Indies, and above all the West Indies opened Europe to the exuberance of tropical vegetation, the effectiveness of

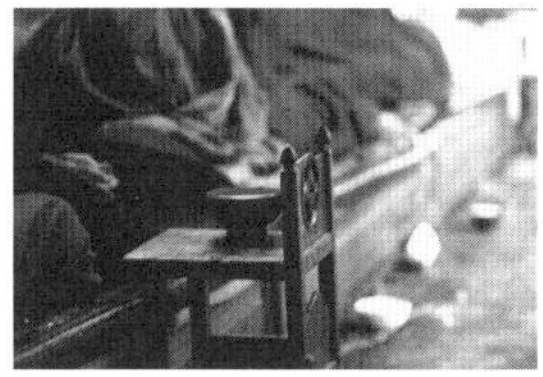

which discredited the garden of simples. What were sage, hellebore, and lungwort to do, any more than the extracted elements of animals (viper, deer, lizard) or minerals (arsenic, mercury, antimony), in the face of strychnine, cocaine, and atropine from the Amazon? Opium alone contains codeine, morphine, and papaverine; it is indeed that which: "Enlarges what is unbounded / Extends the limitless / Deepens time" (Charles Baudelaire). Louis Lewin attempted a first classification of these substances by their effect: euphorica, phantastica (Indian hemp, *Solanaceae*, peyote), inebrantia, hypnotica, excitantia (tobacco, tea, coffee). The psychotropic drugs are now categorized differently, into psycholeptics (hypnotics, tranquilizers, neuroleptics), psychodysleptics (hallucinogens, stupefacients), and psychoanaleptics (antidepressants, amphetamines). Sedatives, perturbators, stimulants. Three ways of supplementing endomorphine and enkephaline, the endogenous drugs of the brain. In fact, each new element extracted or synthesized to complete the medicine cabinet is liable to feed the body's traffic and the underground market. In the case of tea, an insipid drink consumed without counting, the whole of Europe, notwithstanding, became smuggler, then drug dealer.

LSD, GHB, DOB

Before the end of the twentieth century, synthetic drugs infiltrated or irrigated society, concurrently with—and at the same technical level as—computing or genetic biology. Before the introduction of Ecstasy (MDMA or methylenedioxymethylamphetamine) and DOB (MBDB, a hundred times stronger than MDMA), LSD (Lysergic Saür Diethylamide) led the way in the Sixties, at the stage when the first, enormous, electronic calculators were tested. Another molecule, perfected at the same time and rediscovered with EPO and PFC by bodybuilders when steroids were banned, now presents itself as the ideal drug: GHB (Gamma-Hydroxybutyrate). Colorless, odorless, and leaving no trace in the body, GHB circulates in dance clubs in the United States. It is the Date Rape Drug: notices warn that it can be slipped surreptitiously into drinks and render the victim defenseless against sexual abuse. The intense effect and impossibility of detection of GHB, leaving rapes and deaths attributed to it almost unprovable, added to the ease with which it can be made from chemical products harder to control than cannabis, coca, or poppy, have suddenly discredited the classic drugs, which had retained an exoticism owing to the remoteness of their source, their illegality, and associated rituals. The designer drugs can multiply new molecules: to try them out it is not necessary to smoke, inhale, or inject, merely to swallow a pill.

Food & Medicine

Between toxins and nutrients, functional foods have invaded the shelves of the supermarkets, alternative pharmacies, and health food shops: nutritional supplements, foods lightened and enriched in turn, concentrated extracts administrated

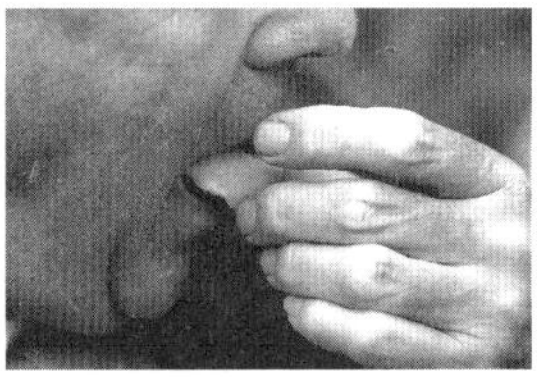

under various forms. The formulation by industry and commerce of products that the human ingests or injects is a restrictive rediscovery of the old thinking of the Chinese in their regulation of daily life. Cosmogony and pharmacopeia were indissociable from everyday activities: no food is neutral, it depends on the moment, the climate, the person, the altitude, the season, the orientation. It is neither pure nutrition nor simple pleasure, and never without consequences. Every food is by definition medication. In this sense, the dietetic debate in the West, based on science or a simple promotional argument, is like a recurrence of the history of tea, which passed from medicinal use as a drug to everyday use as a commodity.

Panaceas

Tea, coffee, and cocoa, like sugar cane, were introduced into each of their spheres as panaceas, universal prophylactics. The processing they underwent—both manufacturing and extraction of the active principal—led, paradoxically, to the disappearance of their medicinal effect, lost with their magic power, which had been reinforced by rarity, cost, and aristocratic use: thenceforth, they were ordinary fare, less communal than common.

Dietetics has now carved out an area, between gastronomy and therapy, in which to practice the new cult of the panacea: clay, seaweed, nettles have been invested with limitless virtues, great powers founded on ancient knowledge. These claims are betrayed, however, by the stereotypes that underlie them: the same words, the same ailments, although the remedy changes. The long protection of trade that tea enjoyed in China, and the country's remoteness and closure to foreigners, have no doubt contributed to this curious development: tea, that "nothing, which is drunk," is the only one of the three beverages to be extensively credited with beneficial properties by women's magazines and scientific research. Green tea has emerged as an anti-coca-cola—which drink began, none the less, as a universal elixir.

Everything and More

In recent books that juxtapose rehashed legends and hypotheses based on pharmaceutical tests, indulge in exotic onomastics, and throw their weight around with daunting scientific terms, tea, green or black, finds itself obliged to answer to everything. Everything and more. Apparently, tea quenches thirst and makes one urinate; supposedly the process needs to be followed right through. Thirst is quenched not only because water is brought to the organism, but also because the polyphenols, free glucids, amino acids, and vitamin C mix with the saliva in the mouth, increase its secretion, moisten the buccal cavity and give a sensation of coolness; meanwhile the aromatic substances, bringing a certain amount of heat as they volatilize, create a refreshing sensation; and the diuresis produced by the caffeine causes much heat loss. The tea leaves also contain alkaloids (theine, theobromine, theophylline), which are diuretic, because they allow the number of sodic and chlorine ions in the

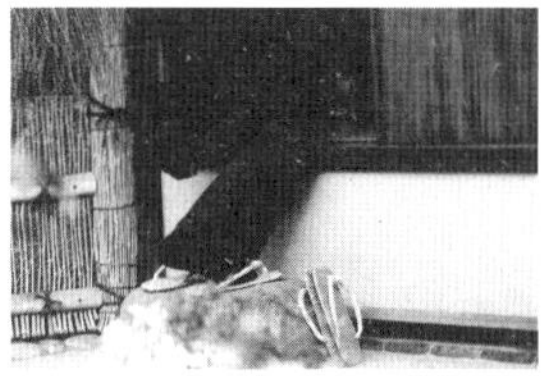

urine to increase by inhibiting renal reabsorption, all while provoking a relaxation of the entire nervous and vascular system, from which the renal vessels benefit. The flavonols, such as quercetin, reinforce the diuresis as a synergic factor, and the compound 6,8 dithio-n-octanoate, also contained in tea, is diuretic and anti-emetic. Amidst all the detail, the explanation passes from tea to its components, three of which constantly crop up: caffeine, vitamin C, and polyphenols.

Free Radicals

Tea quenches thirst, it restores, it stimulates. It activates the nervous cells, it detoxifies alcohol, tobacco (in Japan and South Korea tea extracts are included in cigarette filters), and urban pollution. It fights senescence (in acting against free radicals, which attack unsaturated fatty acids and start a chain of reaction against macromolecules by lipidic peroxidation); it has a sterilizing action against bacteria (dysentery, cholera vibrios, staphylococci, the Yersinia bacterium of enterocolitis, typhoid, trichophyton mentagrophytes fungi and erythrasma); it is an antivirus (acting against herpes zoster, psoriasis, beriberi, and even a plant virus such as tobacco or cucumber mosaic disease); it has a slimming action, in reducing the lipid content of the blood, and also reduces the three cholesterols (low density, hyperdensity, high density), whereas coffee makes cholesterol rise; it has a beneficial effect on atheromas and arteriosclerosis; it helps control hypertension and prevent cardiovascular diseases; it inhibits platelet agglutination and is preventive of thrombosis and cerebral hemorrhage; it acts on angina pectoris, coronary thrombosis, heart failure, and arrhythmia; it is a deodorizer and a digestive; it produces a reduction of glycemia and has a preventive action against diabetes (thanks to tea extracts: diphenylamine, hydrosoluble polyoside, methyl salicylate, catechin); it acts against asthma; it improves visual acuity and helps treat ophthalmic ailments; it has a protective effect on the liver and is preventive of and a treatment for scurvy; an American investigation after Hiroshima demonstrated its protective action against radiation; it is anti-allergic (catechin inhibits histamine); it acts against ulcers; it sharpens the intelligence and controls psychosomatic conditions; it is used to treat constipation; it has an anti-carcinogenic and anti-mutagenic action. Within the disorder, followed here, of a book published in 1995, which forces Western taxonomy in the Eastern system, what stands out is the way it passes from the banal to the radical, from intellectual stimulation to intestinal motions, from a fought cancer to an avoided mutation. Tea is already committed to the advance guard of the resistance to biogenetic manipulation.

Virtues Enumerated

The first European to mention tea, the Venetian Giambattista Ramusio (1485-1557), was relying on an account by the Persian Hadji Mohammed that described tea—*chai catai*—specifically by the health-giving properties attributed to it: "A cup

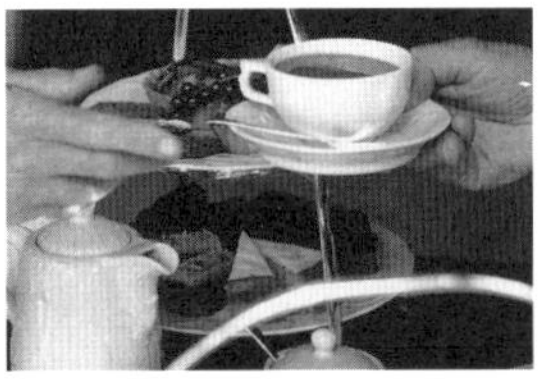

or two of this decoction taken on an empty stomach cures fever, headache, stomachache, pain in the side or in the joints. It should be taken as hot as you can bear it. If anyone feels uncomfortable after eating too large a meal, let him take a cup of tea and he will quickly digest it all. Tea is held in such regard that all travelers carry some with them and are willing to buy an ounce for a sack of rhubarb. The Chinese say that if the Persians and the French only knew about tea, they would stop buying rhubarb and buy nothing but tea." (*Navigazioni et Viaggi*, II, 1559)

In 1642, Dr. Nicolas Tulp wrote: "Nothing compares to this plant. Those who use it are free of all kinds of illnesses entirely because of it and grow to a very old age; not only does it give the body much vigor, it also protects it from gravel and stones, migraines, colds, eye ailments, catarrhs, asthma, a sluggish stomach, and intestinal troubles. It has the further merit of fending off sleep and helping night vigils, which makes it very useful to people who want to spend the hours of darkness writing and thinking."

De l'usage du caphé, du thé et du chocolate was first published anonymously in 1671 in Lyons. The author, Philippe Sylvestre Dufour, alias Jacob Spon, enumerates in a curiously similar manner the virtues of coffee, which "dries up all cold and damp humors, drives away wind, strengthens the liver, helps those with dropsy by its purifying quality; a remedy likewise against gall and corruption of the blood; it invigorates the heart and the heartbeat, brings ease to those who suffer stomachaches and loss of appetite; it is equally good for cold, humid, heavy indisposition of the brain. The steam that rises from it is good for congested eyes and noise in the ear; it is a remedy also for shortness of breath, for colds that attack the lungs, and painful spleen, for worms, and extraordinarily comforting after too much eating and drinking. Nothing better for those who eat a lot of fruit."

A Form of Currency

If the first mention of tea recorded by a European—Giambattista Ramusio, citing the Arab Mohammed—concentrated on its health-giving properties, an earlier account by another Arab, in 851, was more concerned with its economic importance. "To the king are assigned in kind, as important sources of revenue, salt and a herb that is drunk with hot water, which is sold at a high price in each town: they call it *sakh*. It is used everywhere. The Treasury derives its income entirely from taxes, salt, and this herb."

Coffee, cocoa, and tea, like sugar, salt and spices, were each used in their own country as a form of currency: the berry of the coffee tree, coin of the Arab nomads, the bean-coins of the Aztecs, the paper bills of the Chinese representing packets of tea, and later claimed as tax, duty, or tribute, until they were finally quoted on the stock market. Now subject to the fluctuations of the financial markets, the producing countries are left in a position of ultimate dependence on the conditions of the countries that have overturned all their resources. In this reversal, the Indies have

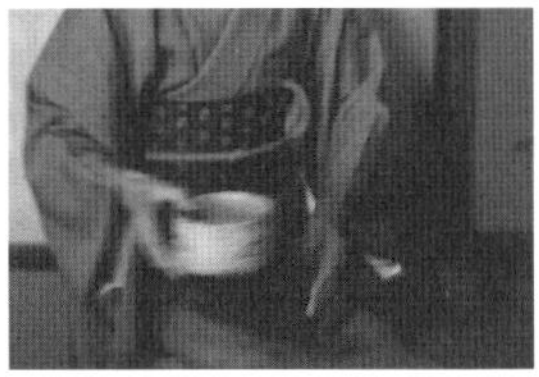

definitively lost their aura as the land which dispatched proofs of a world beyond, exotic flavors, and status symbols.
"Spices like a link to Paradise, Paradise being somewhere in the Orient. Pepper, nutmeg, cinnamon, having come by the long trade route from India, reveal the status of the ruling class, the insignia of power. Sumptuary: moderation or excess." (Wolfgang Schivelbusch)

The Tea Tax

In France today, tea, although of poor quality, is an expensive commodity, for it is not indexed and taxed on consumption, as coffee is. Apart from the metonymic force promoting the drink that has given its name to the café, the fact that coffee is the cheapest item on the menu encourages people to order a *petit noir* when not sure what to have. This is recognized in the market studies for internal purposes of the professional suppliers of CRH (café-restaurant-hôtel). When one considers that the quality of the bag of dust on offer is even poorer than that of the taxed coffee, it is ultimately reassuring that the handicap of price is not overcome.

Term, Text, Tax

In the China of the Tang (618-907), tea gained a name, a text, and a tax: *I.* The mandarin *cha* was officially adopted in place of a variety of other words used until then to refer to tea: *gu, chuan, she, ming, gao lu, du; II.* The poet Lu Yu wrote several texts about tea, water, and the mountains, including the famous *Chajing, The Classic of Tea*, that launched a long series of "books of tea." A genre that modern publishers have tended to trivialize, particularly after Okakura Kakuzo's *Book of Tea*, published in 1906; *III.* Tea tribute was instituted to provide the Son of Heaven and his Court with the best quality leaves. In the time of the Han and Nan, tea cultivation, most often practiced in the precincts of the Buddhist monasteries, was introduced particularly in the south and east of the Chang Jiang (Yangtze) valley. The canal dug by the Sui (589-618) provided between the different kingdoms of the north and south a proper axis of communication, which helped the Tang create political stability and economic expansion, to which their art—ceramics, poetry, painting, and calligraphy—bears witness. With this movement, tea was to spread as a popular commodity from the south towards the center and north, as far as the frontiers dominated by different nomadic peoples. The assignment of public places for serving the drink—the first tea houses, called *chakuans*—was the most obvious indication of the place henceforth occupied by the beverage. A truly national drink.

Tributes & Tribes

More than a simple currency, tea appeared as a new economic sign, as is proved by the role it played in political control and the economic dependence it permitted inside the country—as tribute—and outside, on the frontiers—the tribes. The consumption of tea extended to the Yellow River, and reached the people of the

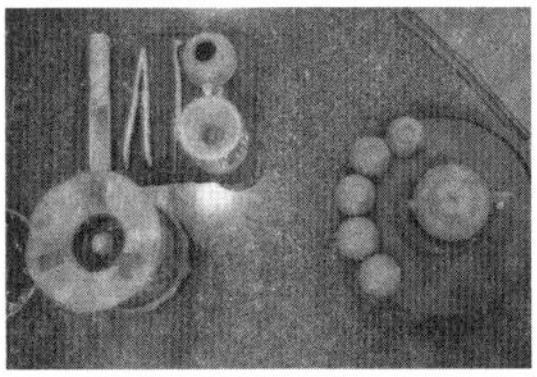

north, whose history symbolically dates the entry of tea to the marriage of Princess Wen Cheng to a Tibetan king. One may point out that the West did similarly in linking the arrival of tea in England to the marriage, in 1662, between Charles II and the Portuguese Princess Catherine of Braganza, said to have brought a tea chest in her trousseau and introduced tea to the Court. The arrival of cocoa in France is likewise associated with the arrival in 1615 of Louis XIII's wife Anne of Austria, a Habsburg brought up in Madrid.

Cha Ma Si

The central power deliberately used the sale of tea to forge an alliance with the barbarians or to settle them in outlying parts: the regions of Xinjiang, Xizang (Tibet), Waimengu (Outer Mongolia), Nemengu (Inner Mongolia), and Qinghai. On the frontiers were held great markets, great fairs, alien to the Chinese style of business, which has always preferred a radial distribution system suited to supplying small streets of shops, without the risks run by large gatherings where strangers would run into each other. For the tribes of the northwest, who fed almost exclusively on meat and animal fat with very little vegetable fiber, tea was an ideal complement to the diet. Tang politics created a need—which is evidenced in the continued use of tea to this day, despite all the conflicts in these regions—for what was as much a primary staple as a stimulant of pressing necessity. With the "tea and horse trade" between China and the Mongols, established under Emperor Su Zong (756-762), the central government gained on all fronts—military, diplomatic, economic. Indeed, through the "Tea and Horse Office" (*cha ma si*), China distributed its tea and secured, in this empire that practiced surprisingly little animal husbandry on its territory, one of the essentials of military control: the possibility of a cavalry.

Tea Tribute

It was also under the Tang that a tax on tea (*cha sui)* came in: the production and trade of tea assumed such importance at this point that it was to supply the financial needs of central government and enter into the different power struggles. At once, on the precedent of salt, tea was brutally taxed at 10 percent. That first tax dates back to 782; the responsible is the Emperor De Zong. At this period, the tea-producing regions already corresponded to the eighteen provinces of today. The manufacturing center for the "tribute tea" lay mainly around Zhejiang, near Huzhou, close to what is now the pottery center of Yixing, which would produce the teapots necessary for *gongfucha*. Over three thousand persons were then hired for over three months to pluck and manufacture the tea.

Narcosis, Comedown, Dependence

At the beginning of the nineteenth century, to meet English and American demand for a commodity priced at twenty taels for a hundred pounds, the tea plantations occupied increasingly large areas, plucked many times in the year, by a growing

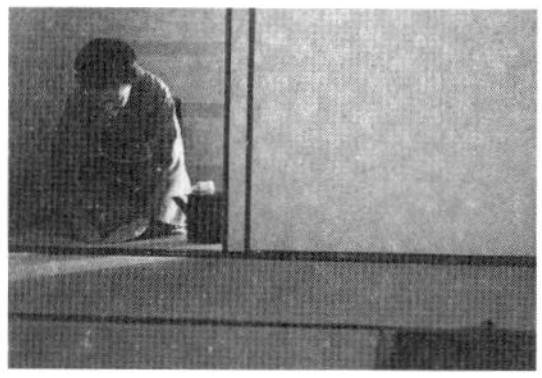

body of peasants who came pouring in from Jiangxi and Guangdong towards the center and north. But this rush was to suffer a reversal before the end of the century, more brutal even than the crisis that affected the export of brocades under competition from the Japanese, Italian, and French silk factories: the industrial methods of the plantations established in India and Ceylon, and the arrival of a modernized Japan, after 1860, led to a worldwide fall in the price of tea. The British had finally succeeded in transplanting the bush elsewhere, namely to that remarkable India, whose name, in the plural —Indies— referred to the various poles to be opened up and cleared with the help of the Companies. The catastrophe awaiting the thousand-year old culture developed in three stages, from gradual habituation to massive demand, and finally sharp comedown. Tea suffered a form of narcosis echoing that inflicted by the Europeans when, for the sake of tea and to avoid total dependence on China, they poured opium into a country that was ignorant of it. Nearly eight-tenths of Chinese tea plantations were abandoned. When Sun Yan Tsen arrived in the legendary Keemun early in the twentieth century, he was sadly surprised: "Anyone who owns bushes harvests them himself with the help of his family. Or rather, he tears off all the green leaves, having other things to get on with, such as rice growing. As far as he is concerned, the quicker he does his work, the better. There is no reward for a good plucking and everyone's leaves are mixed once they reach the factory. Plantations in the proper sense of the word no longer exist."

Fortune's Tea

"I was now out every day, from morning until evening, busily employed in collecting seeds, in examining the vegetation of the hills, and in obtaining information regarding the cultivation and manufacture of green tea. By this means I obtained a good collection of those tea-seeds and young plants from which the finest green teas of commerce are prepared, and much information of a useful kind." (Robert Fortune, *Journey to the Tea Countries of China*, 1952). In 1848, disguised as a Manchu merchant and accompanied by two Chinese servants, Robert Fortune left Shanghai on behalf of the Tea Committee, by night "to keep the matter as secret as possible," and headed for the tea mountains. This was the second of three journeys he made to China, each one full of adventure and observation, which he recounted in three books. On his return to Shanghai, he busied himself overseeing the planting of tea-seeds and young tea-plants in cases, for dispatch to India. "I did not like the idea of returning to Europe without being perfectly certain that I had introduced the tea-plant from the best black-tea districts of China into the Government plantations in the North-western Provinces of India. There may also have been a lingering desire to cross the Bohea mountains and to visit the far-famed Woo-e-shan." (*Ibid.*)

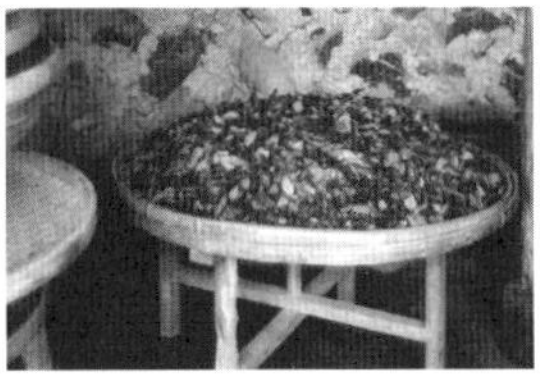

Tea's Fortune

"Beyond a few superficially common traits, the fortune of tea was of a different order to that of other commodities, both materially and psychologically." (Louis Dermigny). Indeed, not only was tea the last comer to the grand series sugar, tobacco, cocoa, and coffee, but it also represented a third stage in Chinese trade. After the Luso-Hispanic phase dedicated to silk, and a second one dominated by precious metals (gold and silver), this third stage was marked both by growth on a different scale to that of the previous two, and by its almost exclusive concentration on what Voltaire called the "little leaf." Thus the Batavia-Nagasaki axis, and the domination of oriental trade in the seventeenth century by the pairing Oost Indische Company—Japan, was overtaken after 1680 by the pairing East India Company—China, as the third pairing China—Japan came back into position. The Portuguese, Spanish, and French had ceded ground or stayed in harbor. At the same time, tea was totally separated from the other remedies imported from China (cinnamon, ginger, star anise, galanga, camphor, borax, alum, sapan wood) and notably the three main ones: rhubarb, China root, and cassia, which were the basis of European medicine. The fashion for tea soon led it to overtake silk and ceramics as an import: porcelain had preceded the drink it was designed to contain, but would thenceforth merely make up weight, acting as ballast at the bottom of the hold. "Gone were the days when China to an extent relieved an America producing insufficient precious metals and sugar; she differentiated herself from America and the rest of the world through trade, or, to be more precise, those personal values, that character of unicity she possessed to the highest degree on the moral plane, were transposed to the commercial plane." So neither cocoa nor tobacco nor coffee played the role of tea, which "is a rather extraordinary article, because it composed 70 to 90 percent of the cargo of all Chinese ships, and in the end mobilized veritable fleets; because, above all, it presents a striking contrast between the vastness of the distances covered and the non-essential, if not artificial, need that they satisfied: in this sense, the most spectacular of the long-distance trades."

Smuggling, Faking, Adulterating

In England, the government of Charles II, at the end of 1660, took advantage of the growing fashion for tea, as it had already done with tobacco, and imposed a heavy tax. Maintained until the nineteenth century, this was to provoke smuggling on a world scale, from which Dutch, French, Scandinavian and, in due course, American companies would draw the bulk of their profits. Smuggling—often controlled by City traders—but also adulteration and substitution of a product that often had no tea left in it, and even fictitious re-exportation to avoid the import tax, before a tax on consumption itself was imposed in 1723. The colonists of the New World would in their turn be heavily taxed in 1763 on sugar, paper, and tea, the third

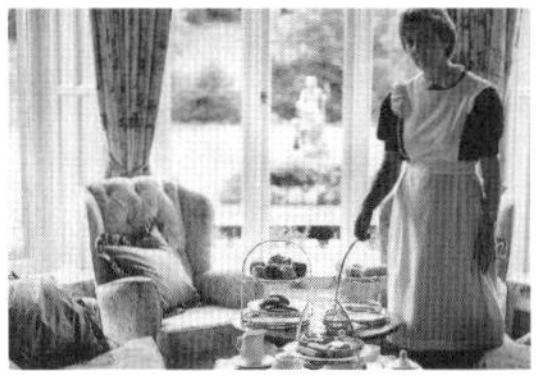

import after textiles and manufactured goods. In an effort to stop the boycott of consumption across the Atlantic, all taxes would be lifted, with the exception, however, of that on tea. By the Tea Act, the Company tried to get out of the crisis, freeing the drink from all taxes, other than that imposed six years earlier on the import of tea to the colonies. The result was the Boston Tea Party in December 1773, when three of the Company's vessels, the *Dartmouth,* the *Eleonor,* and the *Beever*, had their cargo of tea thrown overboard, leading to the American Revolution.

In Three Acts

The Tea Act of 1773 rearranged excise regulations to help the financially troubled Company. The India Act of 1784 placed the latter under the authority of the State, and was accompanied by Pitt's Commutation Act, which hugely reduced the tax on tea from 114 to 12.5 percent. These three acts marked the end of protectionism and mercantilism. As Hugh Johnson has pointed out, in the same way as the Romans brought vineyards to the countries they conquered, so did the English plant tea in India, Ceylon, and Africa. All the history of England makes it a sort of western China, where tea, inseparably tied to tax, is the fluid that links top and bottom of society, official with outlaw, and that ruled all the exchanges between interior and exterior.

Pharmakon & Sumbolon

"Signs of wealth: [...] The noise of medicines being pounded and tea being ground." In his *Za Cuan, Notes*, whose enumerative style Sei Shonagon adopted in her *Pillow Book*, the monk Li Yichan crushed medicine and *cha* in the communal pestle and mortar of a class-based society.

Before it was treated as a foodstuff, a thirst-quenching drink or an entry on a menu, tea was *pharmakon* and *sumbolon*. Drug and Money. Medicine and Valuable. Therapeutic object and economic object. Magic sign and symbolic sign. It is one of the rare things to remain so.

In a paradoxical history, where, although only trafficked between the British Empire and the Middle Kingdom, tea mobilized the economies—governments, banks, and law-breakers—of Europe (smuggling), Southeast Asia (country trade), the American States, and India. In an equally paradoxical history, where, as a minority drink outside England, China, and Japan, when one compares its use to that of coffee, chocolate, and obviously alcohol, it appears to have kept its curative function: after all, to have a cup of tea is to show weakness or admit frailty. There is the further fact that as a substance of consumption tea presents itself also as a sumptuary-libatory object. This makes it *sumbolon*, *pharmakon,* and *ouluchutai*—oulai and oulochutai were whole or coarsely ground barley grains that the Greeks roasted and spread on the sacrificial altar and victim's head.

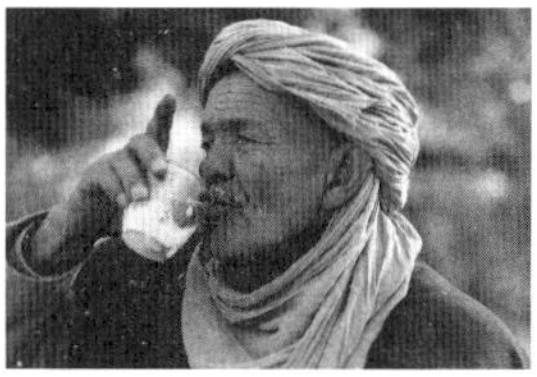

Therapeutic, Liturgical, Esthetic

Therapeutic, then, but also liturgical—the tea offering of the Mongols, the libation of the Tibetans, the ceremony of the Japanese—and again esthetic—the *gongfucha* of the Chinese, the *chadô* of the Japanese, the British pastime of afternoon tea. These three functions come up against the stubborn fact that tea, in these very different parts of the world, and without a sequential genealogy or "natural" necessity to explain it, tends still to be presented not only as a drink but also as a ritual. Ritual to be understood here as the spacing out of a technique: of specific hand movements and tools.

White Powders

Salt and sugar, while they have played a dominant and universal role in the economy of human societies—also exchanged, as a form of currency or a sign of life—, have been obtained either in the way of other animals as a nutrient naturally present in most foods, or separately, extracted, refined into the white powder to which industry reduces them. Drawn from the sea or earth, pressed from cane or beet, salt and sugar in their generalized use have been so abstracted that they can be confused, and are identified both with their chemical elements (sodium chloride, sucrose) and the most fundamentally opposite of the four poles of taste (sweet and salt). This current polarization barely masks the fact that the history of its domestication (from New Guinea, India, and Arabia) recalls: sugar was for a long time considered a spice, and the rule it exerts over modern eating habits perhaps lets us forget that, in animal physiology, sugar operates not in its sweetening version but as complex glucids. The function of salt and sugar, from now on shared— the best emblem being their joint use as taste exhausters in most food preparations—, consists of stimulating and maintaining consumption. The function gains in refinement as the products gain in "purity." This is henceforth the sole rite entrusted to them by the civilization which placed them at its origin: the "salt of the earth" and the "honey of love."

Black Powders

Next to the white extracts, black coffee and cocoa have a place whose history, a shorter one, falls into two distinct periods, which in turn define two spheres of provenance and two zones of influence. Pre-Columbian Mesoamerica and Catholic southern Europe (Spain, Portugal, Italy) for chocolate, Arabia and Protestant or bourgeois capitalist northwestern Europe (England, Holland, France) for coffee.

Kakawa

Cocoa has a form of prehistory that is in fact no other than the pre-Cortés history, which was literally disfigured and wiped out by the *conquistadores* and their missionaries. Long reduced to a few pale fables with echoes of darker myths, this history began to be reconstituted with the deciphering of the Maya hieroglyphs: "cocoa," pronounced *kakawa*, is a word from "the proto-mixe-zoque vocabulary of

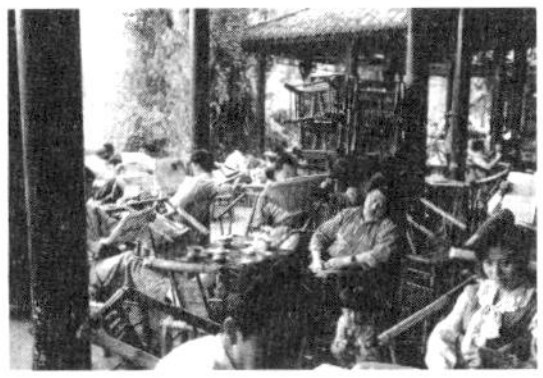

about 1000 BC, spoken at the apogee of the Olmec civilization in places such as San Lorenzo." (Sophie & Michaël Coe). In this region, the extreme humidity of the tropical forest, necessary for theobroma cocoa, is unconducive to archeological preservation; but the existence of the name in the language attests to the domestication of the plant by the Olmecs. The word occurs in *Popol Vuh*, the Maya "book of counsel": "They were delighted when they found a great mountain, full of good food, rich in white and yellow corn, and rich in patashte (*theobroma bicolor*) and cocoa." In the rare bark codices to have survived, some gods are depicted, with cocoa pods and plates full of cocoa beans. On a decorated vase conserved in Princeton, dating from 750 BC, a woman pours chocolate from one vessel to another to make it froth. Chocolate played a central role in Mayan rituals: eminent people served it as a libation-potlach at betrothal and marriage ceremonies, and at a form of baptism, when the child was anointed with a bone dipped in a mixture of "flowers and cocoa thinned with pure water." (Landa) To protect their crop, "in the month of Muan the owners of the cocoa plantations celebrated a feast in honor of the gods Ek Chuah, Chac, and Hobnil, who were their patrons" (Fray Sahàgun). While Aztec warriors made lavish use of cocoa in drinks, grain dishes and porridges, to which they also added herbs and spices (chili, pepper, vanilla, corn, *itsim-te* or *clerodendrum ligustrinum*, achiote or *bixa orellana*, *hueinacaztli* or *cymbopetalum penduliflorum*, ground kernels of marmalade fruit, *mexacochitl* or "thread-flower," *magnolia mexicana*, borage), the Spanish missionaries soon after arrival made confections from cocoa by adding cane sugar they had brought with them. These sweetmeats were marketed and found their way as far as the tables of the Old World, next to water ices and preserved fruits. That sweetener introduced, in place of pepper, by the monks and nuns probably caused chocolate to lose the sacred, ritualistic character that attached to it at the moment of consumption, an experience the very bitter, indeed acid, acrid taste of unprocessed cacao must have helped make rare. Moreover, in the Spain of the Habsburgs and the Italy of the Medici, chocolate was a dietary medicine—owing to its "cold and humid" properties—and a nourishing drink, which "did not break the fast" and was recommended by the Jesuits; but above all it was a fashionable delicacy.

Yerba

Yerba maté, which grows in the same regions as cocoa, did certainly not have the same widespread history as the latter, nor as *cha*, the tea the Chinese at the time of the Three Kingdoms called "herb" or "plant," as the indigenous Tupi-Guarani did maté: *ka'á*, picked up in the Spanish *yerba*. This generic name appropriated by *ilex paraguayensis* indicates already its importance in the region, and its symbolic function. It is one of the many stimulant, intoxicating, or hallucinogenic plant substances in which America is rich—from tobacco (*nicotiana tabacum*) to peyote

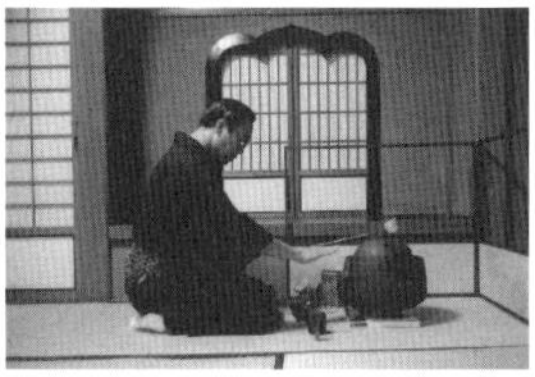

(*anhalonium lewinii*)—and which different ethnic groups used in their ritual practices. A century after the first Jesuit foundations, the undefeated tribes of Paraguay were persisted in these habits. But they also made the most of the physiological effects of this carrier of caffeine, *refresco*, *vomitorio*, or *medicina*. A refreshment, or a medical or ritual emetic, like the related Appalachian tea (*ilex cassine*) drunk by the Indians on the coasts of Florida, North and South Carolina, and Texas. Maté, first eaten in its natural state, then steeped in cold water, was made by the Company of Jesus like oriental tea, as an infusion in hot water: this was *maté cocido*. While the plant's scientific name still refers to its original provenance, the Paraguayan infusion was called not after the Guarani *kayguá* but after its Peruvian neighbor: maté—from the Quechua word for calabash, the fruit of the *lagenaria vulgaris*, in which it is drunk—or after what had become its main method of preparation: "*Te de los jesuitas*" ("the Jesuit's tea"). It was also often assimilated to the Andean plant that played such a large role in the region: coca. In 1594, Juan Romero of the Company of Jesus discovered with suspicion: "a water mixed with grass, which they call Paraguay grass," drunk by the Indians and the first Spaniards; which suggests that the drink developed from a fast cross-cultural exchange in the early days of colonization. Although there were regular attempts at prohibition and prolonged arguments among the Jesuits—as with tobacco, chocolate, and coca—before it was accepted that maté, a lightly infused liquid, did not break the fast as did the nourishing cocoa, it was in fact the Jesuits themselves who conducted the traffic (from the sixteenth century in the region of Guayrá). While coca would never cross over to the Spanish, but only be controlled and encouraged by the caciques, and chocolate and tea would not spread to the poor of colonial society until the republican period, maté permeated every social class in Paraguay and the surrounding regions. "Rich and poor take it in great quantities, the poor in vessels made of painted gourds or guayacán wood and the rich in the same vessels decorated with silver, drinking it through tubes of the same material." (Cardiel, 1731) The only things distinguishing rich from poor here would have been the fresh cane, the gold or silver used to make the receptacles (*bombilla*, *calabaza*, and *caldero*), and the quality of the leaf (*caa-kuy*, young leaves; *caa-mirim*, older leaves; *caa-quaza,* leaves mixed with branches), indeed the provenance of this forest plant.

Caffeine Content

On November 16, 1715 Captain Thomas Dover loaded 147 arrobas of maté at Rio de la Plata, destined for England, and in 1723 Savary des Bruslons recorded that "the English like it or at least pretend to like it no less than tea." But the venture did not prove lasting: maté would have only a limited spread, in Syria, Lebanon, and Israel, where a coconut replaced the gourd as a receptacle; in Europe, its use would be purely therapeutic, a treatment for kidney and urinary ailments, before dietetics

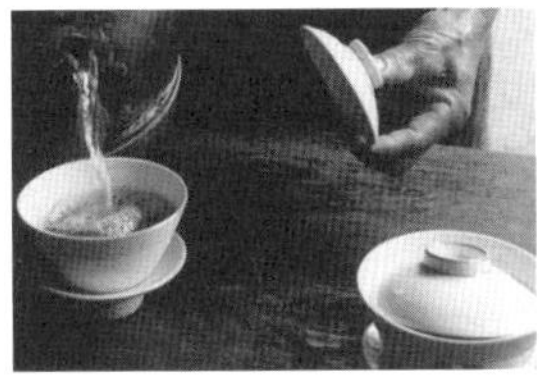

and aromatherapy gave it a place again. "In three of the largest parts of the world, Asia, Africa, and America, people discovered plants entirely different morphologically, but all with a common link: their caffeine content." (Louis Lewin, 1925) Coffee, tea, kola, cassine, *pasta guarana* (*Paullinia sorbilis*), and maté, then, the three last American. These plants have an effect on physiology but also always play a cohesive role in community life, bringing people together round a ritual substance, united both by place and the methods of consumption. The conviviality of maté is expressed not in a tea or coffeehouse, but in a circle gathered round the gourd, which is passed from hand to hand, each person drinking from the mouthpiece. This practice, somewhat alien to European ways, probably militated against the adoption of the Paraguayan drink. But maté would also have suffered here from its ill-defined identity, somewhere between tea and coffee. On the contrary, the steady growth in its consumption in Latin America, which "secularized" it, and sometimes paradoxically—when the Jesuits introduced it as a tea-type infusion—, made it a specialty: the regional version of coffee and tea. In that respect, the ancient Guarani rituals that went with it were absorbed into the specific methods of its tools and preparation. Although the leaf was roasted and ground like coffee and certain teas, and brewed like tea and certain coffees, maté retained its unique vessel—the last element of a forgotten ritual.

Qawah

The various stories that tell how coffee began always link its chance discovery—the intoxication of the shepherd Kaldi's goats on eating the red berries of the coffee bush—with its immediate use: an encouragement to prayer and meditation, as in the fable of Chehodet. Yemeni sufis, Maronite monks, Mocha dervishes. In one of these stories the Archangel Gabriel brings the potion *quawa*, black as the Kaaba stone, from Allah to the prophet Mohammed, who, having thought the hour of his death was come, regains the strength and will to raise an army and satisfy his wives. In the Abyssinian legend of the devout Bata Maryan, or the Yemeni tale of the faithful Omar wandering in the desert, the fragrant bush with red berries is a marvel, a miraculous revelation. One of the earliest recorded mentions of coffee goes back to an Arab doctor and philosopher, Rhazes (850-922). The *cahouah* of the Arabs then re-emerged, carried forward in historical chronicle, in the coffee houses—*kahveh-kanes*—of Constantinople in 1554. From there, less than a century later, they would spread and multiply across Europe, from Venice to London, as if coffee could be of no use except in establishments named after it, demand being such that in France the café swallowed up the traditional bars, the *estaminet, taverne,* and *cabaret.* Although coffee was the first of the exotic drinks to come to the West, bringing in its wake the establishments in which to drink it, which would soon serve chocolate and tea too, it also has the shortest history. Roasting and pulverization, by which the

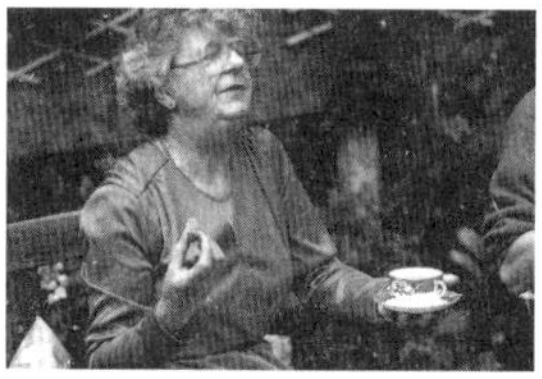

green coffee chewed or brewed with its pulp (*bun* or the present *qisher*) developed into *kahveh* or *qahwah*, came late, and the Arabs did not begin to cultivate the tree until the fifteenth century. Islam accepted its use, as a stimulant that might help keep people away from alcohol, but after much debate set restrictions on it. For this drink, quickly popularized, too often consumed, no tradition managed to establish a ritual, other than the motif of urban and social life, and later the domestic practice, that coffee became.

Chewed Leaves

Qat, betel, and coca further represent the three A's: Africa, Asia, and America, where the Old World went in search of its future. But these stimulants, important as they were over there, were not brought back; nor were they only refined. In each case, the chewed leaf is a "sacred plant" or "flower of paradise," which is reflected in the oldest of their known names—*khoka* for example signifies the tree, as do *ka'á*, the Indian name for maté, and *pan*, the Indian name for betel—with gods, in each case, attributed to the leaf and myths telling of its origin: Mama Coca, the wife of the Inca Manco Capac; the cult of Isis or of the saint Abu Zarbita substituted coffee for qat; Duthagâmini fighting with the Malabars, who thought he was wounded because his mouth was blood red from chewing betel. The taking of the leaves is thus strongly linked to an occasion, to symbolic moments: divination, welcome, rites of passage (birth, marriage, funerals). Ceremonial, magic, religious purposes. Myths and rites. Islam, like Christianity, has tried to circumscribe them, decreeing them *halal* or *haram*, permitted or prohibited. Although these leaves do not each have the same importance in the zones where they are chewed, they have common energizing effects, of resistance to hunger, fatigue, and sleep, of stamina, "well-being," "good temper"; they are mood elevators and tranquilizers, both a stimulant and a light narcotic. A recourse in sickness, boredom, and work, they quickly become a necessity, not like the habit of more powerful drugs—intoxicants, hallucinogens, psychotropics—but as a form of accompaniment to life, the rumination of matter itself, a mastication of the world. This empire is revealed in formulaic expressions, which say that one can manage without food but not without the leaf. It is also reflected by the stimulant's spread to every level of society, having previously been the sole preserve of the noble classes—shamans, warriors, high-ranking officials—for whom it was a privilege and luxury. "The passion for this product is shared by men and women, of all ages, of all social classes: princes, priests, artisans and slaves, of all religions, Christians, above all the native founders of missions, Mohammedans, Buddhists, Brahmins, Fetishists, and yet others, in no category, from every race, Caucasians, Mongols, Malays, Papous," writes Louis Lewin of betel. "It is chewed every day at any hour of the day, during work and rest, walking and sitting, at home and in others' houses." Although qat, seldom chewed under the age of twelve, does

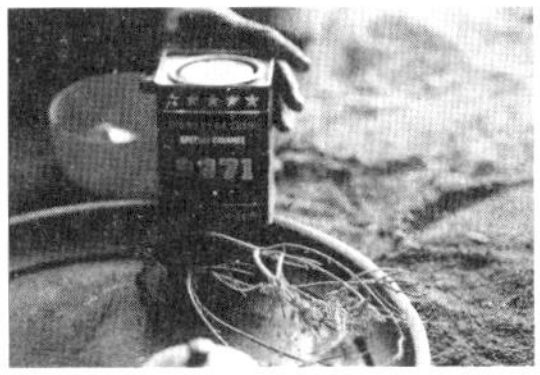

not have nearly as many users as betel, taken by hundreds of millions in Asia, it still has a huge following in the Yemen: "On a Friday afternoon, more than eighty per cent of the nearly five million people in the Yemen Arab Republic are to be found sitting in small groups, chewing the tender leaves of the qat plant." (John C. Kennedy) While the qat session—*majlis al-qat*—is a social institution observing a variety of precise rules and taking place in a room—*muffraj*—specially reserved for it, the leaf is also chewed throughout the day, by individuals: students, housewives, shopkeepers, laborers, drivers, stone-masons, to name but a few. At Potosi, in about 1550, the coca traffic provided as much revenue as that of silver ingots. The huge growth in consumption of the leaf was linked also to the colonists' exploitation of mines, as the peasants recruited to work them relied on the stimulant; it had earlier been given a boost by the Incas, who, during their imperial expansion, paid their army in coca, establishing new plantations to meet the needs of the new garrisons.

Ritual The stimulant's effect on the body itself—perception, sensation, imagination—has always been given a frame by community rites: prescriptions and proscriptions. After the religious or medical controversies, tea, coffee, chocolate, wine, beer, tobacco, stimulants, and even drugs were secularized, adopted, and sold as consumer articles; controlled by the state, science, or traffic, legal and illegal. Attached to most of these substances are identifiable practices or rites—habits, customs, specialties, particularities, routines; one can also identify prescribed tools and assigned places, but few, in comparison with tea, have retained an undeniable ritual all over the world: such different ways of taking it, equally different implements, and such specific places of consumption: the *chaya*, tea house, *chashitsû*, tea pavilion, *salon de thé*, tea room.

Tou In Lu Yu's *Chajing* appears this famous claim: "Tea became a drink by the grace of Shennong and developed by the grace of Zhou Ghong." It is nearly four thousand years since tea was respected in Chinese pharmacopeia and consumed as a food in soup, mainly in Yunnan, Sichuan, and Guizhou, regions where wild tea plants are still to be found, one at least being in its eighteenth century. The earliest written reference to tea supports Lu Yu: tea became a drink during the Zhou dynasty (1121-256 BC). The inscription *tou* (pinyin: *du*: herb) occurs in the tribute list of Pu, one of the small kingdoms of southeastern China reunited by King Wu. From the outset, a valuable commodity, a nutritive and medicinal substance, and a luxury—*sumbolon*, *pharmakon*, and *oulochutai*.

Test But before King Zhou Gong, there was the mythical Emperor Shennong. It is to him, the "divine husbandman," that the first Chinese classic on medical matters, which,

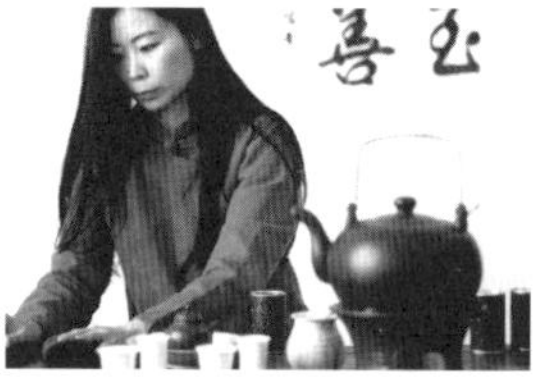

indeed, bears his name—*Shennong Ben Cao Jing* (year 0), credits the discovery of tea. One of three divine emperors, he is the human figure with an ox's head who established, with agriculture and medicine, the therapeutic role of herbs and notably tea. Roaming the country in search of all kinds of plants, Shennong unhesitatingly tasted them to test their nutritional, curative, or poisonous effects, poisoning himself in the process up to seventy-two times a day. At least three versions tell of the occasion, precisely dated to 2730 BC, when he lay down under a tree having been poisoned more seriously than usual, and the leaves dropped dew into his mouth to restore his strength: "Shennong tasted the plants. Every day he discovered seventy-two that were poisonous, but tea protected him from all sickness." On its discovery by this Minotaur, tea immediately presented its paradox and riddle: an anti-toxic toxic. Not only the ambiguity of any substance that dosage or protocol, following the principle of Paracelsus—*Allein die Dosis macht daß in Ding kein Gift ist*—can make beneficial or poisonous. But a property that counters other properties. In a variant of the story, the leaf drops into a pan of boiling water that Shennong had recommended as a preventive treatment. This chance fall, like Newton's apple, recalls another accident that led to the discovery of another product, whose "route," like that of tea, joined up the world: silk was said to have been discovered when a silkworm cocoon, on falling into a cup of tea, let all its thread unravel. In a different version, the Emperor has a transparent stomach allowing him to observe the leaves of a white-flowered bush that he has chewed, and which start to move and visit the smallest corner of his intestines. The name of tea —*cha*—is said to derive from the character meaning "to inspect," "to verify." Each time, however, the myth of tea is a test in the shade of a plant.

ALL OF TEA

The Name of Tea

"It is on Mount Cast-by-the-Sun (*Richu Ling*) that the king of Yue had his sword cast. The tea there has a sharp flavor, a taste of metallic stone. 'Of all the teas of the two Zhe,' said Ouyang Yongshu, 'the best is the tea from Mount Cast-by-the-Sun.' Wang said: 'On Mount Dragon grows the Lucky-Herb. On Mount Cast-by-the-Sun, the Seeds-of-Snow. That is how the tea gets its name. The tea specialists of the city go where there is tea, but they take no notice of Seeds-of-Snow.' They enjoy it as one of the teas of the city without telling the difference. My Uncle San'e, who knew the roasting method of the tea called Umbrella-Pine (a mountain situated in the district of She, the province of Anhui), tried using it with Lucky-Herb tea. It gave out a generous scent. 'Lucky-Herb tea is certainly excellent,' I said, 'but, as when Han Wudi drank a cup of dew, far from satisfying desire, it increases it.' About the store of

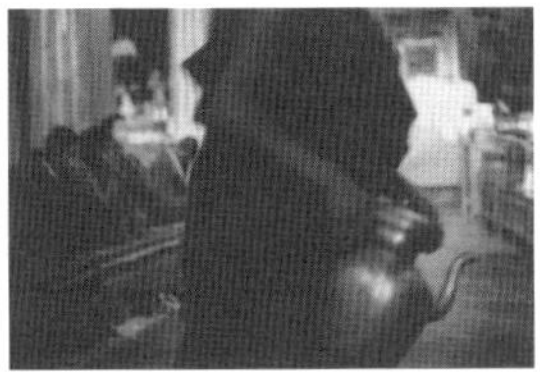

Mount Cast-by-the-Sun tea, one might say: even when it is thin, the ox crushes the pig! So men from the She district were summoned to go to Mount Cast-by-the-Sun. The method of flattening the tea, the method of pinching off (in arboriculture pinching off means severing the end of a young branch to send the sap back into the parts it is wished to grow), the method of transport, the method of scattering, the method of drying, the method of cooking, the method of roasting, the method of conserving, were all done by the rules of Umbrella-Pine tea. Brewed in another spring water, the tea does not give out its scent, but when boiling water from the Spring of Offering is poured into a teapot, the scent is very concentrated. The addition of jasmine flowers must be sparing. In a bell-shaped porcelain cup, one first puts a little water and leaves it to cool. Next, one pours on boiling water. The color of this drink is like the smooth green of the bamboo shoot escaped from its sheath. Or like dawn on the mountain when it falls across the window screen. If you take a white *qingfei* teapot and pour the tea into a white porcelain cup, it is like seeing a hundred white orchids spread in a snowy wave. The name Seeds-of-Snow well translates the color of the tea, but not its scent. I called it Snow-Orchid for fun. Four or five years later, the name Snow Orchid was suddenly everywhere. In Yue, fashionable people stopped drinking Umbrella-Pine tea, to drink only Snow-Orchid tea. One drank Snow-Orchid, but one also drank Umbrella-Pine, of lesser reputation; one bowed before Snow Orchid to be in fashion. Recently, between Hui and She, Umbrella-Pine tea also changed its name to Snow-Orchid. And a strange thing happened, the tea that used to be called Umbrella-Pine also changed the name on its packet. (Zhang Dai, Tao'An mengyi, *Dreamt memories of Tao'An*)

Tou, Cha, Tea

"The Chinese call it Thée, the Japanese and the Indians Cha and Tcha, the Tartars and the Persians Tai or Tzai, and the Europeans Thé." (Philippe Sylvestre Dufour, *Traité du Café, du Thé et du Chocolate*, 1693)
"The characters to describe tea have either the 'herb' key or the 'tree' key or the 'herb' and 'tree' keys together. [With the 'herb' radical one forms the character *cha*. This character appears in the *Kaiyuan wenzi yinyi*. With 'herb' and 'tree' together one forms the character *tou*. This character appears in the Chinese dictionary of objects *Erya*.] These characters are: *cha*, *jia*, *she*, *ming*, *chuan*. The Duke of Zou said: '*Jia* is *kutu*, "the bitter tea."' The official Yang said: 'The people of south-west Sichuan call *cha* tea *she*.' The official Guo said: 'If it is plucked early, it is called *cha*, if it is plucked late, it is called *ming*; sometimes it is called *chuan*.'" (Lu Yu, *Chajing*, I)
The Latin *thea* translates the Chinese *cha*, whose spread into Vietnamese, Greek, and Tibetan (*tsa*, *ts'ai*, *ja*), into Japanese and Portuguese (*cha*), and into Turkish, Indian, Russian, Albanian, Greek, and Rumanian (*chay*, *chaya*, *tchaï*, *chav*, *cai*, *çay*, *ceai)*, follows the overland route of the tea trade. Before the sixth century, Turkish

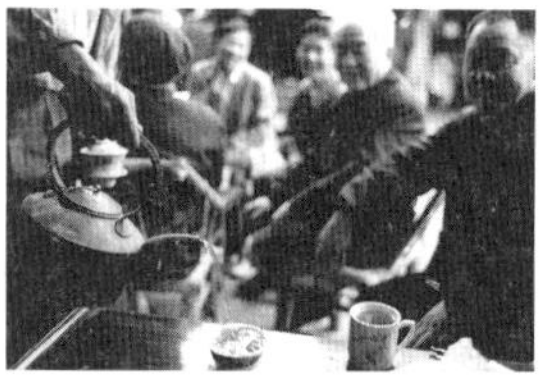

merchants reached the northern frontiers of China through Mongolia and bought tea there. Around 1611, the ships of the Dutch East India Company brought the first tea to Europe; France discovered it in 1636. On the evidence of the first known advertisement in the country, it was around 1650 that England received "that excellent, and by all Physitians approved, *China* drink, called by the *Chineans*, *Tcha*, by other Nations, *Tay alias Tee*." A rhyme by Alexander Pope suggests that up to the eighteenth century the English word tea could have been pronounced "tay," which is how it is pronounced in south Fujian, which is broadly the same as the Dutch (*thee*), Singhalese (*they*), Malay (*teh*), Tamil (*tey*), French (*thé*), German (*tee*), Indonesian (*tèh*), Israeli (*tae*), and also the Italian, Spanish, Hungarian, and Danish (*te*). This alternative voice of *cha* follows the sea passage, the line of the great discoveries in the direction of India and the Far East, by which the West got its tea. It was indeed to the ports of southern China, such as Amoy (Xiamen), that the merchants, smugglers and middlemen of different East India Companies came for their supplies. The way of tea, paradoxically, survived in those regions of southern China where the mandarin ideogram *cha* is articulated *tei*.

Attributes of Tea

The place that tea has come to occupy in the West is reflected in its languages, where *tea*, *tee*, and *thé* have replaced older words such as *tisane*. In English, the word *tea* no longer denotes a specific drink but is synonymous with "infusion." In France, a good many names are attached to "thé," giving an infinite number of derivations. According to Hartwich, there are ninety substitutes for tea in Europe, fifty-seven in Asia, forty-nine in America, eleven in Australia, and three in Polynesia. Here are eighty-one:

Acaena Sanguisorbae V., Rosaceae, Australia, New Zealand; *Acanthopanax spinosum M.*, Araliaceae, "Ukoli cha," Japan; *Adiantum Capillus-veneris L.*, ferns, northern temperate regions; *Agapetes saligna B.*, Vacciniaceae, India; *Akebia quinata D.*, Berberidaceae, "Akabi cha," Japan; *Alstonia theaeformis L.*, Styraceae, Columbia; *Angraecum fragrans P.T.*, Orchidaceae, "Bourbon tea," Mascarene Islands; *Aphloia mauritania B.*, Bixaceae, Mascarene Islands; *Artemisia Abrotanum L.*, Compositae, "citronella," Europe and Asia; *Borbonia cordata L.*, Leguminosae, "Cape tea," southern Africa; *Bursera gummifera L.*, Burseraceae, tropical America; *Capraria biflora L.*, Scrophulariaceae, "American tea," *idem*; *Ceanothus triphylla M.*, Labiatae, "Canaries tea," Canaries; *Chenopodium ambrosioides L.*, Chenopodiaceae, "Mexican tea"; *Chiogenes serpyllifolia S.*, Vacciniaceae, "aniseed tea," North America, Japan; *Cistus villosus L.*, Cistaceae, southern Europe; *Clereya theoides C.*, Ternostroemiaceae, Antilles; *Corchorus siliquosus L.*, Tiliaceae, tropical America; *Croton corymbulosus R.*, Euphorbiaceae, North America; *Croton Eluteria B.*, Euphorbiaceae, "cascarilla," "Port de la paix tea," Antilles; *Cymbopogon citratus S.*,

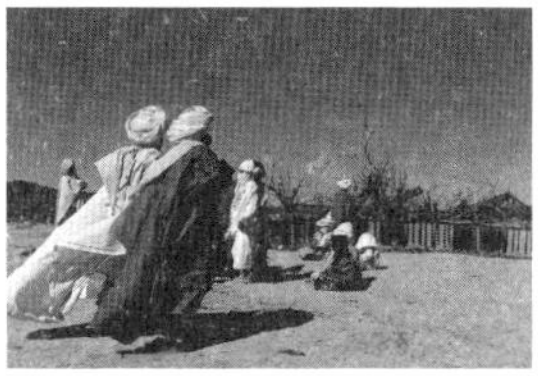

"citronella" ; *Cymbopogon Nardus R.*, Graminaceae, India; *Cymbopogon Winterianus J.*, idem; *Desmodium Oldhani O.*, Leguminosae, Fuji Kanzo, Japan; *Dryas octopetala L.*, Rosaceae, northern temperate and Arctic regions; *Elaeodendron orientale J.*, Celastraceae, India, Mascarene Islands; *Epilobium angustifolium L.*, Russia; *Epilobium hirsutum L.*, Russia; *Eugenia operculata R.*, Myrtaceae, Vietnam; *Eupatorium triplinerve S.*, Compositae, "Aya-pana," tropical America; *Frankenia portulacaefolia S.*, Frankeniaceae, "St. Helena tea"; *Gaultheria procumbens L.*, "red tea," "Newfoundland tea," North America; *Helichrysum serpyllifolium L.*, Compositae, "Hottentot tea," southern Africa; *Hibiscus Sabdariffa L.*, Malvaceae, "Karakadish," "Sudan tea," tropics; *Hydrangea Thunbergii S.*, Saxifragaceae, "Hamartsja," Japan; *Ilex Aquifolium L.*, Ilicacaea, Europe; *Ilex Cassine W.*, Ilicacaea, "Appalachian tea," North America; *Ilex glabra A.G.*, Ilicacaea, idem; *Ilex theaezans M.*, Ilicacaea, Brazil; *Lantana Pseudothea*, Verbenaceae, Brazil; *Ledum latifolium J.*, Ericaceae, "Labrador tea," "James' tea," *idem*; *Lepstospermum Thea W.*, Myrtaceae, Australia; *Lindera Benzoin M.*, Lauraceae, *idem*; *Lippia citriodora H.B.K.*, Verbenaceae, "lemon verbena," southern America; *Lithospermum officinale L.*, Borraginaceae, "Bohemian tea," "European tea," Europe, Asia; *Lycium chinense M.*, Solanaceae, Kuko-cha, China and Japan; *Malus theiera R.*, Rosaceae, China; *Melaleuca genistifolia S.*, Myrtaceae, "New Wales tea," Australia; *Melaleuca Leucadendron L.*, Myrtaceae, " Niaouli tea," New Caledonia, Australia; *Melissa officinalis L.*, Labiatae, "Melissa," Mediterranean region; *Micromelum pubescens B.*, Rutaceae, "Lifou tea," islands of the Pacific Ocean, tropical Asia; *Monarda didyma L.*, Labiatae, "Oswego tea," "Pennsylvania tea," North America; *Muntingia calabrica L.*, Tiliaceae, "Jamaican Guasem," Antilles; *Myrica Gale L.*, myricaceae, "Simon-Pauli tea," temperate northern regions; *Neea theifera O.*, nyctaginaceae, Brazil; *Paronychia argentea L.*, illecebraceae, "Arab tea," Mediterranean region; *Polygala theezans L.*, Polygalaceae, "Carolines tea," Japan and Java; *Potentilla rupestris L.*, Rosaceae, "Siberian tea," Europe, Northern Asia; *Prunus spinosa L.*, Rosaceae, "European's tea," Europe, the East; *Psoralea glandulosa L.*, Leguminosae, "Chile tea"; *Rhododendron chrysanthum P.*, Ericaceae, "Tartars tea," the Daur; *Rhododendron lapponicum W.*, northern and arctic regions; *Rubus arcticus L.*, Rosaceae, "Norwegian tea," northern regions; *Sageretia theezans B.*, Rhamnaceae, India, Burma, China, Vietnam; *Salix Alba L.*, Salicaceae, France, Europe; *Salvia officinalis L.*, Labiatae, "Greek tea," Mediterranean region; *Sassafras officinalis, N. & E.*, Lauraceae, "Sassafras tea," northeastern America; *Sauvagesia erecta L.*, Violaceae, "mountain tea," tropical America and Africa; *Saxifraga crassifolia L.*, Saxifragaceae, "Siberian tea," "Moguls' tea"; *Scoparia dulcis L.*, Scrophulariaceae, "mild tea," tropical America; *Sida canariensis W.*, Labiatae, "Canaries tea"; *Smilax glyciphylla S.*, Smilaceae, "New Holland tea," Australia; *Solidago odora A.*, Compositae, northeastern America; *Stachytarpheta jamaicensis*

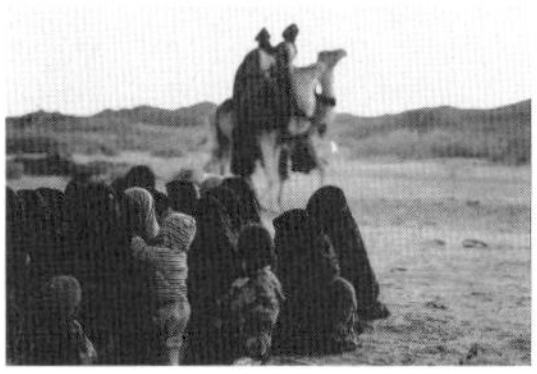

V., Verbenaceae, "Brazil tea," Tropical America; *Teucrium Thea L.*, Labiatae, China; *Vaccinium Arctostaphylos L.*, Vacciniaceae, Armenia, Caucasus; *Vaccinium Myrtillus L.*, "Blueberry," "Caucasus Tea," temperate northern and arctic regions; *Veronica officinalis L.*, Scrophulariaceae, "European tea," "Northern tea," Europe, Asia Minor, northern Asia; *Viburnum cassinoides L.*, Caprifoliaceae, "Carolina tea," northern America; *Viburnum theiferum R.*, Caprifoliaceae, China; *Villaresia Congonha M.*, icacinaceae, Brazil; "Swiss tea," (blend of potentilla, clover, gentian, *veratrum*, rananculus, *alchemilla*, *dianthus*, yew, spruce, gramineae).

Three Teas

In the West, three classes of tea may be singled out on a tea counter's list: master teas, classic blends, and scented teas (sometimes also: Indian tea, Ceylon tea, China tea).

From now on, the most general of lists will include green teas (unfermented), black teas (fermented) and Wulong teas (semi-fermented) in the middle. In the persisting ignorance of the latter, they are systematically reduced to "Formosa" teas with fantastical names such as Fancy Grade Oolong, leaving out the majority of Chinese vintage teas.

Here we suggest another classification: Narrow Tea, Middle Tea, Bree Tannic Tea.

Tea with Flowers

Scented teas have a long history, that of flower teas: "In summer, when the lotus came into bloom, Yun wrapped a few tea leaves in a small gauze bag that she would place into the lotus flower before it shut in the evening. In the morning, as soon as the flower opened again, she took out the sachet. With spring water, we then made a tea with an extremely delicate aroma." (Sheng Fu, *Six Stories of the Fickle Passage of Time*) Teas with flowers were among the scented and decorative presents that used to be given to the emperor. According to Cian Zhuangnian's *Cha Pu* (1539), tea was mixed with jasmine, osmanthus, rose, wild rose, orchid, orange blossom, magnolia, plum blossom, and lotus. Although an indifferent jasmine tea has become the standard accompaniment to Chinese meals outside China, flower teas are not in fact greatly esteemed by Chinese connoisseurs, whose art lies more in identifying, in the great vintages, an aromatic complexity that has developed slowly in the earth, in the plant, and through secrets of manufacture. In this respect, flower teas appear redundant and contradictory in their very aim: the mixing of a particular tea with a particular aroma. So red tea goes specially well with the rose, green tea with jasmine, blue-green tea with the rose or osmanthus, and Pu Er with chrysanthemum. However, one great jasmine Chinese tea—Son Zhen—sold in very small quantities (a world production of 200 kg), is a mixture of white tea and jasmine made painstakingly by hand. This involves laying alternate layers of tea buds and fresh, half-closed flowers, letting them rest for no more than three quarters of an hour,

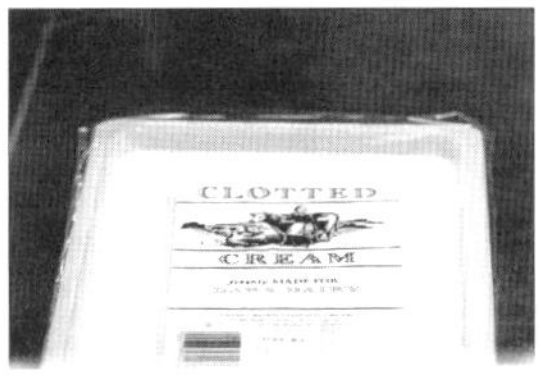

then separating and simultaneously sorting them, which process may have to be recommenced nine times, or even more. The need to have on hand fresh jasmine and a high quality white tea, such as Silver Needles, and to treat the tea immediately after plucking, means that the jasmine fields and tea gardens must be adjacent. This—and the laborious task of repeatedly sorting fragile downy buds and delicate clusters of petals—explains the rarity of the tea.

Scented Teas

The fragrant teas of the West—the commonest are black teas, more rarely green or semi-fermented teas—are scented sometimes with flowers, like the traditional jasmine tea, sometimes with fruits—bergamot in Earl Grey, orange and other citrus—but nearly always with essential oils, synthetic aromas, sprayed on essences. Varieties, fantasies, exoticisms. Their main interest seems to lie in the work given to tea blenders, in the dreaming up of their names—like titles of pornographic films—and the resulting extension of the list in teashops. As a reminder, the great vogue for scented tea began with the idea of Earl Grey whose range Jumeau-Lafond extended: from Imperial Russian—an entirely French invention—to the coca-cola-esque caramel tea of the Paris establishment Mariage Frères, embracing those flavored with cinnamon, apple, or blackberry. The first tea offered by the man who founded the largest French tea company, and has developed the longest tea list in the world, used the same artificial flavoring as orange and lemon Fanta.

Flavors

"Traditional": Earl Grey (bergamot), jasmine, chrysanthemum, orange blossom, lychee, lotus, magnolia, orchid, rose, mint.
"Novelties": almond, aniseed, apple, apricot, banana, bitter orange, blackberry, blackcurrant, blueberry, caramel, cardamom, cherry, chocolate, cinnamon, coconut, fruits of the forest, ginger, ginseng, gooseberry, grape, grapefruit, guava, honey, kalamansi, kiwi, lemon, lime, mandarin, mango, Amazon mango, maracuja, melon, mirabelle, mocha, naranquilla, orange, papaya, passion fruit, peach, peppermint, pineapple, pistachio, quince, raspberry, rhubarb, rum, sakura, imperial sakura, spice, strawberry, vanilla, violet, walnut, ylang-ylang.
"Blends": take the above ingredients, mix them in varying proportions, and give them the names of operas, far-away islands, or holidays.

Classic Blends

So-called "classic" blends are made by tea blenders who mix known vintages of black tea to obtain marriages of flavor, aroma, and color; the chemistry of this is akin to that of perfumery, coffee, and tobacco. The three great places of origin—Ceylon, India, China—contribute to the English Blend. Terai, Dooars, and Travancore will systematically be used as a base for their color, their body, and their neutrality; Assam, Ceylon, and Kenya for their strong, pungent or malty taste; and

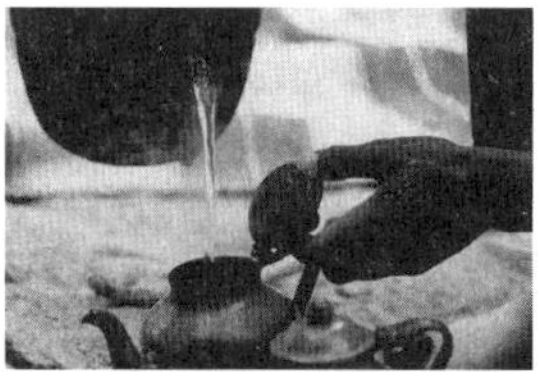

Keemun, Yunnan, and Darjeeling for their mellowness, fragrance, or delicacy. The best reputed establishments carry on this "tradition," which may blend five types of leaf that are very different in provenance and fermentation to produce an inevitably blurred infusion.

Standard Blends

With the exception of the "great masters"—teas from an exclusive garden specified on the packet—most teas on sale are blends. Generally, teas are sold at auction in London, Hamburg, and Amsterdam, but also in Calcutta, Colombo, and Mombasa. The expert taster judges a tea in three different stages of presentation: *I.* The dry tea should correspond to a given grade, and be "clean and uniform"; *II.* The infused leaf should be "regular, brownish to yellowish" according to type, and with no strange smell; *III.* The liquor is judged by its "color, brilliance, smell, density, strength, astringency, and aroma." A single name can refer to a mixture from several gardens that have the same appellation—Castleton, Makaibari, Jungpana—or from several estates in the same region—Darjeeling, Assam, Ceylon. After the tea taster, it is the tea blender who has to draw up the formula for the mixture, which will be adjusted according to the consignment and the condition of the available stock. As soon as one of the teas making up a blend runs out, it will have to be replaced by another, if not several others, to obtain the same quality. The tea blender, his nose, and his palate are again needed, as an insurance system. The expert blend can be made by a dispatcher in the producing country or by the importer from stocks bought at auction or by the actual producer, who packages the tea accordingly.

The Bland Blend

The blend is the basis of the western tea expert's skill, with the exclusive object of maintaining a standard and uniform taste, which the rules of the marketplace entitle the consumer to expect. The whole vocabulary of tea tasting is there only to support this breach of nature: whatever the season, the results of the harvest, the particular garden of its provenance, tea will end up in the same state: black particles with a uniform taste. In this process, the tea taster is there solely to serve the tea blender, and in most cases the same person fulfills both functions. He clearly does not taste to discover what aromatic surprises the new crop might have, and he "tastes" it, just enough to be able to determine the prices on the Colombo, London, or Hamburg markets. In fact the person employed to "taste" is only there to "test" variations of quality, and to correct them repeatedly by blending, which does not add characteristics but on the contrary irons out idiosyncrasies. The comparison with wine or olive oil immediately exposes the stratagem in this operation. Instead of developing a product that brings out or distributes subtleties of flavor, an aggregate is reconstituted, with elements that have been held in check. In general, this reduction starts in the planter's factory, where the different pluckings of the day are

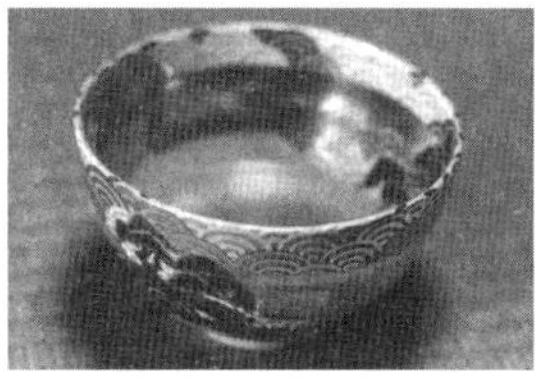

mixed according to grade and made up into lots, perhaps ten or twenty cases of each quality, rendering the product homogeneous. The planter takes a sample from each of these lots and sends them to his broker in Colombo. The latter inspects them, tastes them, and gives an estimate based on their quality and the state of the market. *In situ* or in London, the blenders get to work again: a blend can contain up to thirty different provenances, regions or even countries; the mixture is worked out from samples bought at auction, on the basis of a recipe similar to that drawn up by a nose in perfumery, but allowing for later additions; the blend will be adjusted as necessary to obtain the established taste. When sent to the factory, the formula for the mixture will allow calculation of the quantities to be packed into the rollers. The tea blenders, as with a pack of cards that is cut and cut again, will renew the mix of a tea, whose potentialities have intentionally been cut and cut again in all possible combinations. The blend is only there to be bland—to lose taste.

Great Masters

In addition to the scented teas and the traditional and synthetic blends, there are the great masters from the regions of Anhui, Yunnan, Jiangxi, Guangdong, Zhejiang, Fujian, Taipei, Xinzhu, Nantao, Uji, Shizuoka, Yame, Darjeeling, Assam, Dooars, Uva, Dimbula, and Nuwara Eliya, and so on. This category of teas—which there is little chance of obtaining from a single garden under existing distribution systems—represents the exception that proves the rule, seemingly bent on their extinction.

Green, Wulong, Black

All these teas—all teas—can also be divided into the three main categories of green, semi-fermented, and black. But this classification can be made from three different standpoints: the European, the Chinese, and the Taiwanese.

Wulong, Blue-Green, Semi-Fermented

In Taiwan, where all three types are produced, the semi-fermented teas are clearly of central importance, with the two extremes, unfermented and fully fermented, logically on either side of them. This emphasis corrects an imbalance in the tripartite division of the types of fermented tea in the West and East. Indeed, when exported to Japan, Oolongcha looks in the can or cup like a Chinese version of a commonly drunk local tea, Bancha, the coarsest quality of Japanese green tea using the largest and oldest leaves, known as Hojicha in its roasted form, and as Kukicha with the stalks. Oolongcha, usually drunk cold, survives as a sad reminder of the occupation of the island off Fujian by the Empire of the Rising Sun. In Europe, historical analysis of the adapted names of teas imported by the East India Companies supports the view that Wulong varieties were the first to come to the West: Bohea, from the Wuyi mountains, could not have been a black tea, which would have been compressed, nor a red, which was only developed later, nor a green, as is most often claimed, since this would never have withstood the journey back, lasting over a

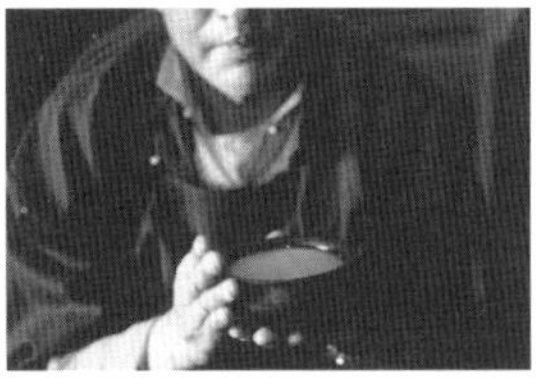

year; this tea would more likely have been one of the many semi-fermented teas cultivated in the region after which it is named. Blue-green tea, however, was absorbed into the family of green teas, because of a confusion arising from the lack of a word to translate *qing* (blue-green, another name for the semi-fermented category) as distinct from *lu* (green); it was not until the end of the nineteenth century that England noticed the difference, and distinguished the teas with the very particular aromas that characterize Formosa teas such as Oriental Beauty. This particular culture, which has kept the art of Chinese Wulong alive on the misty heights of Taiwan, has added new vintages to the already largest category on the continent: nearly three thousand names. The immense variety, which by itself rivals that of wine in the rest of the world, remains unknown in the West, and even in Asia, where semi-fermented tea is seen as a poor cross between green and black, equivalent perhaps to rosé wine, whose indifferent image was long justified by its standard of production.

Whites, Yellows, Greens, Blue-Greens, Reds, Blacks

From a Chinese viewpoint[1], the tripartite division—still observed in the drink lists of the best-reputed establishments of the West—is an abbreviation of a more extensive range, more coherent and richer in promise, which unfolds as a hexagram (or hexagamut) of white, yellow, green, blue-green, red, and black teas. These colors speak at once of the degree of a tea's fermentation, of its effect, and of the manner of drinking it. The first three—white, yellow, green—are unfermented teas; the three others—blue-green, red, black—are fermented to different degrees. Similarly, the three pairs—white and yellow, green and blue-green, red and black—represent three types of plucking (from downy bud to adult leaf), three forms of "work" (roasted or not), and three uses (the effects drawn from the leaf). While a coded system, seen notably on the emerald green cubes that circulate in the Arab desert, identifies the number of the tea factory and size of the grain—as in the case of Gunpowder—this concerns only industrial teas. In contrast to the "verti-quality" of the hierarchical grading of Anglo-Indian teas, Chinese teas are recognized first by their color—as happens with wine (white, *rosé*, red, but also yellow, *verde*, gray) and with Yemeni qat, whose leaf varieties include white (*abyad*), red (*ahmar*), black (*aswad*), and blue (*azraq*). These colors place all teas on a continuous horizontal spectrum. Exceptional teas are distinguished from ordinary ones only in their drinking and reputation—which invites plenty of confusion. Named vintages, novelties, traditions all run into each other. It is not unusual in a Chinese shop for several thousand teas to be listed (by comparison, the largest European supplier might list 450 international teas, including scented ones).

1 – A precise description of all the great Chinese vintages, of their different modes of cultivation and manufacture will be given in *The Colors of Tea* (in collaboration with Yu Hui Tseng), the second and forthcoming part of the *Three Teas Treatise*.

Hexagamut

The classification of teas in China divides them, on the pattern of a rainbow, into six great families. Even flower teas, blended teas, and compressed teas can, as

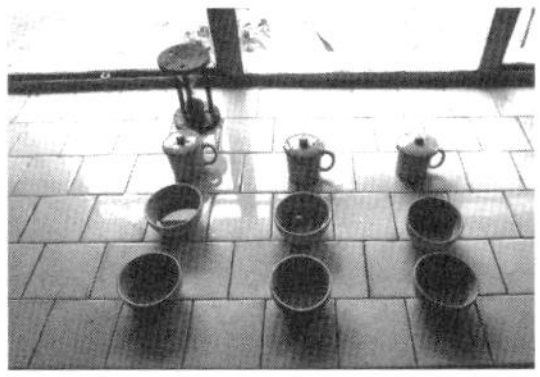

sub-branches, enter this taxonomy or "chromonomia." The latter, determined by the color of the dried treated leaf or the infusion in the cup, relates above all to a method of treatment, and particularly to the degree of fermentation.

White Tea & Yellow Tea

These unfermented teas are the mildest and most delicate in the hexagamut. All the white teas are made entirely of downy buds—Bai Mu Dan, "White Peony," or Yin Zhen, "Silver Needles"—that give the infusion a crystalline hue. Once plucked, the teas are immediately dried in the sun without other treatment. The white teas that come from genuine varieties are rare and each has a world production of less than 300 kg. The yellow teas, even rarer, look similar but have a yellowish tint, like the liquor they produce. The leaves of the yellow teas have undergone a form of light and stewed fermentation in a pan. White and yellow teas will keep for up to two years.

Green Tea

Chinese green teas, in the dry state, are made up of leaves of very different appearance: minute silvery green buds, khaki-green bamboo leaves, emerald "bird beaks." The color of the infusion runs from a crystalline pale yellow to a glaucous shade, embracing every nuance of yellow and gilt. Green teas are not fermented; their buds and young leaves are fragile and should be used from three months to a year after plucking. Fermentation is halted straight after plucking either by steaming—the process favored by the Japanese—or by direct heat in large copper pans. There are few pluckings of green tea in the year; the best are those of the spring. Green teas are those most commonly drunk by the Chinese—inevitably in the lesser of the fifteen hundred known qualities.

Blue-Green Tea

Wulong teas take their name from the color of their dried leaves: a dense green with bluish reflections, emerald with occasional reddish hints. Less fragile than the greens, these are the semi-fermented teas, in reality fermented to varying degrees, depending on type, between 12 and 65 percent. Despite being little known, they represent the largest range of teas in China and Taiwan, numbering several thousand vintages. Their aromatic complexity, the sophistication of their manufacture, and the long history to their development have no equivalent outside the French wine culture. The long selection of varieties, the soils, climates, orientations, the techniques of cultivation, of manufacture, and of tasting are very similar. Blue-green tea differs from wine in its keeping quality: except for a few vintages, it keeps for less than a year, like green tea. The teas also differ in their varying degrees of fermentation—from a Wen Shan Bao Zhong with its fresh aroma of flowers to a Bai Hao or a Dan Cong with a taste of muscat and smells of leather. The altitude of the garden, possible extra roasting, and particularly the season of plucking (from three

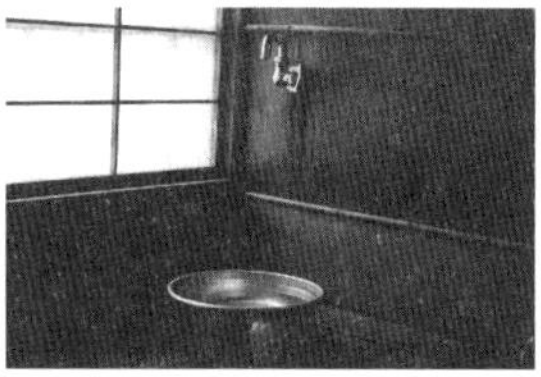

times yearly in China to six in Taiwan) will shape in their turn a great diversity of aromas. Often, taste and aroma are unconnected and, depending on the tea, one will take precedence over the other; there are "mouth teas" and "nose teas." While the Wulong teas reserved for the export market are of very indifferent quality—planted in Vietnam or bought in China before being treated in Taiwan—others to be drunk by connoisseurs are the object of exorbitant auctions: in 1998 a Chinese blue-green was sold for some $37,000 a kilo—for a quantity of 1.2 kg, it is true.

Red Tea

The red teas are the only ones known outside China. Their leaves are reddish, their infusion red, amber, or crimson. Their aromas should be fruity and woody, sometimes chocolatey. They have roundness in the mouth. They are fermented from 90 to 100 percent.

Black Tea

In China, the black tea family is represented above all by Pu Er and compressed teas. These are post-fermented teas: they have undergone an extended period of fermentation, a method of maturation very like that of wine for keeping. During this process, the tea—loose or more often compressed—will completely lose its theine but gain in tannins and flavonols. Pu Er will need to mature in the warehouse for over fifteen years, and as many as ninety. The black teas essentially reveal themselves not in their taste or aroma—they release a smell more than an aroma, of humus and undergrowth—but in their physical effects and sensations. Such teas, very difficult to find, are to be distinguished from most of the Pu Er and the very cheap Tuo Cha, which have undergone forced fermentation in the factory, after being mixed with red tea, and before being sold in the year of their harvest. These aberrant practices, encouraged in the West by pharmaceutical advertising of "slimming tea," have their equivalent in Hong Kong and Taiwan, where Chinese tea-lovers fall victim to counterfeiting and traffic in labels.

Black & Red

From the perspective of the West, where the division green / semi-fermented / black has been laid down, the privileged position of black tea, by which is meant Anglo-Indian tea, is masked by its apparent universality. This blackened tea is not the twice-fermented tea of Chinese taxonomy—Pu Er, Tuo Cha, and various compressed teas. It corresponds to Chinese red, which is fully fermented and made in China almost exclusively for export. Chinese red tea, European black tea, is further to be distinguished from the infusion known in South Africa as red or golden tea; the latter is assimilated to tea, as is maté sometimes, although its plant, the Rooipos Bush—*Aspalathus Linoaris, Aspalathus Contaminos* or *Borbonia Pinifolia*—does not belong to the tea family.

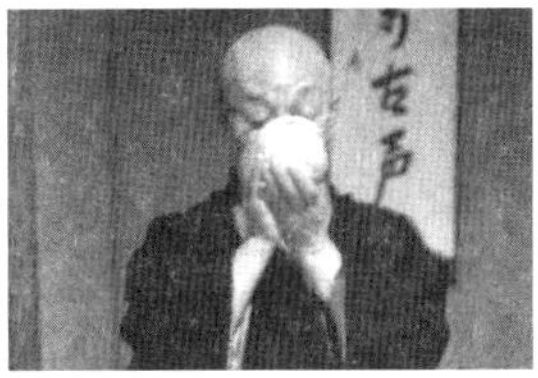

An Orange Dust

But apart from the short horizontal division, made unbalanced by the dearth of Wulong and green teas, which have always been left to the paramount skills of the Chinese and Japanese, the main classification used in the West is a vertical scale of grades—running from SFTGFOP to BOP right down to Dust—which defines each tea by the type of its leaf using terms transcribed into English: "Orange" for the Dutch royal family Orange Nassau, "Pekoe" for Bai Hao, which in Chinese means "White Down," and "Flowery" for a plucking in which the flower plays no great part. Flowery Orange Pekoe—which thus denotes the downy terminal bud and first leaf of each branch—is ranked by the quantity of its fine golden tips and the quality and size of its other leaves. The categories are Special Finest Tippy Golden Flowery Orange Pekoe, Finest Tippy Golden Flowery Orange Pekoe, Tippy Golden Flowery Orange Pekoe, Golden Flowery Orange Pekoe, Flowery Orange Pekoe, and Orange Pekoe. To these can be added Pekoe, Pekoe Souchong, and Souchong—all three without tips and with older or rolled leaves. The range is extended by Broken Orange Pekoe, made of broken leaves, in the categories TGBOP, GFBOP, GBOP, FBOP, BOP, and BPS—which can be deciphered on the basis of the earlier list. Finally, there are BOP Fannings, Fannings—leaves crushed to 1.5 mm—, and Dust, with even tinier particles.

Verti-Quality

The above classification, which would have itself systematic, poorly conceals the uselessness of its main appellation, Orange Pekoe: already rather meaningless, it loses all significance by being attached to every grade. The name of the ruling Dutch family, moreover, exercises something of a divine right in the tea business: how many industrial loose teas, in an effort to distinguish themselves, have boasted the title "imperial," or invoked the European royal court that had long kept for itself the drink and the colony, into which it sought to reduce the world's *terrae incognitae*. Furthermore, the string of letters of the abbreviated categories makes the system of identification if not unworkable at least cryptic, and replaceable by a numbered system. In fact, by protecting the territory of the expert while grading all teas by quality—"verti-quality"—the classification points to something one-dimensional in Anglo-Indian tea. And this approach, which seemed objective, loses all its relevance, effectiveness, and discrimination when it tries to take account of Chinese, Taiwanese, and Japanese teas. For the so-called "China tea," black here, red there, one distinguishes Pekoe (buds or furled leaves), Souchong (young leaves, often with a smoky flavor), and Pouchong (adult leaves, called *Congou* when they are short). The grades of Chinese green teas are denoted by adapting the terms *Chun Mee* for mild, flowery, lightly colored teas; (*Young*) *Hyson* for those that have very young, choice leaves, plucked in early spring; and *Gunpowder* for those with rolled leaves like small lead shot. For Japanese, Taiwanese, and Indonesian teas,

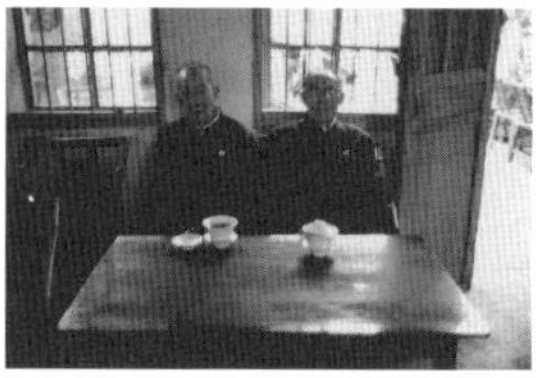

local names of tea categories are imported: Sencha, Tencha, Bancha; Wulong, Ch'ung, Bai Hao; Djikeng, Tulang, Bubuk. These divisions are sometimes accompanied by some distinctions of leaf form: in India, the leaves are whole, crushed, or broken; in Japan, they have the form of needles, commas, or powder; in China, the leaves are flat, twisted, rolled, crushed, compressed, or in bud. Ceylon teas are divided into three categories according to the altitude of the plantation, determined by the site of the factory: low grown teas (about 600 meters); mid grown (600 to 1200 meters); and high grown (1200 to 2400 meters). In Sri Lanka, land of British experiment in industrial tea, on the model of Lipton, the "verti-quality" that measures all the teas in the world is reflected in the topography itself: the different levels of value are made visible in those of the landscape. Robert Fortune already remarked of the final sorting: "This is a part of the operation which requires great care, more especially when the tea is intended for the foreign market, as the value of the sample depends much upon the 'smallness and evenness' of the leaf, as well as upon its other qualities." (*Three Years' Wanderings in the Northern Provinces of China*)

Chinese Choice

Slipped between the Darjeeling and Earl Grey that are *de rigueur* in tea rooms, "China tea" often appears as the only reference to the roughly six thousand vintages that can be distinguished in China. It is rather as if a Japanese menu offered simply "French wine" to accompany a meal, with no clue to its color, region, vineyard, year, producer, or alcohol content. This is nevertheless—except for rare establishments—the general level of attention to tea, its innumerable vintages and its history of thousands of years.

Another Story

At the Maison des Trois Thés, the list of vintage teas is long, yet never stops being amended to reflect the harvests. And the Chinese names, when they are translated, would not disappoint the adept of the East, as they are in no way gratuitous exoticism. Red Robe, Water Fairy and the Phoenix's Sole Plant are not far-fetched inventions by a business trying to reinvent itself, but custodians of tales and myths that made tea culture the companion of a history to be reinterpreted. So the colored hexagamut—white, yellow, green, blue-green, red, black—gives a first glimpse, indicating by the degree of fermentation the type of infusion to be drunk: its family of aromas, its expected effects, the manner of drinking it. But other classifications are possible, which distinguish types "pearl" (*zhu*), "eyebrow" (*mei*), and "needle" (*zhen*); or again "orchid," "cinnamon," and "bitter." The shape and aroma of the leaf thus complement its color like sides of a triangle. The reference points of this typology, especially when they exist in Chinese poetry and painting, can be as valid in one register as in another; "bamboo," for example, can refer to the fragrance of the infusion or to the shape of the leaf. The variety of the tea tree (Tie Guan Yin or Yin

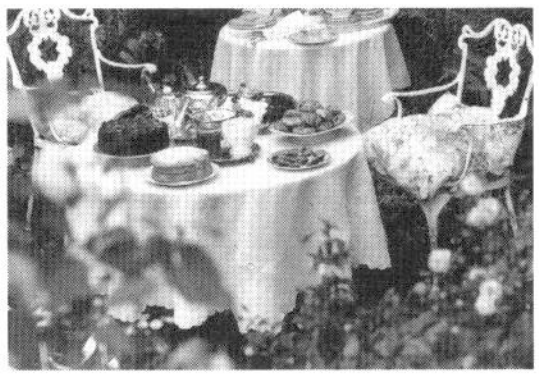

Zhen, for example), its method of manufacture (by steam or in a pan, dried on racks or in the sun), and any link with particular dates in the agricultural year (Qing Ming or Gu Yu) can also further specify the quality of the vintage. The tea's characteristics, not necessarily implicit in its name, are further determined by the time of plucking (spring, summer, autumn), the degree of fermentation, and of course the region, the garden, even the individual tree, that produced it: Qimen (Keemun), Wuyi (Bohea), Dong Ding. In these last respects, tea is subject to much the same influences as wine: soil, climate, year. Finally, as with most alcoholic drinks, the names of the teas may link them to a founding story, a dedication by a poet or scholar, or a myth attached to a place: Iron Goddess of Mercy, Spring Spiral of Jade, Dragon's Well.

Red Empire

It is possible to redistribute all the teas according to a topology, which opens this typology, and which may ultimately cover a technology of the drink. Black tea is linked to the British Empire, in the sense that the tea drunk in the West was invented, cultivated, and traded in that sphere (from the Chinese frontier to the Americas, with the Indian sub-continent in the middle). In fact, the Chinese always reserved their red teas—western black teas—for export, as they did certain silks, and most of the porcelain specially designed for "barbarians"; likewise, bricks of compressed tea were mainly dispatched to neighboring nomadic tribes. China remained until the middle of the nineteenth century Europe's sole supplier of tea, the world storehouse of tea, and hence the "Green and Black Empire," whereas in the eyes of its own population, China was the "Red Empire" before its advent.

Tea for Foreigners

It is worth recalling that Yunnan, which in Western pharmacies represents the paragon of Chinese teas, is only a very recent tea, although therapeutic effects backed up by an ancestral tradition supposedly evidence its quality. When carefully manufactured, Dian Hong Gong Fu—its Chinese name—has whole twisted brown leaves with golden buds. Its infusion is an orange red and its fragrance fruity. Although the mountainous region of its provenance, which remains less known than its name, has on its high plateaux and hidden valleys tea trees several centuries old, it was only in 1938 that a government factory was built there, the first attempts to establish red tea proving a success. As for Keemun, produced at Qimen in the south of the province of Anhui, it was at the end of the last Chinese dynasty, that of the Qing, that a region previously cultivating only green tea saw a retired official, Yu Ganchen, bring from Fujian the techniques for red tea. So well established and commercially successful did these new varieties become, that planters abandoned the traditional production of unfermented tea in favor of Qi Hong Gong Fu—Keemun—, which, having been established in 1880, by 1939 represented one-third of the red teas for export. But it is probably Zhen Shan Xiao Zhong, the

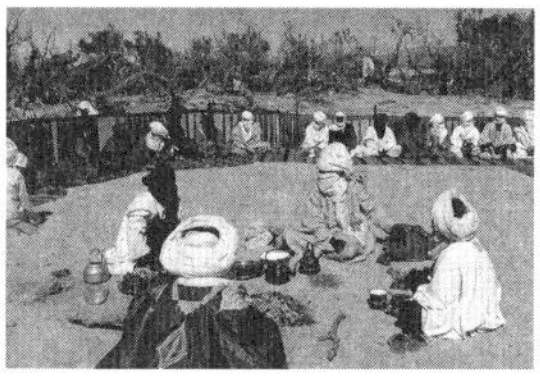

redoubtable Lapsang Souchong, that best illustrates the long misunderstanding with the Middle Kingdom. This tea from Fujian encapsulates for Westerners the characteristics of "China tea," whereas for the Chinese it has never been anything other than a tea for foreigners. The story of its invention is instructive: in the reign of the emperor Daoguang (1821-51), one of the armed occupation forces that crossed the country, deciding to take a few days' rest, stopped at the small village of Xingcun and requisitioned the only building large enough to house the soldiers: the tea factory. This happened in the middle of the tea harvest, but the owner was forced to comply, and watch tons of tea leaves accumulate, awaiting treatment, then ferment and blacken. To stop the leaves rotting with dampness, he asked his workers, who were unable to enter the factory, to light fires of pinewood in an attempt to dry the leaves over the embers. The tea, strongly impregnated with the acrid scent, failed to find a local buyer and was sold at the Fuzhou market, but only to foreign merchants living in the provincial headquarters. The spoiled leaves were presented there as a local specialty—which is exactly what they became when the tea planters all set to making this tea for the barbarians, who took the bulk of its production from the 1820s. It was the main Chinese product to be industrialized on a massive scale in the 1950s, to ensure exports to Europe and the United States where, in the post-war period, the taste for green tea seemed to have been totally forgotten.

Tastes & Colors

Other accounts in the West seem to support the accidental invention of red tea: European taste must also have been shaped by the accommodation to cargoes that, after eighteen months at sea in the hold, had failed to maintain their green, dry state. As is said of wine, the tea would have been *maché* (chewed). Green or lightly fermented teas, nothing short of moldy, would have reproduced in uncontrolled conditions the fermentation of red / black teas. This accident, like its counterpart in the Chinese story, fictionalizes—in the adventure of an uncontrolled technique—a tale of tastes and colors involving East and West. Every time the tea reached its port of destination or distant market, it was in an unintended but opportunely corrupted form. Despite the figures that the history of "Chinese trade" has managed to put together about tea imports to London, Amsterdam, and the East, the categories regularly followed—*Boui, Hyson, Congou*—cannot be precisely recognized; and the tastes of these teas, like those of various wines—claret, malmsey, port—transported across Europe at the same period, can only be imagined, as a very improbable hypothesis. Those tales concerning the Chinese taste "invented" (in the double sense of discovery and fiction) by Europeans, through the hazards of war and sea travel, paradoxically assign to accident the role of fixed determinant of an endlessly repeated difference. In the twentieth century, this difference manifested itself between the green tea of Asia and the black tea of the West, a clear distinction

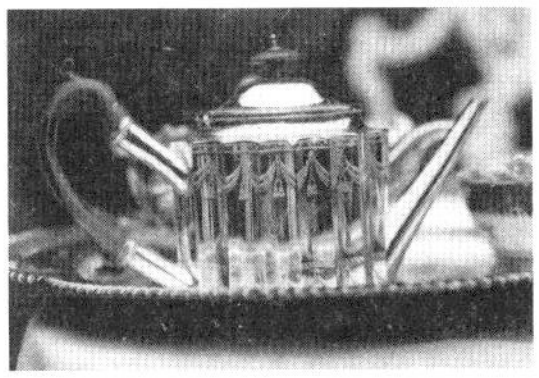

between two zones of large-scale consumption, which is less the survival of an opposition of two civilizations than the result of a constantly missed meeting of minds.

Tannic Brew, Tannic Bits, Tannic Brits

Black tea, then, since red is not a term used outside the Chinese hexagamut. Black tea, strong, tannic, and not very aromatic—a drinking spice, dyed hot water, a form of abbreviated coffee that one can down in greater quantity—was designed for milk, sugar, and the parliamentary monarchy. The colors of Anglo-Indian tea are those of alcohol (brandy, sherry, whisky). The *assamica* variety, which the British developed in Assam, Ceylon, and part of Darjeeling, with its leaves nearly three times the size of the Chinese, its robust, round, spicy aroma—brought out best with milk—and its shining, deep red color, was designed to carry through this policy. The mechanization, like the treatment and packing of tea, was driven in the same direction: by moving from whole-leaf to broken and then crushed tea, there was less and less wastage of the crop, but also more and more robustness, and less and less aroma: the industrialization of tastes. A distaste for tea, the most broken, the most tannic. Great Britain has indeed founded the Empire of Bree Tannic Tea (*Bree*: A thick pottage made of meal, etc. Liquor in which anything has been boiled, or which flows from it; broth, juice.)

CTC

In 1880, the mechanization of the three stages rolling-sifting-drying was introduced in India. The rolling consists of breaking the cells of withered leaves to extract their essential oils, a juice that will impregnate the down on the buds and give them a golden color—golden tips. In China, each tea occasions different work and a succession of sometimes very complex operations, which may be secretly handed down: for instance, many teas are manipulated without being rolled. The work of Anglo-Indian tea, while the plucking continues to be done by hand, was soon have been mechanized and standardized: rolling, which presents itself as the unique treatment of tea, is closer to crushing. The only variation is in the machine used for the purpose: rollers consisting of a table, a box and a brass cap, which break up the leaves; the Legg Cutter, which is simply an adaptation of a tobacco cutter for tea; the Rotorvane, invented by McTear in 1958, is a cutter composed of a cylindrical body, fitted with blades, and an endless axial screw, finishing in a cone; the L.T.P. (Laurie Tea Processor), which reduces the tea to very small particles using hammers and articulated blades turning at great speed (3000 revs / mn); and lastly, the system most in use, CTC (Crushing Tearing Curling), invented by McKercher, consisting of two grooved metal rollers turning in opposite directions and at different speeds, which merges the three operations of crushing, shredding, and twisting and allows the extraction and rapid reabsorption of the juice of the leaves without an increase in temperature.

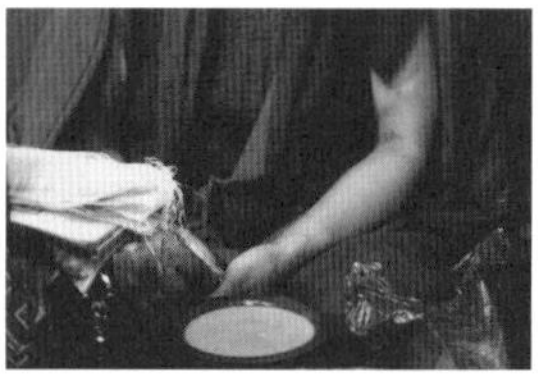

English Style or Indian Style

As early as 1919, broken tea, or dust, composed of stalks and fewer and fewer leaves, was denounced by the Indian Tea Association in a battle against overproduction, falling prices, and competition from Java and Indonesia. The Association recommended a return to the traditional Chinese way of plucking: the terminal bud with the first two leaves. Anglo-Indian tea is thus regularly subjected to a play of industrialization and regulation of a cultivation that has been imposed on a massive scale. In the early days of the Assam and Bengal plantations, the company J. Thomas & Co., which still runs the Calcutta auction center, held the first auction in India in 1861, challenging the monopoly of the City. A controlling body—the Central Tea Board—was set up in 1949 to bring together government representatives, planters, and businesses. While the Tea Control Act of 1933, introduced by the International Tea Committee, set the first quotas for Indian planters as well as the new producing countries (Kenya, Uganda, and Tanganyika). While the internal market has grown tremendously, bodies such as the Tea Research Association are studying methods of cultivation and treatment to obtain even greater profits. But with this tea, introduced and produced in hundreds of thousands of tons, India remains vulnerable to the hazards of the financial markets and to climatic disasters.

India 99

The Financial Times of March 1, 1999 carried a report that at Membai, in Sikkim, a project was under way to produce Rumtek Tea without pesticide and insecticide. Over a thousand acres had just been brought into cultivation by the co-operative of Sang Martam for this tea, considered superior to—its name notwithstanding—"Country's Highest Regarded Darjeeling Tea." The same edition reported that India's Ninth Plan would give a "big boost" to tea, coffee, spice, and rubber plantations. The manufacture of tea by hand, seen to this day as a measure of quality, has surrendered at the rate of 12 percent a year to mechanical picking and treatment. From now on, the CTC that used to handle no more than 65 percent of Indian production, will be the sole technical aid to the drink. India, its artisanal methods and technical efforts to develop new *jats*—hybrids, cuttings, clones—has of course permitted an alternative cultivation of tea, mainly in Darjeeling, the home of the finest Indian vintages, of the *sinensis* variety: for a clear, delicate, flowery infusion. But this cultivation, small in scale, while recently supported by a few German and American businessmen keen to introduce biodynamic methods, suffers from disastrous conditions: impoverished land, parasite attacks (viruses, caterpillars, flies), and a constant turnover of managers.

The Common Health

This empire of "Bree Tannic Tea" is of course not only that of the English, the British or even the Commonwealth—which, subjected to this general diet would be more of a "Commonhealth"—but that where the new culture of tea turned from accidental to Occidental.

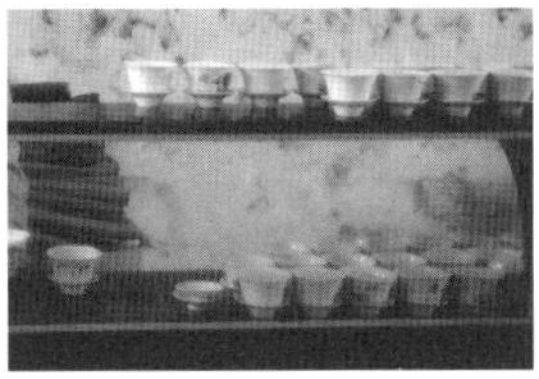

The Three Toms The different stages in which this happened are well-known, starting with the three founding Toms in Great Britain: *I.* Thomas Garraway who, in 1660, at the heart of the City and burgeoning Stock Exchange, first gave publicity and financial potential to tea; *II.* Thomas Twining who, in 1717, opened the first tea counter next door to his already established Tom's Coffee House; *III.* Thomas Lipton, "Tea Tom," who introduced American selling methods, invested heavily in Ceylon, and started to mechanize tea production.

Trade Where trade is concerned, tea has no world equivalent—not in sugar, or the other black drinks—and probably because China for so long kept a monopoly of its plantation and production. The sugar routes, which remain illustrative and central to the complete modification of tastes and eating habits, have in fact been more continuous and prolonged: although sugar was treated for a long time as a spice, there was never a break, even a continental one, in the progressive spread of its trade and use: India and Arabia never severed their links with Europe. As for coffee and chocolate, their adoption and transformation, linked to slavery as with sugar, were almost immediate in the Antilles and the various Dutch, Iberian, and French colonies. But the coffeehouse and the drinks—Protestant *kaffee* and Catholic *chocolate*—were so completely and immediately reinvented in the West that they might never have existed in their original forms. There is nothing to compare with tea when it comes to understanding and following every moment of the history of the trade: the long confrontation of opposing tastes, before the crude impoverishment of "Bree Tannic Tea"; the traffic on a vast scale that involved many foreign interests (smuggling, drug addiction, wars), the endurance of which contributed to successive economic stages: mercantilism, capitalism, commercialism.

Bree Tannic Empire Although, from the end of the eighteenth century, the English were undeniably at the forefront of these politics, as of the parliamentary system, there were also efforts by the French, successfully realized by the Americans, to transform the "little herb" from China. And while England remains at center stage of the history of the tea trade—this is clear from the position still held by the London stock exchange despite its relative economic weight—the contributions of the United States, followed by France in the post-war period, should be recognized. Which applies equally to chocolate, for a long time the specialty of the Latin countries, but then developed also by the Dutch (Van Houten's separation into cocoa powder and fat), the Swiss (milk chocolate), and the French (the raw bean made edible by Michel Chaudin)—all of which processes extended its consumption. While scented teas, "teas of the world," and the endless additions to the list of vintages are innovations from France, the tea bag, iced tea, and instant tea are American in origin. *I. The tea*

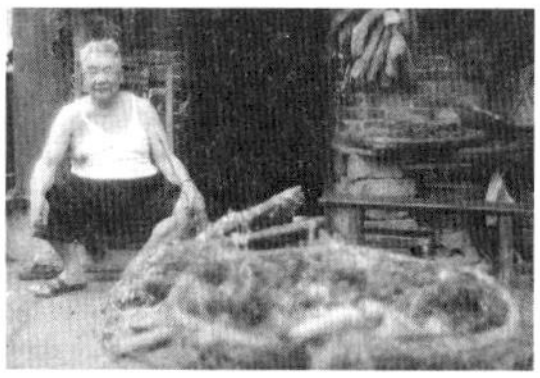

bag, of gauze or silk, was given to customers as a sample by Thomas Sullivan in 1920; *II. Iced tea* was made by Richard Blechynden in 1904, to relieve the torrid heat at the St. Louis Fair; *III. Instant tea*, soluble tea (successively: evaporation of concentrated tea, then pulverization of the solution by blasts of hot air or chilling, and evaporation in a vacuum: lyophilization). The achievement of the "Bree Tannic Teas": first broken, crushed, or powdered, they are then flavored, sweetened, depleted; and also bagged, frozen, and evaporated.

Packaged Brittle Bits

It was in 1826 that the Quaker John Horniman introduced tea in packets to establish his brand name. Until then, tea had been sold loose and weighed on request, in however small a quantity was required. From thenceforth, the unseen tea would need to guarantee a standard weight, cleanness, and non-adulteration. Packaged tea did not properly come in, however, until the 1880s, with Lipton, Twining, and Tetley, when it was sold from a horse-drawn van. After the First World War, a machine was able to measure the tea and automatically fold the packet from a roll of paper. It is highly significant that this stage was reached only when the tealeaf, planted in India and subjected to a highly mechanized treatment, had been reduced to a black powder.

Tea, Coffee, Coca-Cola

The British Tannic Brew—broken, dust or fanning—becomes a black powder in an indissoluble relationship with another commodity that a comparable, but inverse, transformation makes soluble: a white powder—sugar, also grown in India. Moreover, by their common additions of white liquid and crystals—milk and sugar—tea confirms its kinship with another black powder: coffee. It is like a new version of the fermented, roasted, hot, stimulant drink used, in progressively diluted state, all the way from the Levant—rather than India—to Europe. So from the thick decoction of Turkish coffee to Anglo-Saxon dishwater, with the perfect Italian expresso in the middle, one sees that same trend of which tea is the ultimate incarnation. There is also a common thread of flavor that runs from the full-bodied English tea to the American cup of coffee that can be replenished at will (the refill service)—being much like a strong tea—and as far as Coca-Cola. The latter, before the law of the marketplace made it ubiquitous, started in 1866 as the "spark of life" elixir made by a chemist in Atlanta—John Smith Pemberton—who borrowed a cordial from Europe—Ange Mariani's *Vin de Cola*—added the South American stimulant and disguised it with the African nut, to produce French Wine Cola. But the exoticism of unknown rituals quickly yielded to the precaution, made necessary by the Temperance League, of specifying that its secret formula 7X contained neither wine nor coca nor cola—only there in name. However, the bottled, carbonated, sweetened drink, with its caramel coloring and aromatic flavorings, does contain caffeine as its one stimulant. Caffeine, which can be restored to its Linnean

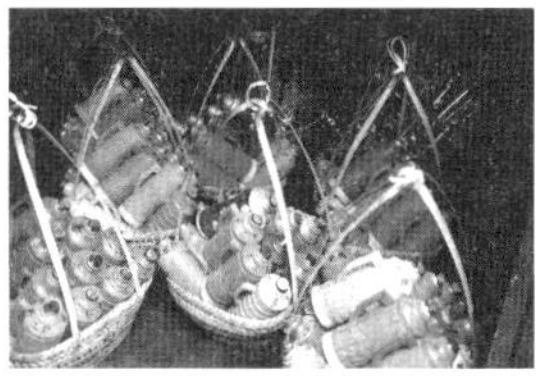

classification of theine, since the chemical industry draws it mainly from tea, has invaded the multitude of "colas" inspired by Coke, to such an extent that the Health organizations are worried: the alkaloid, as pervasive as saccharose, saccharine, and aspartame, invariably causes excitability in children and adolescents.

Green Quality

The bulk of Japanese tea production—97 percent of which is reserved for the internal market—consists of green tea: Ryokucha. Green tea reaches its apex in the land of the Rising Sun. Nowhere else does it have such verdancy, such freshness, such straightness. It is green, uniquely green, totally green. The leaves are green when furled, when infused, even when open. Less well known than the feasts of Hanami and Momiji, when the white cherry blossom and red maple leaves are wildly celebrated all over the archipelago, there is Shinryoku, the new leaf—literally, the "new green"—in the month of May, which marks the appearance of the first leaves, particularly on maples and fluorescent azaleas. This celebration, which has its autumn counterpart in Shin Kôyo, the new red leaf, happens at the same time as Shin Cha, the new flush, the new harvest of green tea. The illustrations and design of Japanese tea packets are also given to green, to images of tea gardens that are almost fluorescent: the very regular waves are depicted in deep color, which contrasts with the faded or pastel tones of commercial color charts. Chinese green teas, in the cup, range from transparent yellow through a rare greenish hue to bright orange; the Japanese green teas, from murky white to spinach green, passing through every shade of green. Their aroma is fresh, iodized, young. Their taste is sharp, raw, bitter. It evokes grass, bamboo, seaweed. For someone drinking it for the first time, the Macha will of course have its look of "jade mousse," but its taste will be closer to that of spinach cooking water. Its verdant quality is all-vertical. Compared to a Chinese green tea that vaporizes, or a Taiwanese Wulong that diffuses, Japanese tea cuts: it comes straight to the tongue, passes the throat, goes direct to the stomach, without impregnating the mouth, invading the palette or lingering on the olfactory bulb. It is best not to have an empty stomach. During a *chanoyu* performed in full—lasting some six hours—a meal is served before the tea. After the meal, and just before drinking the Macha, a sweet based on red bean, rice or chestnut (*omogashi*), a small sculpted sugar cube, or a rice cracker (*higashi*) will be carefully eaten as part of the ritual. But in the case of Gyokuro, a tea so green—its dry leaves are an astonishing deep emerald—that its infusion is a cloudy white liquor, the sweets are eaten afterwards so as not to destroy the aroma of so very delicate, mild and subtle a tea.

Empire of Narrow Tea

That freshness, that greenness, that taste of iodine in Japanese tea are in the image of an archipelago whose dense vegetation still covers nearly two-thirds of its surface, of its economy turned towards the sea, of its cooking, which favors what is live,

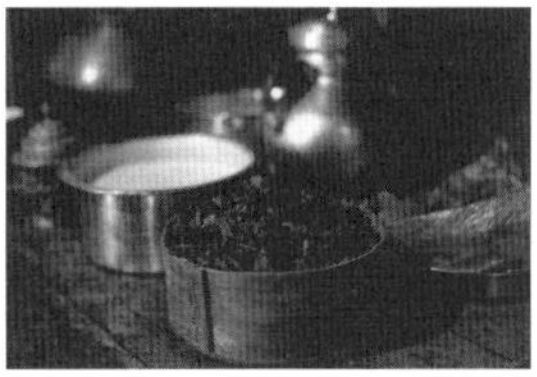

raw, and fish. Curled round the end of the earth—and so at the end of tea, at the end of its empire—this archipelago has deliberately cultivated that narrow, intense flavor that conjures up a world[2]. During the tea ceremony, after the preparation of the hearth, incense is taken from its little box (*kôgô*)—guests are invited to admire the latter—then burnt in an incense-burner (*kôro*): this action signals a Buddhist ambience while denying importance to the aroma of Macha tea, drunk for its taste more than its smell. An astringent taste—like sake or kaki—severe, restrained; this is expressed by one of the terms used—with *wabi* and *sabi*—to define the esthetic derived from the way of tea: *shibui*. The shape of Japanese tea is also very precisely wrought or sculpted: next to ground powder (the Macha of the ceremony) and dust (Konacha: the residues of the good Sencha and Tencha vintages gathered for the infusion traditionally served with sushi), there are needle teas (Gyokuro, Sencha, and Bancha): Japanese tea is always sharpened, drawn out, refined. The Green Empire is the "Empire of Narrow Tea."

2 – A description of the various aspects of Japanese tea culture (vintages, ceremonies, related arts) will be given in *The Narrow Tea*, the third and forthcoming part of the *Three Teas Treatise*.

Three Narrow Teas

All kinds of O-cha are drunk daily in Japan, in restaurants, shops, and offices. However, if one sets aside Kocha, an Anglo-Indian black tea, Oolongcha, drunk mostly as iced tea or in a can, and drinks such as Mugicha, Hatomogicha, Umecha, or Kombucha—recently imported or industrially produced, or non-stimulant infusions (based on cereals, plums or seaweed)—three main types of green tea are commonly drunk: Bancha, Sencha, and Gyokuro. Bancha—sometimes called "three years tea," but which has varieties of one, two or three years—is a green tea made from the last plucking, when little theine remains in the leaf. Bancha exists in three forms: Bancha (leaves and stalks), Hojicha (roasted Bancha) and Kukicha (stalks only). Sencha, the commonest tea, is grown on bushes cut in uniform waves that merge to form a semicylindrical harvest "table." For standard grades, the tea is not protected from the sun. The leaves are steamed for thirty seconds, then folded and finally dried in needle form. The finest tea is Gyokuro, its particular feature—shared with Kabusecha and Tencha, which are ground to make Macha—being that it is shaded with straw for about three months before plucking. The Green Empire has many intermediate types such as Senryu between Bancha and Sencha, but its main typology takes the form of a vertical spectrum, the grades of tea rising from the coarse Bancha to the middle-grade Sencha to the finest Gyokuro. This scale also measures an increasing mildness and decreasing time of infusion.

Green Empire & Black Empire

Between Anglo-Indian black tea and Japanese green tea there exists a similarity not in their tastes, as far apart as they can be—the one full-bodied, the other "cutting"—but in their tendency to reduce the synaesthetic spectrum, to eliminate aromas, to be less of a hollow in time and more of a stimulant to activity. Between the

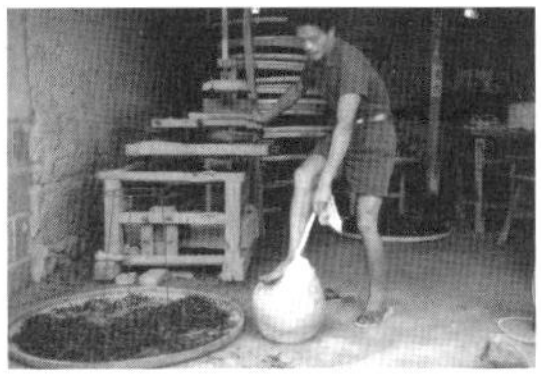

black tea empire and the green tea empire, there is a balance of conformism, manifest in their respective sessions of "teatime" and *chanoyu*, which are as much symptoms as symbols, both seen from outside as odd, abstruse, and even slightly ridiculous rituals. The image of British soldiers, on the battle field, stopping for tea, and of samurai, participating in the tea ritual, before going forth to meet death, are meant to show an imperturbable sangfroid, a calm detachment, but also an incongruous delicacy. As imperative and laughable necessities, teatime and the tea ceremony each reveal and expose a culture, a belief in form, in fact a whole people. A same social and esthetic conformity—the fashion that rages, as nowhere else, in London and Tokyo is its modern outpouring—which draws its ethic from an interpretation—each time unique—of Christianity here and Buddhism there, links the archipelagos of the Far East and Far West. There is a sort of color chiasma between the two empires of black and green: the very vivid, fluorescent, and verdant color of Sencha is the total opposite of English tea, with its wishy-washy hue, almost gray brown, its opaqueness, whitened and dulled with milk, and even its mat quality. The color of the primordial forest against that of the cloudy skies, gray and heavy. The color of Japanese tea finds an echo only in what constitutes the heart of the British countryside, the fields, the well-tended gardens, even the countless sporting grounds: the courses, greens, and pitches (golf, cricket, ball games). And the color of English tea has its justification only in Japanese spatial art: in the famous cob walls exemplified in the tea pavilion and taken over by the most (post)modern of decorative schemes introducing the subtlest, or most kitsch, variations; in the traditional or recent architecture of Japanese cities, which always look so gray, so flat, so subdued; and even in those stretches that could considered the symmetrical opposite of British lawns: the areas of sand in Shinto shrines, the patterns of combed gravel in Japanese Zen gardens. As an obsessive refinement, a widespread practice, and a centering on empty space (of sand from which a spare rock or restrained bush emerges in *karesansui*, or of a lush but shaven lawn edged with wild borders), this art of the garden is, moreover, the emblem most often chosen to represent the two cultures here mirroring one another. In the sense that the Japanese and British see one another as the most estranged, the most alien, the most symmetrical, and each other's counterpart ("One compares the Japanese to the English by the fierce insularity they have in common, by the suicide one believes so frequent at those two ends of our hemisphere," said Voltaire); in this same sense, the Germans, Italians, and French manage to build across that gulf of difference more continuous bridges—technology, culture, food—with the Far East; and those mirroring effects diffract into as many shining surfaces, which Japan has made a metaphor not of narcissistic reflection, like the West, but of emptiness: the glaze of ceramics, the trembling disk of tea, the garden sea.

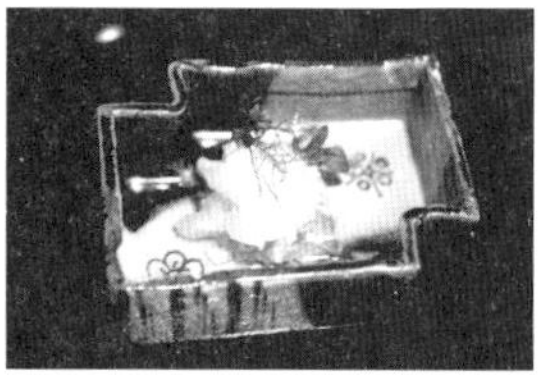

Do we need reminding that the Green Empire had to open up to the world when it saw the black ships that Commodore Matthew C. Perry had driven into the bay of Edo?

The Middle Kingdom

Between the British Empire and the Empire of the Rising Sun there is the Middle Kingdom. Between "Bree Tannic Tea" and "Narrow Tea" there is "Middle Tea"—*zhong*—the tea of "centrality" or "adaptation for ordinary use" (François Jullien). And in this sphere, there is the whole rainbow of Chinese teas—white, yellow, green, blue-green, red, black—that goes beyond even the two extremes: Anglo-Indian tea is less black than the post-fermented, true black teas of China (such as Pu Er); likewise, the white and yellow teas (such as Bai Hao Yin Zhen or Jun Shan Yin Zhen) cross the far limit of Japanese teas. That Chinese teas should embrace all others, is only historical, geographical, and botanical logic. The kingdom of "plains in the middle of mountains," China has expanded under the colors of its tea the empire of the drink that is still the most consumed in the world. At the same time, keeping to the "exact" or "steady middle"—of Confucius—China has preserved the position reached by tea, where, far away from "full-bodied English" and "cutting Japanese" tea, all flavors, all aromas, and all colors coexist; which means that they are still possible, amidst an inexpressible dullness—*dan*.

Dust of Empires

Most teas are sold in tea bags, as aromatic extracts dissolved in a carbonated drink, or at best as loose broken bits. In the West, these particles are inferior in color–flavor–smell to ground coffee or cocoa; in the East, tea is a powder, gathered into a mat heap at the heart of a ritual whose every sign contributes to the loss of meaning. Every time, the action of a stone mill or mechanical roller crushes the fibers and forms of the plant matter; every time, the pulverized matter is subjected, before its final infusion, to serried shifts and processes: crushers, fermentation rollers, drying conveyor belts, packing machines for loose tea or bagging machines, packaging-machines. In China, in the middle, beside the mass production of tea under state control, a few teas keep a special status: the dust of a Bi Luo Chun or a Du Yun Mao Jian is not the mechanically produced residue of the plant, but the fresh down of buds plucked in tiny quantities: over 75,000 buds in half a kilo, hand-picked in a single garden. Between the pinch of the fingernail that has to sever the barely open bud on the bush, and the careful weighing on the sales counter, a tea like this will have been treated to withering, the arrest of fermentation, and drying to preserve its minuscule hairs, leaflets, and stipules.

The Three Empires / The Three Islands

So three scales of measure rule the world of tea: in the West, the "ver-tea-quality" of Anglo-Indian tea; in the Far East, the "verdant quality" of Japanese tea; in the

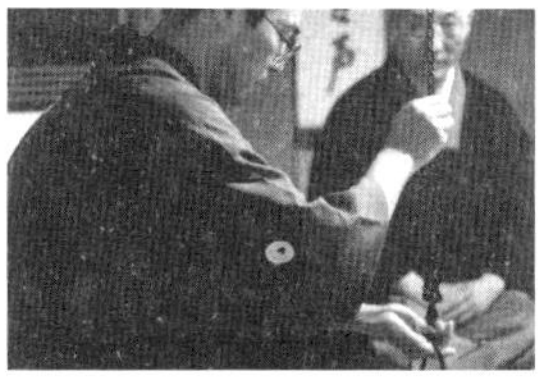

Middle—because in this new projection of the globe, it is not Europe but China that is in the center—the rainbow of Chinese tea: the celestial in that sphere not representing the refuge of a transcendence, as in Western metaphysics, but rather the immanent force at work in the course of nature.

Each of the three empires has annexed or appended to itself an island—with all the political consequences that such notions imply when relating to territory: Ceylon for British India, Kyushu for Japan, Formosa for China. Three islands discovered by the Portuguese. Each of these islands has precipitated, concentrated, and unfurled the qualities of the continent—or archipelago—from which it depended, in the improved conditions of the land, atmosphere, and sunshine needed to establish a plantation. To the point that Ceylon and Formosa, even after becoming Sri Lanka and Taiwan, each continue to be synonymous with the name of a tea, while the oldest customs of the archipelago survive in Kyushu, the third Japanese island.

Kyushu

In the Japanese archipelago, Kyushu is the island with a mythical foundation: the goddess Amaretsu gave her grandson Ninigi three *regalia* (mirror, sword, and magatama jewel) and sent him up Mount Takachiho to found the line of the first emperor, Jimmu. Its beginnings are not only mythical, but also historical; its Jômon pottery is among the oldest in the world (10,000 BC), and carved caves of Buddhas survive with sixteenth-century grottoes of crypto-Christian sects (*kirihitan dôkutsu*). On this island, also, Mongol warriors failed three times to land; and Korean potters invented Japanese porcelain (*Imari, Arita, Nabeshima*), which was distributed, with silver and tea, from the island trading post of Dejima by the Dutch, the only foreigners tolerated. The same circumstances governed the cultivation of tea: it was on Kyushu—in the monasteries of Tendaiji-in and Shôfuko-ji in Hakata—that the monk Eisai (1141-1215) planted the first tea bushes in Japan, having brought them from China with the *sutras* of Rinzai Zen Buddhism. This is also the only island in Japan that has retained the Chinese method of roasting, which produces teas that are curly rather than needle-shaped: Tamaryokucha, Kamaraicha, and Guricha, the favorites of the Korean ceramists. The tea from the southern regions (Fukuoka, Yame, Kagoshima), cultivated on very sunny low plains, is the first of the new crop in Japan. Bitterer and stronger than the others, it is indeed not the finest. As soon as the teas of the higher gardens of Honshû (Uji, Shiga, Shizuoka) go on sale, the previous ones lose the only thing that makes their primacy: their priority.

Ceylon

Ceylon, "the most beautiful island in the world," according to Marco Polo, produces one of the most full-bodied Indian teas. The beginnings of Sri Lankan tea, while often recounted, do not constitute a fable: tea was simply a means of bringing back into cultivation an island devastated in 1869 by *Hemileia vastatrix*, coffee rust. An

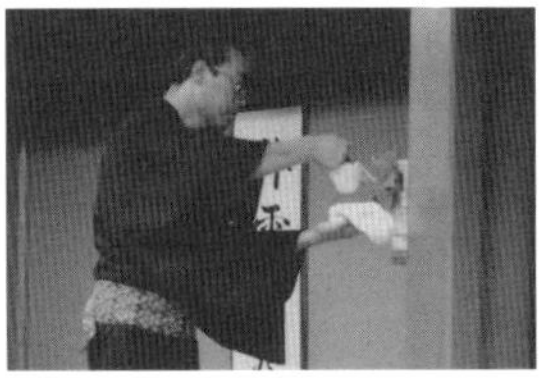

attempt to diversify, by the addition of a third crop, an intensive agriculture based on coffee and the accompaniment to both drinks, sugar cane. Before his compatriot Lipton, it was the Scotsman James Taylor who, in 1866, was sent to test the possibilities of tea cultivation in Ceylon. This was the first step towards the industrialization of production. The hard facts speak for themselves: 12 kilos in 1872 and 22,900 tons in 1890. The British plantations, first nationalized in 1971, were offered anew to private investors, while Sri Lanka fell from first to eighth as a world producer, and the CTC was considered as a last resort. The violent political clashes that continue to threaten the island result largely, as in Darjeeling and Assam, from the English strategy of moving tribal peoples to obtain skilled workers at lower cost. Ceylon tea, cloned from Assam tea, remains, in its finest vintages—those from the high mountains of Nuwara Eliya—a strong, astringent, highly colored tea, falling perfectly into the British mold as a vehicle for milk and sugar.

Wulong Island

In the sixteenth century, the Portuguese, followed by the Spanish and Dutch, occupied the *Ilha Formosa*, previously inhabited by Malayo-Polynesian tribes. In 1661, a rebel Chinese military chieftain took possession of the island, which was to undergo waves of immigration from the southern regions of China, finally becoming a separate province of China in 1886. Already in 1839, Doctor William Jardine, cofounder of Jardine Matheson & Co, the powerful British firm in Hong Kong, recommended to the Minister of Foreign Affairs, as the Opium Wars loomed, that possession be taken of three or four islands, namely Formosa, Quemoy and Amoy, to provide new markets and a foothold in China. Commodore Perry, who was to force Japan to open to the outside world, also advised the United States of Taiwan's strategic importance. British and American trade established itself there in 1860: camphor, tea, rice, sugar, wood for construction, coal. From 1895 to 1945, Taiwan, renamed Takasago, was occupied by the Japanese who created an institutional and administrative infrastructure. Jiang Jieshi (Tchang Kaï Chek) and the KMT (Guomindang) moved to the island in 1949. In modern Taipei, prostitutes, although illegal, continue to practice their profession while selling betel (*bin lang*), which forms a triad emblematic of the island with Wulong and *doujiang* (soy milk, served sweet or salt with fritters or sesame biscuits).

An offshoot of the Middle Kingdom, Taiwan has developed a tea culture whose most distinctive vintages are Wulongs, coming from southern continental regions where exceptional teas had been perfected. The Wulongs, principal representatives of the blue-green family—transcribed "oolong" by Europeans, and translating as "black snake" or "jet dragon"—, are identified with Formosa tea. While most of the stocks have been imported from the continent, some, such as Tie Guan Yin, "Iron Goddess of Mercy," have been carried on, under the same name, or in a derived form, such as Dong Ding. Others have been radically adapted, while the "original" from Fujian—Wen Shan Bao Zhong—has disappeared; new versions have been invented, notably Bai Hao Wulong, the famous Oriental Beauty, very popular with the English due to its strong oxidation. The blue-greens, in their differing fermentation, treatment, and altitude, offer the greatest variety of aromas, from floral to resinous; the largest palette of flavors from mild to bitter; the broadest spectrum of color when infused, from very pale yellow to a deep coppery brown. The six colors of China reappear, not imitated but visited and interpreted by the Taiwanese blue-greens. These teas also release a great range of essential aromas, very flowery, even fruity, or totally woody. So the Island of Wulong, with its spectrum of diffracted blue-greens, is a reduced version of the Chinese rainbow. Between the Black Empire and the Green Empire, is the Rainbow Empire, and not far off it the Island of Blue-Greens, "Wulong Island."

Although Lu Yu was writing at a time when tea was made by the compressed method, and not like Wulong varieties, only the latter fit his description given in chapter three of *Chajing*: "Tea appears in a myriad of forms. To put it plainly, it can be rough and creased like the boots of the Tartars, curly like the dewlaps of a wild buffalo, coiled like a cloud floating at the top of a mountain, barely undulating like water rippled by a light breeze; other teas are like the clay that the potter filters and settles with water or like a freshly plowed field in which a fierce downpour has made rivulets."

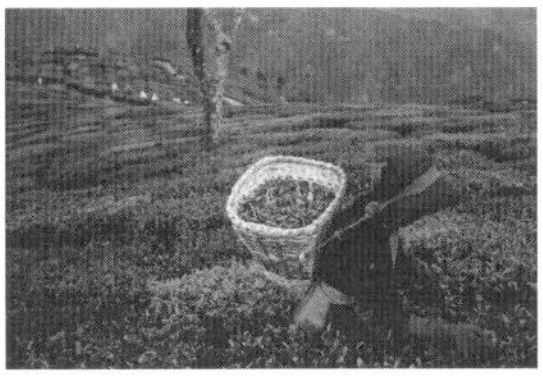

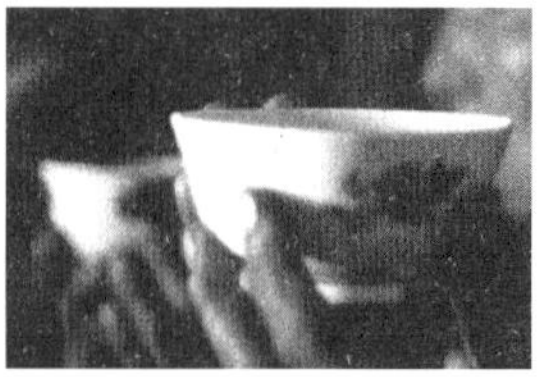

0

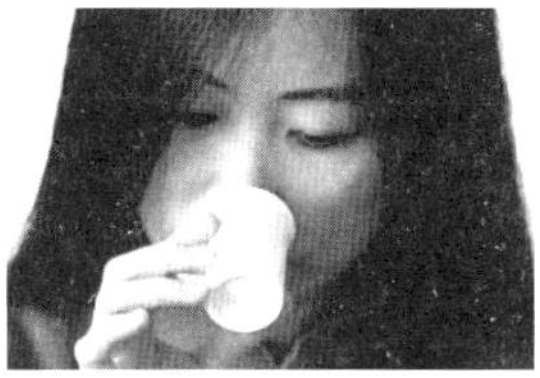

WATER

Water & Coke

It is probably more difficult to obtain a glass of water in our urban culture than it is to find a can of Coke. The water will have taken on the flavor of ice cubes left too long in the freezer alongside inadequately wrapped foodstuffs; it will bear the imprint of its travels along pipes and carry a whiff of its glass or plastic recipient. The economic trick which has ensured the success of the Atlanta-based company, now undermines its own raison d'être: if it is only the secret syrup which is manufactured in the United States, and then sent to be diluted and reconditioned in factories scattered throughout the world, it follows that the final drink will suffer from enormous variations because of the local variations in the quality of water used in its manufacture. Thus the whole idea behind this operation is constantly undermined: total continuity—the *always*-standard taste—is no longer ensured except by the curly white on red trademark signature.

Milk, Water, Air

Already reconstituted by another big company, which had invented powdered milk and freeze-dried coffee, "synthetic" water was at first sent to be tested on a large scale in the Third World, which had also been flooded with powdered milk adapted to simulate mother's milk; a murderous form of charity, an abuse of young mothers, the industrialization of the maternal feeding process working alongside the medicalization of childbirth. The truth is that this "pure" water synthesized by chemical ingenuity, in succession to distilled and sparkling water, marks a further stage in the reconstitution of the element/aliment. This same group, based in a country which has also contributed to the neutralization of cocoa by adding milk to it, has recently relinquished its assets in the white liquid, on which the company name had established itself, in order to acquire reserves of natural water on a huge scale and throughout the world. England, which hitherto had preserved its countryside, has, with the arrival of Thatcherism, recently sold off a large number of its purest springs. In the face of this theft of spring water, another group—called "to live"— from a middle country has, by controlling the subterranean circulation of water, reinforced its hold on the communication and recycling networks. This gigantic but discreet embargo on the element which, as an essential nutrient, is our statistical constituent, does not simply represent a financial redistribution and a worrying prospect, but signals the fact that control is possible over resources that humanity had until now assumed to be inalienable and inexhaustible: water and air—henceforth vulnerable to the same depletion as earth, with its minerals and hydrocarbons.

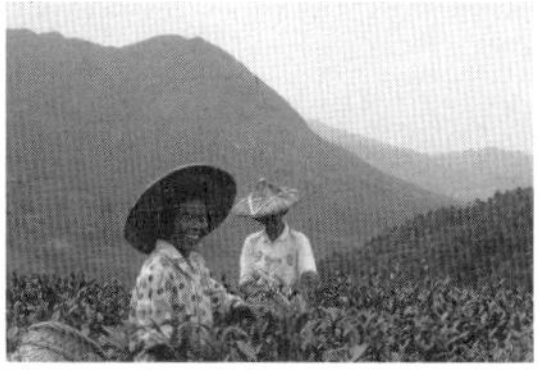

Black Water, Charmed Water, Diluted Water

"The Turks also have a black-colored drink;" (Della Valle, 1615) "they call it *chaoub*: it is almost as black as ink" (Rauwolf, 1582); the Iranians "drink coffee (*coho*); this drink, or rather this black soup… as black as soot" (Herbert, eighteenth century). Coffee is described by the earliest Europeans as blackened water, its nature as a transparent fluid annulled.

"Tea is water bewitched!" (Jonathan Swift) "Charmed water," the exotic drink is a *pharmakon,* as medicine of the apothecary, but also by its color, its artifice, its covering of make-up: *pharmakon* in Greek means magician or doctor's drug as much as color or scent. The word "drug" best reflects the mingled traces of magic, cosmetics and aromatic elements: an Anglo-Saxon *drugstore* is as much a chemist as a perfumery, whilst a *droguerie* in France is a shop in which one can find chemical products and paints. Treatises and descriptions identify the purpose of these unknown drinks in what was seen as their "pharmaceutical" function: as with coffee, the primary aim of tea was to eliminate the nasty color, unpleasant odor and bad taste of the local water. "At Oula-Houdouk, we all noticed the sulphurous taste of the water they gave us to drink, at Heve-Mouhor, this taste became unbearable and caught you in the throat and the nose." (Catherine-Fanny de Bourboulon, 1861) From Syria to the Mauritanian desert, water is described by travelers variously as salty, sulphurous or tasting of magnesium; and that alone, at first, seemed to justify the need for this extremely bitter beverage made from grilled and ground-up beans.

The Abbé Raynal, in the following century, applies this explanation to account for tea in China: "It was not just a mere caprice which originally brought this infusion into fashion. Water throughout the Empire is brackish, disagreeable and unhealthy, especially in the low-lying provinces. Of all the methods they invented to correct this, the use of tea was the only one which proved completely successful." In the nineteenth century, the spread of tea consumption in England arose from a similar motivation. After all, drinkable water only reached London in the sixteenth century, via the "new river," a 60 kilometer long aqueduct: but wine was still the universal prophylactic, as was brandy, or ale, beer imported by the Dutch, made of water and malt to which were added bitter hops and other flavors. "For hygienic reasons, water does not inspire confidence as it is a carrier of germs and illnesses. All medieval literature reflects a deep distrust of it, and the habit of systematically mixing it with wine became a measure of sanitary precaution before becoming a mark of good taste. And also one generally dilutes wine with water to reduce its density or its acidity." (Massimo Montanari)

Water Carrier

A large part of the planet, and in particular its dark continent, that giant reserve in negative of the world and probable birthplace of humanity, Africa, does not live

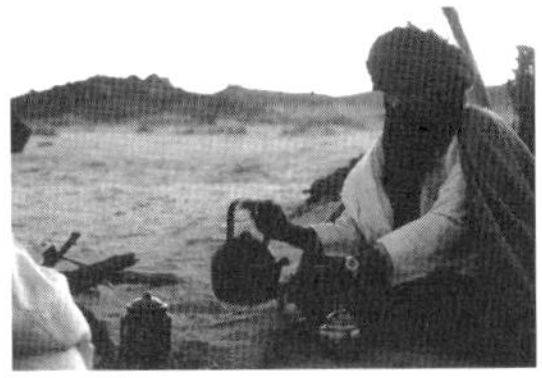

with an abundance of, nor easy access to water. There, water remains a constant occupation and preoccupation: it is work. It is also a pleasure. A description of old Damascus in the 1930s well describes the ebb and flow between exhaustion and reward. In the hot streets of the souk, the itinerant salesman bangs together two brass cups, indicating an offer of "souss," coffee or tea, which will come in these same tiny recipients, which look like two lemon-squeezers encased together. With his tarboosh on his head, and a white or striped apron down to his knees, the man carries on his back two large demijohns made of metal, nickel-plated and padded with linen to retain the heat, and, on his stomach, a copper tray with the cups or a glass box protecting some "simit" cakes. The thermal container can also be carried on the stomach, in the form of a horizontal cask, with a tap topped with a minaret and a crescent, or on the side, when it is a goatskin. The tumbler, held far away from the tap, is filled by stretching the stream of water to its utmost length, without spilling a drop of the precious liquid. A small-embossed silver ewer, filled with orange-flower water, a few drops of which will scent the glass or cup, also hangs at his belt. "A drop, come and drink a drop." Souss—a cleansing maceration of liquorice or tamarind—, *dam'a*—lemonade served with ground ice—, or blackberry syrup, are all scented waters, sweetened and colored, which are drunk, iced, alongside steaming cups of coffee or tea. Other drinks are even more nourishing: *labann*—curdled sheep's milk, as thick as cream; cow's milk curds, floating in whey; goat's milk, very liquid—, which is diluted with water to make *ayran*, chilled with large ice-cubes, or finished off with a grain of salt or a pinch of crushed garlic. *Doundourna,* an ice cream made with milk and *sahlep. Hboub*, a porridge of wheat, lentils, beans, raisins and sugar, is served in little bowls. From Morocco to Afghanistan, there are infinite variations on such drinks, in which water, ice or snow are the basis for various types of gustatory ornamentation.

On the café terraces, alcohol, rarely allowed, appears only in the form of *arak* or *raki*—a spirit made from the resin of the mastic tree, or flavored with aniseed, from the large family of Mediterranean drinks such as pastis, ouzo, anisette—, "water" soon made cloudy by water poured into it and ice thrown in, and which, like orgeat (barley and almond syrup), takes the form of an opalescent liquor: a cross between milk and water. "All liquid is water; and then all water is milk." (Gaston Bachelard) Telling their amber beads, banging their pieces down on the backgammon board, smoking their hookahs, the men sip out of their little Persian glasses tea, black coffee or a decoction of green coffee—*binn, bun* or *buncum*, which is still drunk from the Yemen to Syria. In these cafés, water is everywhere: not simply as the basis for all the drinks, or in the smoking devices, to filter the tobacco or the hashish, but also, as a metonymic supplement, in the water cooler, which, on the table, supplies fresh water between mouthfuls of coffee.

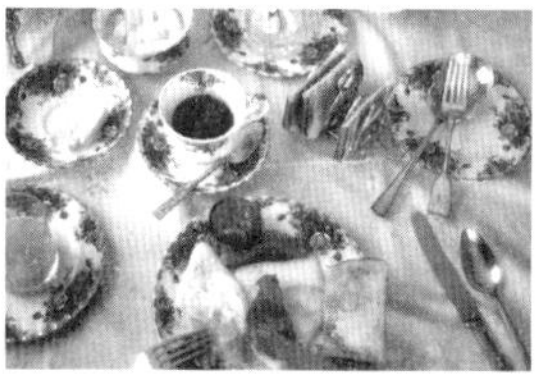

In the streets of Damascus, another purveyor of water would make the dust from the clay on the roofs more bearable: the waterer. He would appear in places where the big municipal water-lorries were unable to pass: " A great water-bag, a whole goat whose head had been replaced by a sort of tube, like and elephant's trunk, was used as a reservoir, suspended by a brace at hip height, as though the animal had slung its feet around the man's back. In rags, with his trousers rolled up to his knees, he scatters the liquid. "O'a ijrek," 'Watch out for your feet' he cries, advancing in the halo of dust that he raises before him." (A. Keusseoglou)

Supply of Water

The Indus, the Chang Jiang (Yangtze), the Tigris, the Euphrates, the Nile, the Rhine: rivers nurture civilizations along their courses or in their basins. Elsewhere and for a long time, water, whether it be water as matter, energy or carrier, has been an object of domestication: to irrigate both human beings and crops, to put its driving energy to use, or to provide its channels of communication. All kinds of expedients have been attempted, from propitiatory rites to ensure the alternation of dry and rainy seasons, to hydroelectric dams, with the whole history of navigation in between. In order to follow water through its cycle—precipitation, infiltration, evaporation—, and to gain access to its sites—springs, ground water, deep subterranean waters (magmatic, fossil, geothermal), machines have been necessary in order to pipe and drill it—building wells, dams, barrages—, to transport it, via supply pipes, tunnels, aqueducts, and to conserve it, in basins, cisterns and water towers. Yet more appliances were invented to harness, or resist its flow: wheels, chain-pumps, locks, turbines, pumps, fountains. "Water is thus the eye of the earth, its mechanism for observing time... " (Paul Claudel)

Water Supplies

Drinking water, cleaning water, drowning water. Water is an environment for human beings: a food, a bath, or an aquaculture. And there are as many actions involving it—canalization, libation, ablution, immersion, aspersion, irrigation—as there are states in which it exists—clear, cloudy, running, still, live, dead, light, heavy, deep. But, as the embodiment of refreshment, water cools or heats; and it quenches thirst. "At certain times, the human being is a plant which yearns for water from the sky." (Gaston Bachelard)

In Dark Waters

The man saved from the waters starts humanity again: Noah, Moses, Jesus. The same water which renews the life-cells or which, in the oasis-island, allows the survival of the nomad, is a danger, notably to the sources of desert religions. Gathering together opposites such as fire, it permits ordeals, purification, baptism. "In liquid, opposites pass more easily into one another. Liquid is the element of the *pharmakon*." (Jacques Derrida) Holy or tainted water, therapeutic or malefic: the

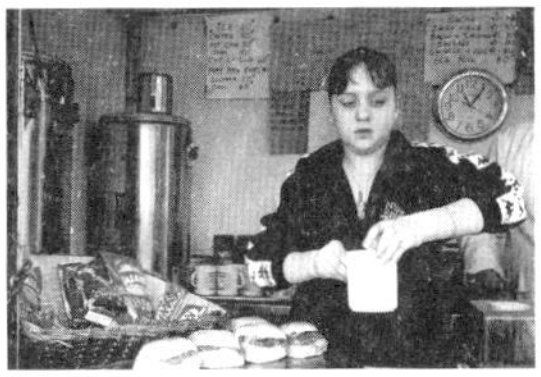

dowser is also a magician. Water allows hydrotherapy: soft water for thermal baths, or salty for thalassotherapy ; while rivers are carriers of epidemics—typhoid, cholera, polio in Africa and in India, and the sea, in seafood, disseminates flukes, thread-worms and bilharzia.
Heraclitus: "Sea-water is both the most pure and the most polluted. For fish, it is drinkable and beneficial, for man undrinkable and poisonous."
Plato: "Water, is of all foods for the garden, undoubtedly the most nourishing, but it is easily tainted: indeed neither the earth, nor the sun, nor the winds, which nourish plants, can easily be lost through drugs (*pharmakeusin*), leakage, or even theft, but water is, by its nature, exposed to all these inconveniences: and so there must be a law to protect it." (*Laws*)

Source of Offerings

"... As for me, I cannot drink sulphated water [*xie lu*: this may be *xie yan*, magnesium sulphate, Epsom salts?], and I cannot afford to have water brought to me from the Benevolent mountain. In the summer of 1614, when passing by the monastery of the Speckled Bamboos, I drew some water and tasted it. It had a sharp freshness, which surprised me. I went to see the color of the water. It was like a white halo around an autumn moon in a frosty sky; or a light mist escaped from the mountain, wafting around the pines, drifting by the rocks, growing paler, about to dissolve. Suddenly I noticed some words engraved on the lip of the well. I cleaned them with a broom, and the words "Spring of the Offerings" appeared, in writing very similar to that of Youjun, which increased my astonishment. I tried making tea with the water, and it revealed its aroma. When freshly drawn it has a faint taste of stone which disappears when it is left to sit for three days. The only way to recognize it is this: take a mouthful of water, just touch the roof of the mouth with the tongue, and pass it over the cheeks. The mouth seems empty, as though there is nothing to swallow. This sensation is characteristic of the water from the Spring of the Offerings. Enterprising people who knew about it would come each day to draw water from it, some to make wine, some to open a tea-house selling tea from the Spring of the Offerings, some to put it in jars to sell, some to give to their superiors. When Dong Fangbo became governor of Yue, he tasted the water. Finding it very sweet, and for fear of it running out, he had the well sealed. And so the reputation of the spring grew day by day. The spring waters from the river Tao at Kuaji, the Branch of the north at Mount Xiao and the Tiger's Leap at Hangzou do not compare with it... One of our yearly workers, through negligence, did not go as far as necessary and brought back another water instead. As I beat him with my cane, he shouted curses at his companions, thinking they had betrayed his secret. I had to tell him from what place and what well his water came from to convince him that he was wrong." (Zhang Dai)

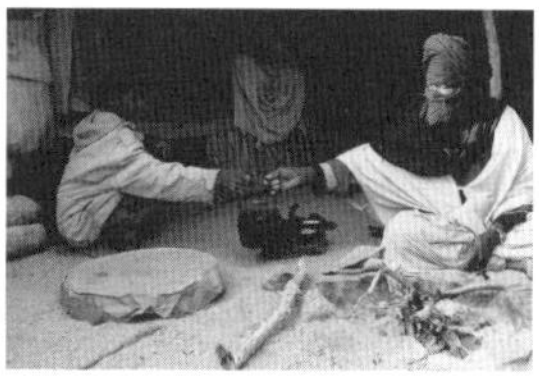

Treated Water

In countries where the water supply is assured to both town and country, the irrigation of crops has been accompanied by fertilizing of the soil and development of the land, with consequences, sometimes catastrophic, which have been the opposite of those intended, bringing an increased risk of surface flooding and of long-term pollution of the subsoil. The rites of passage, mediated by water, have henceforth been applied to things and to the element itself, notably through the other purifying element, fire: disinfection, sterilization, pasteurization. If a part of the treatment applied to water is based on hygienic regulations concerning food in general, such extensive canalization, bringing it to the very smallest of habitats, and making it serve every industrial and agricultural purpose, demands even stricter regulations. This economic control is being shared out on a world-wide scale, on the eve of the third millennium, by consortiums such as Vivendi, Nestlé or Danone, which own huge networks of water conduits and sources of mineral water. In fact the effective management of water depends on mastery of its treatment and recycling: I. Chemical treatments (sifting and skimming): coagulation (with aluminum sulphate, ferrous chloride, silicon dioxide), flocculation (for limpidity), filtration (with silicon sand, or active carbon to eliminate smell, taste and bacterial growth); II. Sterilization, using chlorine, chlorine peroxide and dioxide, or ozone to bleach and deodorize; III. The purification of used water (biological processes, treatments of mud and effluents).

To the natural pollutants—colon bacilli, fecal streptococci, germs—can be added those introduced by industrial waste and agricultural effluent—nitrates, sulphates, chlorides—and their micropollutants: heavy metals (chromium, mercury, lead), pesticides (herbicides, fungicides, insecticides), detergents. And nobody at this time has the slightest idea which will have the most catastrophic effect: the liquid manure produced by pig rearing, the chemical fertilizing of fields or the radioactive waste from nuclear power plants.

Water Treatise

Concern for water. Caring for its chemical, therapeutic and organoleptic qualities has become a permanent feature in the analysis of differences in the preparation of espresso coffee, the manufacture of beer, or, that of whisky or rice wine, yet more patience-demanding—present-day manufacture of sake in Japan depends on the quality of the water for its fermentation. But few cultures have pursued this concern to the same extent as China: there this preoccupation is reflected in poetry, history, and a genuine theory, which echoes the country's entire cosmogony. Lu Yu, the poet, author of the *Canon* (*Chajing*) and *The Notes on Tea*, has, as well as writing over a chapter in each of these, devoted an entire work to the subject of water: the *Shui Pin, The Tasting of Water*. This is only the first of a long list of such treatises, which are mostly composed themselves of lists: catalogues, topographies and chronolo-

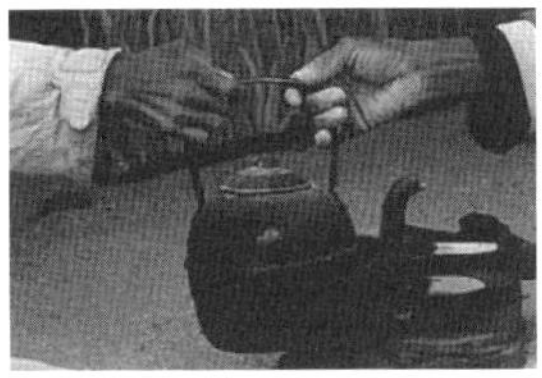

gies of the best sources of water in China. This form of classification likened them to guides for connoisseurs of tea. Alongside the hierarchy of specified springs, a typology would grade the water according to the different forms in which it appears: "As for water, that from mountain springs is the most desirable, that from rivers is of medium quality, that from wells the least adequate." (*Chajing*) To these three sources—spring water, running water and still water—other conditions or places for water are listed in the Chinese and Japanese treatises—dew, snow, rain—, as are its most familiar circumstances—depth, distance from edge, type of movement... Water, in its many forms, can be listed by its cosmogonic meanings: water from a thunderstorm is considered dangerous, whereas water from rain at the beginning of spring is beneficial, and water gathered from stalactite caves is a sovereign remedy. This system allowed people to both adapt treatment and usage to each situation, and to act in consequence: when water was being drawn from a river, it had to be taken from the middle, where the current is strongest.

Water Stories

From its founding myth, tea is linked to water. Even if versions of the myth differ, the discovery of *cha* always included a meeting between the "bitter herb" and the liquid element which received it, cooked it or infused it. One example is the story of the divine emperor leaning against the sapling to rest, causing the fall of three leaves into the water he was about to drink. Another story shows Lu Yu, begged by a high-ranking dignitary to taste the renowned water of the region, obliged to contradict his host: "This may be water from the main river of Nanling, but it has been heavily diluted by water from the edge of the river," obliging the dignitary to admit that the swerving of his junk had forced him into this carelessness... Later, few of the Chinese stories in which tea is the theme fail to fictionalize the importance of water; most of these stories, legends and anecdotes tell of the infallible ability of such and such an illustrious character to detect the origin, nature or method of transport of the water he has been offered. For serving tea it could be brought at great expense from distant lands; and these geographical movements, as well as the expense involved, confirmed the metaphors establishing the legend of the drink.

Master Min's Tea

"Zhou Monong spoke to me endlessly on the subject of the teas of Min Wenshui. In the ninth month of the year 1638, I went to Liudu. As soon as I landed I went to Min Wenshui, at the quay of the Peach Leaves. It was mid-afternoon and Wenshui was out. I was awaiting his return when a trembling old man arrived. I had hardly said a word, when he drew himself up, saying: "I have left my stick somewhere!" and disappeared. "Am I going to return empty-handed?" I wondered. I waited a long time more. When Wenshui returned, the evening gong was sounding. "Oh, you're still there!" he said, looking at me from the corner of his eye. "What brings you?" "I have

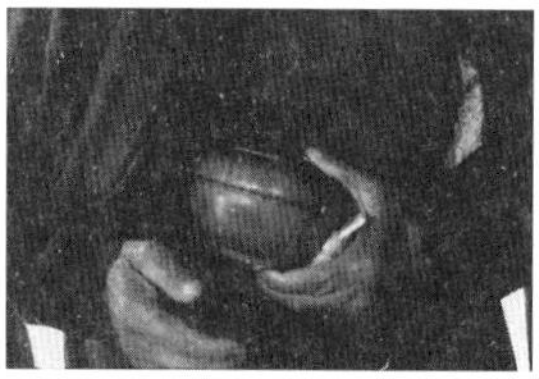

wanted to pay my respects for a long time," I said. "I will not leave today without tasting Master Min's tea." Wenshui, delighted, went to the stove himself and, in the time it takes for a shower of rain, the tea was ready. He led me into a room with a bright window and a small clean table. There were teapots from Jingxi, bowls dating from the Cheng and Xuan periods, more than ten tea sets, all of the finest quality. I examined the tea by the light of the lamp; you could not distinguish it from the bottom of the cup, and yet it had an intoxicating aroma. I cried out that it was excellent. "From what place does this tea come from?" I asked Wenshui. "It is tea from Langyuan," he replied. "Don't make fun of me," I said, tasting it again. "If this is made in the Langyuan manner, the taste is not the same. "Would you know its provenance?" asked Wenshui, hiding a smile. "Isn't it more like the tea of Luojia?" I said, after swallowing another mouthful. "Admirable!" murmured Wenshui, sticking his tongue out in astonishment. "Where does the water come from?" I asked. "From the spring of the Benevolent Mountain." He replied. "You must be joking!" I said once again. "The spring of the Benevolent Mountain is a thousand li from here, how could it be that a tired water could preserve all its sharpness?" "I dare not hide anything from you," he said. "To take water from the spring of the Benevolent Mountain, you must bail out the well, wait in the calm of the night for the new water, gather it quickly and fill the bottom of the jar with stones from the mountain. Finally the boat must not leave until there is a wind. In this way, the freshness of the water develops so well that the normal water of the Benevolent Mountain is a notch inferior to it, not to mention other waters!" He put out his tongue again and said: "Admirable, admirable!" No sooner had he said this than he disappeared. He reappeared a moment later with a full teapot. "Please taste this," he said, pouring out the tea. "It has a lively aroma," I said, "and a strong taste; could it be a spring crop, whereas the previous one was an autumn one?" "I am seventy," said Wenshui, with a burst of laughter, "and amongst all the fine connoisseurs who have visited me you have no equal." And so we became friends." (Zhang Dai)

Fortune's Water

On the high peak of the temple of Kao-Chan: "The old priest now led me to a different part of the grounds, to see a famous spring. This was in one of the most romantic looking dells or ravines that I had ever beheld. We descended to it by a flight of stone steps, crossed a bridge which spanned the ravine, and found ourselves in front of a small temple. On one side of it the water was gushing down, clear and cool, from the mountain, into a small cistern placed there to receive it; while on the other a cauldron or large kettle was always ready boiling during the day, in order that tea might readily be made for visitors. Here a number of priests were lounging about, apparently attached to this temple. They received me with great kindness, and begged me to be seated at a table in the porch. One of them took my cup and

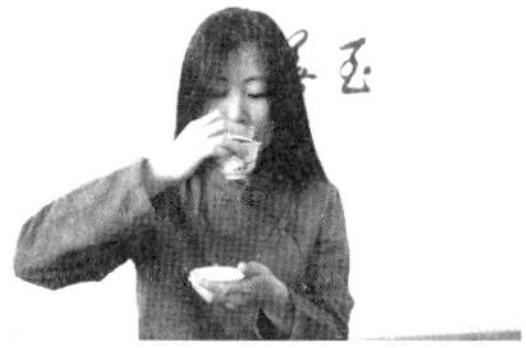

filled it with water at the spring, and brought it to me to taste. They all praised its virtues; and it certainly was excellent water. I told them it was the best I had ever tasted, and they brought me a cup of tea made with water from the same spring." (Robert Fortune)

Wine & Water

Our civilization is not a water-based one. Water, according to the dictionary, must obey a triple injunction: colorless, odorless, tasteless. To be satisfied with it is paradoxical: "Water suffices… *In vino veritas*: it seems that here too I am again at odds with all the world over the concept 'truth'—with me the spirit moves over the water." (Nietzsche, *Ecce Homo)* Those who do not drink are, in this context, "men who know nothing of humanity or nature, artists who reject the traditional means of art; workers blaspheming against their machinery… A man who only drinks water is hiding some secret from his fellow-men." (Charles Baudelaire, *On Wine and Hashish*) In France, wine, the totem-drink, is set against all other beverages; one can, for example, contrast it with milk: "The real anti-wine (that is to say, milk) contrasts with fire by its molecular density, by the creamy, therefore soothing, nature of its surface; wine is cutting, surgical, it transmutes and brings to birth; milk is cosmetic, it binds, covers, restores. And its purity, associated with childish innocence, is a promise of strength, a strength which is neither revulsive nor congestive, but calm, white, clear and equal to reality." (Roland Barthes, *Wine and Water*) However, the real liquid enemy of wine, the "essence of sun and earth," is water: "The vine-stock resists and repels water from earth or river. The stem is a fist preventing water from climbing to the fruit. In its roots it twists the quintessential sap. And the vine shoot, dry in all the fibres of its substance, prevents the humidity from polluting the grape." (Gaston Bachelard, *The Wine and the Vine of Alchemists)* The only water the vine will tolerate is that of the tail of the comet, "rich in smooth and liquid fire, essential and subtle water, long distilled in the firmament." The poor reputation of rosé wines arises, too, from the fact that, even when they have not been made by blending, they appear to be a mixture: neither "drinkable gold" like white wine, nor "blood of the earth" like red, they reveal, in their transparency or grayness, a water content which dilutes the wine, as one does for children.

Empty Drink & Gray Drink

In our sphere, tea represents the perfect neutral, dull, empty drink. Tea is indeed a perfect metonymy of water; it shares all its negative qualities—no color, smell or taste—and, for this reason, is the opposite to wine: even more so than other exotic drinks, coffee in particular, which were greeted in Europe in the seventeenth century by the puritan bourgeoisie as the antidotes to alcohol. But Bree Tannic tea is not simply set alongside water—on the menu, just before the mineral waters—, but in it, mixed with it, warmed up with it, emphasizing the vacuum, the void of the

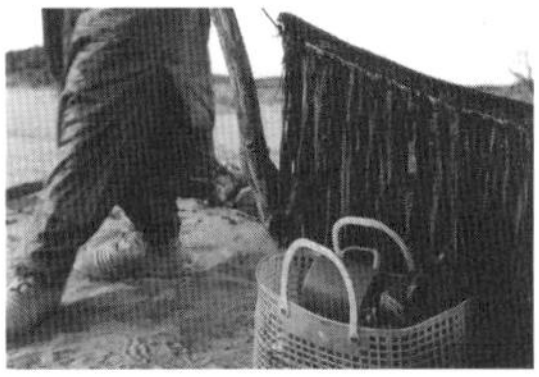

aquatic signifier; tea is, even more than water, dull and blank. After all, the crystal clearness and the sweetness of water—its insipidity lies above all in its non-saltiness—ensure freshness, lightness and purity for the drinker. But these very qualities are removed by the infusion of tea: they are neutralized by a flavorless taste, aroma-free smell and colorless hue. Each aspect is thus diminished, becomes gray, and therefore more apt to be included on a color chart than a watery transparency. As it is, tea perfumed with bergamot, the invention of which continues to be attributed to an English nobleman, though the stories were long ago disproved, is perhaps correctly named after all: Earl Grey. This "title" continues to remind us that even before it is rendered opaque by milk and sugar, and even before it has been sprayed with essences, this Bree Tannic tea is gray.

Tea, Water, Wine

If wine remains a totem, it is because it stands as the opposite pole to water or milk. Tea in China represents not so much an uncontested domination as a point of reference or, better, equivalence. If wine in France remains, symbolically and alchemically, a standard, like gold, tea in China is more of a general equivalent, more like exchangeable currency. Thus it retains a relationship with all other drinks, as currency does with all other commodities: a true general metonymy, it is this "liquid"—in kind—alongside and similar to other fluids. Thus the Chinese art of tea—*cha yi* and *gongfucha*—considers tea in exactly the same position as that of wine in the West: by the euphorid it produces, the complexity of its flavors, or the diversity of its soil. And the poetry of Du Fu, Lu Yu and Lu Tung celebrates tea in exactly the same way as François Villon, Omar Khayyam or Charles Baudelaire sung the praises of wine. But, at the same time and in the same terms, the Eastern poets celebrated both tea and wine. The latter probably referred less to the wine from vines, brought very early on from the Levant and introduced to China, than to all the rice, barley and millet liquors drunk throughout Asia. They are beers or spirits which, through the water in which the fermentation takes place, and through their characteristic limpidity, retain a link with the aqueous element, the enemy of wine. Tea, in China, is so widespread that its name has come to refer to the cup of hot water into which one has lost the means to put a few leaves, or in the bottom of which they have long ago given up their flavor—a liquid which circulates amongst all other drinks and at the same time represents them all; it is a wine, the product of an elaborate process bringing about euphoria, and it is a water, which quenches and refreshes.

If "wine is the blood of the vine or blood the wine of animals" and "between extreme kingdoms, between drinkable gold and blood, wine is the natural intermediary," it is the "creative liquid," which escapes "from vegetable life, so often exhausted, dulled by the effusion of the liquid principle, a life almost always

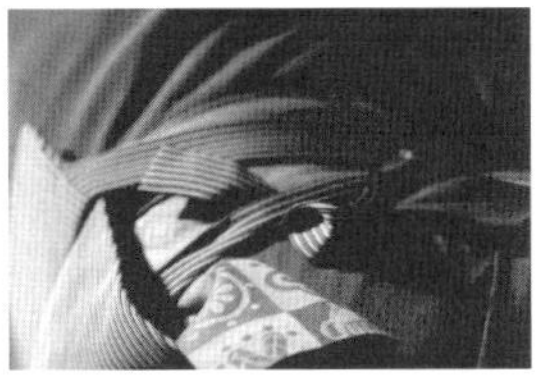

without strength, stimulus or force." (Gaston Bachelard) Milk is the animal's digestion of grass. Tea, once it has been united with the water needed to deploy its flavors, recreates the water of flowers—lilacs, magnolias, orchids—, of fruit—pears, grapes, pineapples—, and of wood—camphor, aloe, cinnamon. And, more astonishing still, that of the earth, damp earth, humus—as one finds in a twenty or thirty-year-old Pu Er.

Tea With Milk, Tea Without Water

The link established from the beginning by China between tea and water has not been broken in the Bree Tannic world—and has even been pushed to extremes in French café-brasseries where hot water without any discernible flavor is served for social reasons—but it has been denied by the addition of milk. This lactic addition represents, for the Chinese amateur, whether he be an ordinary consumer or a connoisseur of fine vintages, a crime in the same order as that of diluting wine with water. A Long Jing, a Tie Guan Yin, a Pu Er would quite simply be ruined by such an interference. Green tea from the most mediocre of sources would be rendered undrinkable. Still, this practice did actually begin in China itself, or at least on its borders, amongst the nomad tribes of the North West. All the different forms of tea with yak butter, tea with mare's milk, churned tea, still in use from Tibet to Iran, along the caravan trails, were perhaps what transmitted the custom to Europe, though the latter got its tea-supplies from the sea. In the Yemen, tea is prepared, in this tradition, in a decoction with other ingredients; cardamom, cinnamon or other spices. But then it reaches another extreme: it is boiled in goat's milk—and without water.

Out of Water

True, the Ionian cosmogonies, like the Babylonian and Egyptian mythologies, regard water—the sea, rivers, rain—as the bath from which the universe springs. In *Metaphysics* and *Of the Sky*, Aristotle writes that for Thales of Miletus the earth floats on water and that water is the principle of all things. For Anaximandros, this principle (*arkhe*) is the undefined (*apeiron*), whilst "the living creatures were born from the humid element when the sun had evaporated it." Anaximenos, however, saw fire, wind and cloud in the rarefaction or condensation of air, and wrote: "as our soul is air (*aer*) and supports us, so a breath (*pneuma*) is air supporting the whole world." In the *Physics of the Milesians*, philosophy is drawn from mythology, being above all geographical and meteorological; water and fire are the forces, movements or fluxes that play on earth and in the air. In this way, the four roots—fire, air, water, earth—of which Empedocles of Agrigento said that their joining or separation through love or hate was the root of all things in the world, are elements not valued in the same system. So, for Heraclitus, movement, which is the substance of the universe, is manifested through fire and water: "All things are opposed to fire, and fire

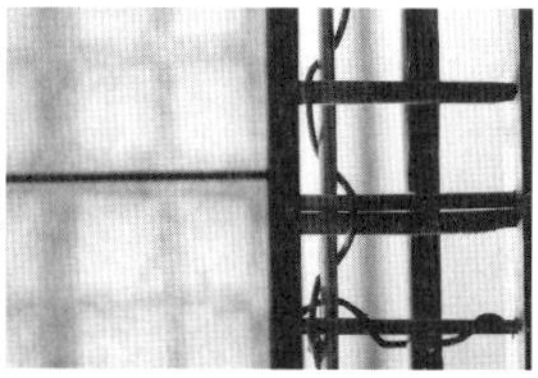

is opposed to all things"; "For souls, to die is to become water, for water, to die is to become earth. And from earth comes water, and from water comes the soul." "The metamorphoses of fire: first the sea, from the sea half becomes fire, half becomes whirlwind." Hippocrates, before the four conditions of Galien—hot, cold, dry and humid—, and the four temperaments—sanguine, bilious, phlegmatic, melancholic—which remained a part of Western medecine until the nineteenth century, would gauge health through the interaction of the opposing forces of driving fire and nourishing water. As for Plato, before "hearing" in the "ether" that "it ran ceaselessly flowing around the air" (*aei thei rheon*), and "seeing better" into the earth *(ge)* the generatrix, gaia, he must "set aside" fire and water, whose words have been "borrowed from barbarians" (*Cratylus*). We should investigate the way in which Western philosophies, physics and religions evolve, beyond the tangible-intelligible paradigm, between earth and air, the stable and the pneumatic. They give a very different account of the relationship between sky and earth to that given in China. The ages in which the great prehistoric periods have been divided are named after stone, bronze and iron—hard elements for the archeological memory. The ages of pottery, wood, rice, bamboo, beer or water would be, despite their less solid remains, equally pertinent designations. In the metaphysical system inherited from the Greeks, in which little is made of intermediary or changing states of matter—fluid, soft, burning—matter is solid and spirit gaseous. The favored transition is sublimation, in the chemical sense of the term.

If wine represents our culture so well—Noah, hardly saved from the flood, plants a vine—it is precisely because it exists between earth and air: "Wine?... a living body in which the most diverse "spirits" are held in balance, flying spirits and weighted spirits, the conjunction of a sky and a soil." (Gaston Bachelard)

Water Landscapes

Our civilization, ignoring the lessons of the Flood, has domesticated water. Rather like one of those officials who, after his town has suffered from a flood, redoubles the fortifications, elevations and dikes without considering their effects on the flow, the variations in the river's cycle, or its alluvial outlets.

Our painted images are made of wax, resin, egg, oil, glue, gum, honey, bitumen, mortar, chalk, graphite, glass. To maintain its stability our art is adhesive, fatty, creamy, pasty, plastic or crystalline. Washes, apart from the preliminary reinforcement of a drawing and watercolor, outside England and the work of Cézanne, have remained minority arts. Water, as a medium, both solvent and binding, has never held the central position that it has done continuously in the pictorial art of the Far East. This is no doubt generally connected with writing (*graphein*) and, at its heart, the connection between writing and painting, where the common tool in China has

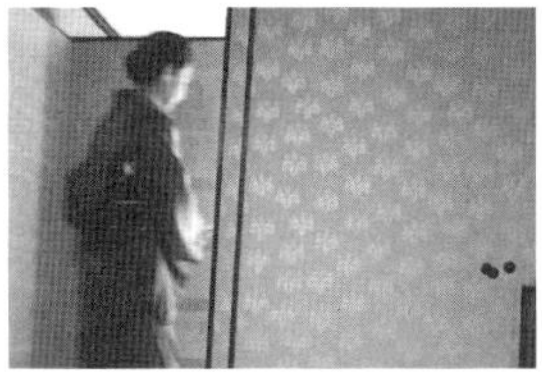

been paintbrush and ink—poetry, calligraphy and representation unfolding in the same space—whereas in the West it is either the stylus, the pen or the pencil—creating an opposition between *colorito* and *disegno.*
Climax, end and beginning: Monet's *Waterlilies*—"water landscapes."

Water, Mountain, Wind

One of the most ancient treatises on Chinese art begins like this: "Now, at the center of the way of painting, water and ink are preeminent. They adopt the nature of the spontaneous, complete the work of that which creates and transforms, bring forth everything that is in proximity, draw light over a hundred thousand leagues, from East to West, from South to North, adapt to what is before the eyes in spring, summer, autumn and winter." (Wang Wei, *Houa Kiue, Secrets of Painting*, Tang dynasty)
Water, in the ink, is, between paintbrush and paper, in the midst of the artistic process, the fluid whose deposited soot leaves a trace. Water, in its diffused metonymy, is everywhere in Chinese representation and articulation: under the hues of cloud, of mist, of fog, of lake, river and waterfall: "When painting addresses mountains, it finds its soul; when it addresses water, it finds its movement." (Shitao)
Shanshui, "mountain-water" (or elsewhere "mountain-river"), is the name of the most distinguished form of work in Chinese ink. What is translated as "landscape" is in fact an ideogrammatic association, in which the three strokes of each character still represent the two poles of the landscape: a peak dominating its slopes and a river between its two banks. Chinese painting and poetry are not linked, as in Europe or Japan, with the theater, but with "geomancy (*feng shui*), the object of which is to determine the value of sites by considering the running waters (*feng*) and the air currents (*shui*), which are always in relation to the mountains." (Hubert Damisch) In fact, they share a number of notions, which can also be found in the representation of the physiological body: bone-structure of rocks, breathing of clouds, water-courses or arteries of the dragon (*long mai*).

Water Courses

Confucius before the continual flow of the river: "To pass like this, without truce, by day and by night!" (*Conversations*, IX, 16)
Heraclitus: "Those who go down to the same rivers are always bathed in new waters. And the souls exhale from the dampness"; "We go down and we do not go down to the same river, we are and we are not."; "One cannot go down twice into the same river."
Kamo no Chômei: "[*Yuku kawa no nagare wa taezu shite, shika mo, moto no mizu ni arazu]* The course of the flowing river never dries up, and yet it is never the same water. The foam which floats on still waters sometimes dissolves, sometimes reforms, and there is no instance of it lasting long. The same happens to men and to

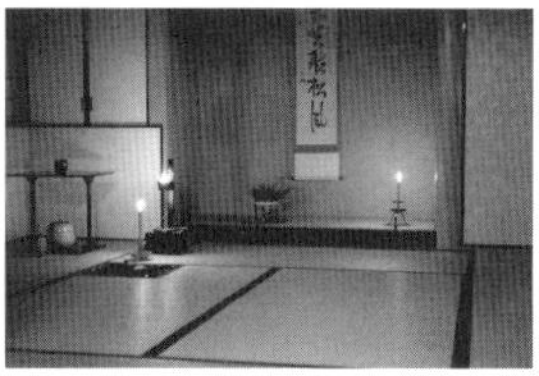

dwellings in this world." (Hôjôki, *Notes from the Hermitage*) Each of the texts, endlessly ruminated upon in its own sphere, is a shared place, an infusion offered to all. But the common ground is not a motif common to the place it comes from. The water course does not have the same value or meaning in every tradition. For the Greeks, as Plato in the *Cratylus* or Aristotle in *Metaphysics* relate it, using a lost formula from the Heraclitian fragments, "everything flows away" (*panta rei*) and "there is no science possible for things thus made." It is totality, it is being, it is the substance which are thus carried along: "Thales saw the unity of the Being and when he wanted to speak of it, he spoke of water" (Nietzsche) "It is the same thing to be what is alive and what is dead, awake or asleep, young or old; because through the changing (*metapesonta*), this becomes that, and, through the changing, that in turn is this." (Heraclitus) In the Japanese tradition, from the first sentence that everybody can recite, it appears as a Buddhist expression, and the archipelago of all catastrophes (typhoons, earthquakes, tidal waves) is its naturalized metaphor: *mujo*, impermanence, transience or "the dissolution of all things in time," (Augustin Berque) "the only notion to which every Japanese adheres to, from the most ignorant peasant to the wisest monk and most subtle philosopher." (René Sieffert) For Chinese thought, as Menzi in particular has interpreted it, it is not a question of "a painful sense of the ephemeral," nor of a philosophy of time and being, but more of seeing in the flow of water the image of the greater "world process," of a "background of immanence," of the "propensity of things" (François Jullien).

The Chinese attitude towards water is neither ontological as in the West, nor poetical as in the Far East, it is strategic. Laozi: "In the world, there is nothing more supple and weak than water, but nothing can surpass it when it comes to attacking what is hard and strong." Sunzi applies it to the art of war: "Just as water tends to avoid heights and flow downwards, so troops will avoid the enemy's strong points and attack his weak ones; just as water determines its course according to the terrain, so troops can determine victory according to the enemy." (Xu Shi) "The ideal gentleman is like water/Water is beneficial to all and a rival to nothing/It lies in the depths that are despised by all/It is close to the way." (Laozi) Water is what brings one closest to Tao, "because it is infinitely yielding, and fluid, it has no form and no backbone, never ceases to flow without ever drying up, water puts us on the way of the Way, it makes us return to the undifferentiated. That which one could never see individually nor name separately; whence everything continually proceeds, where everything continually returns. Of all tangible realities, water could be the one that is least so; it does not stand still in any particular place. The least thing-like of all things—the most alive, the most alert." (Francois Jullien)

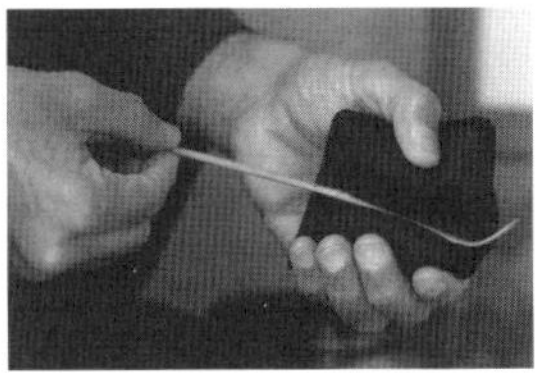

Image of Water During the tea ceremony, the host waters the "steps," the stones in the garden, three times, before his guests walk on them. The gesture simply repeats the general humidity and liquidity: the front garden, the *roji,* is the "dewy path," which offers in a very small urban space all the signs of a deep forest with its mosses and evergreens; before penetrating into the inner garden, or into the tea house, the guests wait beside a basin, from which, before their crouched entrance, they draw water with a bamboo ladle to wash their hands and mouth, to purify themselves and leave behind the profane world. A similar ablution is necessary to enter a Shintô sanctuary, which may consist of a "sea" of sand, or a sacred waterfall, symbolized, on the altar, by a mirror—icy water. The doorsteps of traditional houses and private gardens are still liberally watered. And the truth is that the ground in Japan can seem permanently damp: the interior flooring, whose wood has been polished and rubbed by repeated rinsings; the gravel of "dry" Zen gardens, combed into recurring patterns of concentric waves to symbolize the water they no longer display; sound devices reinforcing the sound of water, like the *suikinkutsu*, a jar buried beneath the mossy basin, and which echoes the sound of the falling drops. After the serious ecological crisis of the 1970s, in order to restore its emblematic amenities, contemporary Japan has had to rediscover its relationship with water. Thousands of kilometers of seafront had been fortified with concrete against tidal waves; hundreds of rivers corseted or covered up by motorways and railways; urban canals walled up and cut off from pedestrian circulation. When in fact "the most remarkable forms of Japanese culture have developed in the vicinity of water." (Jacques Berque) The *ukiyo-e* prints—"images of the floating world"—take up the Buddhist word *ukiyo*, "miserable world," transcribed in other characters (*fushi*) meaning "drifting, changing, frivolous world." Thus named, this world of pleasures—theaters, games, courtesans— was, needless to say, located in tea houses not far from water: the areas of Gion and Pontocho in Kyôto, Dôtonbori in Osaka, Sumida in Edo.

Water-Tea Solidarity If tea cannot reveal its excellence without the pure water in which it infuses, water can not find a more subtle companion than tea, which spreads into it whilst respecting its transparency—with the three exceptions of Japanese macha, Tibetan chai and Anglo-Indian Milk Tea—and its lightness of taste and fragrance. This solidarity, this mutual co-dependency is shown in some appellations, naming a tea grown in the immediate vicinity of the water which will join it in the cup. Thus Uji in Japan or Long Jing in China are both names of most famous teas—a success at their expense when one sees the multiplication of estates and improper appellations—, among the most ancient and those growing near a famous spring.

In each of these countries, the perfection of such names, as evoked by poetry, is founded on water, which both enables the growth of the tea-plants and the infusion

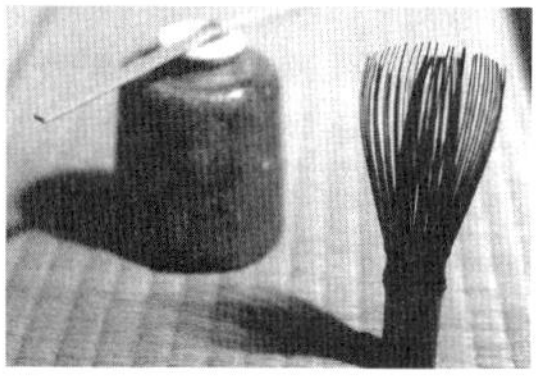

of the teas without the inconvenience of distance or the dwindling of their respective qualities by the time taken for transportation. The closeness between the spring of the Two Tigers and the Well of the Dragon tea (Long Jing) thus multiplies the protection granted, in several myths, by animals in response to the farmers' prayer for rain.

Water Test

Mr Li Te Yu, an official in the Tang dynasty, was in the habit of getting water delivered from the Hui Shan monastery to Changan; it took a month to transport it. One day a monk from a neighboring temple remarked while drinking his tea: "We can find the same water here. What stupidity, replied Mr Li. This water is brought to me from thousands of *li* away[*1li*=576m]. What possible connection could there be between the two springs?" Still, he decided to check the matter by pouring water from ten different springs into separate bottles, one of which contained his special Hui Shan water and another the water brought by the monk. The latter easily recognized them both; Li, tasting in his turn, also found them identical. "He therefore saved himself a great superfluous expense." (John Blofeld)

Tea Test

Chinese accounts describe tea through a testing or tasting process: most often "test" and "taste" are identical. This test is there to establish the proof of tea, its value for the physiological body, and its role in a society whose hierarchy is established not by heredity but by recruitment through the mandarin examinations of the *Cheng Zhu* tradition. Each time, both water and tea are inseparably at stake: all is measured by this concurrence, in this common test, this *contest*. Japan never adopted the Confucian idea of merit to select its hierarchies, but instead, long before its "way of tea," carried the pastimes of the Chinese court: games, competitions, riddles. A Japanese poetry competition: the classical *tanka*, individually composed during a contest, the *renga* ("linked poem") or *kusari renga (*"a chain" of *renga*), by two or more authors who each compose a stanza (*hokku*), named *haiku* in its free form. Games of cards in which images and quotations must be linked. *Monoawase* competitions, in which flowers, fans and incense are compared... Jesting in the form of a blind test, making people guess the best or recognize a given item. The tournament, or *kaicha*, takes a simple form in which one must distinguish between the *honcha,* from Toganoo and then Uji, and the *hicha* from elsewhere; a formalized version, *yonshu juppuku* ("four types, ten portions"), or the popularized form, *unkyaku*: in these competitions, the ten services could rise to thirty or even a hundred cups at the time of Ashikaga Yoshimasa. Now what the accounts of these games enumerate for each participant is not a list of specific vintages—type, season, provenance—to be recognized, but the simple alternative of two possibilities: the *honcha* ("real tea") and *hicha* ("non-tea"). In whichever social class the contest

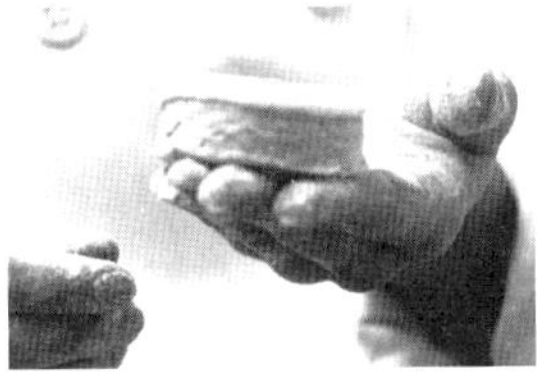

was held, it neither concerned the identification of a geography of taste, nor a test of quality, but a test of existence. It was an ontological pastime.

Taste of Water

In many towns in the USA and most of the states of the ex-USSR, water without a strong smell of hypochlorite—considered unbearable in Western Europe—would cause anxiety concerning its harmlessness and would not be considered as having the taste of water. Thus every region in the world has not traditions, but habits established by sanitation authorities and water treatment centers: criteria of potability; rates of chemical or biological contamination; degrees of limpidity or cloudiness. The taste, caused by dissolved natural salts (calcium, magnesium, sodium) must remain discreet in Scotland, and more pronounced in French or Italian mineral waters. Certain noxious salts (magnesium oxide, ammonia, nitrite), or micro-organisms (*phormidium* algae, diatoma *nitzschia*) cause tastes and smells that are difficult to eliminate, whilst the addition of chlorine or phenolic derivatives produce yet other additional tastes—acquired tastes. The salts, minerals and carbonates will determine whether the water is hard or soft. As well as potability, other criteria are used to establish a simple organoleptic classification between three types: "tastes without smells" (caused by sea salts, metallic salts and alkaline salts), "smells without tastes" (traces of hydrogen sulphides or hydrocarbons), and "combined tastes and smells." A list of reference-flavors allows the judging of spring waters: taste can be salty, sweet, acid, bitter, bitter and salty (magnesian), metallic (presence of iron, manganese, or copper), pharmaceutical, of chlorine, chlorophenol, mandarin (presence of hydrocarbons), must, moldy nut, moldy cork (herbicide, pesticide), earth (chalk). The water-testing procedure then consists, for a team of at least three tasters, in progressively mixing water being tested with a base water, until the flavor is discernible. In France, for example, the base water is Evian which is weak in minerals and considered the most neutral, odorless and tasteless. Today, a master of tea would have to choose between: I. Spring water (collected from near the surface and generally low in minerals); II. Mineral water (from deep underground and high in minerals); III. Table water (sometimes treated). All these waters, as well as carrying their own organoleptic and therapeutic characteristics, are always distributed under seal. Without measuring the inconsistency, Twining teabags and all guides to tea repeat the same piece of advice: "Use pure and fresh water (mineral water preferably)." The Chinese would understand such water to be "asleep" or even "dead," as is water that has been heated for too long: bottled or boiled waters are fluids which have had "their vital force destroyed."

Master Tseng recalls that in China, water for tea must be "sweet, supple, light, alive." For such a master of tea, the discovery of a good spring means the design of a water transformer, with a membrane to filter the running water in conditions precisely

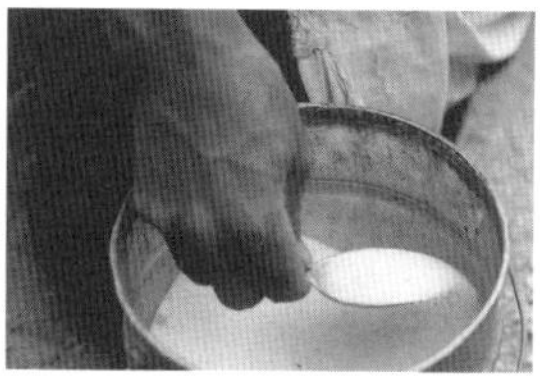

suited to infusion. When these conditions are obtained, it is possible to concentrate on the tea, in order to eventually capture all the aromatic subtleties, alongside which one will be able to glimpse "the taste of water," which is not the specific character of the water containing the infusion, but more a quality that can be perceived behind the taste, brought out by certain post-fermented teas. Some of them—such as Chinese or Japanese DewDrops—have been treated so that they lighten the water, making it sweeter and lighter, and in a word more subtle.

Water Cycle

The tea plant grows in tropical and sub-tropical regions, subject to the monsoon, strong rains followed by dry seasons. Only the clones of *assamica* grow outside this zone, but the *sinensis* was never acclimatized in the way ornamental camellias were. The harvesting of tea consists in breaking off the tip of the twig, with the bud—or even fishleaf—and the two youngest leaves. Apart from a few Indonesian teas, Japanese *bancha*, and the Chinese Dan Cong or "unique tea" plants, from which one can gather older leaves, the gathering of tea is concerned exclusively with the renewed part of the bush, the young shoots. It can only take place, up to seven times a year in exceptional years in the particular climate of the high mists of Taiwan, with the new growth of these shoots. Tea is thus made of the solidified water, the gelled sap, the green growth by which the bush recreates itself. On the mountains the tea-plant awaits its water, strategically placed within the great cycle established by Claude Perrault, brother of storyteller Charles: evaporation above oceans and continents; storage in glaciers, lakes and underground sheets; outflow through rivers from the mountains to the sea.

Tea Cycle

There are many deviations in the cycle of water: small closed circuits (sea to sea, lake to lake, river to river), circular passage through living creatures (vegetable and animal), surface or subterranean accumulation and direct return to the atmosphere. These are repeated, after the harvest, in the cycle of tea: the different stages of its manufacture are designed to bring about a progressive increase in the aromas, through the elimination of vegetable moisture. It is wilted in the sun and air; fermented in a drum or stopped from oxidizing in a hot vat, dried on wattles or in an oven, sometimes roasted on baskets, sometimes smoked under a hood. This process continues as tea matures, and is then reversed when tea is prepared: the infusion, the decoction or emulsion of tea bring about its reunion with water. It is only in water that tea retrieves all the richness it has stored and modified in waiting. Rehydration of the vegetable matter previously dried.

The preparation of tea displays the great cycle of water in a series of tiny movements and minuscule circuits. All the possible conditions of water are reviewed; running water (rivers, streams and rivulets) from one vessel to another, stagnant

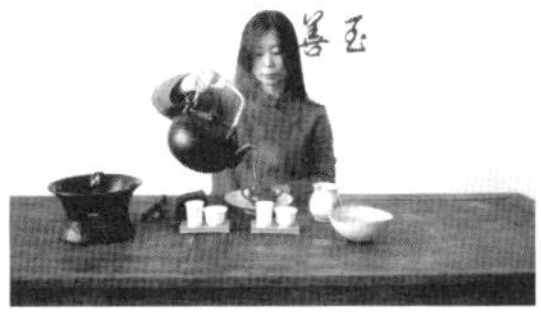

water (lakes, marshes, ponds) in the jars of water and reserve teapots, sea water (three oceans, seas, lagoons) in the "boat" of the *gongfucha*. Water exposed (in the cup) and hidden (in the teapot), invisible water (in the atmosphere of the tea house). It touches on the utensils and the leaves by the different ways in which it is poured: irrigation, aspersion, immersion. In the serving of the tea, water circulates, between earth and sky, in the three times of its labor: mobilization, transport and even sedimentation. Indeed in the same way as it travels through the living being (one absorbs and rejects three liters in a day), a "chemistry" takes place, by which the water is integrated without reversal: the tea leaves gorge themselves with water, return to their original live appearance and keep, after soaking in the infusion, the humidity they lost during their processing. A similar process "swells" the *Yixing* teapot, whose stoneware retains a minute permeability, which enables it to reach the right temperature and to absorb the perfume of the tea into its very pores. Capillarity of a fluid which penetrates the tiny fissures and fibers, thanks to its surface tension, the highest of all liquids after mercury, conducive to alchemy.

Cycle of Fluids

"[Tea] had other virtues. People persuaded themselves that it was an excellent solvent which purified the blood, strengthened the head and the stomach, eased digestion, blood circulation and perspiration; that it cleared the kidneys and the bladder, protected from chronic illnesses, or even slowly cured them." (Abbé Raynal)

Vademecum of Tea

Before he went mad, Nietszche collected his life and its cycles in a vademecum, with the choice of food and posture coming before "the choice of place and climate and the choice of recreation." Tea, reinforced water, is the prominent fluid: "A couple more signposts from my morality. A big meal is easier to digest than one too small. That the stomach comes into action as a whole, first precondition of a good digestion. One has to *know* the size of one's stomach. For the same reason those tedious meals should be avoided which I call sacrificial feasts, those at the *table d'hôte*. No eating between meals, no coffee: coffee makes gloomy. *Tea* beneficial only in the morning. Little, but strong: tea very detrimental and sicklying o'er the whole day if it is the slightest bit too weak. Each has here his own degree, often between the narrowest and most delicate limits. In a very *agaçant* climate it is inadvisable to start with tea: one should start an hour earlier with a cup of thick oil-free cocoa. *Sit* as little as possible, credit no thought not born in the open air and while moving freely about—in which the muscles too do not hold a festival. All prejudices come from the intestines. Assiduity—I have said it once before—the actual *sin* against the Holy Spirit." (*Ecce Homo*)

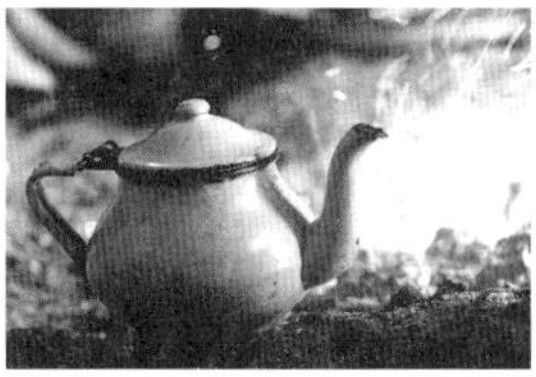

Steam, Mist, Cloud

The island where tea was re-invented in this century, Taiwan, is that submerged mountain in the shape of a tobacco leaf pointing towards Japan. More than sixty peaks tower over three thousand meters, and the highest, the Yu Shan (Jade Mountain) is almost four thousand meters high. In the semi-tropical climate of the North and the tropics of the South, the humidity of the air is more than eighty per cent; the geographer Elisée Reclus noted that "the trees grow right up to edge of the salt water and even the cliffs, carved by the sea into a thousand fantastic shapes, are draped with vegetation." The island is a volcanic formation, and contains numerous hot water springs. There are winter and summer monsoons, floods and typhoons. These are the conditions that the Chinese exploited when they introduced the culture of tea almost three centuries ago. The tea plant grows from the lowlands right up to heights rarely attained for its cultivation: two or three thousand meters up. The frequent mists which envelop the heights and bathe the jungles are what ensure the particular excellence of the Wulong vintages. Between twelve hundred and eighteen hundred meters, the mist filters the rays of the sun and supplies the necessary humidity to the tea bush. As they develop slowly, the leaves remain tender and rich in caffeine, amino acids and essential oils.

From the tea-plant's long bath in the mist to the steam rising from the kettle beside the tea table, a cloud floats over the tealeaf. This tea cloud—fog, coil, smoke—, is the visible manifestation of that invisible vapor which forms the greater part of the atmosphere, and is a fundamental part of the water cycle. Everything in the world has, at one time or another, been a cloud... The tea drinker may therefore ponder on that—physical—part of him that will water the tea that he will one day drink.

"They communicated to us their enthusiasm [for tea] & this enthusiasm steadily increased in the North of Europe, in countries where the air is coarse and filled with vapor, especially in Great Britain and the Northern colonies of America." (Abbé Raynal) "The cloud is the synthesis of mountain and water." (Han Chuo, *Shan Shui Chun Chuan Xi,* Song dynasty). The "mist-cloud" (*yen yun*) is a central element of Chinese landscape painting, which is neither strictly ornamental nor strictly iconographic. The two characters "mountain" and "water," which put together make "landscape" (*shan shui*) are in effect, like *yin* and *yang*, the two poles of cosmic order, the two principles of the world's process. The cloud, as an element in the figurative space, gives concrete expression the alternation of the *dao* around tea.

"The doctor dipped into a cup of tea the tip of a little stick of ink and let it slowly melt on a disc of black stone; he took a paintbrush and began writing the prescription on a large sheet of paper." (Hévarist Huc, 1845)

Hot Water

If water is the "friend of tea," fire is the "master of tea" (Blofeld). Shennong, the inventor of medicine and pharmacopoeia, also invented the prophylactic precau-

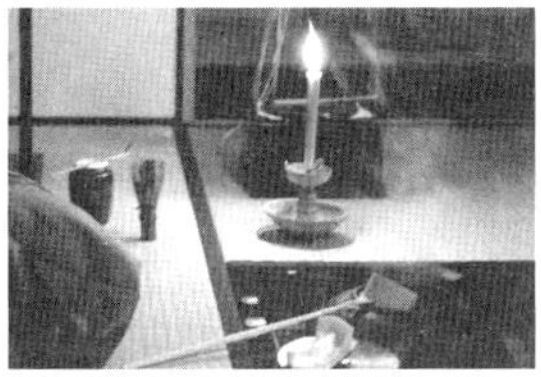

tion of boiling water before drinking it. This precaution, still practiced, has three objects: to sterilize the liquid, relax the stomach through the heat, and to increase the effects of the rehydration. "[The Chinese] drink everything hot, be it water, wine or boiled rice. They always dip the famous herb, which they call Cha, into these liquors, or into boiling water, and drink it very hot. Once I became accustomed to it, I began to strongly disapprove of those in Europe who like to drink cold liquid, as the Chinese by drinking it hot, quench their thirst and dry out the humors." (père Martin Martinus, seventeenth century) In the nineteenth century, in Northern China, a traveler quoted by Fernand Braudel, observed that "the people from the lower classes… sniff hot water with the same pleasure as that with which the richer people take their infusion of green tea—they are happy to call it tea." The omnipresent Thermos bottles in present-day China, in offices, railway stations and schools, continue the age-old work of the peddler of boiling water. In the Roman civilization, hot water was sold in the army and in the towns, under the name of *calda*, still mentioned in the fifth century in *The Master's Rule*, which advises Italian monks to drink a mixture of hot water and vinegar (*posca*) after meals. In a Taiwanese tea house, one determines the quantity of tea before paying for the water, as often as will be necessary; the price varies thus both through the quality of the vintage chosen and the amount of water consumed. Rather as in an Italian trattoria, the bill begins, before the dishes have been ordered, with the number of place settings and breads, thus establishing the number of table companions.

"I can suffer neither tea, coffee nor chocolate; what would give me pleasure would be a good beer soup, but one cannot get that here: beer in France is worth nothing." (Palatine princess at the court of Louis XIV, letter of the 8th of December 1712)

Whereas it sometimes happened in Europe that wine, following an ancient usage, was mixed with hot water, or beer mixed into soup, there was a "rule that everything had to be drunk hot in China as in Japan: tea, sake, rice or millet liquor, water itself?" (Fernand Braudel) In Japan, the hot bath (*sento, furo)* was an urban practice similar to the hammam, in which the community took part every day. While thermal hot springs (*onsen*), with their complexes of traditional inns (*ryokan*) remain favorite weekend destinations, the institution of the public bath has begun to disappear from the Japanese suburban megalopolis: and yet they can still be found in the alleys of the most congested business areas, a fact confirmed by the clomping clogs of those who come even when they have a bathroom at home, in order to prolong an experience of sociability and urbanity, whose only equivalent might be a European café. The entrances for each sex are shown by blue and red split half-curtains (*noren*) with, in the opposite color, the knot of the *"Yu" hiragana*: "hot water." This word/syllable is the last in the Japanese name for the tea ceremony, of which tea is just the genitive: "*cha-no-yu*" ("hot water of tea").

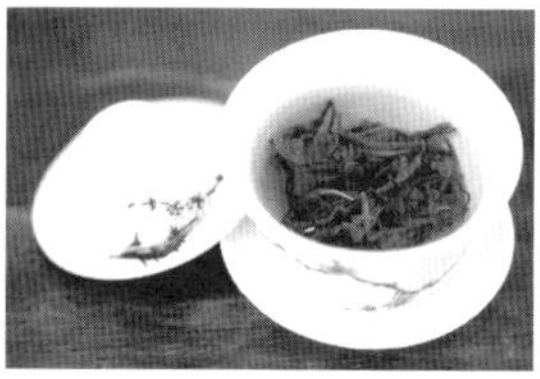

Burning Water

In Cairo in 1600-1601, the Toulousian Henri de Castela remarked on "the large number of taverns and cafés, where a certain black drink is sold, and drunk very hot by the Moors." In the seventeenth century, G. S. Figueroa mentions that the Persians in Isfahan "pour coffee into little porcelain cups; as it is burning hot, they drink the coffee in little sips after blowing on it for a moment. It is so hot that it is impossible to drink it without blowing on it." According to Th. Herbert in 1628, the Iranians of Gombroon drink a lot of coffee "especially in the evening"; "this black soup [...] is so hot that it could well hurt their mouth ."

Coffee surprised and frightened the earliest European travelers as much by its heat as by its blackness. The beverage reminded them of soot, or ink, but also of pitch, which was still in use as an instrument of torture and weapon of war. It is precisely because it is "burning water" that it enters the Galenist tetrad of temperaments as dry rather than humid: according to Prosper Alpin, the Egyptians use it "to fortify a too cool stomach" and " they use it successfully, sometimes for several days, for cold tumors of the liver and the spleen, and for chronic obstructions. This decoction is also much recommended for the uterus, which it warms up and protects from obstructions. It is therefore in such current usage amongst Egyptian and Arab women that they drink it a great deal, very hot, with little sips, during their periods, to facilitate evacuation." (1584). On the other hand, the Persian Shirâzi in his *Alfâz-e Advyah, Treatise on Remedies*, says of coffee that "it dehydrates and hardens the skin, worsens hemorrhoids, tuberculosis, coughs and breathlessness, and taints and darkens the skin." (1629). In 1679, a memoir from the Faculty of Médecine at Marseilles describes the journey of coffee through the body in a most graphical manner: "The burnt elements in which it abounds are in effect so subtle and move so fast, that having spread into the blood mass they take all its serosity into the urine reservoirs and other parts of the body. [...] Attacking the brain, after first dissolving all its humidity and its bigger corpuscles, [...] the bitterness and dryness of the blood becomes like a river bed at the height of summer, all the parts together become so much sucked dry, that the entire body is reduced to a horrible emaciation."

The Turks, Egyptians and Iranians could consume coffee together with something sharply contrasting in temperature: "It is the custom to give *cahwe* to all those who come to see what is before the house; & if they are persons of honor & quality, they are offered a sorbet, or even jams" (Jean de Thévenot, 1665). But also together with a superfluity of fire, particularly with the three following hearths: hookahs, opium and tobacco (*tchoubouk*): in Syria, Turkey and in Cairo, in restaurants and souks, coffee was served by a neighboring café. Similarly, after a bath, massage or depilation, in the first room of the hammam, it was a general habit to take "on a divan, a pipe and a cup of coffee" (Chabrol) Like the Japanese *yu*, boiling water is both bath and beverage.

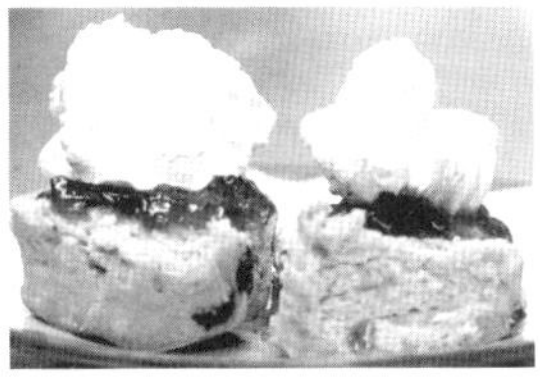

The Spring & the Hearth

Tea cannot be prepared without the other element which provides the consumed constituent: water. Its container is different according to the locality. In the nineteenth century, the serving of tea in Europe still included a utensil, which, because of its size, dominated the table: the water urn. This has now disappeared, like the kettle on its flame burner, because the preparation of tea in the West now largely takes place in the pantry or the kitchen. Other forms of storage for those still confronting more desert areas are gourds, leather bottles or jerry-cans: the preciousness of the liquid can be measured by the simplicity of the containers. The Japanese, on the contrary, display the preeminence of water in the tea ceremony—*o-chaji*—through the formalized approach of the tea house: the entrance to the garden and the path of the *roji* are watered three times, before, in the middle and at the end of the ceremony; the guests are waiting by the *tsukubai*, a stone basin of varying height covered with moss, with cold water in its hollow, that will allow the guests to purify themselves with several ablutions; the host will bring out, as the first utensil, and on his first appearance from the tea chamber, a vase of fresh water.

Since the infusion can be made with cold water, the latter does not necessarily have to be heated—this is the case with a rare Japanese Ryokucha, heavily steamed, which is infused in summer for several hours with ice; however, the circumstances of the preparation are also defined by a specially prepared fire, a hearth that is portable or cut in the flooring. Amongst the Tuaregs, the descent from the camels is immediately followed by a search for kindling in the area around the stopping-place: building the fire straight on to the sand takes priority over all other activities, indicating the preparation of tea: the distance between two halts is measured in numbers of teapots, just as in the Andes, walks are calculated by numbers of *cocada*, coca leaves lodged in the cheek. Something similar is at stake amongst all nomadic tribes: the tea that one swallows is the finally enjoyed refreshment by the hearth, whose making marks the beginning of a moment which is both a necessity for survival, and a ritual. Japan has no doubt gone furthest in the elaboration of the fire-making process: surrounded by a frame—*robuchi*—sometimes richly lacquered and gilded, cut in a tatami—*ro*—in winter, or set up as a brazier—*furo*—made of bronze in summer, placed on the same tatami. Located in the center of the tea house—*chashitsu*—this device will summon all of the master of ceremony's gestures after the entry of the participants through the *nijiriguchi,* both at the beginning of the tea gathering as well as after the *kaiseki* meal and the guests' pause in the garden. Few details escape attention: even the cooled embers from the fire, bright white and familiar in shape, are arranged solemnly on wood charcoal, each log outlining a dark chrysanthemum in section. When these sacred combustibles are raised "like Mount Fuji" on the combed ashes, and the tea master has, with a long feather, dusted the different parts of this sunken frame, the guests assemble to

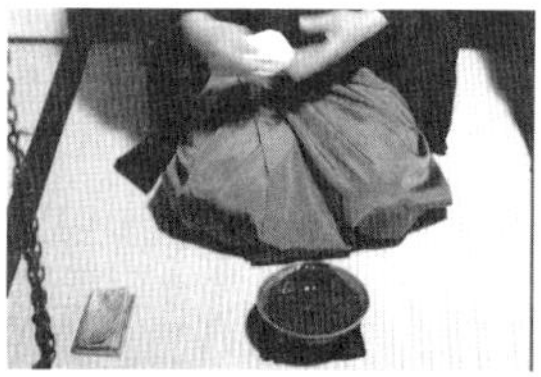

contemplate it on their knees. Between tea-hearth and theater. In China, in Japan, as in Argentina with *yerba* mate, this scene, previously organized around the fire, has given way to the inevitable Thermos bottles, hot water taps or electric kettles which are left to be used at people's discretion in public or private places. This hot water now at everyone's disposal, distributed everywhere, continues a tradition—the *feng cha*—which used to take place alongside Buddhist temples or to mark stages on mountain routes: casks of tea, from which one could help oneself with a goblet hanging on a chain. This free and running hot water comes for everybody, as well as hot and cold water from the tap, which will only be used for cleaning the utensils. This hot water, also provided in Russia in the form of the built-in samovars with their chrome machinery obstructing the corridors of trains, is the proof of an achievement: the mastery over fire and water, and the meeting of the two.

Boiling Water

On the road from Chang Shan to Yuk Shuan, in an inn: "The good lady of the house set down a teacup before each of us, into which she put some tea, and then filled each cup up with boiling water. I need scarcely say she did not offer us any sugar or milk. Other tables were crowded with people, most of whom were coolies going to Chang Shan with tea, and whose chests nearly blocked up the road in front of the door. We drank our tea, which I found most refreshing, in its pure state without sugar or milk. Now and then some one connected with the house came round and filled our basins again with boiling water. This is usually repeated two or three times, or until all the strength is drawn out of the leaves." (Robert Fortune)

Warm Water

"But the repast provided in this case was all vegetable—vegetable—vegetable; precisely similar to what the priests had entertained me with a week before, but got up with more care and at greater expense. It was very, very tasteless to be sure, and utterly devoid of relish. Such an attempt to imitate animal diet may please the fancy, but it will not gratify the palate. As the Chinese conclude by eating rice with a light soup, rice came on the table in the regular course, and some liquid in a center bowl intended to represent a dish of soup; but, could anything be more emetical? It was nothing save lukewarm water—genuine, limpid, unadulterated *warm water!*" (William Charles Milne, *Life in China*, 1857)

Water & Fire

In the highest plantations in Darjeeling, on the slopes of Georgia, on the hills of Japan, the tea plant can survive snow undamaged as long as it is not followed by a sharp rise in temperature, which will burn and redden the leaf: the scorch. The temperature which is so necessary to tea can be high but must not rise sharply. The tea plant must also not be exposed to direct and prolonged sunlight: the exposure of

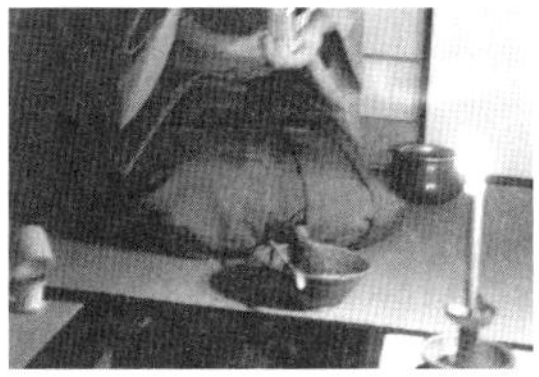

the land and its conditions must be constantly studied in its effects, in a similar manner to viticulture.

Heat conditions are no less important when it comes to the preparation of tea; a green tea, in order that its delicate aroma and perfume be diffused in the cup or the lid of the *zhong*, must not be subjected to boiling water, nor must it be stewed in a closed teapot. Its water must be tempered—from sixty degrees for a Gyokuro to seventy for most of the Chinese vintages—by a quarter of cold water or by waiting in an intermediary vessel. A Wulong, on the contrary, must receive the water as it boils, and be confined in a *yixing* teapot, with a hermetically sealed cover made of heavily metallic stone in order to sharply raise in temperature.

"One does not know which is working: is it fire, is it water, is it time? This triple uncertainty allows one to have a reply to everything." (Gaston Bachelard) For tea, water is a solvent, a medium both cooling and heating. In the cycle of water and tea, the motor forces are gravity and the heat which takes the place of solar energy. Water "tempers the other elements" whilst fire sets them in motion, animating the water molecules or initiating the aromatic releases. At the beginning of the Japanese tea ceremony, the hearth, cut in the tatami floor, is arranged and activated, whilst the first instrument brought by the host is the jar of water. Opposite earth and air, substance-elements, water and fire are vector-elements, whose active power can be measured by the threat they can carry even in their domestic roles (mistrust of baths, fear of fire), and in their roles in rites of purification. This dissymetry, as much apparent in the Greek scheme as in the Chinese (the four cardinal trigrams of the Yijing are also the sky, *qian*, the earth, *kun*, fire, *li*, water, *kan*) is emphasized by Hippocrates in his conception of health as a balance between two opposing forces: the energy of fire and the nourishment of water. If the West has no trouble integrating tea into its "four temperaments" theory of medicine (sanguine, bilious, phlegmatic, melancholic), inherited from Galen's "four qualities" (hot, cold, dry, humid), it is because tea immediately puts into play the roles of fire and water.

Here one must once again measure the difference from and the link with alcohol. Tea could only achieve such a position in Northern Europe by offering a possible symbolic substitution for spirits—*aqua ardens* : firewater—, the sap of the earth—wine—, or for liquid breads such as beer, gruel and porridge. In India tea knows rain; in China, mist; in Japan, hot air ventilators.

Steam & Ice

Of the three possible states of H_2O, the liquid one is that which has had the most technological use; ice is only used for dwellings and transport in the Arctic and, before the modern era, for refreshment in some regions such as Iran or China; steam plays an effective corollary part, but has only lately been mastered for cooking and in the work of coopers. Some Japanese teas, which one will remember as

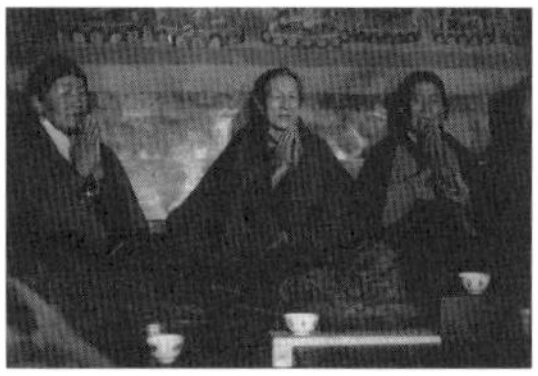

being inactivated in vapor, are prepared in the teapot, not with hot water, but with steam; whilst a rare Sencha is treated—oddly by a treatment of reinforced steam—in order to be infused in ice. In the case of the latter, the resulting liquor is very thick, almost gelatinous and crystalline. Here too, Japan carries out every possible exception to a principal, extremely formalized, rule.

Heat & Coolness

Wine is "the best quintessence," coming from the vine, "queen of herbs" and maintaining "the dialectic of the subtle and the nourishing"; it "warms a cool and humid temperament and cools a hot and dry one." Again: it galvanizes as well as it quenches thirst; it is "a means of change, capable of turning round situations and conditions, extracting their opposites from things, making, for example, a weak man strong, a silent person talkative." (Gaston Bachelard and Roland Barthes) Tea always maintains the possible alternatives of giving the body heat—as with a Pu Er—or coolness—as with a white or green tea, of being dehydrating—a sign of poor quality—or refreshing. In China, the choice of "a" tea will be made taking into account these thermal effects, whilst in the West, "the" tea—thus heralding its monolithic and gray nature—, as universal panacea and following the model of wine, is supposed to do both.

OXIDATION

Gardens, Fields, Hillsides

The ideogrammatical sign-language of a vineyard, vainly interpreted by the horizontal lines of vine props to which the human hand must necessarily tie the shoots in preparation for the wine harvest.

The oceanic and uniform depth of a field of wheat whose mechanical and yet random order again displays nature in process, right down to the waves drawn by the weather through the crops, whilst a bird's-eye view reveals the geometry of the harvest.

The waves of tea plants in neat fluorescent half cylinders outlining the convoluted curves of the terraces, lined and covered by the undulations of dark screens, or hidden and contradicted by walls and roofs of thick straw, before the harvest.

Gardens in which tea bushes are grown may take three guises: in China, the bushes, close to the soil, seem scattered through the plot of land, their cross-fertilization defying any kind of alignment; in Japan, the little trees, at hand-height, melt together, overlapping, forming undulating spaces like swollen vineyards; in India or Sri Lanka, the picking "table" is kept flat, and forms a cracked surface, dotted with shady trees—like a dry but somehow luxuriant lake-bed.

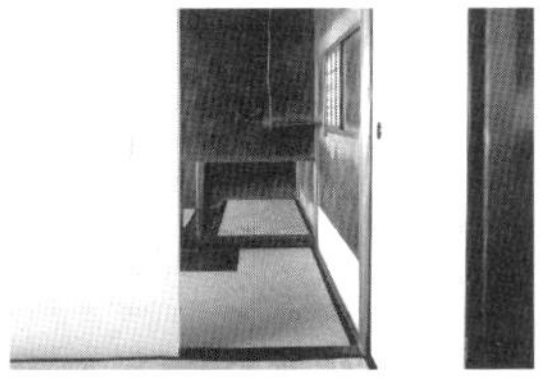

A New Plant

"Tea is a leaf which grows in China and Japan. [...] It is dried and then transported to Asia and Europe. The little tree on which it grows, which is depicted at the beginning of this Treatise, is so little known by our Botanists that it seems to me to be prudent to tell the public what travelers have reported about it before telling them of the feelings I have about it." (Philippe Sylvestre Dufour, 1684)

"However I cannot withhold three or four things unknown to our people. The first is the little tree the leaves of which are used to make the famous drink of the Chinese, Japanese and neighboring peoples..." (Matteo Ricci, *Story of the Christian Expedition to the Kingdom of China,* 1610)

"Tea, which is the favorite drink of the Chinese, is here called *theca.* It is the leaves of a bush which resembles the pomegranate, but which has a more pleasant odor, even though the taste is more bitter. [...] The shrub which produces it spreads out small branches: its flower is yellowish and has the odor of the violet. This smell is apparent even when the flower is dry. The first leaf grows and is picked in spring, because at that time it is softer and more delicate..." (Giovanni Laureati, letter, 26 July 1714)

Soils for Tea

The tea bush is a robust plant which thrives on the following soils: I. Alluvial; II. Sedimentary rock; III. Volcanic. Also: soils reclaimed from the jungle, rich in nitrogen, provide teas of good quality. A rock tea in China grips onto cliffs where erosion will have filtered the soil, providing a taste as complex as a great Bordeaux.

In China, in the noteworthy circumstances created by the geomantic art of Feng Shui, the culture of the tea plant has given rise to a knowledge of place and weather, the only European equivalent being viticulture. In order to ensure a successful culture of something as uncertain as tea, it has been necessary to acquire a similar body of knowledge of climate, soil and exposure, as that of the Burgundian monasteries where subjects only much later officially designated as sciences were assembled and studied (geology, topography, hydrology, meteorology, physics, chemistry).

Surface of Tea

Tea is cultivated in gardens and not in fields. Intensive cultivation is a contradiction, as the tea-plant needs to be surrounded by the aromas that will impregnate it. At a time when flowers are grown industrially in fields, tea resists agriculture (the field of cereal crops sown and harvested in bulk, a result of the near-Eastern Neolithic revolution) and remains within the realm of horticulture (the kitchen garden consisting of fruit, leaves and roots individually planted, treated with care, and harvested one by one, traditional in the tropics), demonstrating the necessity of maintaining *hortus* in the face of *ager*. The tea-plant, which numbers among the most ancient cultures (dating back four thousand years according to Candolle) and whose cultivation surface covers one of the largest of all cultivated areas in the

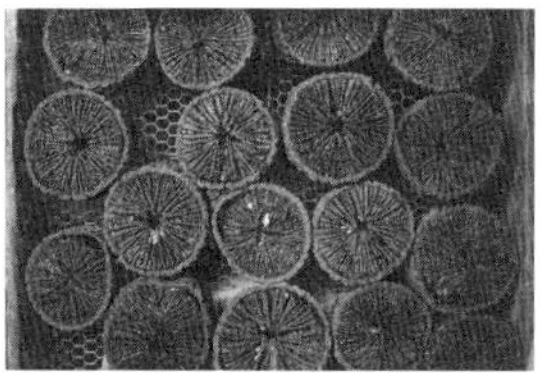

world, finds its natural habitat in a large zone within the limits of Assam, Burma, China and Indonesia. "It grows in a zone limited in the North by the 43rd parallel—the tea-plant reaches Georgia in the USSR—and in the South by the 27th parallel—there are tea-plantations in Corrientes in Argentina." (Denis Bonheure) The main places of origin of the cultivated plants were found in regions situated in tropical-equatorial zones (Java and part of Ceylon), tropical zones (Uva, Annam, Taiwan) and subtropical zones (Japan, China). But this preponderance did not happen uniformly, or by threatening a culture. With 1.2 million hectares under cultivation, China owns more than half of the tea-growing area in the world. It produces a yield of 0.3 ton per hectare whereas India, with a yield of 1.5 ton to the hectare, is the largest producer though with less than a third of the surface. The third largest producer is no longer Sri Lanka, but Kenya, where the British introduced the tea-plant just after the First World War.

Of all the world's great crops, the tea-plant is the most labor-intensive in relation to the surface cultivated. The soils which produce the greatest growths also have the lowest yield. Only vine-cultivation could compare, but whereas the mechanization of the wine-harvest can have advantages—the picking-machines shake the plants, leaving the stalks on the branches, thus avoiding a later sorting process—, doing the same with tea can only damage the leaf by chopping it: a type of curved clipper which crops the "table" or waves of tea-plants has been perfected in Japan for the green teas, where the leaf is broken anyway. But a great Chinese or Japanese tea must be picked by hand. For a pound of fresh leaves, there must be several hundred pickings, up to 75,000 buds for a Bi Luo Chun, where each tiny leaf must be cut with a sharp fingernail, without crumpling its bloom or damaging its down.

Tea for Tea

The three plants of the Far East—rice, soy and tea—complement one another as food, condiment and drink. China, Korea and Japan depend on three crops: rice, which provides food, alcohol and straw, bamboo, which has a thousand uses and soy, a food in which nothing is wasted. Three simultaneous epochs, three ancient civilizations (the other ages of the world).

Rice is the most often quoted, as a type of general equivalent (a nutrient-standard), like bread, or the potato in Europe. And elsewhere, there is millet, cassava and maize. But no Western plant, matter or technical commodity is equivalent to bamboo. And no foodstuff over here comes in the same variety of forms as soy. Opposite the generic representation of rice, which in Asia is the full white *yang* sign of food, there is the hollow black *yin* sign of soy as condiment/complement. And between the two comes the empty translucent *yin* or *yang* sign of tea. If one confronts the culture of tea (from plantation to consumption, via fabrication) with that of bamboo or soy, one perceives how unique its function is, how directed and hypertelic:

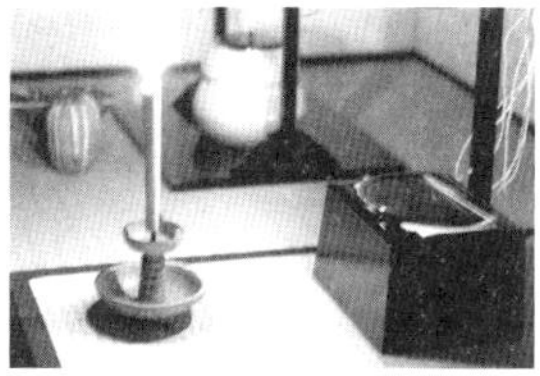

the tea-plant, with its enormous acreage of world cultivation, is grown exclusively for the use of its leaf (and only the most tender leaves and buds at that), and with the sole aim of making a drink, whose image and spell are universal—welcoming, awakening, relaxing. Only the infused leaves, as left-overs, are sometimes recycled as compost, or re-dried in the sun to be used as absorbent sawdust for cleaning floors, or for stuffing pillows.

Soy First cultivated in the North and center of China, and now concentrated in the United States which has two thirds of world production. Although the plant is an excellent green fertilizer—this is its main use in the West—and provides the highest yields of any cereal crop, it was one of the first to be subjected to the genius of the genetic engineers. The whole irony of industrial research is summed up in this first trial: soy has been genetically modified to resist chemical fertilizers. One of the principal derivatives of the soybean, tofu, is a foodstuff more ancient than cheese, first recorded three thousand years ago. It is mentioned in the *Seiroku*, in the Song dynasty. It is a specialty of the Fujian, a great tea-growing region. Tofu was exported to Japan, as was tea, by Buddhist monks, and was a great success at the court. Already before the ninth century, the function of "tofu-master" was created to take in charge all the techniques involved in the preparation. The *chan* (zen) monks opened restaurants within the precincts of temples in order to spread the vegetarian manner of eating, which was maintained by Japanese society until the Meiji era. The plant provides its beans, but also its foliage used as forage and, when buried, as a natural fertilizer. The soybean can be eaten fresh (*edamame)* when just picked, like the flat bean (*soramame)*. Boiled and salted in the pod, it becomes an aperitif. The bean can be germinated, fermented or cooked; it can be ground, pressed or crushed; many heterogeneous derivatives may be obtained: flour, oil, milk, fermented nutrients, concentrated proteins, spiced condiments. In the time of tofu, three products follow one another: the bean (*fukumame*), the filtrate, or soy milk (*tonyu*) and tofu. Similarly, the making of soy milk produces a "poor" remnant of the filtering of the soaked soy beans, cooked and pressed in muslin: *okara* (which is used to feed pigs, thicken fish soup, or mixed in Korean fashion with minced meat and leeks); and when the *tonyu* is heated up, in order to curdle, with *nigari* salt (the liquid which falls drop by drop from sea salt when it is kept in a damp place), making the tofu curds, the skin which is formed on the surface forms the "rich" remains of this process in which nothing is lost: the *yuba*. Following these endlessly drawn-out arborescences means displaying a real theory of soy—a range with no waste—, as it has been elaborated in Japan in the Chinese tradition. From soy as a green manure, re-fertilizing the soil with its decomposing foliage, to *koya tofu*, in which the bean is successively cooked, crushed, filtered, curdled, frozen and dried,

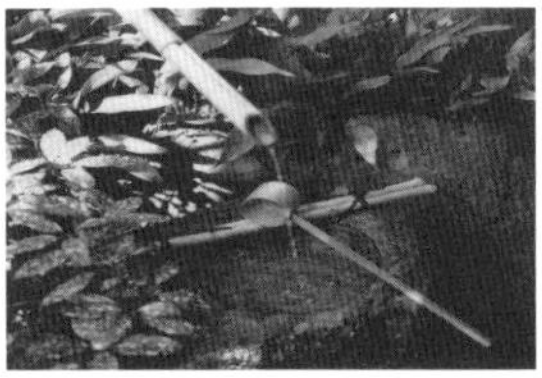

and via various forms of remains (*okara, wazumi, yuba*), the plant is taken in a totally waste-free economy, in which the possible re-use of a substance is maintained by exhausting its meaning, usage and effect.
Tofu, miso, and *yuba,* which are an essential part of the Japanese tea ceremony, can thus form a sort of reserve of taste—of meaning—in the face of tea, whose hypertely—but not its intensive monoculture—indicates the vanishing point.
Arborescence of "Glycine Max.":
1,0: green manure (soy has the same property as other leguminous plants such as peas, lentils and beans, of being able to fix large quantities of nitrogen in the soil, through symbiosis with a bacteria called rhizobium, which multiplies in nodules on the rootlets of the plant. Therefore, once the pods have been gathered, the foliage is always buried in the ground, enriching it with nitrogen as well as humus). 2,0: forage (the use for which soy was first cultivated in the West in 1908). 3,0: beans, dried or freshly consumed (fresh, boiled or grilled). From the dried soybean are derived: 3,1: lecithin. 3,1,1: health food. 3,1,2: emulsifiers in the food industry. 3,2: soy proteins used in the food industry. 3,3: soy cubes. 3,4: (ground) soy flour. 3,4,1: industrial bakery products. 3,4,2: culinary uses. 3,5: (sprouted) soy shoots. 3,6: (fermented). 3,6,1: *miso* (soy ground and fermented with *koji,* itself a cereal—barley, rice etc—inoculated with *aspergillus oryzae* and salt), which, like soy sauces, *natto* and *tempeh,* contains a lot of vitamin B, notably B12, and comes in almost thirty varieties (with the addition of wheat, barley or rice). 3,6,1,1: white (*shiro miso).* 3,6,1,2: red (*aka miso* or *aka dashi*). 3,6,1,3: black, very black indeed (*kyozakura* from Kyoto). 3,6,2: *natto* (yellow beans cooked, cooled and fermented with *bacillus natto* at a constant temperature for 15 to 24 hours): 3,6,2,1: as a fragrant, sticky, fragrant puree. 3,6,2,1,1: *otsubu*, large beans. 3,6,2,1,2: *kutsubu*, whole beans. 3,6,2,1,3: *hikiwari*, broken beans. 3,6,2,2: *daitokuji natto* (a speciality of the Kyoto temple, consumed during the tea ceremony). 3,6,2,3: *hama natto* (which strongly resembles goat droppings). 3,6,3: (beans fermented by the same spore as *miso*, in brine): 3,6,3,1: *tamari* (a sauce of soy, water and sea salt fermented with *koji* for 6 to 18 months). 3,6,3,2: *shoyu* (like *tamari*, with the addition of grilled and crushed wheat). 3,6,3,3: *usukuchi* (a lighter and more delicate version of *shoyu).* 3,6,4: *tempeh* (a cake made of whole beans pealed, simmered and fermented with the spores of *rhizopus oligosporys* which agglomerates them with its filaments), consumed throughout South-East Asia, particularly Indonesia. 3,6,5: *ketjap* (a sauce of fermented soy, concentrated and with sugar added). 3,7: (roast and ground): 3,7,1: *kinako*. 3,7,2: soy butter. 3,7,3: a texture-giving agent in bakery. 3,8: (pressed) soy oil: 3,8,1: margarine. 3,8,2: ground. 3,8,3: fertilizer. 3,9: (soaked, crushed, filtered): *gô*. Using *go*, cooked and with water added; 3,9,1: (diluted at 11 parts to 1) light soymilk, *tonyu*, much consumed in Taiwan and the whole of South East Asia.

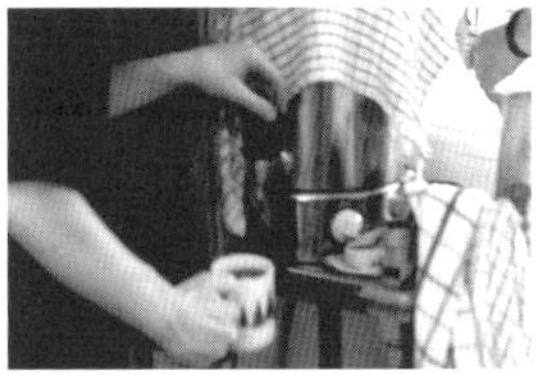

3,9,1,1: (remains) *okara (kirazu* or *unohana*). 3,9,1,1,1: culinary uses. 3,9,1,1,1,1: (fermented, dried and powdered) *meitauza*. 3,9,1,1,2: animal fodder. 3,9,1,1,3: household wax. 3,9,1,2: (residue) whey (*wazumi*): 3,9,1,2,1: soap, shampoo. 3,9,1,2,2: gentle detergents. 3,9,1,2,3: animal drink. 3,9,1,3: curdled: 3,9,1,3,1 (gently crushed) the soy bean is the only leguminous plant, indeed the only vegetable which produces a milk whose proteins can coagulate to the point of producing curds thick enough to compare with soft white cheese: *tofu* or *do fou*. 3,9,1,3,1,1: "cotton" (*momendofu)*. 3,9,1,3,1,2: "silk," containing more water. 3,9,1,3,1,3: with the consistency of jelly (*kinugoshidofu)*. 3,9,1,3,1,4: *zarudofu*, filtered in a bamboo basket, the creamiest. 3,9,1,3,1,5: *yosedofu*, this is "reassembled" *tofu*, the curds of soymilk, gathered when it has just taken, and which must be eaten without delay. Three types of *tofu* elaborated and sold by the *tofu* manufacturer: 3,9,1,3,1,6: the *tofu* is packed fresh, grilled, braised, simmered, served as a fritter, a pancake, a *ganmodoki* croquette, in sauces, desserts etc. 3,9,1,3,1,7: fried *tofu* : 3,9,1,3,1,7,1: *abura age*, thin slices of fried *tofu*, forming a fillable pouch. 3,9,1,3,1,7,2: *atsu age* (or *nama age*) larger slices or fried dice. 3,9,1,3,1,7,3: *yakidofu*, soy paste dried further and grilled. 3,9,1,3,1,8: *frozen tofu* (one of the rare foodstuffs that not only can be frozen, but is actually improved by this method of preservation). 3,9,1,3,1,9: dried frozen *tofu (koya tofu* or *kori dofu*, the highest in protein—53%—of all known foodstuffs), a sort of freeze-drying before its time, alternating natural freezing by exposure to cold at night and defrosting by exposing to the sun in the daytime, for 6 to 9 days, before a final drying process (in the North of Japan, they would bury it in the snow, or, as the samurais did, hang it to the overhang of a roof exposed to icy winds, attached by straw plaits). 3,9,1,3,2: (heavy pressing): 3,9,1,3,2,1: (broken) firm *tofu* for grilling. 3,9,1,3,2,2: *sufu* or *doufu-ru* (*tofu* cubes fermented by *actinomuco-elegans,* and macerated in red wine, spices and sodium chlorate). 3,9,1,3,2,3: *do gan (tofu* pressed, simmered in *tamari* and dried). 3,9,1,3,2,4: *chù doù fû (*stinking *tofu*). 3,9,1,3,2,5: *mapo dofu* (extremely spicy *tofu*). 3,9,2: thick soy milk (4 to 1 dilution): 3,9,2,1: powdered milk. 3,9,2,2: yogurt (made with the same bacillus as for cow's milk). 3,9,2,3: *yuba* (skin of soymilk, very high in protein—52%—and also high in calcium, sodium and phosphorus): 3,9,2,3,1: fresh *yuba, hiki age yuba* (which is eaten as it forms on the milk being cooked). 3,9,2,3,2: raw *yuba*, *nama*. 3,9,2,3,3: dried *yuba*.

Bamboo

"Bamboo is neither a tree nor a grass. It gives neither flower nor fruit. It holds within it the pure breath which animates the Sky and the Earth." (Zai Hsi, Qing dynasty) Tea is cultivated in order to be drunk. Bamboo, with its multiple varieties (more than 1500 species and 75 types, the three principal ones being *arundinaria, phyllostachys* and *sasa*), and an ill-defined vegetable identity (is it weed, grass, bush,

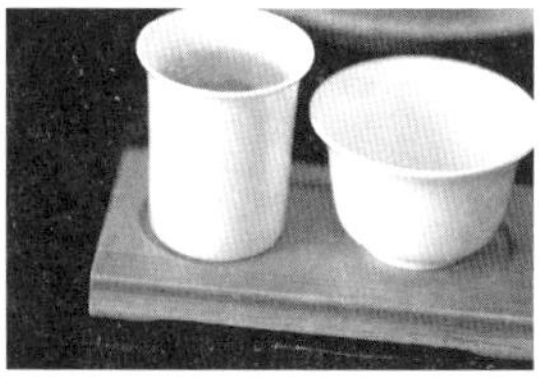

shrub, hedge or forest plant?) has been found to have almost unlimited practical uses, thanks to its tensile strength, its capacity to split straight, the particular nature of its cross-sections, and its speed of growth. Simply in its tea-related uses, bamboo goes from being the first to the last receptacle for the leaf: hip-basket for the pickers, withering tray, drying wattle, strainer, sieve, framework, support and windows of the tea-house, flower vase, water ladle, teaspoon for the *chanoyu*. (In 1903, Spoery listed 1047 uses for bamboo, taking only examples from Japan, to which could be added 498 ornamental uses...)

In his Chinese botanical inventory, Robert Fortune did not fail to note the importance of bamboo, and even to recognize its use as a strategic pawn, next to tea and rhubarb, whose importance in Europe then is hard to imagine now: "At the time of the last war, when the Emperor of China, no doubt in a pre-emptive strike, wished to overcome the English by blocking their supplies of tea and rhubarb, without which it was imagined they could not survive for long, we should have returned the compliment, by, had we been able to, destroying all their bamboo. With all due deference to His Celestial Majesty, the English could have survived without tea or rhubarb, but it is inconceivable that China, as a nation or anything else, exist without bamboo." Fortune, to show its importance, goes on to list its uses, ending with those involving tea: "The bamboo is one of the most valuable trees in China, and is used for a thousand purposes. It is employed in making soldiers' hats and shields, umbrellas, soles of shoes, scaffolding poles, measuring instruments, baskets, ropes, paper, pencil-holders, brooms, sedan-chairs, pipes, flower-stakes and trellis-work in gardens; pillows are made of the shavings; a kind of cloak for wet weather is made from the leaves, and is called a *so-e*, or 'garment of leaves'." On the water, it is used in making sails and covers for boats, for fishing rods and landing-nets, fishing-stakes and buoys; catamarans are rude boats, or rather floats, formed of a few logs of bamboo lashed firmly together. In agriculture the bamboo is used in making aqueducts for conveying water to the land; it forms part of the celebrated water wheel, as well as of the plough, the harrow and other implements of husbandry. Excellent water pipes are made of it for conveying springs from the hills to supply houses and temples in the valleys with pure water. Its roots are often cut into the most grotesque figures, and its stems finely carved into ornaments for the curious, or into incense-burners for the temples. The Ning-po furniture, the most beautiful in China, is often inlaid with bamboo figures of people, houses, temples, and pagodas, which form most correct and striking pictures of China and the Chinese. The young shoots are boiled and eaten, and sweetmeats are also made of them. A substance found in the joints, called tabasheer, is used in medicine. In the manufacture of tea it helps to form the rolling-tables, drying-baskets and sieves; and last, though not least, the celebrated chopsticks—the most important articles in domestic

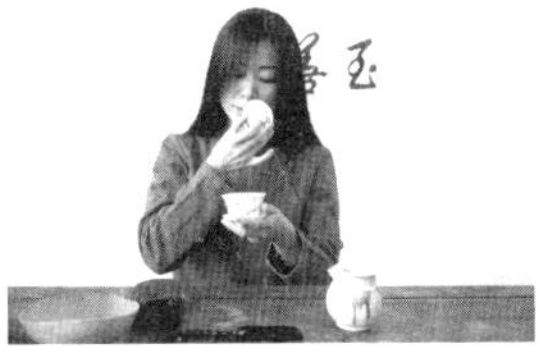

use—are made of it. However incredulous the reader may be, I must still carry him a step further, and tell him that I have not enumerated one-half of the uses to which the bamboo is applied in China. Indeed it would be nearly as difficult to say what it is *not* used for. It is in universal demand, in the houses and in the fields, on water and on land, in peace and in war. Through life the Chinaman is almost dependent upon it and it even accompanies to his last resting-place on the hill-side, and even then, in company with the cypress, juniper and pine, it waves over and marks his tomb." (*Two Visits to the Tea Countries of China...*, 1852)

Appropriate Bamboo Catalog, 1985: A-frame houses, activated charcoal, acupuncture needles, airplane wing members and stress skin for fuselage, alarms, alcohol, anchors, *angklung*, TV and radio antenna supports, aphrodisiacs, axles, mandrels, arrows, arrow tips, ashtrays, tents, awnings, tarpaulins, baby carriage, bagpipes, barrels, baskets, pearls, rosary beads, beanpoles, beds, beehives, beer, bicycles, bilge pumps, blinds, blowguns and darts, boards, panels, boat hoods, boats, boots, nuts and bolts, screws, bookcases, books, booms, bottles, bowls, bows, boxes, bracelets, bridges, brooms, brushes, brush holders, buckets, buttons, cages (for birds, crickets or tigers), candlesticks, canes, canteens, store-rooms, carts, castanets, catalyst (*tabasheer*), caulking, chairs, charcoal, chisels (for carpenters, masons or sculptors), chopsticks, churches, cigarette holders, clothes racks, clubs, colanders, combs for hair and hand looms, cooking vessels, coops for chickens and ducks, couches, cowbells, cradles, crates, cribs, crosses, crutches and equipment for the handicapped, cultures (for bacteria in lab tests), cups for drinking and waterwheels, curtains, dams, defensive fortifications (palisades, revetments), deodorizers (dried leaves), desks, diesel fuel, dikes, dirigible, dolls, domes, dowel pins and forelocks, dredge (fishing), drogues, supports for drying and storing, dustpans, egg-cups, fans, farming uses, fences, fenders (for ships or docks), fertilizer, fiesta assistant, fifes, firearms, fire starters, firewood, fireworks, fishnets, fishpoles and traps, flagpoles, flails (for nut harvesting and so on), floats, flooring, flowerpots, flutes, kites, food (the shoots), animal fodder, forms (for bean meal in oil presses, and for reinforced concrete), frames (for pictures, silkworm culture, and so on), fruit pickers, furniture, *gabions*, wattles, games, garments, gates, gate springs and bars, grain storage, graters, greenhouses, guns, gutters, gypsy vans, hairpins, hampers and trunks, handles (rake, hoe, umbrella), hats, mooring ropes, hawsers, hay, hedges, helmets, hinges, hen houses, hoops, hookahs, houseplants, houses, humidors (tobacco), hummers, iceless cooler, incense sticks, insect cages, irrigation waterwheels and pipes, jackets, jars, vases, joss sticks, junks, kiosks, lacquerware (plates, cups, boxes, trays, bowls), ladders, ladles, lamps, lampshades, landing docks, landscaping, lanterns, lathing, laundry poles, levees, light-bulb filaments, lofts, looms, *marimbas*, markers, masts, *mattang*, matting, mattresses, medicines, mills,

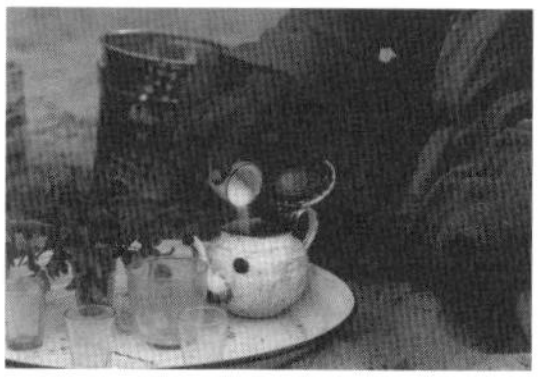

mobiles, mushroom culture houses, musical instruments (*shakuhachi, gambang bambu, rengkong, kohkohl, hatong, kolecer, celempung* etc), nails, napkin rings, net floats, sewing and netting needles, pins, *netsuke*, organs, ornaments, outriggers, ox cart beds (balance-beams, yokes, harnesses and couplings), ox goads, oyster cultivation, packaging, paper cutters, paper pulp, pegs, pen and pencil holders, pens (ink and animal), pillows, pipes (drains, gas, irrigation, opium, organ, tobacco, water, etc), plant labels (shades and stakes), plates, plybamboo, poison, poles, props, plates, supports (boat, carrying, clothes, flag, gardening, telephone, tent, TV, vaulting), polo balls, polo mallets, posts, printing pads, propellers, props, instruments of punishment, racks, rafts, raincoats, rainspouts and guttering, rakes, rattles, toys, bells, rayon, record needles, reeds (for woodwind instruments), reinforcement (for concrete and adobe), rings, ritual objects, jewels, trailers, roofing, cables, ropes (towing, drilling salt-wells, hoisting brine), carpets, hammocks, rulers, sailcovers, sails, sailstays, sake, salt well drilling, sandals, scaffolding, scales, scarecrows, scoops, baskets, ladles, spades, bailers, scratchers for backs, screens, room dividers, papermaking screens, scrubbers (for washing, brushing, rubbing), sedan chairs, shades, shavings (for pillows, mattresses and boat caulking), sheaths (for knives and swords), shields, masks and protective screens, shingles, ship design, shoehorns, shoesoles, shoots for food, shovels, shuttles for weaving, sieves, skewers for grilling food, ski poles, slide rules, sluices, snow fences, spears, splints, spouts for watering cans, spray guns, springs, stakes, barrel staves, stilts, stools, string, sugar, sunning floors (for fruit, beans, fabrics), swimming pools, tables, tallies, tea houses, tea strainers, tea whisks, temporary structures, camps, tortures, towers (for water windmills or rope-making), toys, trailers, transport, stalking or trapping (fish, rats, birds, tigers), textiles, thatch, theatrical uses, theodolite, thole-pins, threshing boards and machines, tiles, floor tiles, tinder, *tipis*, tokens, tongue depressors and cotton wool applicators in hospitals, toothpicks, ear-cleaners, torches, trays, tree guards, tree houses, trellises, curtains, trestles, triumphal arches, chariots, trolleys, troughs, water-barrels, trumpets, tubs, tug and tracking cables, twine, umbrellas, parasols, *valiha*, wagons, walking sticks, walls, water pistols, water storage, wax, weapons, weirs, well sweeps, wheelbarrows, whetstones, whips, whistles, wicks, windbreaks, windmills, wine storage, winnowing machinery, writing brushes, xylophones, yurts, zithers.

"Laid on my table is the virgin paper, as white and smooth as the skin of a young girl. I am taking advantage of the early hour to draw this bamboo: who wishes to taste its secret flavor? Later, when the tea has completed its infusion, giving out its sweet scent, I will be alone, there, contemplating it as I drink." (Chin Nung, 1687-1763)

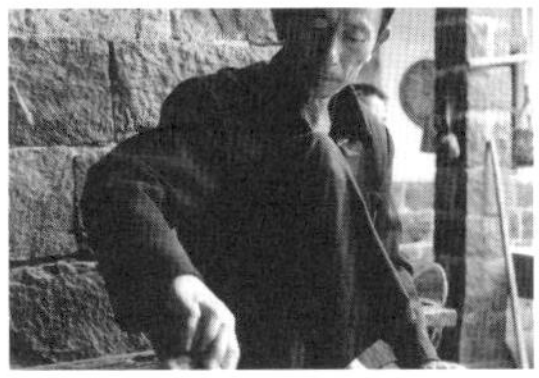

Vine Plants

The products of the vine are less numerous than those of the soy or the bamboo, and mostly derive from its fruit: vine-shoots, ashes from shoots (medicine, ceramic glazes, heating), soaked inflorescences, the verjuice of immature grapes, fresh grapes, dried raisins (wipe off the bloom, soak in a solution of potassium carbonate and olive oil, dry for between 7 and 12 days), grape juice, grape juice reduced by half (*sapa*) or a third (*defrutum*), clarified juice (by filtration or sterilization), new or *primeur* wine (*bitzler, federweisser*), young wine, fizzy wine, fortified wine (*retsina* with pine resin), sweet wine, wine for keeping, marc.

Of all the tens of species scattered around the world, most of which are in America or Eastern Asia, it is the one—and only one—of Europe and Western and central Asia which produces the greatest wines: the species called *vinifera*, of the sub-genus *euvites*, of the genus *vitis*. Thirty of its varieties—or *cépages*—are currently in use for wine production. At the beginning of this century, an ampelography listed 24,000 names or synonyms for 5,200 varieties. One can list the three hundred most important ones:

Abouriou, Affenthaler Blauer, Abrst Blauer, Afus Ali, Aglianico, Airén, Albalonga, Aleatico, Alfrocheiro Preto, Alicante Henri Bouschet, Aligoté (Plant de Trois Grappes), Alphonse Lavallée, Altesse, Alvarihno, Amigne, André, Antão Vaz, Aramon Noir, Arinto, Aris, Arnsburger, Arvine, Assario Branco, Aubun, Augster Bleu, Augster Blanc, Aurelius, Aurora, Auxerrois, Babeasca Neagra, Bacchus, Baco Blanc, Baco Noir, Baga, Barbera, Baroque, Blauburger, Boskoops Glorie, Bouvier, Findling, Brachetto, Breidecker, Buffalo, Cabernet Franc, Cabernet-Sauvignon, Canaiolo Nero, Cantaro, Cardinal, Carignan Noir, Carmina, Castor, Chancellor, Chardonnay, Chasselas, Chasselas Rouge, Chasselas Cioutat, Chenin Blanc, Ciliegiolo, Cinsaut, Clairette Blanche, Clairette Rose, Colombard, Completer, Comtessa, Concord, Cortese, Corvina Veronese, Cot, De Chaunac, Dalkauer, Diana, Deckrot, Docetto, Dog Ridge, Domina, Dornfelder, Dunkelfelder, Edelsteiner, Ehrenbreisteiner, Ehrenfelser, Elbing Blanc, Emerald Riesling, Faberrebe, Fer, Fernão Pires, Fitzrebe, Flame Seedless, Folle Blanche, Fontanara, Forta, Freisa, Freisamer, Kiraly Furmint, Gamaret, Gamay Noir, Gamay Teinturier de Bouze, Gros Mourot, Gamay Teinturier Fréaux, Gänsfüßer Blauer, Garanoir, Garganega, Gelbhölzer, Gloria, Goldburger, Goldriesling, Graciano, Grenache, Grando, Grignolino, Grolleau, Gutenborner, Harslevelü, Hegel, Hefensteiner, Heroldrebe, Weißer Heunisch, Roter Heunisch, Gelber Heunisch, Hölder, Weißer Honigler, Humagne Blanc, Humagne Rouge, Huxelrebe, Isabella, Italia, Jubiläumsrebe, Jurançon Noir, Juwel, Kadarka, Kanzler, Kerner, Kernling, Blauer Kilianer, Knipperlé, Kolor, Königin der Weingärten, Korinthiaki, Koshu, Kyoho, Lady Downes Seedling, Lagrein, Lambrusco di Sorbana, Laska, Léon Milot, Lemberger, Len de l'El, Maccabeo, Madeleine Angevine, Madeleine Royale, Madeleine Céline, Malingre

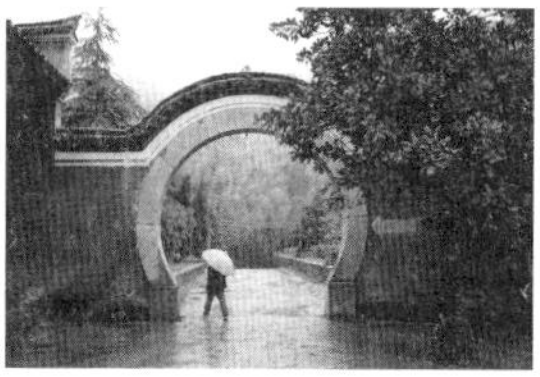

Précoce, Manteudo, Mariensteiner, Marsanne, Mauzac, Melon, Merlot, Merzling, Monastrell Mourvèdre, Montagna, Montepulciano, Moreto, Morio Muskat, Müller-Thurgau, Mourisco Tinto, Multaner, Muscabona, Muscadelle, Muscat d'Alexandrie, Muscat de Hamburg, Muscat Blanc, Muscat Rouge, Roenmuskateller, Muscat Ottonel, Nebbioilo, Négrette, Neuburger, Niagara, Noblessa, Nobling, Ohanes, Weißer Olwer, Optima, Orangetraube, Gelber Orleans, Ortega, Osiris, Osteiner, Pais, Palomino Fino, Parellada, Periquita, Perle, Perlette, Perle von Csaba, Perrum, Petit Manseng, Phoenix, Picolit, Pinot Blanc, Pinot Noir, Samtrot, Pinot Meunier, Pinot Madeleine, Pinot Gris, Pinotage, Pollux, Portugais Bleu, Primitivo, Primus, Prosecco, Putzscheere, Rabaner, Rabo de Ovelha, Rabose Veronese, Weißer Räuschling, Regent, Regner, Reichensteiner, Gelber Rèze, Ribola Gialla, Weißer Riesling, Roter Riesling, Blauer Riesling, Rieslaner, Rkatsiteli, Rotberger, Rotgipfler, Roupeiro, Ruling, Saint Laurent, Sangiovese, Sauvignon Blanc, Savatiano, Scheurebe, Schönburger, Sémillon, Septimer, Sercial, Seyval, Siegerrebe, Silcher, Sirius, Sissi, Staufer, Sulmer, Sylvaner, Sylvaner Bleu, Sousao, Süßrot, Sultanina, Syrah, Tamara, Tamarez, Tannat, Taylor, Teiturier du Cher, Tempranillo, Terrantez, Thurling, Tibouren, Tinta Amarela, Tinta Caiada, Tinto Cao, Touriga Francesca, Touriga National, Roter Traminer, Gewürztraminer, Weißer Traminer, Savagnin Blanc, Trebbiano Toscano, Ugni Blanc, Tressot Panaché, Blauer Trollinger, Groß Vernatsch, Klein Vernatsch, Blauer Urban, Roter Urban, Grüner Veltliner, Früher Roter Veltliner, Roter Veltliner, Verderlho, Verduzzo Friulano, Verduzzo Trevigniano, Vermentino, Vernaccia di San Gimignano, Villard Blanc, Villard Noir, Viognier, Wanner, Welschriesling, Blauer Wildbacher, Witberger, Würzer, Xarel-lo, Xynomavro, Roter Zierfandler, Zähringer, Zalagyöngye, Nero, Blaue Zimttraube, Blauer Zweigelt.

Varieties

The Bruce brothers, entrusted with the development of tea growing in India, discovered a new species of wild tea bush in Assam, which confirmed the challenging of Linnaeus's distinction between *thea bohea* and *thea viridis*: "The leaves of green tea are not harvested in the same way as those of black tea, although the tree is exactly the same; there can be no possible doubt about this, because, at this very moment, I am picking leaves to make green and black tea on the same plantation and from the same tree. The difference is in the method of production and nothing more." (1839). In China, Robert Fortune, entrusted, after G. J. Gordon, with the other part of British the enterprise—spying on Chinese techniques—was more specific: "It appears therefore that the black and green teas of the Northern regions of China [those regions where most of the tea exported abroad is grown] both come from the same variety of plant. This variety is *thea viridis*, more commonly known as green tea plant. Besides, the black and green teas made in considerable quantities in the

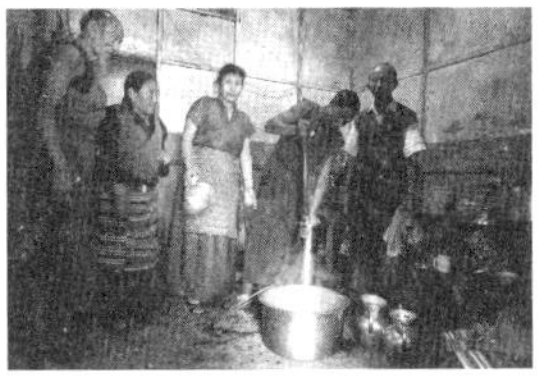

area of Canton are obtained from *thea bohea*, or black tea plant." Fortune, who had observed these plants in botanical gardens in London, notices that the black or green color derives from the treatment applied to the leaf, not from the variety of tree, but, contrary to what has always been stated since, he does confirm the great botanist's distinction between the two varieties. In this he remains alert to the often very great differences between the many Chinese varieties. Most Western observations in the nineteenth and twentieth centuries are made about the tea trees of India, Indochina or Java. Highly eccentric systems distinguish between several subordinate varieties of "China tea." Thus, according to these classifications, we find *camellia* or *thea sinensis,* var. *asamica Pierre, thea hongkongensis P., thea Dormoyana P., thea Piquetraya P., thea amplexicaulis Pitard, thea flava Pitard, thea tonkinensis Pitard, thea Gilberti A. Chevalier, thea Fleuryi A. Chevalier, thea Sasangua, thea bohea Pierre, thea viridis Pierre, thea pubescens Pierre, thea cantonensis Pierre, thea integra, thea parakansalakensis, thea nilgherrensis, thea cochinchinensis, thea japonica stricta, thea japonica diffusa, thea japonica rugosa, thea japonica macrophylla,* the wild varieties *mieng-luang* and *mieng-noi Eberhardt.* In later classifications, three perspectives prevailed. According to the Western botanical point of view, a certain confusion still remains after the varied adjustments made by Linnaeus, the main tendency being to simplify the system following Fortune and Bruce: "The observations I have made on certain cultivars at the museum, of which two have flowered abundantly, have been enough to convince me of the rigorous precision of those made by Koempfer, Thumberg and Lettsom, who only recognize one single species of tea plant." (Desfontaines) Science regards the tea plant as a part of the *camellia* species, of which it is a variety, and of which the main sub-variety is the Chinese: *camellia sinensis var. sinensis.* Three *jats* are thus distinguished with *camellia sinensis var. assamica* and *camellia sinensis var. indonesia*. From the point of view of industrial production, tea has become a vast bank of clones and hybrids, only distinguished by numbers. From the Chinese point of view, the principal denomination *camellia sinensis* is, as *vitis vinifera* is in Europe, subdivided into several types of tea-plants with very different qualities. In China one can count fifteen large families and more than three hundred and sixty varieties, whose names and characteristics have not yet been translated. This system, if it were adopted, would impose a re-evaluation of the botanical classification of tea, and particularly its relationship with the *camellia* species: the question of the classification of tea (by varieties, types and methods of treatment) will be more completely developed in the subsequent volumes of the *Three Teas Treatise (The Colors of Tea* and *Narrow Tea).*

"Where did the tea plant originate? The Chinese have never been in any doubt that it was in China, but when Major C. A. Bruce, Jenkins and Charlton discovered the

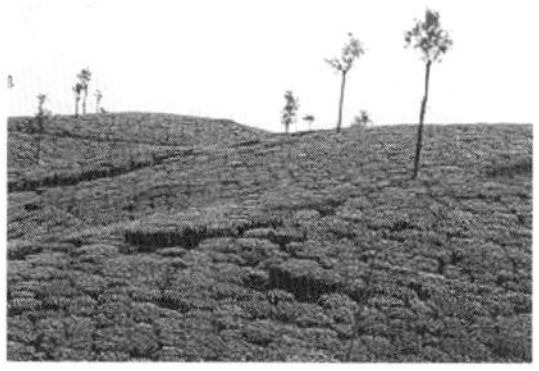

wild tea plants in Assam, at the beginning of the nineteenth century, the English loudly proclaimed that Assam was where tea had originated from. They said that the tea plant had been introduced into China from Assam in prehistoric times. All the English have energetically defended this theory, because it favors the propaganda for Indian tea." (Emile Bois, 1932) Auguste Henry invalidated the British theory in 1897, when he discovered wild Chinese tea plants in the mountains of South West Yunnan, in the forests of Menzi and in the North of Sichuan. Since then, the recognized domain of the wild tea plants spreads from Yunnan to Assam, and probably into Taiwan and Japan, where *yamacha* were found in certain primordial forests. The controversy over the Indian origin of tea took place mostly in Berlin after 1899, and lasted for several decades. Koempfer is one of the first to mention the story, always told in most works on tea, of a Boddhidarma who discovered tea by chewing the leaves of a little tree under which he had fallen asleep in the middle of his meditation. The "Indian" tea enterprise can begin: tea consumption in England increased tenfold between 1800 and 1900, reaching 120 000 tons, whilst in the last fifteen years of the same century, having peaked at 78 000 tons, the importation of China tea dwindled tenfold, then a hundredfold by 1939... In the meantime, tea from India and Ceylon was benefiting from more than just publicity: it was exempt from the taxes which continued to be imposed on China tea; a legend was invented to root it in local religion; science helped by hiding the transplantation of a Chinese tree behind an invented "origin," reversing the truth. In less than a century, the Britannic Tea enterprise invented a whole culture in England, India and even, indirectly, in Morocco; but it missed one detail in its revision of the history of China: there is no Sanskrit word for "tea" and the Hindi word *chai* derives from the Chinese *cha*.

Planted

There are three ways of obtaining a tea plant: growing it from seed, by generative selection, or by vegetative propagation. The last method is the most popular, as the tea plant responds excellently to vegetative propagation, from generative clones—layering, grafting or suckering—but the production of clones is usually done by the simplest method: propagation by cuttings. After the elimination of the bad breeders, generative selection, on selected seed-bearers, growing freely or in nurseries, allows the production of *jats*, from which higher yields will be obtained... Growing from seed is practiced less because it yields "heterogenous vegetable matter, caused by the cross-fertilization between the species." (Denis Bonheure) There is enormous variety in the quality of the trees, and in their yield and propensity to fermentation. This great instability in tea is no doubt what has allowed people, throughout Chinese history, to profit from so many different varieties, constituting the several hundred listed there. These variations, no doubt, also ensured the continuation of the long debate over the botanical classification of the tea plant, ever

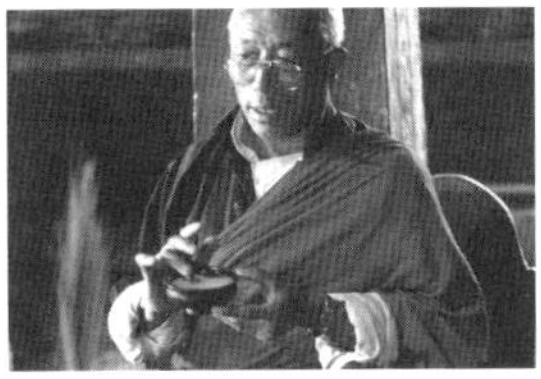

since the time of Linnaeus, who divided the tea plant into the *viridis* and *bohea* types, and called it *thea*; then came Koempfer's corrections in the nineteenth century, and then Bruce's reports, which reduced it to a single variety, related to the camellia and now being increased by modern agronomy with its impoverished *jats*. It was this very heterogeneity that removed tea from a market insufficiently able to control its vagaries: if the London Tea Exchange was forced to close in 1998, it was because the future market, on which other raw materials or exotic must be traded, is very difficult to predict in the case of such an irregular crop.
Koempfer, one of the very first botanists to have studied the plant in the nineteenth century, described the peculiar features of its cultivation: "In Japan, tea plantations are not found in gardens or particular enclosures [...], the seeds are not sown in any regular or symmetrical order. [...] It often happens that two or three shrubs grow together and are so tightly interlaced that, on first sight, one thinks they have a single stem. [...] The leaves can only be picked in the third year, when they are abundant and at the height of their beauty."

Straw

Mulching protects the soil from the rays of the sun and drying winds, considerably reduces the loss of water through evaporation, and allows the maintenance of sufficient water on the surface during the dry season. Mulching is done with gramінaceae such as *Pennisetum purpureum, Digitaria sp., Tripscacum laxum,* etc, but also in China with rice stalks. In Japan, the mulch is put in place a few weeks before the harvest in order to increase the greenness of the tea by preventing the photosynthesis of the chlorophyll, and is prolonged as one rises up through the quality scale, with Sencha, Tencha, and above all Gyokuro; it manifests itself in the cup by the sweetness of its taste.

Picking, Harvesting, Storing

Tea is a foodstuff and vegetable stimulant, harvested by picking, and cultivated—with the exception of recent industrial plantations—in gardens rather than fields. In the Taiwanese mountains and some continental regions, certain professors of tea go out in search of wild tea plants, from which they bring back a parsimonious harvest they submit to a manual treatment in the hope of finding an exceptional tea. This exploration of areas where the tea plant may have survived outside cultivation, developing aromatic powers that generative selection destroys, is surrounded by secrecy in the same way as the hunt for truffles and morels over here, allowing exploration of the potential of wild food, which our art of wine has long since abandoned.

Bud, Axillary, Leaf

"When a tea plant has been pruned and starts reforming its leaves, these early leaves are not normal ones, but axillary leaves (called *kèpel* in Java and *janum leaves* in British India). The axillary leaves change as they go up the stem, getting bigger

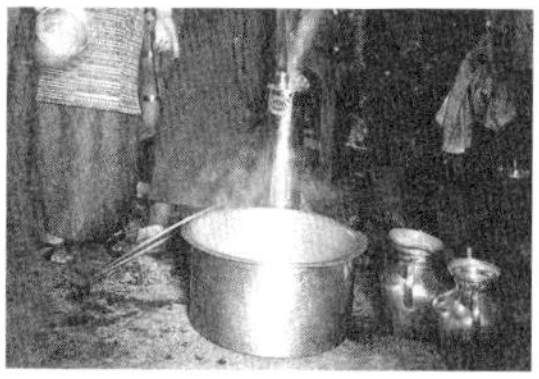

and bigger and more and more indented, until they reach a more or less constant size. After the formation of a certain number of such leaves, comes a period of rest and the final bud no longer forms a "*pecco*" but becomes dormant (*boerong* in Java, *banjhi* in India)... After this period of rest the terminal bud swells again and becomes active. One can then see the axillary leaves appearing, then intermediate leaves between them and the normal ones, and finally the normal leaves. There will then be another rest period, and so on." (Dr J.-J. Deuss)
The wine harvest in France remains one of the last great community rituals, because it is still done by hand, still subject to the vagaries of the climate and timing, and still holds continuing fascination for tourists. The intensity of the timescale, with the variations of region and climate, reflects the very real risks that make it such a gamble: a whole winemaking economy, and thus a whole tradition, can be overturned by adverse circumstances. A late harvest will produce an increasingly flabby wine, and one which will keep badly; an early one will produce an acid or bitter white, or a red with too much tannin, which will show in an undesirable dry, bitter or sharp taste: compromises often have to be sought between physiological and chemical maturity, which do not always correspond with one another—an imbalance between the berry and its tannins.
Already in the Song dynasty, two categories were distinguished in the fabrication of tea for taxation in the region of Bei Yuan: the Zhen Pei (coming from the original soil and reserved for the emperor) and the Wai Pei (from the neighboring regions and for the connoisseurs). The picking takes place in early spring, before sunrise, and with the nails only, so that sweat on the fingers will not contaminate the aroma. The leaves are immediately divided into five categories: *xiao ya* (little bud), *zhong ya (*medium bud including a leaf), *zi ya* (purple bud), *bai he (*a bud with two large leaves), *wu dai* (large leaves with twigs).

Dew & Sun

Too much watering—fear of hail or a downpour before the harvest—excessive exposure, corrected in America by intensive irrigation, and over-fertilization can be bad for the vine. One must prevent the roots of the vinestock from spreading out before pushing downwards into the soil, or the foliage from becoming too luxuriant, or the bunches of grapes from being too watery, thus lacking in flavor and aroma. In the same way, the picking of tea must be done after the dew has dried, but before the midday sun appears, in order to avoid the humidity and the heat that would both affect the fermentation. This delicate and demanding harvest has been the cause of centuries of servitude in China; in India, when the English wanted to industrialize the process and hire qualified workers, this caused the incessant displacement of tribes, with one terrifying consequence: the first concentration camps, which caused more deaths than during the whole period of African slavery. It also brought about

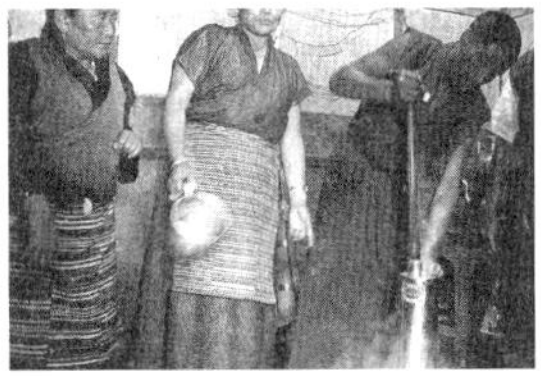

religious and tribal wars, conflicts still reflected in the present situation in Darjeeling, Assam and Sri Lanka. This picking has given rise, as though to soften the image of toil and labor, to all sorts of technical and symbolic expedients, building up a legend around tea cultivation—monkeys sent to pick inaccessible teas, young women chosen as virgins so that they would not pollute the aromas, music played during the gathering... "The Chinese... are very fond [of watermelon], and claim that, to be perfect, they must be picked at night, before the dew has evaporated. They also say that when they are picked in the gardens where they abound, the operation must be carried out in total silence. Because, they say, when the watermelon has reached maturity, the slightest movement of air will split the ones with the thinnest skin, and the fruit will be lost." (Comte d'Hérisson, 1859-1861)

Fermented, Dried, Infused

When a Dong Ding Wulong has been infused several times in its teapot, or a Tai Ping Hou Kui in its *zhong*, the pickings have unfurled. The bud, the leaves, and the stalk have rediscovered, through the water that is nonetheless exuding them, the sap that gives them life. In this brief moment, when they give of themselves like a hologram of what they were on the tree, these vegetable wisps regain texture, color and shape. This tealeaf will nonetheless have endured all kinds of adventures, not the least of which is to have surrendered both its aroma and its effect. The leaf will have been cut, collected, transported, reassembled, sifted, spread out, withered, tossed, prevented from oxidizing or assisted in the process, heated, cooled, manipulated, worked, shaped, sometimes rolled, sometimes roasted, dried, sometimes worked again, even sculpted, dried, sorted, packed, stored, transported, stocked, packed, boxed, sold, portioned out, washed, infused, rested, infused again and again, perhaps examined and then thrown away. The three basic situations that take the leaf from raw to almost raw—from picking to the post-infusion stage—are fermentation, drying and infusion. These three situations are, each time, intermediary stages between the recognized states of raw and cooked, fresh and rotting, cold and hot, dry and damp, soft and hard, stable and unstable. The three situations are actually transitions between these different conditions, but they are stabilized processes; each one marks the end of the preceding one: fermentation threatens the freshness, the drying stops the fermentation, the infusion ends the drying and restores the freshness. Each process of fermenting, drying and infusing is the play—passing—of time. The time of tea—its three-stroke engine—is this strange technique which lets time do its work: in the oxidation of the leaf cells, in the dehydration which fixes the aroma, and in its eventual diffusion in water.

Dried

A white tea is a dried tea. The down-covered buds—for a Bai Hao Yin Zen—or leaves—for a Bai Mu Dan—, undergo no treatment, no handling, only a long

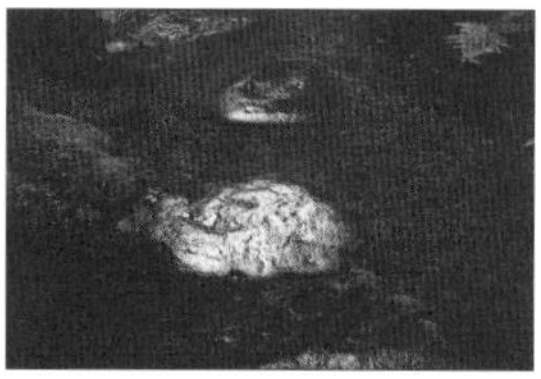

withering process which consists in leaving the leaves spread out in storage for one or two days, then drying them in the sun or under gentle heat. In one of the earliest mentions of tea, the Jesuit Matteo Ricci summed up the fabrication in terms of drying only: "They pick the leaves in spring, dry them in the shade and keep them for their ordinary decoctions, which they almost always use in drinks, not simply at meals, but whenever a guest arrives to visit a friend."

Drying is the simplest of the processes used for preserving food, although it was only slowly mastered in different civilizations: it delays, through the heat of fire, the prolongation of life, of which water and air are both the vectors and possible corrupters. But it is very rare to achieve dehydration without fermentation: neither white tea, which gives out the most crystalline of liquors, nor yellow tea, which undergoes a version reinforced by actual stewing, nor green tea can escape from a period of withering before the drying process.

One of the etymological roots of the word "drug" suggests that it derives from the German word *trocken*, which means "dried." In ancient apothecaries, which only Chinese chemists can give an idea of, drugs—root, sap, leaf, capsule, petal, mould—were above all dehydrated substances, a matter whose principle element or virtues had been concentrated by the elimination of water.

Oxidized, Withered, Fermented

As soon as it has been picked the tealeaf begins to oxidize. An enzyme—polyphenoloxidase—is responsible for the oxidation on contact with air, which implies that the treatment of tea must begin as soon as it has been picked, and that the tea manufacturing sheds must be located as close as possible to the gardens. In Ceylon, Tom Lipton had a kind of cable car constructed to bring the tea to the factories. In China or Taiwan, the transformation is carried out on the spot, and keeps the planters and their many seasonal workers going for up to seventy-two hours without sleep. Situated in the epidermis of the leaf, the polyphenoloxidases can be activated by the slightest folding or crumpling of the crop, and transformed into theaflavins, while the leaves turn brown.

The theaflavins are responsible for the flavors of tea and, already at the withering stage, begin to give off a heady aroma that fills the atmosphere of the factory and impregnates the workers' clothes. So it is through the development and control of the oxidation process that tea is able to acquire all its organoleptic characteristics. Since the activity of the enzyme is lower in mature leaves, a "delicate" harvest is necessary to permit the modulation of its effects. This natural and inescapable oxidation has been controlled in three ways by traditional methods: the time of withering (which all types of teas undergo, including the white and yellow teas) consists in spreading the leaves in a thin layer on large flat round bamboo baskets, regularly shaken; the time of fermentation (of blue-green, red or black teas), which is

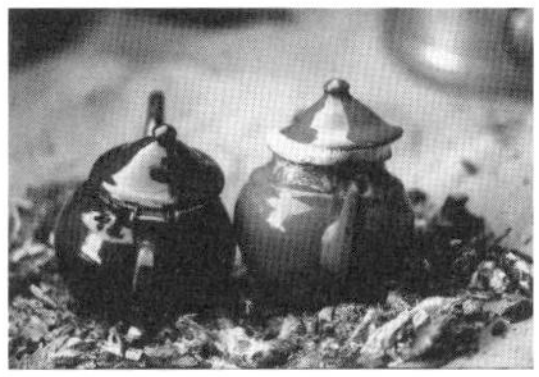

brought on and carried through in a heated atmosphere and by different types of handling; and the optional time of inactivation (for green teas), achieved by heating the leaves to 40°C, thereby destroying the enzyme.

One must observe that, through being such a tender leaf which oxidizes so fast, particularly in tropical climatic conditions, tea differs from its two usual partners, coffee and cocoa, both of which can be stopped in mid-development at the berry or bean stage, in order to be later transported and treated by the agri-food industry in the country of consumption. From this point of view, tea is similar to the wine grape, which must be crushed, pressed and made into wine in a very brief interval after harvesting. These common demands have no doubt created a divide in their respective cultures, between, on the one hand, the arts of tea or wine, for a minority, and, on the other, mass produced teas and wines, whose profitability has left them with only their names. Coffee and cocoa are raw materials more easily absorbed into the process of commercial exchange and in their case the divide is not so much that between an art and an industry, as a break in the production process between definitely unreconcilable techniques and traditions.

The Secret of Tea

"The first leaf grows and is picked in spring, because at that time it is softer and more delicate. It is dried on a low fire in a coarse clay pot, and then it is rolled on matting covered with cotton. It is transported throughout the Empire in lead boxes lined with wicker and reeds." (Giovanni Laureati)

"The Anglican minister, the Reverend Mr Medhurst, who lived there for twenty two years, from 1816 to 1838, even says that the roasting process is kept secret not just from strangers, but also from the majority of the locals. What makes one think that this art is not completely assimilated in the public domain in China is that, in the early days of the plantations in Java and Brazil, Chinese farmers were brought over, at great expense, and that, even so, the roasting process worked only moderately well. The produce of these factories looks as fine as those of China; their appearance is often even more appealing; but once they are infused, it becomes apparent that they are markedly inferior, and the difference is necessarily caused by the roasting process." (Houssaye, *Monographie du thé*, 1843)

The term roasting—or torrefaction—, always used in specialist literature, emphasizes the fact that tea, alongside cocoa and coffee, belongs to the category of "fermented and roasted beverages." But if there is such a thing as the roasting of tea, it is of lesser importance in the process; what Houssaye, following C. A. Bruce, names the roasting is in reality the fermentation process, by which tea acquires its shape and color. It is on this point that Fortune and Bruce, on their respective missions in China and India, thought they had the final word invalidating Linnaeus's distinction between *thea "viridis"* and "*bohea*," bringing it back to a single tree. However, if

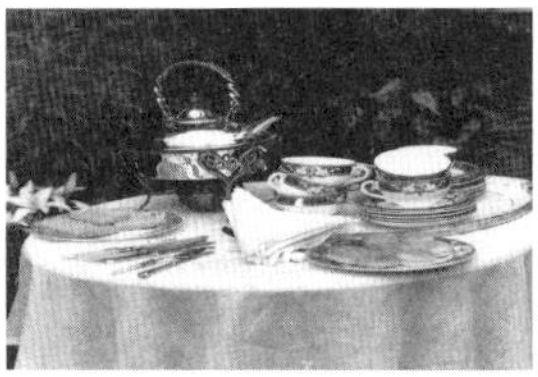

the leaves from the same tea plant can in effect be brought to different degrees of fermentation, producing either green tea or black tea, the Chinese technique, as with wine, selects different varieties of tea-plants—out of the many that exist—for different families of tea; the different ways of handling the tea are so numerous and varied according to location that they cannot be summed up by the reports of the two explorers on their missions. But their descriptions are still the first accounts of a mechanical and thermal process: "After this, the workers lightly work the leaves in the palms of their hands, without using their fingers, passing them from one hand to the other, dropping them in the basket, picking them up again, continuing like this for ten minutes. Then they are laid out on the wattles again for half and hour. The operation is repeated three or four times, until the leaves are as supple as skin; this has the effect of turning the tea a dark color. [...] When the pan is red hot, the roaster throws in about two pounds of leaves, spreading them evenly, so that they are all equally roasted. He repeatedly tosses them in every direction with his hands, until they are so hot that he cannot bear it; this operation is extremely painful, as much because of the high temperature of the place, and the suffocating vapors which fill it, as because of the corroding sap which oozes from the crackling leaves on their contact with the hot metal, and which eats into the skin. But this manipulation must continue without stopping, as the leaves can only be rolled when they are hot." (idem)

Under the Nose

The three principal conditions of food, which make up the algorithm of Levi-Strauss's *Mythologiques*, can be described in terms of the types of odor released: a scent from raw food, a flavor from cooked food, and a stink from rotting (corrupted) food. It is nevertheless at the moment of fermentation, and because of it, that tea acquires its particular aromas, which, according to the type, will vary from a green scent, or floral aroma, to perfumes of wood, fruit or grilled chestnuts or smells of humus or decomposing soil. Thus tea, in the process of withering and during oxidation—a putrefying process—can recreate the most subtle shades of flavor in food, from freshness and rawness, to total vegetable maturity, passing by the diverse possible cooking methods; grilling, stewing, smoking.

The length of the withering process varies according to temperature, humidity and ambient ventilation and also depends on whether the tea is stored in a sheltered storage place or one exposed to the sun. The tea, after picking, will rest in large open-work bamboo baskets—or in vats or ventilated tunnels when the process is industrial—that are gently stirred, as if being winnowed, carefully avoiding damage to the epidermis of the leaf. The leaves are thus dehydrated, and they also acquire a parchment-like pliability, so that they can be manipulated without being broken. This intended and measured pause is the pose of the harvest: a moment

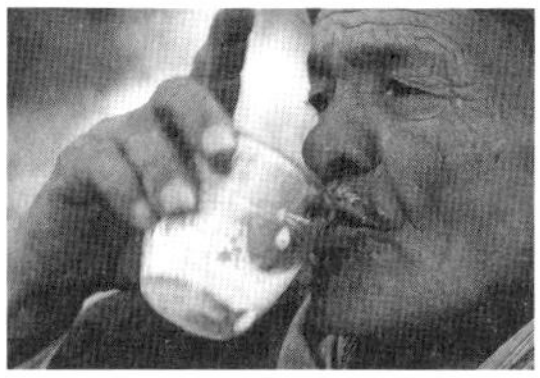

when everything has already been determined, though everything is still to do. During the fermentation, when the crop is pressed, folded or sometimes crushed, the cell constituents come to the unprotected surface of the leaf, and into contact with oxygen. Chemically, the oxidation, operated by the enzymes, is prolonged by a fermentation caused by the techniques and temperatures applied to the tea. As in the cases of wine and cocoa, the numerous molecular reactions are still far from being understood. What is mainly formed during this process is the oil of tea, made up of polyphenols transformed into theaflavins and thearubigins. With the release of the aromas this transformation can also be measured by the change in the color of the leaves, which pass from green to yellow to orange-brown, the change beginning on the serrated edge. The atmosphere must be slightly damp, well ventilated and of a temperature favorable to the activity of the enzymes. Oxidation and fermentation hardly modify the caffeine level, but they diminish that of tannins, thus modifying the efficiency of the former. In general the leaf must remain supple, warm and of the right color for its type. Its herbal odor has given way to a flowery and already characteristic aroma.

This is a phenomenon that depends on three parameters being exactly and proportionately balanced: humidity, temperature and duration. The traditional Chinese methods of controlling this stage were not, it is true, perfected until the Ming period—with white, yellow and red teas—or even under the Qings for the more sophisticated Wulong teas. This is the time when the *chashi*, the tea experts, come into their own: according to the climate, the season, and the quality of the harvest, they decide on the necessary adjustments to the temperature and humidity levels, then fix the intensity levels for the manipulations, and then the exact moment to stop. The professor of tea, who combines the abilities of a master of wine and those of a "nose" in the perfume industry, cannot, at this stage judge the tea by its taste—even if he sometimes bites into a leaf—, but only by the color and the aromas released, in which he must distinguish what they will become after the final treatment, the maturation and above all, the infusion. At this stage, he has to adapt to the given outside conditions to accompany and control—accelerate or slow down, avoid hurrying or stopping the process—this oxidation, which inexorably affects the leaf from the moment it is picked. As it progressively dehydrates and ferments, this leaf turns yellow, and then, when it has been spread out and cooled, green again, before returning to yellow under the effect of further manipulation...

Fermentation, Preservation, Putrefaction

Fermentation replays the balance of opposites in the vegetable pulp: the tea oxidizes and preserves itself, it becomes consumable whilst decomposing, it must lose its freshness to gain its fragrance. Fermentation maintains this delicate balance between the disgusting and the delicious, this edge of value and taste, as with sex

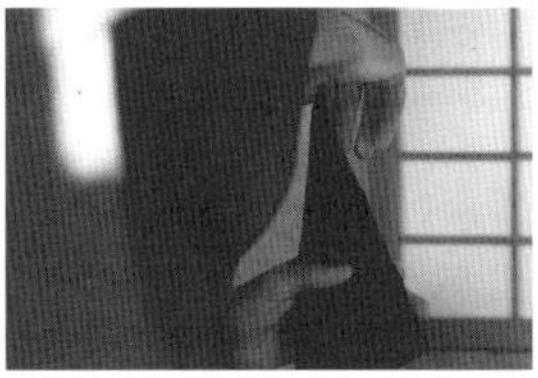

or cooking. This cooked-raw—or raw-cooked—initiates the culinary and provides the history of our food with a constantly questioned material: from the Pythagorian or the Islamic proscriptions against all fermented foods, right up to present-day sanitary regulations in international commerce, which attempt to ban cheeses made with non-pasteurized milk, Cornish clotted cream and non-pasteurized wine. The alimentary threesome which has come down to us from Antiquity through the Middle Ages, down to the nineteenth century is a commonplace: wine (ale or beer in Northern Europe), bread and "what accompanies it" *compagnium (companatico* in Italian, *comapanage* in French). These three complementary items are for the most part a result of fermentation. A traditional Russian peasant welcome would include the serving of *kvass*, with rye bread, cheese and pickled cucumber: the three foods and the drink were all fermented. This human survival kit shows, by its very endurance—fast food still bears its traces—age-old efforts to ensure an always-uncertain edibility. Ritual prohibitions, mistrust of raw fruit or standing water, culinary techniques. The preparation of food consists first of all in removing its toxicity, making it digestible and keeping it edible: washed, soaked, pounded, sliced, filtered, boiled, roasted, grilled, fried, dried, fermented, baked, smoked, salted, preserved, seasoned, marinated, cooked. Cooking cannot be summed up merely by the cooking process: between the lengthy soaking of the food and its long simmering, the transformation displays all its mechanical, physical and chemical properties. Fermentation plays an exemplary role in this transformation: the verb "to ferment" derives from "*fervere*" which means "to boil," and comes from the bubbles of carbon dioxide emerging from the fermenting liquid. It is a spontaneous boiling of raw vegetable matter, a sort of natural foreshadowing of cooking. Fermentation is the most inevitable cooking accident and the most reversible technical expedient: a fruit, abandoned after falling off a tree is destined for putrefaction, whilst any attempt to control the behavior of yeast may cause the development of undesirable bacteria. It is a paradoxical technique, which allows time to do its work and operates in an underhand way alongside it, until another device—most often dehydration—brings it to a halt.

From fragments of a press found in Syria, dating wine at six thousand years before the Christian calendar began, and the four thousand-year-old jars of Mesopotamian beer, right up to the use of yeast and enzymes in biogenetic research, micro-organisms have placed the question of technical advance in the midst of potential toxicity. The process which previously maintained a fermented food at the stage between putrefaction and preservation, between decomposition and improvement—wine on the edge of becoming vinegar—is nowadays torn between a desire to act both at the level of microtechnology and also at the global level, which results in an increasing preoccupation with hygiene: bactericides,

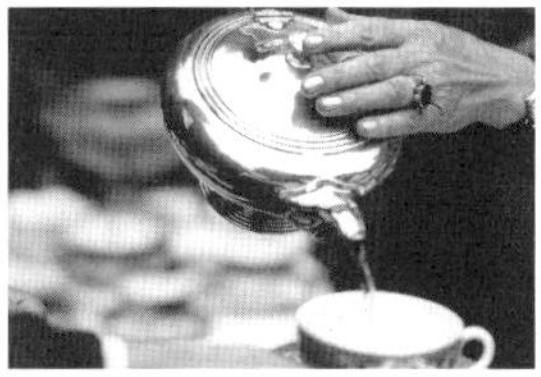

fungicides, antibiotics, antiseptics, sterilization, pasteurization, irradiation, ionization, refrigeration, deep-freezing…

Bacteria, Yeasts, Moulds

Fermentation links the great renewal of forms and substances of the world—the decomposition of organic matter and the maintenance of the soil's fertility—with constituent regeneration—digestion by a living organism. The enzyme (or diastase) works on a triple level: synthesized by the microorganism, it crosses the membranes of the cells and feeds them, induces the nutrition of the organized body (*lactobacillus acidophilus* and *lactobacillus bifidus* of the intestinal *tractus*), and enables the earth to find its nutrients. A change of scale whose potential is shown by the enzyme-producing bacteria: reproducing by cellular division, a single one, if not interfered with, could in three days equal the entire volume of the Earth. Three types of organisms generally carry out fermentation: bacteria, yeast, and moulds. The bacterium is a micro-factory measuring a thousandth of a millimeter (a micron), weighing a billionth of a gram, which manufactures enzymes. In unfavorable conditions it transforms itself into a spore, which can survive for many years. Bacteria appear in many different forms: round (coccus), rod (bacillus), convex (vibrio), spiral (spirillum). The yeast cell, which measures from five to ten microns, and divides by septation or budding, is used, for example, in wine-making, brewing and baking. Finally mould is a microscopic mushroom whose mycelium is made of long filaments, sometimes with reproductive spores; known as *penicillium*, it contributes to the manufacture of Camembert or Roquefort.

Vinification & Vaccination

Between vinification and vaccination, Pasteur linked food and medecine via the new route of bacillae and viruses, and also confirmed the role of air in the processes. Fermentation can be aerobic (in the presence of air), or anaerobic; thermophilic (with an optimum temperature of 30°C) or cryophilic (less than 20°C). It can be alcoholic, lactic, acetic, butyric, or propionic. Often mixed, most fermentations none the less derive from the transformation of starch into maltose, of maltose into glucose, and of glucose into pyruvic acid.

Fermentation takes three main forms: alcoholic, of fruit, cereals and saps (wines, beers, hydromels); lactic, of vegetables, leguminous plants, milk, meat, fish, cereals (sauerkraut, sauces, cheeses); and acetic (wine vinegars, cider, rice).

Fermentation has three main uses: predigestion, transformation of flavor, and preservation. Decomposition of proteins and lactose, hydrolysis of starch, synthesis of vitamins and amino-acids; development of flavors and aromas; manufacture of a transportable and storable foodstuff (bread, cheese, sausage, lacto-fermented vegetables, olives, anchovies, soy or fish sauces). In its non-alimentary uses, these mingled functions can allow a transformation of matter, texture or color: the

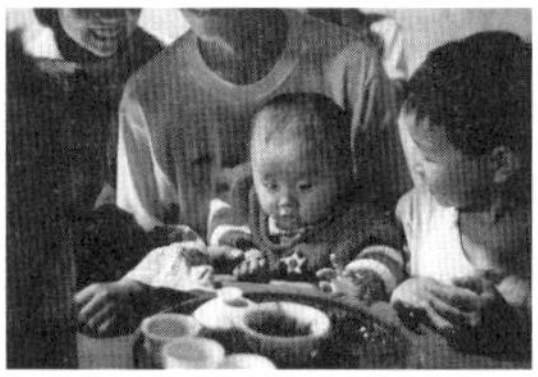

separation of textile fibers (the retting of flax, nettles or vegetable sponges), the impregnation of adhesives, and the stabilization of color (indigo).

Bread, Wine, Cheeses

Innumerable breads, wines and cheeses.
But also: thousands of beers, salt-provisions and pickles.
And also: *braga* (millet porridge, cooked, diluted and fermented), *geislitz, zur, ogi* (Nigerian maize porridge), *uji* (a Kenyan drink made of fermented maize, served at breakfast and as a welcome to guests—up to three liters per day—, now supplanted by tea), *takammart* (Sahara, goat's milk), *angkak, puto, balao-balao (*Philippines, based on rice and shrimps), *trahanas (*Greece and Turkey, wheat and ewe's milk), *burong dalag, kishk* (Middle East, *bulghur* and *laban*), *kisra* (Sudan, a sorghum cake), *ontjom* (Indonesia, a peanut pancake wrapped in a banana leaf), *chiang-yu* (the ancestor of all soy sauces), *shoyu, tamari, miso, tempeh,* natto (Japan), *meitauza* (China), *inyu, falafel* (chick pea ball, fried after a few hours fermentation), *kenkey* (Ghana, ball of maize in plantain leaves), *taamiah* (Egypt, broad beans, pressed, fermented and fried), *jamin-bang* (Brazil), *injera* (Ethiopia, pancake), *barszcz* (Poland, red beetroot), *maz*, sauerkraut, *naveline, brovada, misozuke* (vegetables fermented in *miso*), pickled cucumber, *tsukemono* (Japan, vegetables in rice bran: *daikon*, turnips, cucumbers, carrots, peas, aubergine, celery, peppers, and leaves), *kimchi* (from Korea, with cabbage, *pe-tsai,* cucumber, radishes), *sajour asin* (Indonesia), *tien mien chang, hum-choy* (Chinese sauerkraut*), netetou, iru, dawadawa, soumbala* (West Africa, condiment from the grains of *nere*), fermented cassava (*gari, attieke, foufou, farinha*), *popoï (taro), chuno* (potato in Peru), *aya-bisbaya*, yoghurt, *kefir, koumiss, longfil* (Scandinavia), *kjaerdermelk* (Norwegian cellar milk), *laban* (Middle East), *arroz amarillo* (Equator), *thumba, appam, dahi, rabdi, jalebi, lassi, khaman, dhokla, idli* (India, rice with *mung* bean*),* cream, butter, buttermilk, *aoules* (Sahara), tidbits, *gaffelbitar, surstömming* (Scandinavian herrings), *rakørret*, anchovies, fish sauces and pastes *(patis, budu, nampla, kaomi, ounago, bagoong, trassi, prahoc, mâm, belacham, katsuobushi, nuoc-mam), nahm* (Thai sausage), *chicha* (Inca maize), Mexican *tesguino, munkoyo* (Zambia*), dolo* (Sahel), *kaffir beer* (South African *sorghum), pito* (Nigeria), *busaa* (Kenya) *mbege* (Tanzania), *ikagage* (Ruanda), *talla* (Ethiopia), *sake, amasake* (Japan), *pachwai, madhu, ruhi* (India), Malayan *topai,* Philippine *topuy*, Korean *yakju* and *takju, thai* in Thailand, *bousa* (the pharaohs' wheat beer), *kvass* (barley, wheat, buckwheat, sometimes with apple), *kefir, koumiss* (fermented mare's milk)*, tarhanas* (in Greece and Turkey, a mixture of wheat and fermented milk), *garum* (used by Roman athletes, based on fish), *kiesiel*, beer, *pulque,* palm wine, wine, cider, perry, water melon wine (in Russia and Africa), hydromel, *trojnack* (Poland), *tej* (Ethiopia), vinegars (from wine, cider, rice, bananas, dates, palm wine, sugar cane, coconut milk,

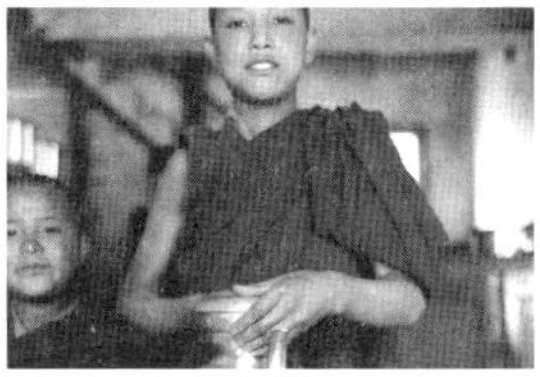

pineapple juice), *ogiri* (fermented water melon seeds, a Nigerian condiment), coffee, cocoa, vanilla, tobacco, silage (fermented grass for animal feed).

Fermented Tea

"What a strange drink this is! We are not speaking of black tea, which has undergone fermentation of a different type, but of a beverage obtained by fermenting, with the help of a special fermenting agent, an infusion of tea with sugar added. One can find this drink in numerous countries of Asia and Europe (China, Japan, Indonesia, Russia, Bulgaria, Poland, Germany) under various names: Teeshwamm, Tea Fungus, Kombucha, Wunderpilz, Hongo, Cajnij, Teekvass. This tea has antibiotic properties which are used in medecine in the USSR." (Claude Aubert, 1992)

Fermentation & Oxidation

The diastases—enzymes or soluble ferments—can be clearly distinguished from the bacteria, yeasts or micro-mushrooms which synthesize them and produce the fermentation of *miso*, wine or cheese. The diastases, which can be found in the cells of the vegetable matter itself, can be divided into separate types. The hydrolyzing diastases dissolve a body into other less complex ones, with the addition of water; amylase transforms starch into maltose; lactase; lipase, involved in the saponification of fatty substances. The diastases, which break down substances, include the zymases, lactases and carboxylases that induce lactic or alcoholic fermentation, or decompose the organic acids. Finally, the oxidizing diastases, or oxidases—connected to the proxidases, reductases and catalases—which are responsible, for example, for the darkening of certain mushrooms, of apple juice, and for the *casse* of wine.
The phenomenon of tea oxidization, which belongs to the third category, if it continues into fermentation, is thus a specific one: the oxygen activates several elements particular to the cells in the tealeaf by direct contact and not through yeast or mould: enzymes—thease or polyphenoloxidase—, glucoside, and polyphenols. Within the little understood reduction of these tannins, a synthesis takes place in which several hundred aromatic elements can then be analyzed. The essential oil of tea, which must be fixed on the leaf by the drying process, is formed at the moment of enzymatic oxidation, and thus not just at the moment of the induced fermentation, but already at the withering stage, something that has long been ignored by scientific research (cf. Van Romburgh, Mann, Bois). This withering process, which simultaneously causes a strong reduction in the humidity of the leaf and a clear increase in oxidizing diastases, already brings about an aromatic synthesis, of which anyone who visits a tea factory at this stage will be powerfully aware.

Breathing, Photosynthesis, Oxidation

The phenomenon of oxidation is a form of putrefaction quite distinct from alcoholic or lactic fermentation, or bacterial breakdown. It is closer to breathing than to digestion or distillation; indeed oxidases are the active agents in animal respiration.

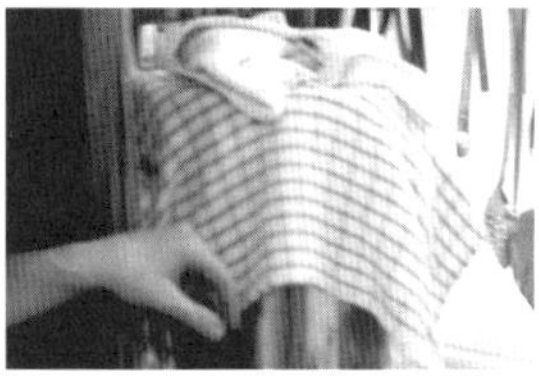

A vegetable leaf is equipped with a lamina, of which the upper surface is generally smooth, while the underneath, sometimes downy, is punctuated by the orifices of the stomates. The gas exchanges take place through these ostioles: photosynthesis (absorption of carbon dioxide and release of oxygen) and breathing (absorption of oxygen and release of carbon dioxide). The plant, irradiated by the sun, combines the carbon dioxide, which it absorbs with the hydrogen it draws from the water; it manufactures organic substances, mainly glucids, at the same time releasing oxygen. The primeval atmosphere, constituted mainly of carbon dioxide, nitrogen and steam, only became breathable for animals thanks to this exchange, and thanks to the fact that, even though photosynthesis stops at night whereas plants carry on breathing, there is still more oxygen released than absorbed. Plants create large molecules from small mineral molecules and manufacture sugar through the action of solar energy on the chlorophyll contained in their chloroplasts; most living creatures, on the other hand, through aerobiosis, use oxygen to transform sugars, turning them into energy.

Photosynthesis, anaerobic at first, solely used by bacteria at the bottom of the sea, probably appeared three billion years ago. Respiration, made possible by photosynthesis, appeared several hundred million years later. One might advance the hypothesis that enzymatic oxidization is no more than a third form of exchange between a body and its surroundings, in which air, water and energy all come into play. This third basic metabolism would find its accompanying ritual in the manufacturing techniques of fermented drinks, its volatile proof in the developed aromas, and would offer all cultures its basic essence through the paradox of incorporation only.

Tea, Coffee, Cocoa (again)

The three black drinks have long been associated, both by their common period of introduction to Europe, and by three aspects of their production: tropical culture, fermentation and roasting. If the difficulty of new implantations has quickly been exposed by the randomness of the results, the same vocabulary has been applied to very different situations, implying a similarity between the operations and processes. In reality, the role of roasting and fermentation for each of these products can sometimes be reversed in terms of their necessity. Tea is only rarely roasted, but the metabolism of its cytoplasm makes oxidation inevitable: it already starts in the withering process—which the greenest of tea cannot escape—, itself a form of fermentation, essential to the aromatic development. Coffee, on the contrary, can do without fermentation, but absolutely must—with the only exception of *bun*, the Yemeni green coffee—undergo roasting, which is the only way to release its flavors. As for cocoa, it must undergo both the fermentation and roasting of its beans, otherwise their astringency and bitterness would be unbearable.

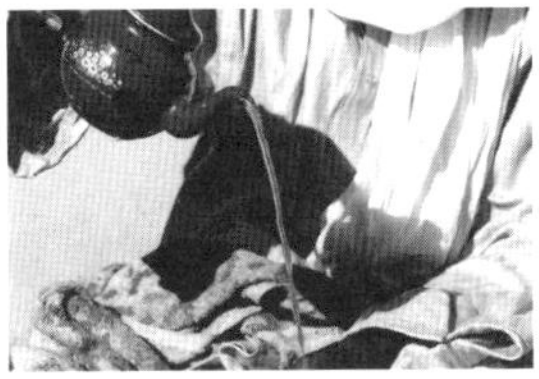

The fruit of the coffee bush is a drupe, whose skin (exocarpus) is garnet-red when it is picked, and whose kernel is formed of two flattened grains lying face to face. These are covered with a membrane described as a "silvery skin"; beyond that is a pale yellow envelope (cellulose endocarp), and, finally, a viscous pulp (mesocarp). To pass from the berry stage to the green coffee stage, and get to the grain itself, the pulp, envelope and skin must all be eliminated, and for this the choice must be made between the dry or wet methods. The dry method consists in spreading the berries out over vast surfaces, where they are turned over with spades, or sometimes with a hot air machine. When the fruit is dry, the hulling takes place, performed with a pestle in the past, nowadays with a machine with a rotating cylinder and a system of blades which break the envelopes and release the grains from the husk and envelope. This procedure leaves traces of the skin, which give a bitter taste, and therefore necessitates the use of a machine to rub and polish the grains. The wet method operates through a sifting process in water, which eliminates impurities by floating them off, then a passage through a pulper, which shreds the mesocarp and releases the grains in their envelope, with some of the pulp still adhering to it. This gelatinous and non-soluble pulp is softened by fermentation for between six and thirty-six hours in a bath, which disintegrates it. The coffee, still yellow rather than brown and still in its envelope, will then be dried for ten days on wattles laid in the sun, and this finally allows the grain to be extracted from the easily removed envelope. A third method, known as the semi-damp one, treats the just-ripe red berries with the wet method, but with a shorter spell in the water, followed by sessions in the pulper and polishing machines. The fermentation of coffee, traditionally done by massing the grains together, begins with an enzymatic and exothermic reaction, causing the destruction of the pectins and the hydrolysis of the sugars; this is followed by the apparition of yeasts after successive fermentations: alcoholic, lactic, acetic; and finally come the putrefying bacteria. This final stage of fermentation, in which a crop can be damaged by a "stinking bean" which ruins the taste, is nowadays better controlled in the sorting bins by the addition of enzymes and selected yeasts. The wet method gives the coffee a finer appearance, but is used only for certain arabica growths. Experts are still divided on the real effects of fermentation on the taste of coffee; in practice, it affects the envelope rather than the grain itself, and that only in order to get rid of it; in the end the dry method is the most frequently used, notably for the enormous production of robusta.

After the cocoa beans have been picked, they are extracted from the pulp, destalked, and put into hundred kilo piles; they are wrapped in banana leaves, and placed in huge baskets or wooden boxes, for a three to six day fermentation. In the case of cocoa, three different types of reaction follow one another, with an alcoholic fermentation at the beginning and an acetic one at the end. The temperature rises

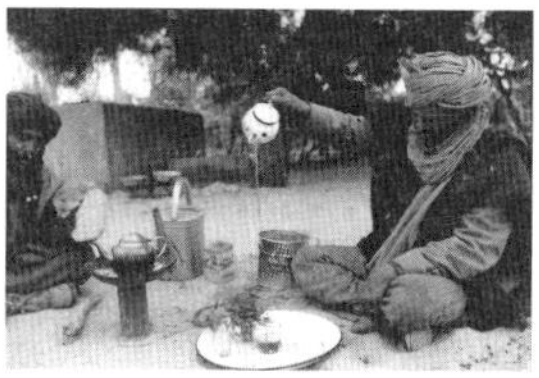

to 45°C, and the beans must be aerated by regular mixing: a great deal of carbon dioxide is released. The beans are then put out to dry on the ground or on wattles. Of these three exotic commodities, the stages through which the cocoa bean passes, from agricultural site to chocolate factory are without doubt the most numerous; but, before roasting and shelling, the fermentation is what establishes most of its organoleptic characteristics.

Wine & Cigars

Being a leaf, tea is in some ways closer to tobacco, although it is never far from wine in its aromatic complexity: the fermentations in both cases play a crucial part in the resulting flavors.

Tobacco from a great cigar develops its scent through the alternation of drying, fermentation and rehydration. There are three successive fermentations, the first lasting three weeks and the last in a barrel more than a year, before the drying, stripping and rolling. Although the enzymatic activity on the much larger tobacco leaf is different from that in tea, the general process remains similar, especially if one compares it to the treatment, without fermentation, of the coca leaf, which is simply dried, or the *qat* leaf, which is chewed when still fresh.

Wine is the juice of freshly pressed grapes which has fermented under the action of yeasts—*saccharomyces cerevisiae,* var. *ellipsoideus*—which proliferate spontaneously in the natural surroundings of the crushed grapes. Immediately after the wine-harvest, the grape is carefully transported from the vineyard to the *chai*, where it is de-stalked, the berries crushed, and the juice is squeezed out in a press. The must (pulp, skin and juice) is poured into huge fermentation vats—wooden casks without lids, vats made of glazed cement, or enormous stainless steel cisterns. The fermentation will last a few days or several weeks, according to the type of wine, light or full-bodied. All kinds of corrections are practiced, according to the different climates, to achieve the right balance between alcoholic content and acidity. According to the locality, all kinds of exceptions are made: only partial destalking in Burgundy, total in Bordeaux; no pressing in the Beaujolais. In the case of red wines, the skins must remain submerged so that the coloring element, the tannin and the bouquet can be absorbed into the liquid. This head does in fact rise to the top, forced up by the carbon dioxide released by the yeasts. When the wine has been drawn off and separated from the skins, these are pressed. In the case of white wine, which can come from black or white grapes, the must of skins and stalks is separated out before the fermentation, gathered by decanting, sometimes by clarification, or by centrifugal force for ordinary wines. During the pre-fermentation cold soaking, the skins are left for a few hours in contact with the must to extract more aroma from it. Manufactured like white wine, rosé wine takes on its color from a short fermentation with the skins, or, after fermentation, by the squashing

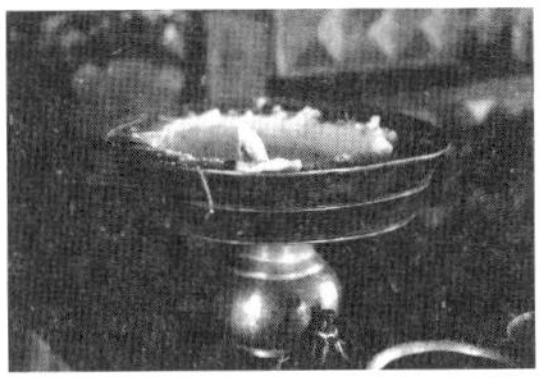

of the grapes, which are left to soak. The fermentation of the wine is first of all alcoholic, through the enzymes converting the sugars (glucose and fructose). The length of time and temperature, closely balanced with one another, are the parameters by which the wine-grower can control the process, avoiding an overheating of the must which would produce a "cooked" wine or would kill the yeasts before the complete transformation of the hexoses. The oxidation, which is necessary for the white wines, will be prevented in the case of the reds with a little antiseptic. These bio-chemical reactions are prolonged with a malolactic fermentation, by which the astringent malic acid is transformed into lactic acid. This stage, which happens spontaneously with the arrival of spring, can nowadays be brought on with the addition of bacteria.

Ale, Rum, Whisky

Aqua vitae, brandy, was called *uisge beatha* in Ireland, where the Arab method of distilling was used for barley beer. Apart from wine, most alcoholic drinks are made from the fermenting of cereals, so that, unlike the product of the vine and sap of the earth, they begin in a bath of water. Since cereals do not contain the natural sugars of fruit, one must, in a chemical preamble, have them germinate by soaking them, thus producing the enzyme (amylase) which, by transforming starch into sugars, will allow alcoholic fermentation to take place. For an actual beer—white, lager, ale, stout, porter or bock—the germination is interrupted by the kilning, at a stage which determines the main categories of beers: pale (slow roasting at 50°C), brown (rapid roasting at 100°C) and amber, in between. The reduction to flour of the germinated grains produces malt, in which the enzyme is activated by long mashing in water. This procedure is sufficient for the making of barley beer. For ordinary beer, hops are added, which have a triple effect: they give beer its bitter flavor, they clarify it and they also have an antiseptic effect.

Highland *whisky*, Irish and American *whiskey* (straight, blended, Bourbon) are based on all kinds of grain: maize, rye, millet, sorghum, barley, wheat. Whisky, like beer, has many different origins and identities. Scotch even bears several designations in the course of its manufacture. First of all it is made with barley, which comes variously from Great Britain, America or Australia. It is sorted, stored, and put to soak in large vats. Spread out on a floor, and turned over by the malters, it germinates on the third day, dries out on the ninth, and is then turned into malt. This malt is then spread in the baking room on sheets of perforated metal, above a peat fire, which heats, dries and smokes it. After resting for two months, it is separated from the dried up roots, and is then ground in a circular mill. This pulverized material is then mashed and dissolved in four lots of hotter and hotter water: the malt turns into *wort*. The third and fourth lot of water serve as *sparge* for a last extraction. The *wort*, as it comes out of the vat, is cooled to 24oC, to allow the yeast

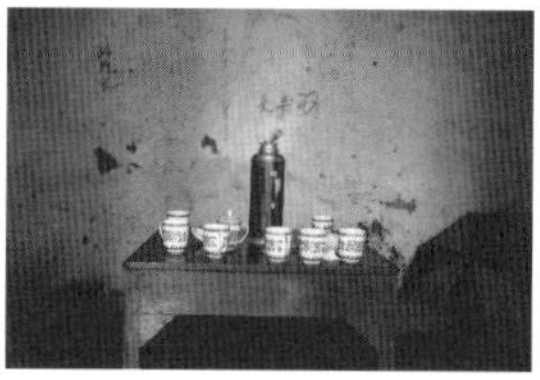

to work, and then placed in fermentation tubs—vats made of pine, larch or steel—, where the sugar is transformed into alcohol. The liquid then changes its name again: the *wort* becomes the *wash*. It is the wash, which undergoes the first distillation, flowing out into enormous copper vats, becoming low wine, so called, because it has not reached full strength. Another distillation takes into the spirit receiver vat what can finally be called whisky. This 60° proof whisky will again need to be diluted with spring water, making Scotch, from beginning to end, an alcoholic drink most dependent on water.

Rum, of all spirits, is closest to sugar, and so lies outside the great family of processes that use roasting and malting. It thus embodies the fermentation-distillation process at its purest, and best preserves the aroma of the distilled product, sugar cane. Since it doses not derive, like vodka, gin or whisky, from starch, this spirit does not need to undergo a very lengthy distillation, nor any supplementary chemical processes. Its fermentation lasts only between twelve hours to a day and a half. The addition of water—as with whisky—, flavoring—such as juniper for gin—, or tannins from the barrel—as with cognac—all remain possible but not necessary. The finest rums are made from molasses, the uncrystallized residue of sugar; country rums are made from cane juice—or *vesou*; others from sugar.

Degrees of Fermentation

The colors by which the Chinese have classed teas are determined by the color of the infusion in the cup as much as by the color of the dry product, but they are, above all, indicators of the type of treatment the tea has undergone: the yellow, red or black teas are that color because oxidation turns the leaf yellow, red or brown. This means that such discrimination by color between families implies important differences in preparation and effect. It also means that the color can provide information both on the strength of the tannin and the aromatic type of the tea. From this point of view, wine which provides a much simpler choice of color, must specify on its label its alcohol content, the percentage of pure alcohol in the volume of liquid: Italian wine provides the widest possible range, from 5.5% in a fizzy *moscato* to 15.5% in a *recciotto della Valpolicella.*

Tea offers a huge palette, from the crystalline transparency of a white tea, which can only be distinguished by the increased brilliance of the colorless water, to the deeply layered darkness of black tea. It passes through all the possibilities of yellows, greens and browns—sea greens, ambers, fawns. But, within each color, and for each particular growth, the shade of color will also specify the state of freshness, the type of harvest and whether there is a down on the leaf. As for a particular vintage of wine, where the blueness or copper-color will indicate the age of the wine, whether it is full-bodied, how much tannin it contains, how much acidity, astringency or "length." In the case of beer, the blond, amber or brown color will indicate just as

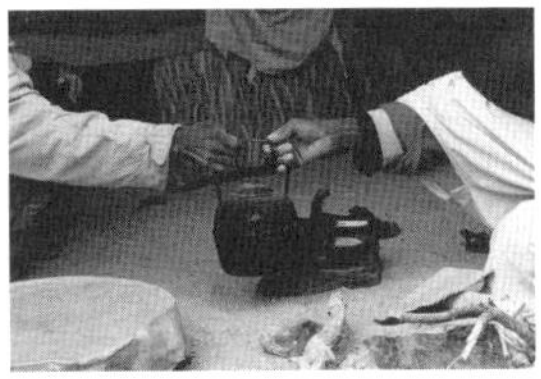

much about its alcoholic content as its bitterness, and thus provide information about the nature of the brewing and hopping process. Nevertheless, one would have to add the whole range of beers, wines and whiskies to approach the chromatic scale of tea: the lightest teas are paler than the palest champagnes, whilst the most post-fermented are as dark as the darkest port or Irish stout.

There is a tendency in the story of spirits—carried out by gin, vodka and *arrack*—, which is to bring together alcohol and alchemy—etymological kins—in the process of distillation. Vodka, originally from Poland or Russia, fashionable on the West Coast of America after the war retains no trace of its base material—potatoes or cereals—after its extreme vaporization: no color, no smell, no taste. Dutch gin (*jenever* or *geneva*), British gin (*hollands* or *schiedam)* and American gin (*London dry*) permute names but the basic ingredients—barley, hops, juniper berries—are no longer primary but secondary, no longer the base for extraction, but simple aromatic supplements. These spirits, for a long time manufactured in Anglo-Saxon kitchens with devastating consequences because of poisonous residues, embody the progress of distillation, double distillation and rectification: the achievement of the simultaneous volatilization of all constituents. In this closed-circuit chemical process, the production of gin consists of simply adding essential oils to neutral, colorless and insipid alcohol: the distillation takes place with already distilled material. Hence, no trace of past times or promise of a time to come: a rectified spirit cannot age, as it does not contain any amyl alcohol. From Egypt to Greece, the water of fire-water is a sweat or a juice (from the Arabic *arrack, arraki, raki*), which varies in versions and ingredients while the name endures: distillations of the fermented sap of the palm tree, of the essence of rice, barley, dates or grapes. Each time, alcohol as crystal-clear as water, which alone can cloud its transparency.

Limits of Preservation

No doubt because of all exotic products it was the most difficult to preserve, since it needed to be protected against humidity and heat, and could rapidly spoil, tea, as it was actually drank in China and Japan, only became known outside these countries very late. In one the most heroic episodes in the history of shipping, the famous races between the tea clippers took sailing by wind to the limits of speed, before the coming of the steamships; the clippers also broke the normal rules of commercial freight, by being built in light and streamlined form, unlike the heavy big-bellied Indiamen demanded by the tonnage laws. Before this, Chinese and Japanese tea could only reach Europe in damaged, even ruined, condition. To a certain extent, when it is possible to access a large selection of exceptional growths in rare places, such as the Maison des Trois Thés in Paris, one can even state that tea is the one drink which still remains to be discovered.

Fermentation can take place on its own, allowing the preservation of a product,

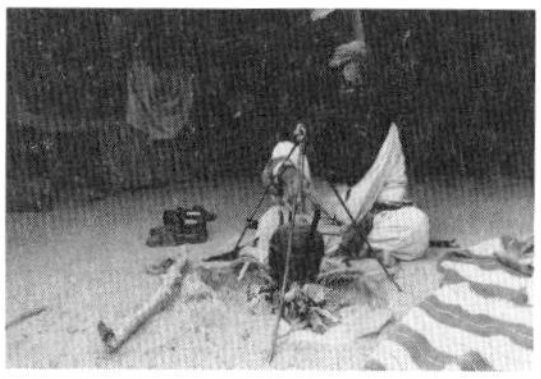

particularly a vegetable one—, all the alcohols, soy sauce, pickled vegetables—whilst adding nutritional qualities absent from the raw product, and eliminating toxic substances. Before Nicolas Appert's discovery of sterilization in the nineteenth century, which destroyed micro-organisms through heat, and before the twentieth century development of the deep-freezing process, which inactivates them through cold, lacto-fermentation was one of the most ancient methods of preservation, and one which, unlike more recent inventions, did not destroy vitamins or spoil flavor. If the transformation of sugar into alcohol allows the fruit to remain in the volatile aroma liberated by the liquid when it is drawn off, one must prevent the wine from drying, or the fruit would disappear, leaving a sour after-taste. In the development of beer, on the contrary, the drying time—in the kiln—is a crucial stage, as it is for all barley-based alcohols, in that it halts the germination of the grain in the water, and allows the formation of malt, the yeast producing the subsequent transformation into alcohol. In this sense, the drying process, and indeed the peat baking of whisky, is an interlude between soaking and fermentation. The treatment of tea is the combination of these two fundamental operations—fermentation and drying—, often used together and each leading to preservation: salted meat—sausages and hams—undergoes an enzymatic transformation during the curing process. In the case of tea, these two operations remain independent, but alternate and correlate with each other. The withering process is the decisive stage, during which the leaf simultaneously begins to lose its humidity and slightly oxidize; this happens precisely because the natural desiccation, by breaking up the epithelium, facilitates the activity of the enzyme. This drying process in the treatment of tea brings the fermentation to an end and fixes the essential oils, which have been expressed by the handling of the leaf: it determines aroma, taste and color. But drying is the goal, the final aim, of this progressive reduction in the water level of the leaves which motivates the entire process of tea after it has been harvested.

Inactivated, Steamed, Dried

"By its presence, the kitchen fire avoids total disconnection; it unites the sun with the earth and saves man from the rotten world which would be his lot if the sun really disappeared; but its presence is also something that has been interposed, which is the same as saying that it obviates the risk of total conjunction, which would result in a burned-up world." (Levi-Strauss) Cooking holds the balance between the consumed and the putrid, the fire that destroys, and the absence of fire, which also destroys. In the course of the treatment of tea, fire does not simply prevent putrefaction, but also determines the process of fermentation. Indeed, the oxidation of the leaf causes it to heat up, just as alcoholic fermentation raises the temperature of the must; each time, the *chashi* and the wine-maker must be careful to maintain the temperature between 18 and 20°C for tea, and 21 and 28°C for wine,

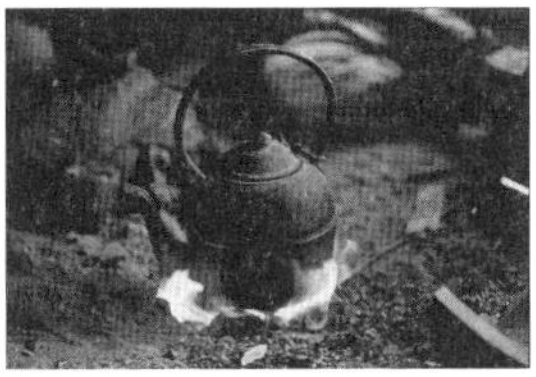

the respective temperature zones in which the micro-organisms flourish. The enzymatic metabolism is sustained by heat, which also has a contradictory effect on tea: it stabilizes it, enabling preservation, but also immediately blocks the course of its development. The principal types of green tea are actually classed according to the method used to block oxidation and the type of drying process (cooking pot, oven, sun).

In the case of unfermented teas—the whites, yellows or greens—, only the pre-oxidation which takes place during withering is allowed to take its course, but after that the enzyme must be prevented from doing its work: in this case the temperature must rise above 40°C, in order to destroy and not simply deactivate the thease. The Chinese language refers to "finishing" or "killing the green"—*sha qin*—, an expression used to describe the end of the shooting of a film, also an announcement of its future success. This practice appeared during the Tang dynasty, using steam (*zhen qing*), heating in a pot (*chao qing*) or on wattles (*hong qing*). One must notice too that, at this stage, the heat conductor can equally well be the copper of a cauldron, heated air or vaporized water. Water can intervene for one last time, in a process designed to eliminate it, and which has some effect on the type of tea aimed for: the extreme greenness of Japanese tea, its herbaceous, iodized nature, and its lack of any kind of roasting are caused by this method of steaming. But whether it is done by cooking in a pot or by steam, the blocking of tea is a decisive moment, when all the factors upon which the tea-grower can act are assembled: the temperature, quantity, and duration, variations in which can lead to the most different results. If the temperature is too low, the enzyme will continue its activity unabated; if it is too high, the aroma will be affected by a burnt taste; if the bulk of leaves is too great, a sort of stewing process will take place, in which the leaves will become difficult to shape because the water has not sufficiently evaporated. The halting of the fermentation is thus not simply a matter of eliminating the enzyme, it also has a decisive effect on the quality of the tea: by further reducing the humidity of the leaf, eliminating undesirable odors, and increasing its suppleness. This work, which was traditionally done by hand with a paddle, is nowadays performed by mechanical drums which pass from a slow rotation at high temperature to a faster one at a lower temperature, the whole process not lasting more than nine minutes.

After the final drying, the residual humidity should be lower than 3%, in order to stabilize the tea and allow it to undergo handling and transportation. This operation is generally carried out by a progressive raising of the temperature from 52° to 98°C, for about twenty minutes, on wattles placed over a fire or in an electric oven. If it is too low, the tea will become moldy, if too high it will lose its aroma. Some teas are dried in the sun (*shai qing*): these are destined for nearby regions, for aborigines or nomads, and are compressed into bricks or cakes. In the industrial arena,

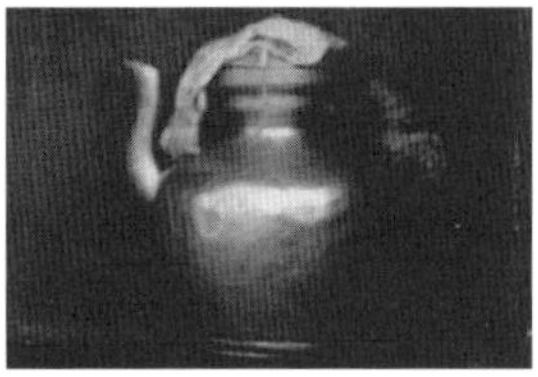

different types of drying machines have been perfected, and these can take loads of 150 to 400 kilograms per hour: they are hot feed, two stage dryers, and dryers with fluidized beds.

Roasted, Grilled, Smoked

"Smoking produces foodstuffs which resist putrefaction longer than those cooked in any other way." When Levi-Strauss is trying to define what comes between roasting and boiling (as in the raw-rotting-cooked sequence), he suggests smoking "which, like roasting, is an operation which does not require a medium (no recipient and no water), but which, unlike roasting, and more like boiling, requires slow cooking, and so is simultaneously deep and steady." One must pay attention to what is always active in the elementary transformations of food. Thus, cultural development can be measured by attitudes to food: savage (raw), barbarian (grilling, roasting), and civilized (stewing, boiling, simmering); one could also index cultures according to their relationship with tea; Japanese tea (unfermented), Chinese tea (unfermented, semi-fermented, post-fermented), English tea (fermented). Such or such a fashion can spread throughout the world, for example as recounted by this traveler who, crossing the Gobi desert in the nineteenth century, encountered smoked food everywhere: "I have one other observation to make: it is impossible to eat fresh mutton that has been grilled or roasted over yak dung; it takes on an unbearably nasty taste. Food that has been boiled over this type of fuel, the only sort available in the desert, is just about possible." (Catherine-Fanny de Bourboulon)

"Roasting provides coffee with all its properties, the dark color of the infusion, its taste and its aroma. And green coffee, powdered, extracted or boiled, has only ever been used in Russia... in certain cases to replace quinine." (*Grande Encyclopédie*, 1890) The reason why *bun* is only consumed in regions close to Abyssinia, and coffee only began to spread from the Middle East to Europe in the seventeenth century, is that it is completely defined by the roasting process. The role of the drying and fermentation processes undergone by the coffee bean after harvesting is only to remove the pericarp; it is no more than a physical preparation, which is nowadays carried out by machines, making the processes redundant. Roasting, on the contrary, is the fundamental moment in the transformation of coffee, the beginning of its existence, as baking is for bread, or pressing for oil. In the case of cocoa, heat intervenes in different ways throughout a long process, rather as with tea—fermentation, drying, grinding, pressing, shelling, the Dutch process; it is nonetheless the case that the roasting stage remains crucial as it has three important effects: it reduces the level of humidity, evaporates undesirable odors, such as that of acetic acid, and causes the formation of aromatic elements or pyrazines, through reactions of the Maillard type. Yerba mate also achieves the development of its charac-

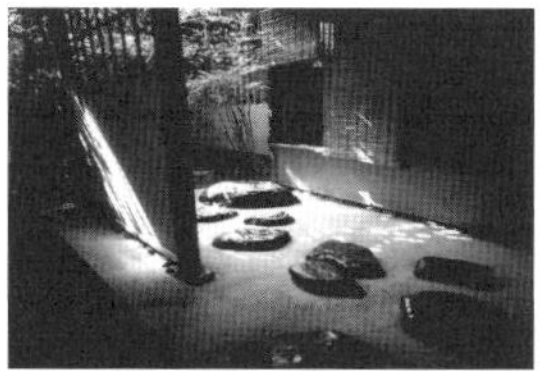

teristic flavor through being put through a large fire to wilt it, and then, before pulverization and ripening in the *perchel,* being roasted in a scaffolding built on the same place as the harvest—the *barbacao*: this adds a grilled taste which softens the bitterness with the sweetness of licorice. But in neither coffee, cocoa nor *yerba* will one find such infinitely varied uses of fire as one does in the making of tea.

Although the drying process marks the end of the long desiccation of tea, begun with the withering, it is not necessarily the final heat to which the leaf is submitted. One might, on this point, suggest that tea, in its *time*, is the constantly postponed experience of heat. Industrial procedures, under the pretext of bringing the process under control, have extended the use of heat to every stage. During the withering stage, in bins or chambers with netted or perforated floors—withering troughs -, the leaves are subjected to pulsating air or sucked up by reversible ventilators equipped with heaters to correct the level of ambient humidity. During fermentation the leaf heats up if it has not already, before this, been blocked by steam or in the cooking pot; the drying process fixes it again through heat. The manufacture of tea is its repeated exposure to heat with such various results, though obtained from similar sources: cooking pot, wattle, drums placed over grates, and, nowadays, every kind of open or closed oven. It is probably the similarity of all these procedures that for a long time allowed the distinctive stages to be confused with one another, or subsumed under the general category of roasting. However, certain Chinese teas, in order to bring out their excellence or, on the contrary, to hide their mediocrity, undergo further heating: the roasting of certain Wulongs, such as the Tie Guan Yin, in order to release certain aromas; the smoking of some red teas, such as the Zhen Shan Xiao Zhong; the grilling of some green ones, such as the Japanese Hojicha. In the case of tea, therefore, there is a true roasting, which is neither a stage of fermentation, nor of drying, but a type of heating on wattles, which takes place after the end of the treatment, and sometimes even several months or years after its manufacture, in order to bring out, at the moment of infusion, some hidden characteristic, enclosed in an exceptional growth. There is also a grilling process, which is applied, just before drinking, to rough grade tea—such as the Bancha, made with aged leaves—, in order to obtain a refreshing tea, by giving it a roast taste which, in a certain rarer type from Kyoto, can even approach a strong scent of cold tobacco. Finally, there is smoking, which people in the West insist on believing is the main characteristic of Chinese tea, and which is industrially produced in China purely for export. The too notorious Lapsang Souchong is said to be the result of the unfortunate action of a planter who, wanting to save his crop from an impending war, tried to accelerate the drying process with a fire made of pine branches, and who then passed off the resulting smoky taste to credulous English merchants as a specialty of his village. The use of barrels with scorched staves on the inside for whisky and

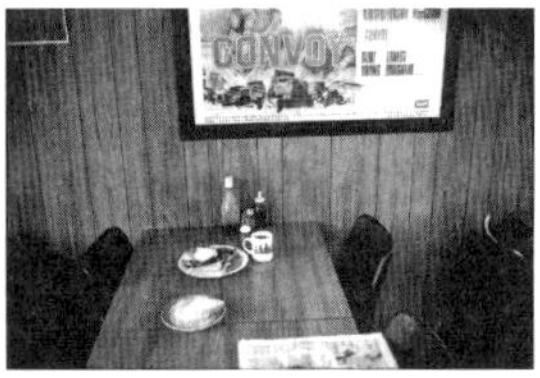

rum has its origin in a similar story: the accidental burning of warehouses in India in which the rum was aged. One might observe that these stories sum up, between China and India, between tea and rum, between subject and object, the story of England's dependence on the products, necessarily imported, on which its empire was founded. Similarly the French habit of burning the staves in order to bend them cannot just be explained by the occasion which caused it, but by a technical reason: the more the oak is burnt, the more empyreumatical aromas are released by the cask. Therefore this accident (accidents often being at the origin of inventions) of Lapsang Souchong is no fluke: it ties the relations between East and West, founded on a sustained misunderstanding about the taste of smoke. That tea, beneath food, should retain the ancient use of smoke—hemp, poppy, tobacco— that one "drinks," and that tea, the produce of the Middle Empire which so long evaded the British Empire, should still be defined by the sensation of an evaporated matter, makes for a perfect metaphor.

THE WORK OF TEA

The Method Used

In the early 1840s, Robert Fortune was one of the very first to describe the general procedure of tea manufacture: "The mode of gathering and preparing the leaves of the tea plants is extremely simple. We have been so long accustomed to magnify and mystify everything relating to the Chinese, that, in all their arts and manufactures, we expect to find some peculiar and out of the way practice, when the fact is, that many operations in China are more simple in their character than in most other parts of the world. To rightly understand the process of rolling and drying the leaves, which I am about to describe, it must be borne in mind that the grand object is to expel the moisture, and at the same time to retain as much as possible of the aromatic and other desirable secretions of the species. [...] The drying pans and furnaces in these places are very simply constructed. The pans, which are of iron, and are made as thin as possible, are round and shallow, and, in fact, are the same, or nearly the same, which the natives have in general use for cooking their rice. [...] When the fire is applied, the upper part of these basins, which is formed of *chunam* [lime], gets heated as well as the iron pan, though in a less degree. The drying pans, thus formed, being low in front, and rising very gradually at the sides and back, the person, whose duty it is to attend to the drying of the leaves, can readily manage them, and scatter them about over the back of the basin. [...] The heat immediately affects the leaves. This part of the process lasts about five minutes, in which time the leaves lose their crispness, and become soft and pliable. They are then taken out of the pans, and thrown upon a table, the upper part of which is made of split pieces

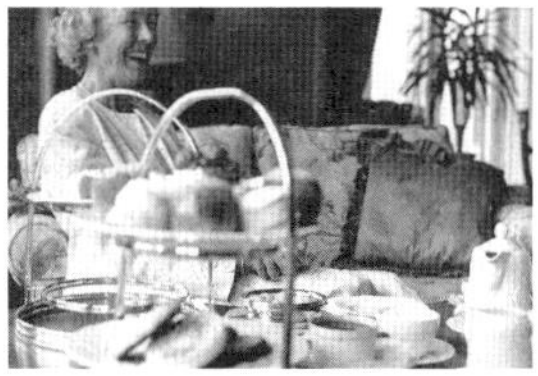

of bamboo. [. . .] Three or four persons now surround the table, and the heap of tea leaves is divided into as many parcels, each individual taking as many as he can hold in his hands, and the rolling process commences. I cannot give a better idea of this operation than by comparing it to a baker working and rolling his dough. Both hands are used in the very same way; the object being to express the sap and moisture, and at the same time to twist the leaves. Two or three times during the operation the little bundles of rolled leaves are held up and shaken out upon the table, and are then again taken up and pressed and rolled as before. This part of the process also lasts about five minutes, during which time a large portion of green juice has been expressed, and may be seen finding its way down between the interstices of the bamboos. The leaves being now pressed, twisted, and curled, do not occupy a quarter of the space that they did before the operation. When the rolling process is completed the leaves are removed from the table and shaken out for the last time, thinly, upon a large sort of screen, also made out of split pieces of bamboo, and are exposed to the action of the air. [. . .] Having in this manner got rid of a certain part of the superfluous moisture, the leaves, which are now soft and pliant, are again thrown into the drying pans, and the second heating commences. [. . .] The leaves, as they part with their moisture, twist and curl, and consequently take up much less room than they do at first, and mix together more readily. The tea leaves being now rather too hot for the hand, a small and neat brush, made of bamboo, is used instead of the fingers for stirring them up from the bottom of the pan. By this means the leaves are scattered about on the smooth *chunam*-work, which forms the back of the drying pan, and, as they roll down on this heated inclined plane they dry slowly, and twist at the same time. [. . .]

The tea prepared in the manner that I have just described is greenish in color, and of a most excellent quality. It is called by the Chinese in the province of Chekiang, *tsaou-tsing*, or the tea which is dried in the pan, to distinguish it from the *hong-tsing*, or that kind which is dried in flat bamboo baskets over a slow fire of charcoal. [. . .] After the drying is completed the tea is picked, sifted, divided into different kinds and qualities, and prepared for packing." (*Three Years' Wanderings in the Northern Provinces of China*, 1847)

Form, Work, Hand

During its fermentation, tea undergoes all kinds of manipulations, times of rest, and varying sequences of thermal and mechanical activity. The most complex teas were not in fact developed until relatively late: the earliest reference to Wulong locates it at Wu Yi, in Fujian, in the early eighteenth century, while yellow and smoked red teas could only have appeared in the seventeenth and eighteenth centuries, when the techniques of steaming and smoking replaced what were then the habitual treatments of tea. Indeed, the sort of stewed fermentation used to obtain

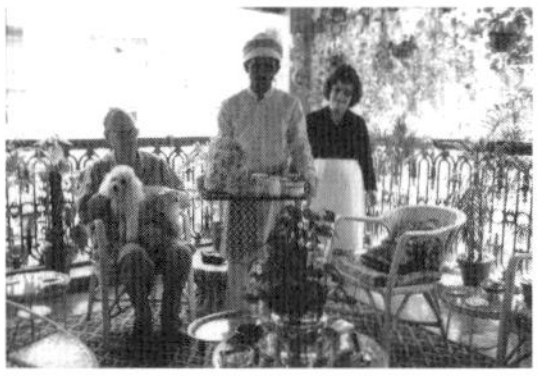

yellow tea restarts oxidation without an enzyme after having stopped its fermentation as in the case of a green tea; the procedure is paradoxical, as it inverts current logic, or combines two alternative methods. In the case of the thousands of Wulongs, the main stages of manufacture—withering, fermentation, blocking of fermentation, working, shaping, drying—will be combined in a great variety of ways according to the vintage, *chashi*, and time. Each stage can be performed, repeated, or omitted; it can be progressive, reversed, or operated in alternation with the previous or the next stage. To grasp the range of these variable techniques is to enter an unknown world, one that makes specialist Western books on tea seem crude and clumsy approximations.

On the one side, there are the assessments of the *chashi*, who observes and smells, and on the other, the actions of the tea workers: in the heated vat of green tea, their movements are strangely like those of a potter working clay or a baker kneading dough. Here again, the variations are endless and reflect regional differences. For the Wulong teas, this stage is physical: rotation in a bamboo drum, transferal, spreading, piling. Its mechanization, by machines with startling movements, joints and extremities, apart from providing consistency and yield, enables the treatment to be continuously monitored, avoiding uncontrolled withering of the crop.

In the course of the manipulation—the stage of *rou nian*—the tea produces its essential oils—the effects of oxidation-fermentation—that are at the same time exuded and fixed to the downy leaf. So this involves work to and by the leaf: the hand is there to work the tea, knead, fold, roll it; but the plant also works, on its cells, through its chemical reactions, and the lamina works morphologically, as is said of wood: its form, its color, its texture all undergo extensive metamorphosis. In a sense, all the other points of concern are the framework to the manual operation: temperature control, permanent protection against exterior odors, resting periods. The working of the plant modifies its biological structure, shapes its future, gives it a new appearance. That tea has always been linked to the hand, as to the tradition of the country that invented it, is because throughout—from picking to brewing—the hand happens to be its most necessary tool: able, in a single action, to select, pinch, and sever its tiny picking, with a nail kept long and sharp to prevent strange smells; and to perform the very complex and varied movements of *rou nian*, as well as the very measured ones of the preparation of *gongfucha*.

Formed, Fashioned, Rolled

If the Chinese prefer to "kill the green" in a pan rather than with steam, whereas the latter has become the main method in Japan, it is probably to allow a more varied working of the tea: the hand can continue to operate in the hot copper bowl, which would be impossible in burning steam. The scents and flavors can thus be modulated, by eye and nose, according to the degree of depth reached in the plant matter

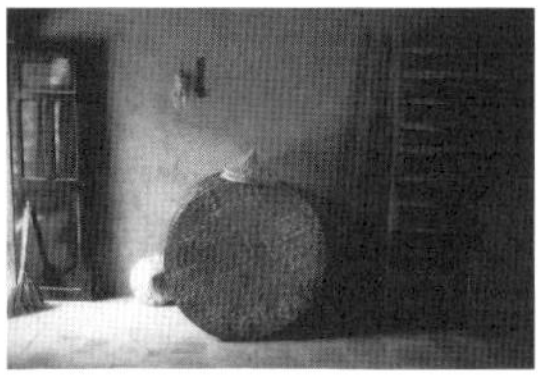

and also to the manner of impregnation that deposits, encrusts, or folds in the essential juices on the leaf. These possibilities show in the extremely varied forms, mostly unknown outside China, that tea displays when loose.

So, depending on the manner of work in the pan, one obtains three main types of tea: long, ball-shaped, or special. The first two are everyday qualities, usually and henceforth machine-made, while the third includes all the great vintages (Bi Luo Chun, Long Jing, Tai Ping Hou Kui). Within the three classes, there are different types of shape, sometimes forming part of the name of a vintage: sword blade, bird beak, dragon fly, and frog, which add to the ranks of silver needles, white peony, and jade spiral, specifying not only the appearance but also the color of the leaf. A similar diversity is found in the dry tea leaves and arises not only from differences in the stool, type of picking, season, or degree of fermentation, but also from the actions performed at this stage. From the long and narrow, alternate leaves of the Tai Ping Hou Kui, which even before it is rehydrated retains the appearance it has on the tree, to the symmetrical lance-shaped and flattened leaflet of a Long Jing, then to a very tightly rolled Zhu Cha, all variations seem to be allowed. They let one deduce the movements that made them possible: from the hand that mixes without crushing, to the hand that presses again and again in a regular kneading. Even the foot can play a part in the rolling of a Wulong: while the leaves are still hot, they are wrapped tightly in gauze and rolled underfoot, applying pressure from the leg. This has to be alternated with times when the leaves are spread out, left to rest, and cool. The shapes obtained at this stage are not the result of a figurative imagination, but the morphological state that accompanies the desired aroma and taste: more delicate or sharper; rounder or longer; with or without down.

If, in the sphere of Britannics, simplification and confusion have reigned over the stages between withering and drying, this is because no general rule of procedure applies to all green, blue-green, and red teas, even within a single family. For instance, there is no systematic order that will govern the times of work, rest, and shaping. Just as the West often assimilates all applications of heat to roasting, all the operations possible at this stage are counted as rolling. This confusion is no accident: it stems from the quasi-unique treatment inflicted on tea in the Anglo-Indian manner. This is how a technical book describes it: "Rolling consists of twisting and breaking the leaves to extract the juice, prepare them for fermentation and turn them into particles that correspond to the type wanted by the tea dealer." And indeed, the leaf, once it has undergone this astonishing rolling, is reduced to broken bits whatever the machine used: rollers, designed to produce orthodox grades in the form of pellets; the Legg Cutter, which compresses the leaves and cuts them into thin strips, for "teas of good color with strength but little quality"; the Rotorvane, which twists the leaves by friction and cuts them for average teas; the CTC, the most

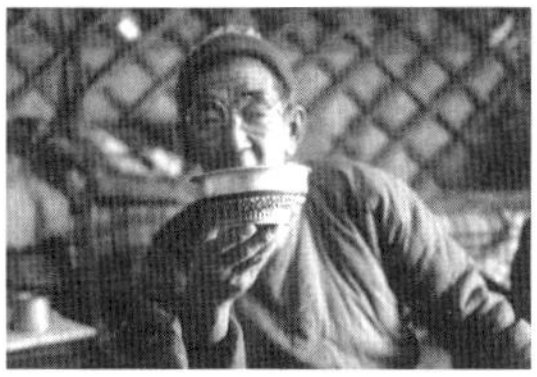

commonly used, although it gives only "low grades with very bright red liquor"; the LTP (Lawrie Tea Processor), which reduces the leaves to very small particles.

Compressed The oldest preparations of tea in China involved softening the leaves in steam, crushing them, and making them into a cake, which could be kept. For consumption, the tea was pulverized, then thrown into boiling water, and cooked alone or with cereals and spices. This treatment of tea is still found among many aboriginal and nomadic tribes in Southeast Asia and is the longest established of the Chinese methods, being applied also, there and elsewhere, with other goods: dry sheets or cakes of seaweed, dried cakes of dung used as fuel, sugar loaf. The practice goes back to the elementary techniques of food preparation by humans.

This in fact brings in all those methods—in which symbolic protocol, technical dictates, and reasons of toxicity/nutrition are indissociable—by which a thing taken from nature is turned into a food, by which a drupe, grain, or leaf is made edible. This involves a domestication that now embraces for us the whole chain from agriculture and horticulture to *haute cuisine* and "life-style," and including all the farming, food, and pharmaceutical industries, as well as the drug traffic. But more specifically, it relates to techniques that still linger among the aborigines of various continents (Australasia, the South Sea Islands, the American Indians): a phase between the Paleolithic and Neolithic, where, before food was even cultivated or cooked, it had to be made consumable, edible, durable. So the procedure consists of eliminating or transforming substances in the wild plants, simply because they are unpleasant (astringent, bitter, acid), indigestible or irritating (lignin, cellulose, hair), or even poisonous. These procedures involve separation (hulling, peeling, cutting, grating, crushing, sieving), and/or water (washing, sedimentation, hydrolyzation) and/or heat (grilling, roasting, cooking in an oven, over hot stones, over cinders, stewing, boiling in water, frying, fermenting, drying, smoking, preserving). And the recipes result in soups, porridges, purées, pastes, cakes, pancakes.

Between the legend of Shennong and the first treatise on tea, by Lu Yu, the commonest mode of production was compressed tea (*Jin ya cha*) in its different forms: bricks, cakes, balls, mushrooms, birds' nests, and plaits. And the commonest mode of preparation was to crush it into a more or less coarse powder, and cook it in soup, adding ingredients such as orange peel, ginger, and other spices. The increasingly heavy duty imposed on tea, from the time of the Tang and the Song, no doubt contributed to the transformation of this mode of treatment, which involves much time, difficulty, and labor, and which from a modern perspective has mainly disadvantages: the pressing into cakes and the immersion of the leaves in boiling water contributed to the loss of what is, for us, the point of tea: its aromas and phenolic components. Loose tea (*san cha*) and the methods of green tea began to make an

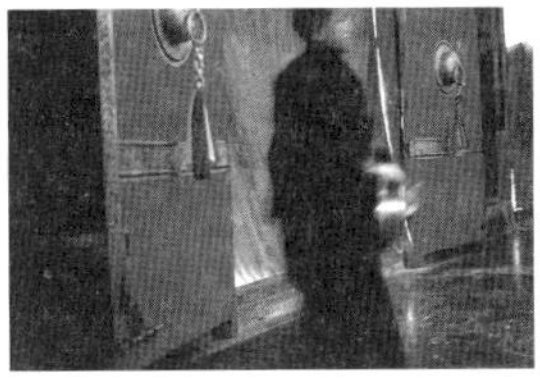

appearance at this period. But it was the first emperor of the Ming dynasty, Zhu Yuan Zhang, who was to give the order to stop the cakes, and allow the manufacture of loose tea, which had started tentatively under the Tang. Similarly, steamed green tea was slowly replaced by tea inactivated in a pan. The new varieties and new colors of tea would emerge with the less limited techniques.

One perhaps needs to consider how the long history of tea—whence it becomes an art—lies in the long transition from compressed tea to the multitude of teas of very varied colors and appearances. This is the history of the opening of a world and the infinite divisibility of its qualities, nuances, and previously unknown subtleties. The beauty of a Bi Luo Chun, of a "rock tea," or a real Pu Er, is that ability to conjure up, in the loose state, but also in the infusion and rehydrated leaf, a landscape of features that vanished long ago at the hands of a too crude technique, which abused the leaf from the moment of its compression into a cake to the moment when it was broken down, for consumption. One has to consider how it came about that only China—Taiwan, and to a lesser extent Japan—kept such a way of tea open, and paradoxically from the Ming period, which was the moment when tea spread beyond the Middle Kingdom. The overland distribution of tea, across Mongolia and Azerbaijan towards Moscow, would in fact take the form of bricks of compressed tea, even up to recent times. Whereas the maritime traffic of the Dutch, Portuguese, and English, because of the need for commercial categories, was to reduce the diversity of teas, soon rationalized to the one, red, Indian tea.

A further point of note is that tea was, in the beginning, made by a similar process to coffee and cocoa, in that the green leaf, after its treatment and preparation, ended up as a decoction of blackish powder. Here, the histories of coffee and cocoa diverge fundamentally from that of tea, because the former drinks consisted not of a gradual vegetal dispersal but of the grinding of their substance, in an increasingly inexorable and thorough manner. The history of cocoa is exemplary in that the bean, totally uneatable in its natural state, has to undergo a process whose logic is carried further with each technical advance. This logic is a machine logic: it goes from *molinollos*—the chocolate mills with toothed grinding mechanisms of Nicolas Blegny's engravings in *Le bon usage du thé, du caphé et du chocolat*—to Marcel Duchamp's *Broyeuse de chocolat*. The proofs are the separation of the manufacture of cocoa from that of chocolate, as well as a procedure that involves several machines, even in the case of the most artisanal great vintages, and a history fully integrated to the industrial advances of the late eighteenth century onwards. The year 1746 saw the first industrial venture, Chocolats et thés Pelletier et Cie; in 1778, came the first hydraulic machine for grinding, mixing, and agglomerating; in 1825, Antoine Brutus Ménier built the first chocolate factory equipped with machines, at Noisel-sur-Marne.

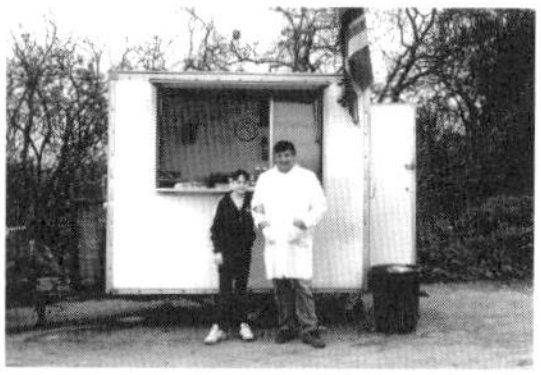

The manufacture of chocolate requires a large infrastructure to cater for storage (in silos where poison gas or natural insecticide can be injected: methyl bromide, pyrethrin); sorting (ventilation, brushing, sieving, extraction of metallic particles); roasting; hulling (removal of kernel shells); the Dutch process (invented in 1828 by Van Houten to extract the cocoa fat, by solubilizing the cocoa butter on one side and the cocoa powder on the other, the use of sodium or potassium carbonate to eliminate residual flavors of acetic acid, attack the tannins and destroy the yellow pigments); blending of cocoas (African or Brazilian cocoas serve as a base, with the addition of *criollos, trinitarios,* and *arriba* from Ecuador); grinding (to break down the structure of the grain in a centrifugal mill linked to four grinding cylinders with heating of fifty to seventy degrees Celsius, to obtain the pure cocoa paste—"mass" or "liquor"); blending of ingredients (additions to the paste, of icing sugar, a small amount of cocoa butter and, in the case of milk chocolate, powdered milk; work done in kneading machines in a partial vacuum to give a homogeneous mix and the requisite plasticity); refining (to obtain a totally homogeneous mix in grinders with cylinders that reduce the size of the solid particles to less than 25 or 30 thousandths of a millimeter); steaming (the chocolate paste, flaky because of the solidifying butter content and lamination, is maintained in heated vats where it matures for twenty-four hours or more, becoming softer and suppler); conching (to eliminate all residual traces of moisture and disagreeable smells, to give the paste a creamy, smooth consistency, using numerous machines that turn and throw the paste onto the sides; to cause maximum friction between the particles and those of sugar: caramelization of lactose, polishing of sugar crystals; addition of soya lecithin to cover the sugar particles, then the rest of the cocoa butter); tempering (to stabilize the continuing emulsion of small grains of dry matter in suspension in the fat matter, which do not crystallize identically at the same temperature); molding (to fill molds mechanically while controlling temperature, then pass through cooling tunnel to contract and solidify the chocolate, which is then channeled into wrapping machines).

Piled, Molded, Tied

Tea, in the beginning, was piled, packed, and compressed. Before attaining all the shapes of what is in effect a plant representation—a way of recreating nature, by the work of the hand, an art that finds its culmination in green and Wulong teas—the leaf, reduced to paste, was molded, given a shape; the tea was "in-formed." It is no accident that at the same time as the industrialization of taste reduces its qualities, tea is delivered up, in a visual equivalent to its supplementary flavoring, to "*chinoiseries*" that are presented by prestigious establishments as traditional rarities.

Tea can, for instance, be kept in the mold into which it is packed, which serves as a

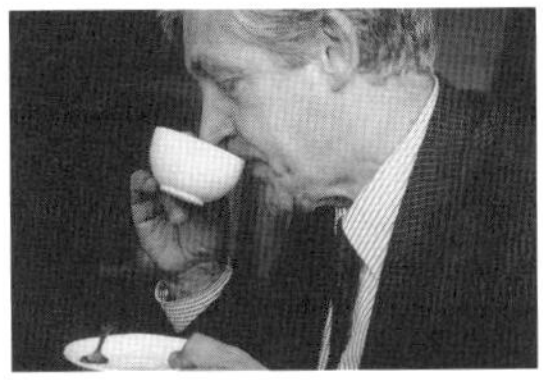

case and also an aromatic complement. An example is Yiou Mi Cha, a product of the regions of Miaoli and Xinzhu in the island of Taiwan; the ethnic Kejia remove the flesh of a very bitter wild citrus, *fangan*, mix it with tea and a little licorice and lemon, and return it to the shell. The preparation is steamed, tied with a little cord, and put to dry in the sun. This traditional manufacture lasts forty-five days. Zhu Tong Cha also is the work of ethnic groups, the Lahu and Tai, who live in Xishuangbanna, a region in the province of Yunnan, on the frontier with Laos and Burma. The preparation, going back two hundred years, makes use of a base material of Asia, bamboo, which is filled with fresh tea leaves that have been heated in the steam of glutinous rice. This softened tea, lengthily flavored, is dried in its case on the heat of the embers for several days. But side by side with these local specialties, where the tea is as if set, there is a multitude of teas whose leaves and buds are tied in a great variety of shapes. Long Xu Cha, which appeared in 1717 in the province of Fujian, is one of the rare ancient "shaped" teas; most of the other shapes in this category are very recent. These teas are fashioned into all kinds of knots, made from the leaf itself or using thread, to obtain balls, pompons, bundles, acorns, corollas, nails, bow ties, buckles. These little structures are held tightly in check in the dry state, which conceals the new forms or figures they will reveal when put into the hot water of the infusion. New spectacle, new pompons, new corollas. This is a device akin to the paper flowers that open in a glass of water, or even the pictures discovered at the bottom of the cup of rice wine; it is the expertise of Chinese floral art, *hua yi*. Most of these teas are scented with jasmine essences, true to the principle of metaphorical supplementation on which they are based, and which also disguises the excessive manipulation that the leaves have had to suffer in their meticulous shaping.

Aromatic Synthesis

While certain aromas are released spontaneously, to ensure reproduction or provide the defenses of the living thing, others will be so only after a transformation that affects their substance. The distinctive aroma of bitter almond is only caught by the nostril of whoever bites into it, at which point a cyanogenetic glucid and an enzyme (emulsin), contained in separate cells, are brought into contact, provoking a release of the prosthetic cyanic group.

Similarly, the pod of the vanilla plant on its tendril has no smell before it ripens. It then dries, turns black, and gains a scent; next it splits, spills its contents, and is no longer a saleable commodity. So it is necessary to pick it before it ripens, heat-treat it, and induce chemical reactions that involve a glucoside, a hydrolyzing enzyme and an oxidase. The enzyme breaks down the glucoside, releasing coniferylic acid, which is transformed in its turn by the oxidase in vanillin. This chain reaction between three substances is anticipated and deferred by picking, which controls its

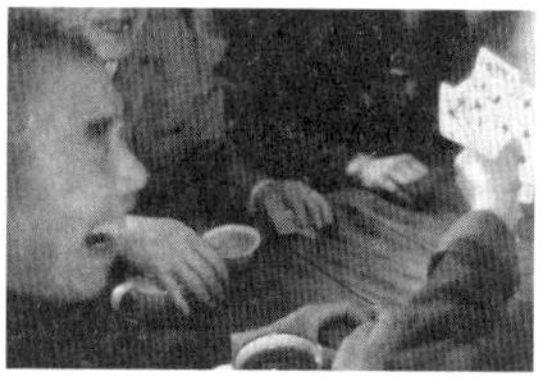

progress. We know that transplanting this orchid to the Antilles and Réunion, because of a similar division of functions, for a long time made its reproduction uncertain.

Various plant stimulants—wine, tobacco, cocoa—develop the character of their tastes and scents in this way, not when they are still attached to the wood and earth that grew them, but at the moment of treatment. The stages of such treatment are diverse and complex, on a scale with the physico-chemical transformations made possible by the components of the plant, possibly supported by catalyzers, additives, or outside agents. The technical operation juggles the different ways of obtaining this effect: reinforcement, concentration, and organoleptic synthesis. From the picking of the aromatic plant, to the work it may occasion, particularly fermentation, embracing all the modes of extraction, expression, and distillation.

In this way scents are drawn from the animal, vegetable, or synthetic source. Animal essences are mainly secretions: ambergris from the sperm whale, musk from the musk deer or civet, castor from the beaver. The plant gives out its aromas from all ends, from its most diverse organs: bud (clove, orange); flower (jasmine, rose, lavender); fruit (bergamot, lemon, mandarin); seed (angelica, celery, nutmeg); rhizomes (ginger, iris); roots (angelica, valerian, vetiver); leaves or stalks (cinnamon, geranium, patchouli); wood (cedar, sandal, rosewood); bark (birch, Ceylon cinnamon); resin (tolu, cistus, myrrh); moss (oak, beech, pine). In the case of synthetic preparations, the formulae are clearly numerous: terpenetic carbides, terpenetic alcohols, sesquisterpenetic alcohols, aromatic alcohols, aldehydes, ketones, phenols, esters, nitro-compounds. Three ways of obtaining natural essences can be distinguished. The oldest and most direct method is expression, such as that of fresh fruits and zests—citrus—yielding scents of the Hesperides. A less direct method is extraction by volatile solvents—hexane—which gives either solids and then absolutes after the separation of waxes by washing in alcohol, or resinoids obtained by ketonic, alcoholic, infusion of resins or animal products, then evaporation of the solvent. The cold or hot saturation of oils or fats with scents of flowers comes in this category. (Cold saturation harnesses the power of a fat to absorb an essence: a fresh bed of flowers is laid on refined animal fats every one to three days, to obtain a pomade, which will be decanted and treated with alcohol. With hot saturation, flowers are macerated by immersion in a melted mixture of the same fats.) The last method is distillation, which uses the movement and condensation of water vapor to obtain essential oils and aromatic waters, exploiting their different densities.

The art of tea, the art of wine, the art of flowers are other practices by which people try to draw off, to outwit, to isolate aromas by associating them with other synesthetic effects. It is no coincidence, however, that a particular technical mode—that

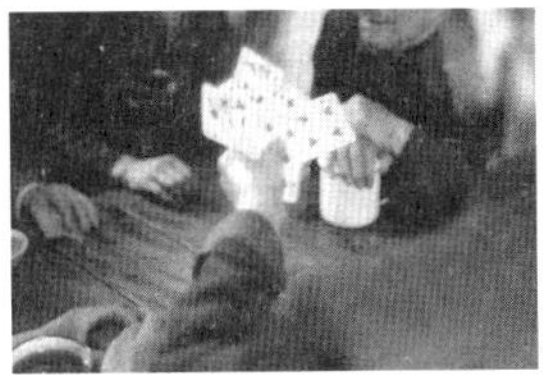

of expression, concentration, and distillation—has produced the paradox where one both separates and joins, divides in order to recombine. Bunches of flowers sprinkled with essences before being sold, alcohols rectified before being redistilled with aromatic oils, and of course the never-ending litany of odorless black teas, supplemented with the most conventional of fragrances. The same dizzying range of combinations, of which tea has been forerunner, is now applied to water ices and incense.

Harvested, Fermented, Infused

Tea is that singular journey or long labor that, in order to release all its aromas, starts with the selection of the rootstock and lasts until the moment of final preparation, covering a patient wait of at least three years, for the plant to produce buds or leaves for picking, and a treatment that brings into play manipulation, heating, oxidation, and a more or less long conservation period. A vegetable growth, it will not release its flavor until it has been first picked, then fermented, and finally infused: these are the three great stages of the synthesis of its aromas. This is the journey, in the form that an art, albeit a minority one, has mapped out in China; this is its particular synthesis, this is its time.

Time, Air, Tannins

"In the depths of the cellars, wine never forgets to re-embark on the sun's journey across the 'houses' of the sky. It is by marking the seasons in this way that it discovers the most astonishing of the arts: the art of aging." (Gaston Bachelard)
The question of time, in relation to wine, almost always relates to its period of conservation. This is the point when technique intervenes, not by default, but in retirement; in this suspension, which is like a forced neglect, something happens: an activity, a labor, a phenomenology whose latency leaves no visible, or rather identifiable, operator except time. When one cannot identify the actor in the play, the subject of the plot has to be time. As another name for the spontaneous.
The evolution of a wine depends on so many factors: region, year, château, vine, blending, diluting, climate, time, viniculture. These circumstances create the conditions for a change, the catalysis of which will occur in neglect, in a residue, in a vacuum: the small quantity of undissolved oxygen in young wines, which is at once the hazard and opportunity of wine, the stake in the game. Indeed, it is this bit of remaining air that will react with the tannins and other anthocyanins (coloring substances), acids, and alcohols during a process of polymerization and esterification, respectively provoking sediments and more complex aromas.
So time is the subject of a process, inside a short interval left vacant, in a place with tannins at its core. One knows that tannins determine both the tasting qualities of a wine and its length of conservation. This is where one finds the biggest difference between white and red wines. It is by their dosage in the liquid

that the body, the smoothness, the astringency will be controlled; it is in them that the pharmaceutical power of wine will now lie, beside the alcohol, which has lost its pre-eminence with the general restraints advertising it. The wine's fate is modulated respectively by the role of stalks, skins and seeds, of the *vin de presse* added to the *vin de goutte*, of the function of the additional tannins in the wood barrels. Choice of young or old oak, changing of the casks, latency of the melted tannins, resting of the wine on its dregs, gluing, filtering, stabilizing in the cold. All these operations are carried out with the tannins in mind.

When the great families of tea brandish their colors, they are showing variations in the proportion of theine and tannins that are transformed by oxidation. The latter plays the role of fermentation in wine, when oxygen comes to reinforce or elicit an active substance—caffeine or alcohol—and work a metamorphosis in the tannins that will potentially appeal to the senses. The chemical composition of tea varies, once again, with climate, season, horticultural practices, the stool of the bush, the age of the leaf, its position on the branch. It also varies at each stage of treatment, from the withering to the final drying, where, each time, new aromatic components develop. However, it is in operating the rupture of the cells during fermentation that the polyphenol-oxidase catalyzes an oxidation of the epicatechin by-products, and that the catechins are converted mainly into theaflavins and thearubigins. This involves a polymerization that also brings in biflavonols and other oligomers. Thearubigins and theaflavins thus appear only in semi-fermented and fermented teas, at the cost of a reduction in catechins. In this respect, the components of the dry extract of green tea remain closely akin to those of the fresh leaf before treatment: over 30 percent of these components are polyphenols, which include flavanols (monomeric flavan-3-ols), flavandiols, flavonoids, and phenolic acids. The principal flavanols are catechins, epicatechins (EC), (–)-epicatechin-3-gallate (ECG), epigallocatechin (EGC), and (–)-epigallocatechin-3-gallate (EGCG).

All these are the polyphenolic compounds that scientific research now submits to tests in order to measure their antioxidant nature on the organic cells; they are in effect active as anti-inflammatories, anti-carcinogens, and anti-mutagens. The capsules of *French Paradox* have thus been produced by the isolation of flavanols in red wine. If there is a paradox here, it is not simply that the diet of Southwest France contradicts all dietetic logic by its richness in animal fat and alcohol, but that the antioxidant substances are synthesized during an oxidation, and that the part most active in the protection of the body against the inroads of time is situated in the very thing that pleases the senses.

Another well-known paradox founds the time of tea: the weaker the color, the stronger will be the stimulant effect and, inversely, the stronger the color, the weaker the stimulant effect. During infusion, the theine diffuses very quickly in the water

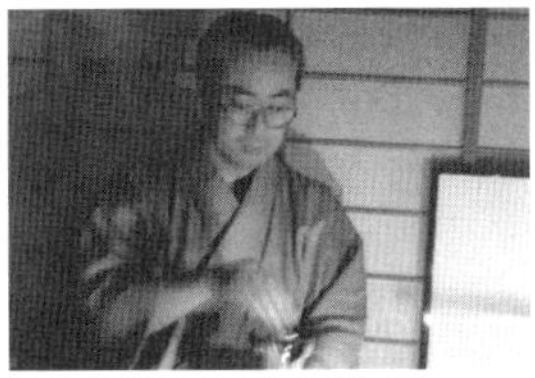

while the tannins come more gradually, darkening the liquor and counterbalancing the effect of the theine. While a similar phenomenon in the aging of wine sees the degree of alcohol decrease and that of tannins increase, tea presents a shorter and more outright version of this process in the single moment of infusion. There remains to describe the more complex movements exemplified in the whole family of Chinese tea: Japanese and Western analyses concentrate mainly on green tea, in the former case, and red tea in the latter. And without specifying provenance, types, or qualities. There have been too few tests on old Pu Er, white teas, and aged leaves to discover the way in which tannins change over time.

Correction, Addition, Adulteration

Wine was for a long time pressed—that is trodden—in a ritual of violence and impurity that introduces the process of fermentation. Tea too is subjected to a ritual, but one that has multiplied instead the signs of politeness, which run from the delicate cut of the fingernail at the moment of picking (fable has it that this should be done by young virgins) to the often formalized care taken in serving it. Tea is, however, subject to all kinds of risks, not least the addition of water—which wine, by getting it from its fruit, knows only as juice. This water, necessary and crucial, is the addition that enables tea to become a drink and return as a plant fragrance. The absolute need for water in tea puts it on such a par that the tea master is traditionally also the water master. Water is tea's ultimate additive.

But tea, in its production, will have occasioned quite as much technical output as wine. Wine, in the course of its manufacture, can be spoiled, specifically by exposure to air, doctored, diluted, improved, ullaged, agitated, gallized, deacidified, reacidified, colored, decolored, chaptalized, maderized, decanted, fortified, muted, sweetened, blended, concentrated, cooked, boiled, pasteurized, frozen, reverse osmosed, cryoextracted, distilled, rectified, evaporated in a vacuum. And a thousand substances can be introduced: sugar, aqua vita, honey, resin, beetroot, elderberry juice, sulfur, charcoal, yeast, must, unripe grapes, *vin de presse*, water, sea water (the Romans), snow, egg white, molasses, raisin, opium (the Arabs), aromatic plants (including *artemisia absinthium* which is infused in it), tartaric acid, antiseptic, carbon dioxide, coloring, and any number of chemical compounds. In these different operations and notably in the endless finishing, it is hard to limit the technical activity: only a court can define what is allowed within the definition of a name: the limits of a vineyard, of a château, of a *terroir* (AOC, *appellation d'origine contrôlée*), of the quantity of a vintage, of actions, of additives, and of possible supplements. The liquid carried by the wine, as grape juice, will, indeed, be that water seen by Plato as an invitation to substitutions, hazards, and imitations: in this colored, odorous, and flavorful fluid, foreign and surreptitious additions are not immediately spotted; illegal practices and traffic are the very history of the drink.

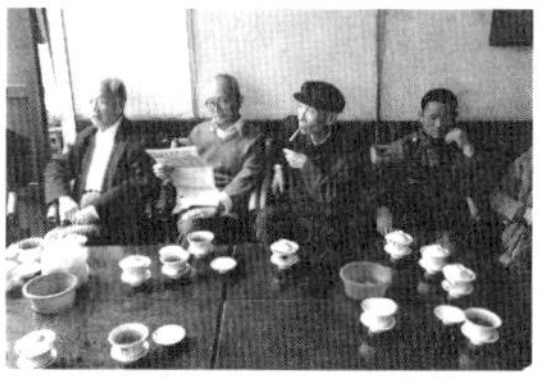

Chocolate, cocoa butter, cocoa powder. Taken from the same bean, these three states of matter cause endless hesitation over the nature of the product. Moreover, the three bases appear as the principal or subsidiary ingredient in a long list of manufactured goods. Here again, names need to be fixed and then controlled by law—decrees, orders, regulations. Leaving aside cakes, biscuits, flavorings and the three main types of chocolate—fondant chocolate, covering chocolate, milk chocolate—over a dozen categories are distinguished by minimum or maximum levels: whole dry cocoa, defatted dry cocoa, cocoa butter, dry matter of lactic origin, butyric fats, whole fats, whole or ground or chopped hazelnuts, almonds or walnuts, saccharose. Under French regulations, the minimal proportion of cocoa in a preparation entitled to call itself chocolate is 56 percent, but this is undermined by other international practices, which use the terms cocoa and chocolate with as little regard to content as the terms "coca" and "cola," branding an over-valued drink. The blackness and opaqueness of the commodity, as eaten and drunk, will no doubt have contributed to this confusion.

Coffee's black powder, like that of cocoa, lends itself to much falsification: abusive use of brown sugar to conserve its aroma, reuse of coffee impoverished by washing and drying, mixing or diluting, artificial ground coffee made from resinous solutions, addition of water by condensation, addition of powdered acorns, almonds, figs, or cereals. Gourmet coffee, malt coffee, barley coffee, Yankee coffee. Substitutions, *ersazts*, the black market of black coffee. In wartime, replacements had to be found for coffee, as for tobacco and sugar. A fresh paradox: the thing that falsifies coffee is, in fact, the thing it had replaced—*ptisina*, the ancient decoction of roast barley; and the substitute can offer advantages: digestive chicory.

"British Tea"

The long exclusivity of its provenance—China—the equally long hegemony of its trade—the East India Company—and the consequent internationalization of its contraband—the whole of Europe followed by America—ensured the continued adulteration of tea. And in a manner even more systematic than with coffee, helped by the fact that tea, in the forms of its native culture, was unknown in the West until relatively recently. The "Britannic" tea, as it developed through the hazards of long journeys, by adaptation to new tastes, or by the accidents of its reimplantation, parallels or indeed surpasses the other black drinks. In its history and its route: coffee and chocolate were wholly reinvented by Arabia and Europe—Abyssinian *qishr* and Maya *cacahualt* were customs that remained vernacular—whereas tea was reinvented in China itself specifically for export. There is a progressive degradation of the thing in the course of its history, as well as a counterfeiting that can become comically repetitive. In the hands of the many intermediaries who took it from producer to consumer, broken red tea was exposed to all kinds of abuse: from the

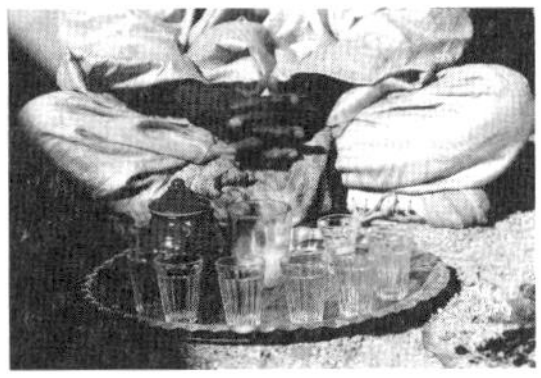

Hanists, who managed to sell the European middlemen leaves that had already been infused and redried, to the English servants who topped up their wages by selling their employers' dregs, also previously infused and redried, there was something of an inexhaustible exhaustion of the plant. The tea, which at least eight London factories in the 1840s manufactured in "second-hand" form, by drying previously used tea leaves, was sold under the name "British tea."

In 1714, in his instructive and curious letters, Giovanni Laureati had already observed: "It is noticeable too that the Chinese keep the best tea for themselves, and what we bring to Europe has been boiled more than once in Chinese teapots." According to Entrecasteaux, in 1787: "Having wanted suddenly to double, triple, even quadruple this export, the English to achieve their end poisoned the source, driving the Chinese to denature the product by mixing it, and decreasing the quality to increase the quantity and meet all the demands that were made of them." Robert Fortune was to notice the difference in the tastes of the Chinese and foreigners: "I have stated that the plants grown in the district of Chekiang produce green teas, but it must not be supposed that they are the green teas which are exported to England. The leaf has a much more natural color, and has little or none of what we call the 'beautiful bloom' upon it, which is so much admired in Europe and America. There is now no doubt that all these 'blooming' green teas, which are manufactured at Canton, are dyed with Prussian blue and gypsum, to suit the taste of the foreign 'barbarians': indeed, the process may be seen any day, during the season, by those who will give themselves the trouble to seek after it. It is very likely that the same ingredients are also used in dying the northern green teas for the foreign market; of this, however, I am not quite certain.... The Chinese never use dyed teas themselves, and I certainly think their taste in this respect is more correct than ours." (*Three Years' Wanderings in the Northern Provinces of China*). From China to England, tea became a business of adulteration, using leaves of elder, ash, sloe, beech, hawthorn, wild rose, and campeachy wood. "In 1813, an official report estimated the volume of this 'detritus' at 2000 tons, a comparable total to the 3000 tons of tea of Chinese origin imported by the East India" (Paul Butel). In these circumstances, the added scent—jasmine, mint, catechu—may appear to have been a necessity, in the same way as polishing or dying—talc, gypsum, indigo—for a "blue tea", still available in the nineteenth century. When the Quaker John Horniman in 1826 set about selling tea in closed packets, this was primarily to avoid adulteration. Likewise, Indian and Ceylon tea would be offered for sale—justifying Lipton's famous "directly from the tea tree to the tea pot"—as an alternative guaranteeing the consumer a commodity that was "pure and original."

The tea blend, by which the Britannic art of tea singularized itself, required the ability to identify, among the samples at a tea tasting in the London Market, those that

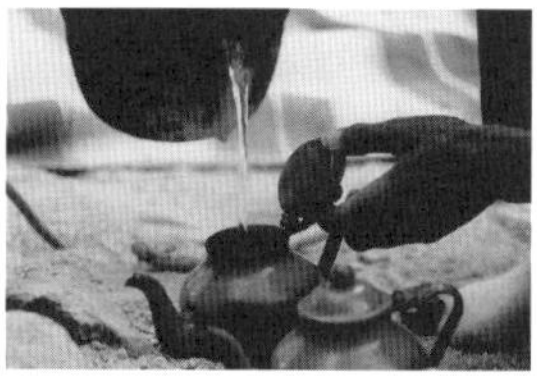

would, in combination, correspond to a given recipe, and possibly, according to the characteristics of the harvest or the season, and the ability to amend it to restore its flavor. A blend can thus embrace up to thirty provenances: gardens, estates, and even different countries. There is a to-and-fro between the different dealers and experts, between the producing and importing countries, between the samples and the tons of tea poured into the drums of the blending machine: the last rotation to be inflicted on this broken Britannic, which had begun its sad odyssey under the cylinders of the CTC rollers, and which, if it is not sold loose, within the single luxury of folded paper, but, like most teas, in a sachet, will find itself in a fast-moving tea-bag machine.

Tea of Time

Tea, none the less, when it presents the spectrum of its dry state in its great Chinese vintages, allows examination of its qualities as well as its possible faults and adulteration: an unbroken tea shows these in its aspect, odor, or homogeneity. That traditional tea gardens in China remain very inaccessible—secret, sacred, or controlled by the government—is because a great tea is offered like a named vintage wine. The pleasure of tea, like that of wine, is the tasting of a soil, a climate, an orientation, in other words not the rediscovery of the sensations of a defined product, but the discovery of an extract of space and time. In this respect, the legal definition of a vintage is not the guarantee of a standard taste but the guarantee that nothing—in the enjoyment—is guaranteed. Each year, each season, each production can hold its surprises, the excellence or the failings of a vintage.

Tea is, even more than wine, a play of time and weather. Its production risk is concentrated on its provenance: a stock, a garden, a harvest. The great Chinese vintages have no equivalent to the blends of vineyards that define the character of, for example, most of the great wines of Bordeaux (Cabernet Sauvignon with Merlot, Malbec or Petit Verdot), or the blends of the same year, like the merchant who systematically mixes the production of different growers in the same region (the 12.95 hectares of Chambertin), or the blends of different years, as happens with the best reputed port, cognac, and champagne.

The production of Chinese tea is so very specific that it can be traced to the picking of a single tree: the Dan Cong or "rock teas," from trees centuries old—between 100 and 1700 years, in other words planted under the Ming or Song—are collected in quantities that rarely exceed three kilos. Without the correctives that go into producing the stock of commerce, the consumer is exposed to a true *meteorology of taste.*

Beaten, Boiled, Infused

"Even as the difference in favorite vintage marks the separate idiosyncrasies of different periods and nationalities of Europe, so the Tea-ideals characterize the various moods of Oriental culture. The Cake-tea which was boiled, the Powdered-tea

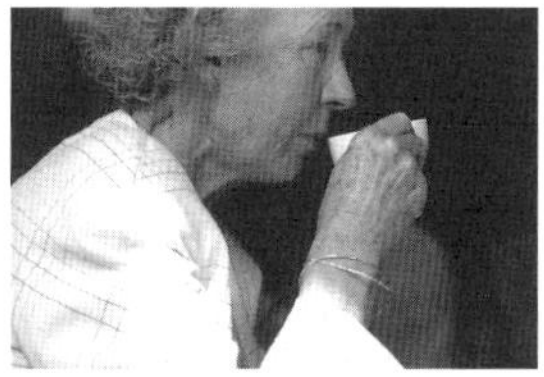

which was whipped, the Leaf-tea which was steeped, mark the distinct emotional impulses of the Tang, the Sung, and the Ming dynasties of China. If we were inclined to borrow the much-abused terminology of art-classification, we might designate them respectively, the Classic, the Romantic, and the Naturalistic schools of Tea." (Okakura Kakuzô, *The Book of Tea*)

Before Kakuzo, Matteo Ricci, one of the first Westerners to take account of these practices, distinguished two modes of tea: "In Japan [...] people use it slightly differently than they do in China, because the Japanese mix these powdered leaves in a cup full of hot water, a quantity of two or three spoonfuls, and drink this mixture as a potion. But the Chinese throw a quantity of these leaves into a little vessel of boiling water and after this, when it has drawn out the goodness and the power of the leaves, they drink it hot, throwing away the leaves." (*History of the Christian Expedition to the Kingdom of China*, 1610)

Hypotheses have been advanced about the oldest ways of taking tea, based on comparison with other plants. In the fresh state, tea would have been chewed. Later practices suggest that the leaves were consumed in stock, in soup, and even in a type of salad. In the Mao Cha, "the vegetable tea," chives, ginger, orange peel, dogwood, and mint was added to tea that had been crushed and reduced to powder. Lu Yu, in *Chajing*, favored a new method of preparation, the *jian cha*, which involved roasting the tea, reducing it to powder, and boiling it in water. With the first bubbles—when the "fish eyes" appear—one adds salt; at the second coming to the boil—like "a spring of pearls"—one sets aside a ladle of water, stirs the liquid in the receptacle with wooden sticks, and throws the tea powder into the vortex thus created; at the third coming to the boil—like "foaming waves"—one puts back the reserved ladle of cooled water, to slow down the decoction.

This method was developed under the Song into a more precise form, using finer tea powder and producing a denser mixture; the operation was performed first with a wooden spatula and then with a *chaxian*, the bamboo whisk (*chasen* in Japanese) of the *chanoyu*. The manner is called *dian cha*—"poured over tea"—because, in contrast to its predecessors, such as *chu cha*, the tea is not thrown into salted boiling water in pinches or a stream, but placed at the bottom of a bowl, into which water is then poured from a ewer. Incidentally, the Latin *mescere*, in the double sense of mix and pour, would correspond quite well to this *dian cha*. It is this method that was progressively codified, and adopted for the *dou cha* (*tocha* in Japanese), the tea tournament, where participants are required to prove their perspicacity, as much as their skill in obtaining a fine "jade mousse"—thc smoothest, the finest, the most pleasing in color. The actions of pouring and whipping were subject to the most detailed specifications: the order of the water and the tea, co-ordination (*dian/tang/ping/jifu*), the number and place of the pourings. The

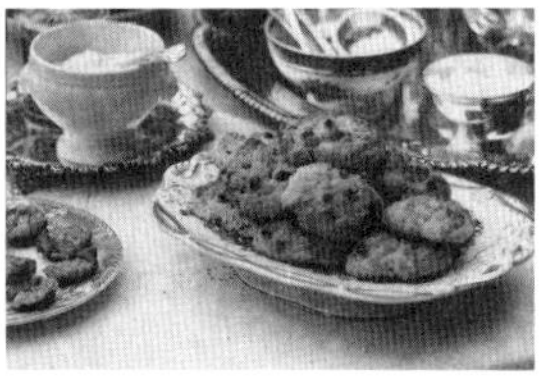

ceramic of the bowls in which the preparation is made assumes a technical and esthetic importance: for contemplation of the whitish froth—and the patterns that appear in it—dark or black glazed bowls are preferred, particularly those of the "hare skin," "tortoise shell" or "drop of oil" type, the *temmoku* that are so highly regarded in Japan. The beaten mode was in fact that which the Chinese and Japanese monks, visiting the archipelago or returning from the continent, brought back with Chan (Zen) Buddhism, to prepare the drink as an aid to meditation. It would provide the imperial court of the Heian, whose refined customs found no equivalent until the sixteenth and seventeenth centuries in Italy and France, with an occasion for increasingly sophisticated practices. This was to remain the central mode of the "way of tea." Although the last wave of Zen, Obaku at Manpukuji, brought across by Chinese scholars and monks fleeing the Manchu regime at the end of the seventeenth century, made the infused method known, it was to spread only as an everyday form, leaving beaten tea its symbolic pre-eminence in Japanese culture.

Until the Ming dynasty, the powdered forms predominated, whether compressed or not (*cu cha, san cha, muo cha*). The coarse loose teas, mixing the leaves and stalks with the buds, and the more selective ones, using only the laminae, were put into soup, but remained in the minority. These modes would none the less persist and are still practiced by many aboriginal and nomadic tribes in western China. In the south, in the depths of Xichuanbanna, where the oldest tea trees and the most archaic rites of preparation survive, the leaf is one of the raw materials of various culinary dishes and is used in its fresh and all fermented forms. In the north, from Mongolia to Tibet, tea is the main ingredient in a staple liquid food, consumed almost exclusively as a decoction of compressed tea flavored with spices, salt, and a milk product (yak butter, mare's milk, camel's milk), to which are added little balls or dumplings made of barley and mutton or beef. This tribal tea is an essential food, being the main source of vitamins, minerals, and vegetable fiber as well as theine, which in their combined effects add balance to a diet based on meat and carbohydrates; but it is equally a luxury: the cakes of compressed green tea are a prized product that has to be brought in from the tea regions.

Under the Ming, and then the Qing, the new way of preparing tea was infusion.

Froth Certain coffees, notably cappuccinos, are accompanied by froth. Desired and induced, by plunging the steam nozzle of a percolator in milk to create an emulsion, this is now identified with the drink of coffee, and even contributes to the enjoyment of it—as when one turns the cup to recover all the froth. Which is curious, as it adds nothing to the flavor or aroma. This extra unctuosity, which modifies the body of the liquid, takes coffee into the family of Maya *cacahualt*, "jade mousse,"

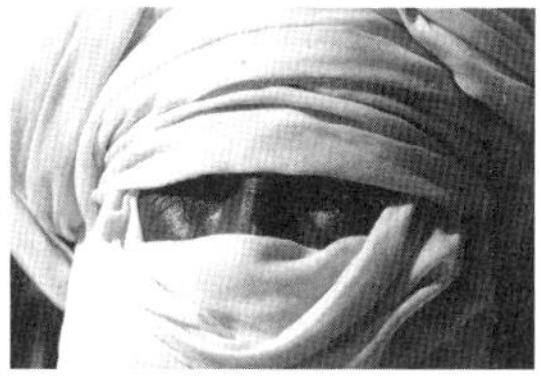

(Tang *dian cha* or Japanese *macha*), and indeed Moroccan mint tea. It is a trivialized version of an archaic ritual, where the drink is crowned by a protective layer—curiously like that which forms on some alcoholic fermentations—where the mass is self-increased by froth, where the liquid becomes solid by incorporating air. In Okinawa, at the far end of Japan, people make *bukubukucha*, the "bubble bubble" tea, a form of tea ritual where rice and water are beaten to a froth with a huge bamboo whisk. Among drinks, it is particularly beer that is accompanied by froth. In contrast to coffee, this is the effect of the liquid itself, charged with gas by the secondary anaerobic fermentations of the yeast. Nevertheless, this froth is not very abundant inside the bottle, but is much increased, as with coffee, when the drink is handled by a machine. The beer pump is an even more complex system than the percolator: it conveys the liquid from pressurized containers in the cellar, through a system of parallel tubes, crossing the walls like an electric circuit or water pipe, up to the tap controlled by a valve and lever. From the seventeenth century, beer was manufactured industrially to cater for mass consumption. Seltzers, sodas, and colas hold reserves of another froth—effervescence—retained by the liquid under the pressure of the mini-container, can or bottle. This gasified commercial product is not, as with the *champenoise* method, a controlled return or supplementary effect of fermentation, a live surprise lurking in the drink; it is rather an accentuation of the drink's sensation in the mouth: so the carbonated sparkle represents not the passage of an airy liquid but the trace of a detestable absorption.

Treatment, Conservation, Preparation

Throughout the process of tea, in its journey from the tree to the cup—to amend the advertising slogan "from the tea tree to the tea cup"—there is the same tendency to increase the synthesis of aromas: to eliminate herbaceous odors and make flower and fruit aromas appear; there is also the same recourse to heat, which is needed for oxidation, desiccation, and preparation of the drink. But there are, all the same, three distinct stages: treatment, conservation, service. Three periods, the middle one involving rest and risk together—suspense. This period is the most hazardous and least defined: everything in the treatments is done for the purposes of taste, but also to avoid deterioration during the conservation period. The different vectors of heat—vapor, pan, racks, in other words humidity, cast iron, and hot air—lead to modalities that recur in the conservation procedures: drying, preserving, steam-cooking. Smoking has inevitably joined the list. In each case, a material and a type of cooking perform an intermediate function. A function re-enacted in the conservation period, which is one of latency for the tea leaf, rather as a photographic film, after its time of exposure, has registered a latent image that will need to be processed in the laboratory. During this latency, the tea is transformed again, but more slowly, sometimes in undesirable ways, when it is not provided with the

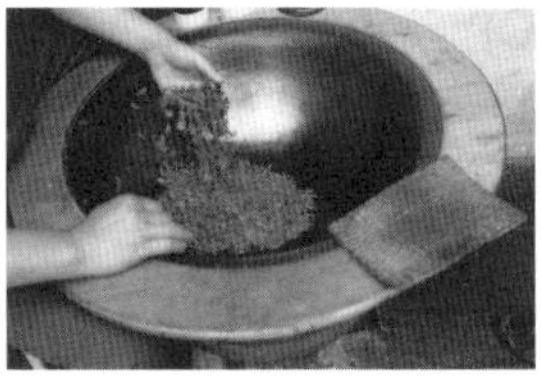

best storage conditions, but also beneficially: there is a maturation that ranges from a few weeks for green teas to decades for black teas. It is during this wait, very like that of alcohols for keeping, that the tea develops excellence or inferiority. The tea can then be tasted by a new form of cooking, a decoction, a mixtion, or an infusion: a new intermediate operation, where utensils will play the role previously allocated to the hand or machine. The tools of tea are insulants or intermediary instruments of a ritual and technique; they make it possible to avoid direct exposure to fire. The boiling vessel, bowl, whisk, spatula, teapot, and cup are the main ones, but each method of preparation can increase the categories: here, the Japanese *chanoyu* and the *gongfucha* of southern China have extended the list, as much out of technical as ceremonial need: ewer, mill, smelling cup, linen, dusting feather, receptacle for used water.

Decoction, Mixtion, Infusion

When the three exotic drinks were adopted or adapted by seventeenth-century Europe, each had virtually a single method of preparation: chocolate was milled, coffee was a decoction, tea was infused. This means that each of the three historical modes of tea was in effect assumed by one of the three beverages; but Europe, although it received the China tea of the Ming, never made beaten tea, or boiled tea, or "poured in" tea (when the tea is added to the boiling water).

The contiguous status of tea, coffee, and cocoa put them for a long time in a class of their own: in the 1930s, Desiré Bois distinguished three categories of drink for his great taxonomy of plants, fruits, and vegetables: "1° Unfermented drinks: saps; cold-pressed fruit juices diluted with water and sweetened to varying degrees: syrups. 2° Unfermented aromatic drinks made by infusion or decoction: coffee, tea, and so on. 3° Fermented or alcoholic drinks: wine, cider, beer, and distilled drinks: spirits and so on." After this, there was rather a tendency, although always a very imprecise one, to class the black trio among "fermented drinks," "stimulating fermented drinks," or again "fermented and roasted drinks." Yet Bois distinguished his categories by the method used to obtain the drink—cold compression, infusion, fermentation—, which it was possible to specify. Cocoa/chocolate tends to have a number of material states—powder, butter, mass—for a mode of preparation that is almost exclusively mixtion: in this respect, although the ancestral recipes have been forgotten, cocoa perpetuates the oldest Mayan representations that showed pouring from a height, which was a way of producing froth by passing the liquid from jug to jug.

Coffee, for its part, while obliged to pass through the state of the ground bean, or indeed the freeze-dried granule, is made by three main methods: decoction, filtration, and hydro-compression. In reality, these methods, as they are sometimes differentiated, in fact all amount to the same thing: brewing. Of course, having come

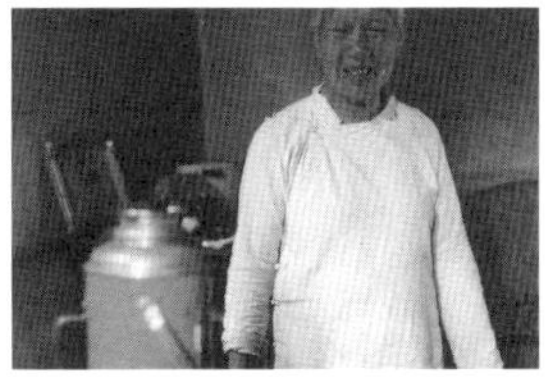

via Constantinople and Venice, coffee reached Marseilles and Oxford in its "Turkish" mode, that is to say "boiled." But this boiling, which removes coffee's essential ethers and intensifies an unpleasant bitterness, was gradually abandoned (cf. Michel Vanier). Even for a "Turkish coffee," the water one pours into the cup over a layer of finely ground coffee has to be maintained at a temperature of between 85 and 96 degrees centigrade to preserve the aromas. All the mechanical variants of the coffeepot—relying on gravity, air pressure, and steam pressure—merely modify the way in which the hot humidity passes through the ground coffee and modulates the infusion.

In this context, tea will have retained its three principal modes—cooking, mixtion, infusion; not, like coffee and cocoa, as alternative techniques of individual choice, but by rooting them to local practice: for example, churned Tibetan tea, beaten Japanese tea, infused Taiwanese tea. This technical rooting of tea is probably the best indicator of the ritual observed in each case: that is to say, the material state of the tea consumed—comforting soup, homogeneous mousse, or subtle liquor—, the actions required by the method of preparation—churn of human height, large bowl that fits in the hollow of the hand, or teapot that can be held between the index finger and thumb—, and the status of the drink ingested—a need that marks out the day, a ceremony governed by formal rules, or an esthetic tasting.

Steeping, Cooking, Infusing

"The water is brought to the boil and poured over." (Sulayman, 851). This is the earliest written reference to tea in the West. Infusion is caught between several defining boundaries that already slightly differ from it: between steeping and cooking; between mixture and decoction; between scalding water and stock. The word infusion, as its Latin etymology recalls, derives from boiling; it has, however, come to suggest the opposite: "*café bouillu, café foutu*" (coffee boiled, coffee spoiled); probably because the operation of boiling is often a culinary or technical action—used for glue, varnish, and chemical compounds—that moderates a natural food or raw material. Indeed, water, in which the latter are immersed, is a vector of heat, in the same way as the cooking vessel, the roasting spit, or the gridiron for smoking. It is also an agent of physico-chemical transformation: dissolution, impregnation, softening. In boiling, the combined effect of fire and water, like the double action of water and the cooking vessel, operate a fundamental transmutation of the immersed solid elements: and so Claude Levi-Strauss put boiled foods on the side of civilization, in opposition to the roast, which in its implied treatment is rather on the side of nature.

The term infusion, moreover, implies that the liquid in which the heat operates is a vector, agent, or catalyzer, but itself the object of the operation: the word retains the double sense of the action and the thing that results. To make an infusion is as

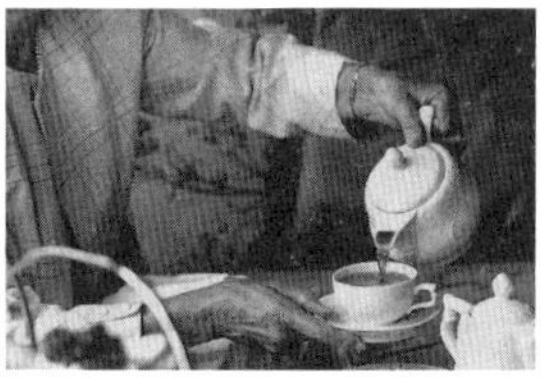

much to effect a mix between a solid and a liquid as to bring about dissolution of one in the other, and to obtain the consequences of a thermic increase. Heat plays a flexible role, the modalities of that are both very determinant and entirely modulable. Indeed, a very satisfactory infusion of coffee, tea, or indeed opium, can be achieved in cold water; however, it will require much more time—over nine hours for coffee. Apart from the practical and timesaving advantages of the hot infusion, there are other aspects to consider: the role of heat in the aromatic development of the drink, the synesthetic elements in the tasting, and, no less important, the symbolic and ritualized function of the absorption of fire. And thus, the infusion is the assimilation and incorporation, by the action that is there accomplished and by the body that accomplishes it, of water, of fire, and of the wood that has been thrown in. To the extent that the infused liquid will be ingested, without distinction between fluid and solid, without separation of berry or leaf on one hand, and water on the other, this will consist as much of endo-cooking as of exo-cooking. Which perhaps contributes to the character of intimacy or hospitality associated with tea and coffee.

Infusion is thus distinguished from dissolution by heating; from decoction by the limitation of the heat; from mixtion by the retention of a residue. Indeed, the fact that the infusion appeared so late, at the end of the sixteenth century, whether in the case of Turkish coffee or the tea of the Ming, reflects the fact that it is a more complex and more refined method of preparation: it is neither an abandonment in water nor an uncontrolled subjection to fire nor an unmeasured mixture. The modifications made in the last thirty years to *gongfucha*, practiced in Fujian, Guangdong, and Taiwan, suggest that there is no possible end to the refining and perfecting of the infusion: it will constantly adapt itself to new methods of cultivation, new water treatments, and the qualities of the clay of the teapots.

Infused Water

Today, in some regions of China, three dishes still include tea as a foodstuff. Among ethnic groups in the regions of Guangdong, Guangxi, and Guizhou, such as the Miao, the Yao, and the Dong, tea is consumed in preparations called *da yio cha*, which are used as seasoning: they involve lightly frying the tea leaves, adding peanuts and sesame, then making this into a soup with chives and ginger. In Sichuan, Hunan, and Hubei, the tribes prepare *lei cha*, in which the fresh tea leaves are crushed in a mortar with ginger and uncooked rice, then cooked in water, and finished off with peanuts, puffed rice, and salt or sugar. In Yunnan, people eat a sort of tea leaf salad, *liang ban cha*, for which the fresh leaves are heaped in a jar, left to ferment for several months, and seasoned before eating.

From *cu cha* to *muo cha*, tea was still a food: the leaves were eaten crushed, steamed, or emulsified. Apart from some local practices in China, the tea leaf is no longer consumed today, with the notable exception of Japanese *macha*, a preparation

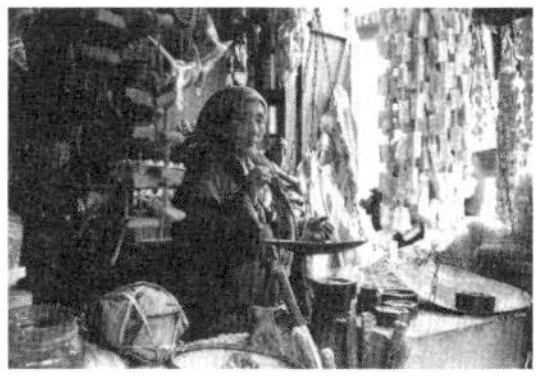

closely akin to cocoa or drinking chocolate: in some modern preparations—ice cream, cakes, cold drinks—where the green powder is mixed with milk and sugar, the resemblance to the Meso-American bean becomes even more striking. In Tibetan butter tea, the fragment of compressed tea can also be eaten, as one might swallow leaves of thyme or oregano in an Italian or Provençal dish: tea is less a foodstuff than a flavoring there, and while its role as a nutritional adjunct is certainly fundamental, and its symbolic function remains central—it gives its name to the drink—it none the less remains one ingredient among others more dominant or more basic: barley and water.

In the infusion, water has performed its part, all its possible effects, all the technical functions that the human has put to use—washing, impregnating, dissolving, refreshing, heating, carrying. In China, the first water poured onto the tea leaves is thrown out: it prepares them to swell with liquid, and washes them. This first function, omitted in the West and in Japan, is nevertheless determinant in the infusion. By impregnating the dry tea, water accomplishes what the treatment after plucking has achieved in a different way, and what is usually expected of it: to soften, swell, tenderize matter (stone, wood, earth, skin, foodstuff, field). By dissolution, water also accomplishes what the manufacturing process has achieved by heat and manipulation of the leaf: a cellular transformation, a change of color, a conduction of its components; something that it also brings about elsewhere—in dyes, varnishes, slip, agglutinants, coatings, sauces. By heating, water accelerates the molecular dissolution of the plant and brings its effects to bear even on animal matter. The dynamic effects of the infusion are not spectacular, masked as they are by the material of the opaque receptacle: after it is brought to the boil and in the course of its canalization through forced conduits or its pouring into vessels, there is a time of pause, of liquid rest, during which an agitation occurs on a minute scale. It is the chemical effects that dominate, as with the majority of the "substances of the chemical arsenal of our people [that] have water as a carrier" (André Leroi-Gourhan) Between the sap of the root and the tannic bath, the fermented and infused drink works an alchemy: of dosage, composition, and secrets of manufacture.

Infusion & Diffusion

When the tea leaf is infused, it expresses its best part, or in any case what has become its best part: everything that has been synthesized in the course of the plant's growth, in the course of its withering, in the course of its oxidation; that is, all its acquired organoleptic qualities. It has to be said that the ancient methods of treatment and preparation did not allow this part to be drawn out: the compression of the leaf into cakes expelled the essential juices in order to eliminate them and obtain the whitish drink and froth that was sought; the decoction at the other end of the process caused the loss of aromatic exhalations, fixed the taste, and brought

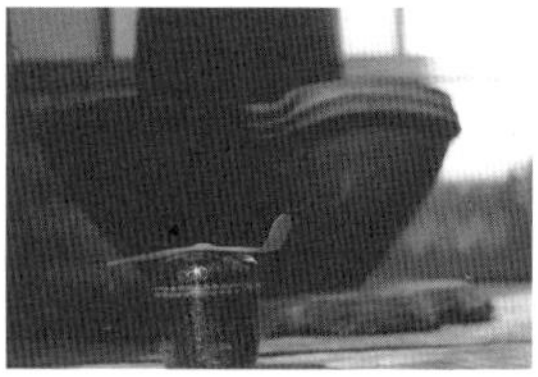

out astringencies: in traditional cooked teas, from Maghreb to Mongolia, salt, sugar, and spices are used to compensate for these deficiencies.

The in-fusion is a delicate diffusion of tea in water and, at the same time, a registering by the water of the memory of the plant. There is a dissolution and an enrichment, the subtlety of which has established itself in increasingly fine teas with complex tastes and smells: the nuances of color, taste, and smell are in fact only possible with the measured process of infusion. The dosage of dry tea, the temperature of the water, the length of immersion, will be the three most important variable elements in the infusion of a given vintage, although other things play a part, namely the weather, the type of receptacle, the season of picking, age in the case of an aged tea, and specific treatments such as roasting, or tailoring to specific consumer tastes.

Infusion, in this respect, takes after and stands apart from other methods. In the course of its rather late global spread by sea with the East India Companies and overland with the caravans, tea proliferated in mixed and intermediate forms: sometimes boiled-beaten, as in the churned tea of the Tibetans; also boiled-infused, as in Arab tea with mint, artemisia, or cardamom; and infused-mixed as in English milk tea and cream tea. In addition, infusion can be practiced as a secondary stage with tea made by another method: the *konacha* served in Japanese sushi bars, made with the recovered dust from *bancha* to *gyôkuro*, is a tea half-way between *matcha* and *sencha*. In mint tea, the tea has been boiled several times with sugar, as a decoction, but the bunch of fresh mint added at the end is, rather, an infusion. In the Russian samovar, the tea is prepared as a strong infusion and kept at the top of the stand on the fire. It is then turned almost into a decoction, before being fed with more water from the hot tap to restore its dilution when it is served; this is in effect a stage two infusion, or a postponed infusion. Incidentally, this method, while it generates great conviviality around the samovar, is only suited to ordinary compressed tea and is not capable of bringing out the delicate fragrances of a great Chinese vintage.

Remains of Infusion

After the infusion, there are remains: the grounds of coffee, the dregs of tea, if not a tea bag. This means that the nutritional or complementary function of tea has disappeared, or at least been greatly diminished. The infused carries the trace of a plant presence, the exudation of its work, or evidence of its passage. But the leaf that has been the object of much work, much waiting, even much expense, is in the end abandoned, and has to be thrown away.

"Teabags tend to be preferred these days because the disposal of the infused, spent, soggy tea leaves in the cold pot is difficult. You cannot swill them down the kitchen sink without risking the clogging of the drains. To pour them into the toilet and

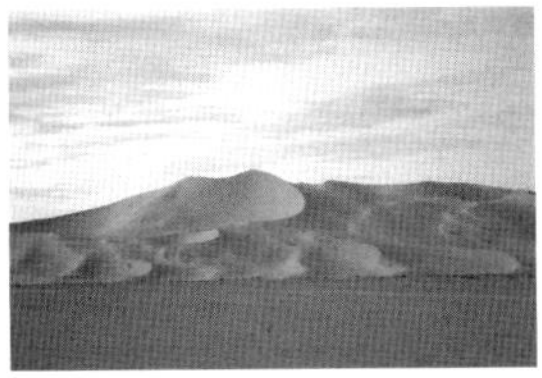

flush them down lends an excremental flavor to what has been a civilized potation. Hens like them mixed with old bread, but few people keep hens. You can spread them lightly on the floor and sweep them away along with the dust they attract. You can keep them in the teapot and bring them back to life with boiling water, but their vitality has vanished and you are drinking a ghost. They are a nuisance when their usefulness is past, just like people. But to prefer teabags to real tea is to exalt the shadow over the substance." (Anthony Burgess, *The Book of Tea*)

In China, where people do not yet use tea bags, the infused leaves are dried to make stuffing for pillows that soothe migraine. Partly because it has been only very lightly fermented, the leaf of a Taiwanese wild blue-green tea, when it is infused, before being dried again into a fibrous curl caused by the loss of juice, looks for a moment very much as it did when it was picked: green, whole, fresh. Very thick, with an oil that gives it a parchment-like strength when it is dried, this leaf can be separated into three layers, or more precisely into three skins, of which the outer two are transparent cellulose films and the middle one, colored molecules. The leaves of Chinese teas—white, yellow, green—paradoxically recover their plant-like appearance when put into hot water, which draws out their aromatic, vitamin, or alkaloid elements, and launches them into their final adventure: the variations of their successive infusions.

Translation of Infusion

The importance assigned to a thing by a people is reflected in the richness of the language that refers to it. In Great Britain, different regions have their own word for "infuse." The general English term is "brew," which recalls how tea came to be adopted in the country, as a replacement for beer. In the North of England, "mash" means infuse, and in Scotland, "mask," which is reminiscent of the *pharmakon*; in Cornwall the word "soak" is used, and in south-western dialects, "wet." In each case, the infusion is an almost mechanical operation, physical in any event, more than a chemical transformation.

Infusion of Water

Tea infuses like the meaning of a text. It is one of the vehicles of aromatic transport, one of the media for the extract, like resin (an easily melted solid or semi-fluid that a plant produces normally or as defense), balm (benzoin, styrax, *tolu*), or oil. It is a collection of volatile essences, over six hundred of which have been identified by chemical analysis in coffee and tea. It is a collection but at the same time a dilution. Because infusion is also a period of latency, of waiting, with risk of loss. It combines a number of aspects mostly associated with loss or watering down: liquidation, dissolution, dilution.

An infusion is water, but water that has lost its transparency, its clarity, its purity. "Sperm, water, ink, paint, perfumed dye: the *pharmakon* always penetrates like a

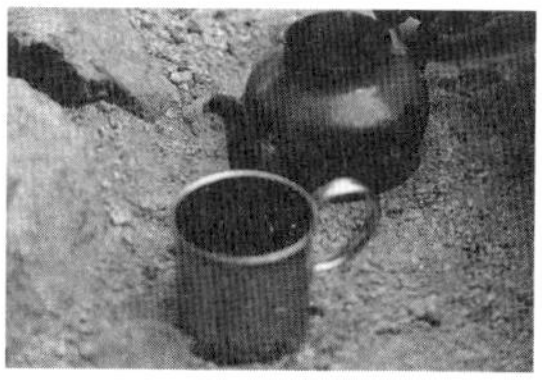

liquid; it is absorbed, drunk, introduced into the inside, whitch it first marks with the hardness of the type, soon to invade it and inundate it with its medicine, its brew, its drink, its potion, its poison." (Jacques Derrida, *The Dessimination*) Thus tea also serves to disguise brackish water in Arab countries and in China itself, where it remains difficult to find water without an unpleasant taste. In one of the versions of the legend of Shennong, tea is used to purify water and counter the effect of "seventy-two poisons," by its capacity to reach and check the smallest corner of the internal organs. The emperor-god, thanks to his "transparent stomach," is able to examine the tea leaves "inspecting" his intestines without difficulty, and the first character from which the name *cha* derives denotes this examination.
Tea's tour of inspection in those far-away times established both a veritable "pharmaco-kinetics," concerned with the way active elements would operate in the body—absorption, metabolism, excretion—, and a "Galenic" theory, guiding the choice of the best adapted pharmaceutical form—suppository, capsule, or syrup. The infused water is here the form of tempered fluid that will best infiltrate the body, to the furthest possible extent; the infused water giving the metonymy of a material that itself carries, without overload, the powers of another material. There is a long history to this, a slow advance from chewed tea to brewed tea—moving through whole tea, compressed tea, crushed tea, ground tea, beaten tea, boiled tea—in a progressive reduction of the wild plant, a stripping of its nutritional content, a passage from solid to fluid, from substance to impermanence. And therefore, the worst tea served in the poorest bar, a dust bag of no quality, will still accomplish this process. Infusion of water and water nullified.

Scented Water

"But when from a long-distant past nothing subsists, after the people are dead, after the things are broken and scattered, taste and smell alone, more fragile but more enduring, more unsubstantial, more persistent, more faithful, remain poised a long time, like souls, remembering, waiting, hoping, amid the ruins of all the rest; and bear unflinchingly, in the tiny and almost impalpable drop of their essence, the vast structure of recollection." (Marcel Proust, *A la recherche du temps perdu*)
The chemistry of infusion is an elementary chemistry; that of theine infusion, particularly, is all lightness: it does not produce those biting, coloring, or tanning substances that can modify the appearance of the matter. It involves, rather, obtaining simple scented water. Not, however, what could be called a "simple water": lavender, jasmine, or orange-flower water. The latter are, in any case, all manufactured by distillation or saturation of the plant in oil. Tea, that "scent which is drunk," remains a drink, which needs to preserve both a smell and taste. A great tea is of course one in which the taste as much as the smell will provide interest, body, surprise. In Taiwan and Japan, the recent revival of interest in tea often leads to the forcing of

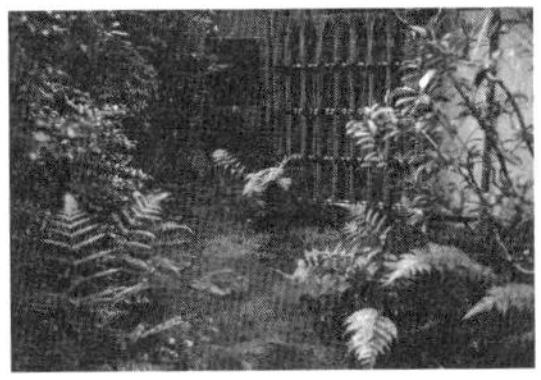

one or other trait of character in an unbalanced way: Wulongs with too much in the nose and no length in the mouth, pseudo Gyokuros that are sickly sweet. In the West, this tendency shows itself not in the development of forced vintages but in the addition of essences to give scent to impoverished teas. The latter have no characteristics apart from their robustness and fast release of color in the cup, instantly assuring the eye and tongue that they are a theine infusion, which serves as a base for standardized flavors. Apple, cinnamon, violet, coconut, cocoa, almond, cherry, verbena, rose. It may be pointed out that these same flavors now appear on ice cream and water ice lists, in ranges of soaps and cosmetics, and even in incense shops, where the new fragrances now accompany incense sticks, cones, and resins from India, Japan, and the Maghreb. In each case, a synthetic scent in effect replaces a synthesis of scents and the same permutations or combinations replace what could have been a real choice.

From this point of view, only *gongfucha* offers the opportunity to enter and explore a complex world of tea infusion. Only its technical apparatus, in the range, precision, and material of the instruments, is equipped to bring out what patient cultivation, favorable weather, and careful manufacture will have made possible in the tea. *Gongfucha* will produce, for he or she who knows how to perform its actions and recognize its effects, a spectrum of qualities, which will bring all the more sensation because they emanate from a fluid that is neither essence nor ether but simple water. Indeed, while the bouquet of wine is carried by emanations—the "vapor"—of alcohol, tea gives out its qualities only through water and heat. In a synesthesia of tastes, scents, and colors, tea presents a reconstituted, reinvented, and disassembled nature. It achieves this by the distinctive transmutation of the infusion, combining extraction and diffusion.

Tisane

The Arab, Persian, and Turkish countries enjoyed a great variety of drinks made from water, fruit, and sugar—syrups, electuaries, water-ices (liquid and solid)—as well as acid juices based on vegetables and decoctions of plants of medicinal use—such as barley water. Others are *boza*, *musselès*, *pekmèz* (cooked wine), *bal souyou* (mead with hops), *raki*, and orgeat, a list soon completed by coffee and tea. These two would play a similar role, and substitute for each other according to season or their availability as imports. This role, after much debate by the learned minds of Europe, was defined by the properties they were recognized to have: curative or harmful powers, in different dosages and mixtures, and above all a "hot" or "cold" nature. The words *qahveh* and *çay* in Persian or Turkish soon came to signify, like tea or *tee* in English and German, not so much a specific drink as its particular method of preparation and consumption. At the end of the eighteenth century, *çay-e-shirin* ("sweet tea") meant in Persian an electuary, heavily sweetened, which could

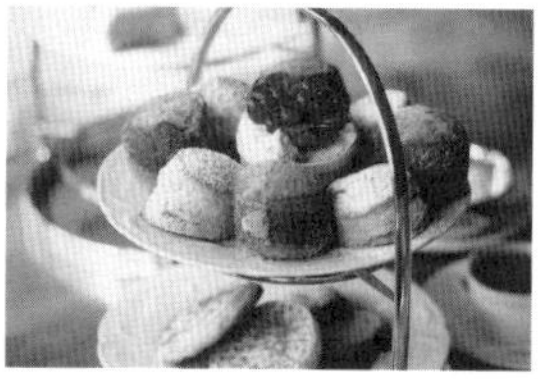

be made out of many ingredients with the exception of... tea. "Tea" became in these latitudes a liquid that was heated or cooked (infusion or decoction), and drunk while still hot, if not burning.

In the pharmacy, where alcohol is found only as a disinfectant and chocolate as a "diet product," tea is shelved next to infusions such as sage, veronica, and verbena: they are "hot waters," which have kept an effect in aromatherapy and are still sold by the pharmacist. Had it not been for the British, who, by acclimatizing tea in a subject India, managed to reduce the drink to a black brew, tea in the West would have remained what the French court, Dutch doctors, and German ecologists pronounced it: one more tisane. Or, in view of the synecdoche that has made tea or *tee* embrace all infusions, the tisane *par excellence*. The French language, which has not adopted the usage of its English and German neighbors, in maintaining the Greco-Latin derivation (*ptisanê, tisana*) has brought about a gradation that ranks "tisane" (*tisaine*, eighteenth century) as a diminutive of "tea." In this intricate dance, the decoction of hulled barley (from the Greek *ptissein*, "to pound," "to hull barley or grain," from the Sanscrit *pi-nà-sti)* is no longer imbibed here, while *maicha* or *mugicha* remain refreshing drinks still consumed during the summer in China and Japan.

Bitter Water

With the manna from heaven and the water from the rock, the waters of Marah reflect the difficulties of finding food and water during the exodus in the desert: "So Moses brought Israel from the Red sea, and they went out into the wilderness of Shur; and they went three days in the wilderness, and found no water. And when they came to Marah, they could not drink of the waters of Marah, for they were bitter: therefore the name of it was called Marah. And the people murmured against Moses, saying, What shall we drink? And he cried unto the Lord; and the Lord showed him a tree, which when he had cast into the waters, the waters were made sweet: there he made for them a statute and an ordinance, and there he proved them." (Ex 15:22-25) Wine, in the Judeo-Christian tradition, is always caught in a triangular exchange with water and blood: river water metamorphoses into blood, water is transformed into wine, wine is transubstantiated into blood. This does not preclude there being a question mark over its invention: the renewed fall of man is the drunkenness of Noah, as a consequence of his first action after the retreat of the waters: the planting of the vine. This does not preclude the fact that the third monotheist religion rejected that *kawah*, which many of its followers none the less continued to enjoy. In the episode of Marah perhaps another way was used, which the three black drinks would make possible. Except that, the plant infusion or maceration, while it aims to eliminate what is noxious, does not suppress but on the contrary brings out a bitterness (*mar* in Hebrew means bitter).

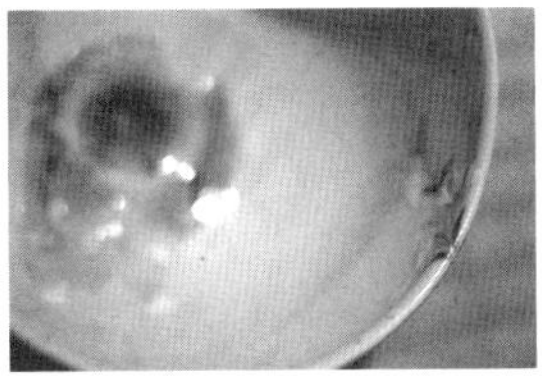

Moreover, the oldest name for tea in China, as it appeared in the dictionary of objects, *Er' Ya*, is *tou* (*du*) or *kutu*, which means "bitter herb." Similarly, the oldest text in the West, an *Account of China and India* written in 851 by Sulayman, identifies the plant as a "herb that has more leaves than clover, a little more scent too, but is very bitter." In most of the practices linked with tea, bitterness is always the limit of play. Used in the Moroccan mint tea, Gunpowder, or Zhu Cha, is a fierce, aggressive tea and many of the steps of its preparation are designed to combat the bitterness and astringency: the rinsing of the leaves, although this is not usual with tea outside China, the crushing and pressing down of the mint with a spoon, the addition of a large dose of sugar. In England, milk is deliberately added to counter the bitterness and robustness of Assam tea. In *gongfucha*, care is taken to make the water spill over the teapot, to "expel the froth that carries bitterness."

We know that while a baby or toddler, with a smile or the word "more," shows a liking for sweetness—shared by the young of other animals—, the bitter taste is systematically rejected, as if from an innate suspicion directed at toxic substances. In Chinese medicine, "bitterness is related to the three hearths. An excess of foods and tisanes with a bitter flavor stops the proper functioning of these three hearths. The energy repels this bitterness and so provokes vomiting." This sensitivity to the noxious probably fosters the neophobia that precedes every initiation, and establishes in opposition to it the negative pleasure associated with domestic toxins, the commonest instance being the nausea of the first cigarette, repeated with each subsequently inhaled puff. In this respect, the bitter drink, the water made bitter, can only amount to a prophylactic ritual and an act of mediation with the "elements."

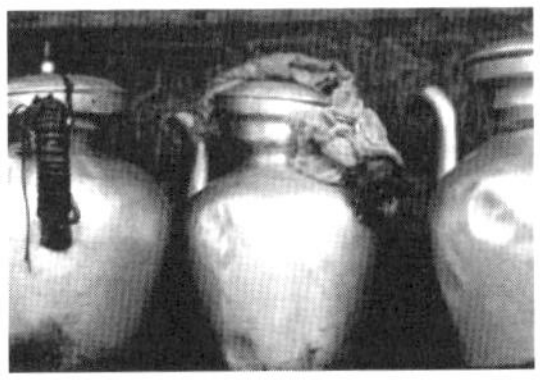

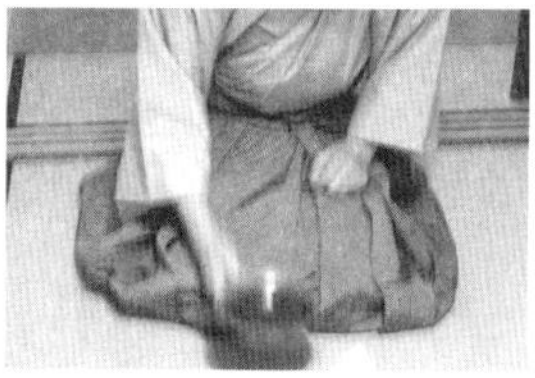

U

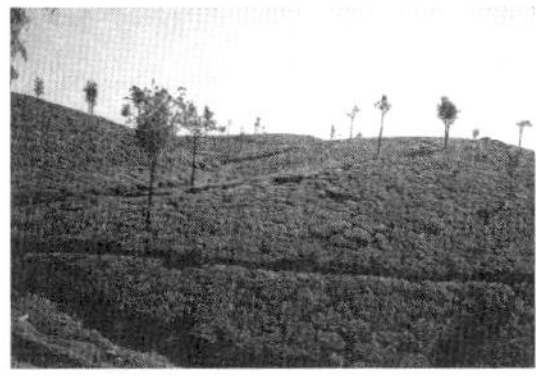

USES

Under Milk Tea

A fastening of twisted copper fixes a rough square of print to a white thread emerging from the chubby, convex pot and indicates at its heart—barely floating in tap water and already covered by a dark skin—the sachet of bleached paper, swollen with fragments of tea. We also have, at the bottom of a cup, milk which, in its whiteness, redraws the concavity of the china, at the risk of raising, to the coagulation at its surface, the minutes fibers of a cloth or even some unidentified particle which has become stranded there at the whim of a draft; milk with a film which, soon perforated by a rain of brown sugar, is ruffled once more by the cascade, also brown, but boiling, from the teapot as it is eventually upturned. Finally, we have this cloudy liquid, made still more murky by its color, somewhere between gray and brown, and its disturbing opacity, given that this is a fluid mass that one is about to ingest, inevitably too fast, without the protection of the teeth which when they chew solids, act as a kind of frontier post, checking them as they pass.

Mixing

Golden and hot, this long jet of liquid before you is disturbing: and shrinking back seems to be what the person officiating expects; the feeling that you have does not only come from the fear of being scorched or your appreciation of the performance, which takes aim at the little receptacle from so high, but is connected with the ritual; and despite the tourist setting, the meaning is clear: you are being given to drink the image of what the organism will give back. And the sort of uneasy panic that grips you, which one wrongly ascribes to the stereotypicality of the situation, is inspired by this sacred urine beneath which one must remain passive and acquiescent. The gestures, which are on the one hand too many and too precise to appear trivial, yet too rapid to aspire to being ceremonial, have both delayed and prepared you for this moment: your body is about to be caught up, not so much in a simple closed circuit in which, as in the case of certain coprophagous practices, it is a matter of reabsorbing the thing excreted, as in some vast circulation in which, by color and gestural language, the element of which we are essentially made up becomes signifier. Tea with mint, tea in a tent, tea in descent. Hence the teapot, shaped like the dome of a mosque, is itself constantly subject to the reversible conductivity of the liquid: upstream and down are interchangeable, source and estuary not defined. After it has been filled with tightly packed grains of Gunpowder, (its cardboard box bearing a mixture of Arabic and Chinese calligraphy—a sort of abbreviated East), then, contrary to the usual practice in most countries, with sugar in large quantities, water will complete it. Later, mint or fresh artemisia will serve as filling for the shiny, dented utensil. In reality, the infusion, reheated more than once, is a decoction: the liquor will be thick and cloudy. But often, in order to maintain the

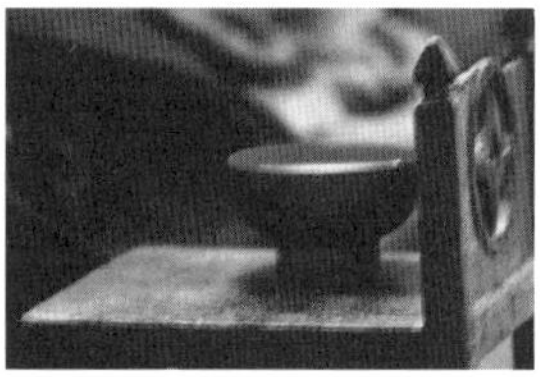

homogeneity that the beverage is constantly about to lose, one must pour the tea into the glasses, then pour the contents of these back into the pot. This coming and going, while it captures the attention, disturbs the expected order. And if the pouring is carried out with those back-and-forth movements that take the pourer dangerously far from the receptacle, this is because micturition maintains mixing. One is surprised, at last, to be served: the tea is gathered up in little glasses, oddly combining the mechanical form of canteen cutlery and the finely worked ornament of gold arabesques.

Emulsion A burning sensation in the back, heaviness in the lower limbs and a chronic feeling of being a foreign body, detached: all these induce a contradictory concentration, the least expected outcome of which is to produce an effect of continuous hesitation in the most self-assured. This awkwardness, a matter of etiquette, which returns as though programmed, is often to be found in the Japanese archipelago; it may charm the visitor, but irritate the businessman in a hurry because, following rather brutal first contacts, it shows itself in those Japanese with whom you are starting to have some feeling of complicity. Something that goes beyond manners, etiquette (*sahô*) and politeness, this reserve and lack of self-assurance even has a name: *enryo*. The *kaiseki*, the Chanoyu meal—"hot stone on the stomach"—has already been the occasion of a long and formal service; its ambiance was more relaxed than the gestures that from now on will engage the host. The figures are well-known, the imperceptible pauses that freeze them help to recreate them, as does the precision that constantly adjusts them: fingers extended and joints broken, the stiffness of the readjusted kimono and the placing of objects on an invisible grid. But—and the whole methodology of the schools of *Sadô* rests on this paradox—the more often one witnesses it, the more the clarity of this sequence of events for a summary, archaic preparation escapes one. At first, the host, who has left the guests in silence, opens and shuts the screen several times on its runners to go and fetch utensils, which are a mixture of the rustic and the refined. Some are already on the shelf, others join them: a basin of cold water or vase for used water, a carved bamboo spoon or ladle, a bowl or tea container… In the most rigorous sequencing of the movements, delivered like martial arts strokes, it is a matter of developing, in a single séance, which may last several hours, a narrative that is none the less brief: the water is poured into the bowl, where the fluorescent green powder has been placed, before being beaten, with the frayed bamboo whip, to make a purée or thick emulsion.

Churn The water has long grown musty in the large rusty kettle when the fragments of tea, also rusty, are scattered by a hand that seems still to be grinding them, after breaking them off the compressed brick, brought from China and preserved for safety's

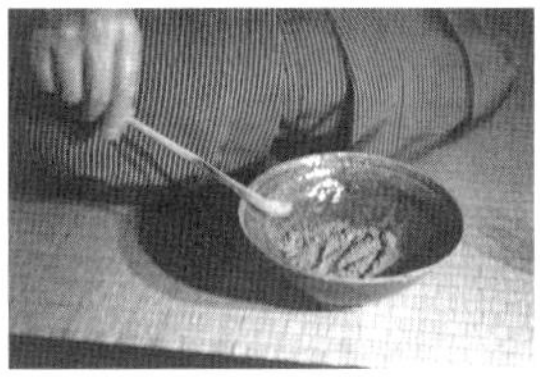

sake in its leather case. While marketing in the West has recently and inappropriately confused the recipient for boiling with that for brewing, by molding the latter in cast iron, in this monastic sphere the kettle is also a receptacle for preparation, since tea is a decoction. Sometimes the theine mixture is accomplished in an open saucepan made of tin. After long boilings, reinforced or countered by the rotation of a spatula, the rancid yak butter is added, together with salt and, when these are available, other spices. The mixture is then decanted via an intermediary pourer or a simple recycled oil can, into the *gurgurchaï*, the tall, narrow churn made of wood circled with iron hoops. Then the pestle makes a *choc, choc, choc* sound, like an amplification of the one made by the winch in the chocolate pot— anticipating, no doubt, the stirring of the drink in the stomach. Two or three women operate the contraption, holding the main part of the churn and driving the vertical up-and-down movement (which, for tea, seems violent and mechanical), corresponding to that of other women like these ones, in Africa or Asia, who still grind millet or rice, or which the same ones use for churning butter, in a slightly different device with a similar method of operation. The lama's tea is thus a sort of liquefied expansion of whipped cream, less tea with butter than butter with tea, in that this is introduced as a seasoning in the passage from one churn to the other. The tall instrument is then tipped by several hands into a great ewer or pourer, which looks more like a kettle than a teapot, because of its capacity and because of the tin, or even incised copper, of which it is made. Supported by the handle which rises above it, this is what will be used to serve the tea into the rough wooden bowls, sometimes trimmed with silver, which the "red bonnets" and "yellow bonnets" have taken out of the pockets on their chests. The bowl of tea seems poised on the tips of the fingers of the left hand, while with the right hand they take the rice that makes up their only meal and has been poured directly on to the stretched cloth between their legs. In the pantry, tea, which is the only distraction from prayer, will be constantly prepared so that they may drink up to ninety cups a day.

Sprinklings

There are numerous minute recipients of every shape, laid out on a little carpet, the most prominent object on which is the stoneware kettle on its lighted stove. There is a sudden movement of all these objects that are alternatively grabbed, grasped or tipped by hands that are agile, swift, but relaxed. The different materials circulate among these instruments: imposing tea leaves, almost baroque in their folds and contortions, solid green in color; but also steaming water which passes from the sonorous kettle to the various containers that are filled from it, filled to overflowing, and abundantly watered. From the outset, this activity is fascinating, not because it gives the impression that one is observing a ritual in which every action is prescribed, but rather because of the reasoning that seems to be behind the

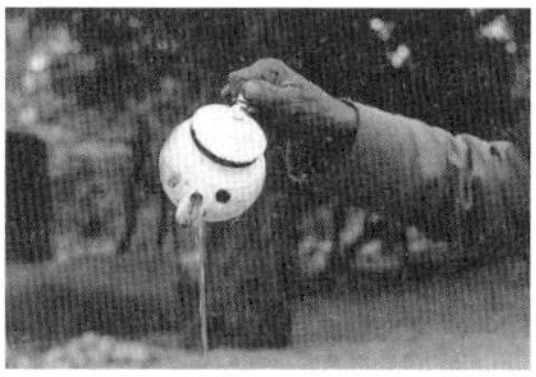

succession of gestures and the various comings and goings. Before being amassed in the place where one would expect it least, around the teapot, in a species of deep dish, the water has been poured into the smallest and most varied cavities and pipes. Even before the tea is measured out, thanks to the only utensils, which, by virtue of the wood from which they are carved, stand apart from the great family of ceramic utensils, this boiling water damps and rinses the "purple" clay; after that it impregnates the leaves which foam with it, but never stagnates. What might appear to be the most precious liquor, the first drawn, is pitilessly discarded, while the minute cups with their varied outlines are each in their turn put to soak and turned beside the teapot. The following infusion barely lasts a few seconds. The teapot, which is so tiny, is abandoned and emptied into another pourer, without a lid. But the little dishes, enameled in brilliant white inside, which seemed designed to serve as cups, remain in the end empty, while some kinds of tall thimbles are filled with tea of a previously unimagined color. These tall cups, spilled into their lower neighbors, are grasped vigorously and held beneath the nostrils, which discover in them mellow fragrances of flowers and fruits. These perfumes are striking in their subtlety, their delicacy and their volatility: they brush past and, even the most essential of them, do not stay; they pass or wait to be perceived. And when the tea enters the mouth, still other aromas arrive to accompany it on its journey—on the tongue, in the mouth, as an aftertaste and even in the throat. The tea is a vintage Wulong. The manner of preparing it is called *gongfucha*. The setting is a Taiwanese tea house.

"The Different Manner of Preparing Tea"

"As for the manner of serving Tea, it must be observed that the Japanese and the Chinese are very different one from another in this respect, by reason of the fact that the first reduce the Tea to powder, grinding it against stone and afterwards mixing it well with hot water; but the Chinese boil it in some liquid, adding only a few grains either of salt or of sugar, and this decoction being still warm, they present it with much courtesy both to those whom they have invited to dine, whom they entertain in their homes, and all those who visit them. And this they do with such care and application that even persons of the highest quality among them do not disdain to take of it. On the contrary, they hold it an honor to prepare the decoction of this herb for their friends with their own hands, or at the least to assist in properly mixing and preparing it, and to this purpose they expressly reserve in the middle of their Palaces peculiar chambers in which there are little stoves made with the most precious stones and most exquisite woods, all of which are particularly devoted to the aforementioned preparation, and they keep rather curiously in these same places the pots, tripods, funnels, tumblers, spoons and other utensils for this sort of cookery, all perfectly made, on which they readily spend some thousands of

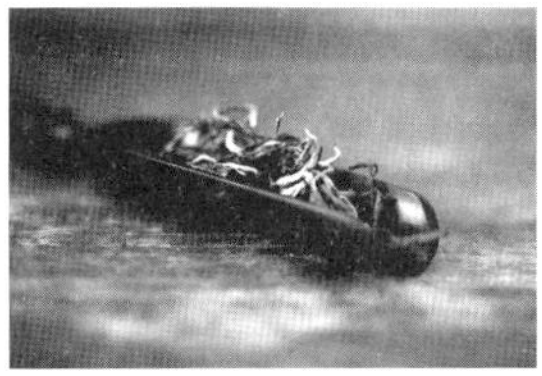

écus, keeping them properly wrapped and folded in silken stuffs and letting them be seen by only their most intimate friends. Thus they attach no less great importance to this than we might to diamonds, precious stones and necklaces or pendants of pearls of the highest price." (Tulpius, Dutch doctor, quoted by Philippe Sylvestre Dufour)

Twenty-Four Things

Tripod for the fire (*fenglu*), woven bamboo basket (*ju*) with the ash container, poker (*tangzhua*), metal rods for the fire (*huoce*), boiler (*fu*), stand for boiler (*jiaochuang*), tongs (*jia*), paper sachet for tea (*zhinang*), mortar (*nian*) with its roller (*fumo*), bird feather to collect the tea powder, sieve (*luo*) with grinding box (*he*), tea measure (*ze*), water receptacle (*shuifang*), bamboo and silk water filter (*lushuinang*), water ladle, made from a gourd (*piao*), bamboo tongs (*zhuce*), pottery salt box (*cuogui*) with its spoon (*jie*), receptacle for boiling water (*shuyu*), tea bowl (*wan*), vertical basket, for ten cups (*ben*), palm brush (*zha*), vessel for waste water (*difang*), vessel for dregs (*zifang*), tea towel (*jin*), shelf for utensils (*julie*), "hold-all" basket (*doulan*). These are the tea objects in the *Classic of Tea.*

Tea Things

Under the Tang Dynasty, from the time of the *Chajing*, emphasis is placed on the tea utensils. Twenty-four are announced and prescribed. In fact, twenty-seven are listed if one distinguishes the accessory objects (the mortar and roller, the salt box and its spoon, the sieve and its container). Some thirty are depicted. Lu Yu devotes the whole series of prints to them, the entirety of the middle chapter that concerns those for preparation and before that a sub-chapter dealing with the tools for cultivation. The Japanese way of tea will be based on these: the taxonomy of the Chinese poet, even though it was to become obsolete for later preparation of tea in China, and the same to a lesser degree in Japan, established a technical, formal and symbolic paradigm for tea. Long before the accounts of tea tournaments, instructions in the matter of tea or Victorian manuals of etiquette, the times of tea were made subject to lists, to classification and to theory. Rare archeological evidence was necessary for the recent discovery of the princely preparation of *cacahualt* among the Maya; the endeavors to claim that a ritual comparable to the Japanese tea ceremony connected with Turkish coffee—*kahve ikrami töreni*—required an element of nationalist folklore; and one would have to return to the cult of Bacchus, secularize the mass or sanctify enology to give back a symbolic dimension to the consumption of wine. The need for the ritual surrounding tea can be measured in the greater extent of variations that it exhibits by comparison with other drinks when it comes to preparing, serving and consuming it.

Pourers, containers, bowls, conveyers, supports, cloths, spoons, measures, pikes... There are many technical objects. Sometimes these are utensils, sometimes instru-

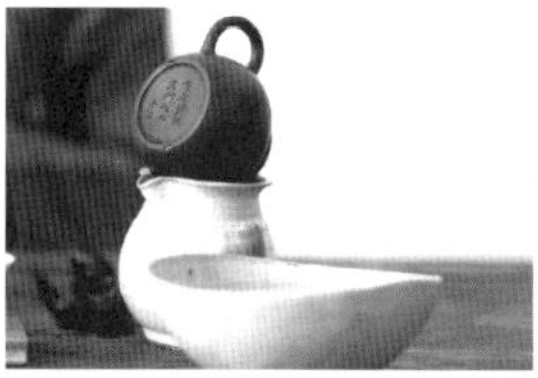

ments, sometimes tools, according to what is being considered: in that they transform matter—the infusion of tea in water, achieved by the Yixing teapot or the *zhong*; in that they allow it to decompose—the analysis of tasting permitted by the *zhong* or smelling cup; or in that they serve for preparation—the tea service. While the samovar constitutes the integration of all the instruments for preparation—the water container and its heating, the teapot, even the cup—in a single unit, the teabag or infuser represents disintegration: the receptacle is rendered inconsequential, be it teapot, saucepan, cup, mug, glass, or plastic cup, and the hot water is treated as already supplied, being external to infusion—hence the student expedient of taking hot water from a tap. The churn perhaps stands as a third pole in relation to the utensils for tea: like a tool, it takes its place at one point of the preparation, both as a temporary receptacle and as a machine for grinding/mixing. While the samovar produces a strong concentration of the infusion, which will be diluted at the moment when it is served in the cup, the tea bag keeps the ground leaves, contained in the gauze or paper, separate from the liquid in which they necessarily bathe clothed and which merely impregnates them. In one case, the tea is concentrated to the limit of remaining a dry extract—which is also the first phase in manufacture of freeze-dried tea—while in the other it is a powder parceled out for rapid diffusion; in the domestic percolator, coffee is also nowadays contained in paper capsules. The churn and its pestle suggest a still further relationship by mechanically intensifying the general concentration of the mixture/decoction. Seen from this point of view, the samovar, the tea bag and the churn form three markers defining the technical process of tea preparation: in each case, in point of fact, they indicate the boundary beyond which tea may vanish: as a sort of coffee, as gray-tinted water and as soup.

European Ware, Chinese Ware, Japanese Ware

European tableware consists in an ensemble of strongly unified and structured components. A round shape prevails for cups, plates and dishes. Porcelain also predominates as the most frequently used material, with earthenware for the most common and silver for the most luxurious. When that metal is used, it is adopted for particular sets, such as a travelling or picnic service where the items are arranged in a hamper or case. Silver and pewter are usually reserved for the serving elements—urn, kettle, teapot, milk jug, butter dish, jam dish, spoons, knives, dishes—while china is preferred for the elements that are served—cups, saucers, plates for pastries. A sort of hierarchy governs the different sizes of the implements. But the decoration as a whole, whether painted, incised or embossed, is unified: an overall iconographic theme—rural, hunting, historical—may be developed; a decorative motif—floral, Oriental, geometrical—will be subject to slight variation; a color or gilding will be systematically repeated.

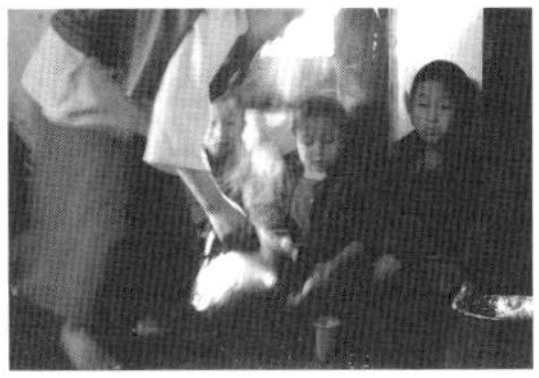

In China, one meets a greater variation in shapes: round, oval, square, rectangular, hexagonal, octagonal. However, the tableware is usually unified by its decoration. In *gongfucha*, both the cups for drinking and those for smelling will be of the same china, with the same designs. Only the Yixing teapot, the choice of which will have been decided by the variety of tea for which it is designed, is distinguished by its purple clay. However, common *gongfucha* services are available with the radical uniformity of a single stoneware for all the items, white enamel covering only the inside of the cups to allow the drinker to observe the color of the liquid.

Japanese tableware exhibits a very great variety of shapes, colors and materials, in accordance with an esthetic which is sufficiently generalized for it to be manifest even against the uniformization of contemporary space; this is a characteristic one always meets in a Japanese family kitchen: the cupboards have a sort of ceramic museum in them, exhibited or piled up. This quite general feature may be traced both to the *wabi* morality of the Muromachi period and to the more exuberant fashions of Edo merchant society. The very heterogeneous appearance of Japanese tableware derives from the components of the meal: the basic meal, *gohan*, is made up of rice and soup, nowadays most often *misoshiru*. However, the two vessels used to serve them are strongly differentiated: rice is piled up in a porcelain bowl with a bell-shaped rim, while soup is poured into a deep bowl of lacquered wood with a lid. These two vessels are practically the only ones that are round. Shortly afterwards they are joined by all sorts of elements—*hachi* or *mukôzuke*—for fish, cooked vegetables or macerated items which will be distributed among the corresponding bowls: *sa-hachi, donburi-hachi, tsukemono-hachi*, in fine china, in glazed stoneware or in rougher enameled earthenware, with regularly curved shapes, or elegantly dissymetrical, or completely "de-formed." The utensils are no longer subject to the general law of a dominant shape or material, but simply to the constraint of containing or offering a specific foodstuff: in fact, they take the name of this food which they carry—raw fish, fermented vegetables or confectionery. This rule, anticipating "form follows function," is so strict that the styles resulting from it are quite alien to the international modern esthetics corresponding to the slogan: dishes in the form of a flower—*kikyô-zara*—flat tiles or composed of indefinable debris of porcelain, as well as perfectly designed bowls in the very finest china. The assemblage of such disparate object on the same table in the course of a meal never ceases to surprise and enchant: the *kaiseki*, the reception meal and the meal of the tea ceremony, is designed around a constantly renewed diversity of numerous dishes bearing small portions but many ingredients. No doubt this manner of gathering together in movement whereby dissonant things are brought together for the time needed to drink tea or share a banquet, is long established; and, a little like the Japanese language itself, whole segments have been borrowed from abroad. The

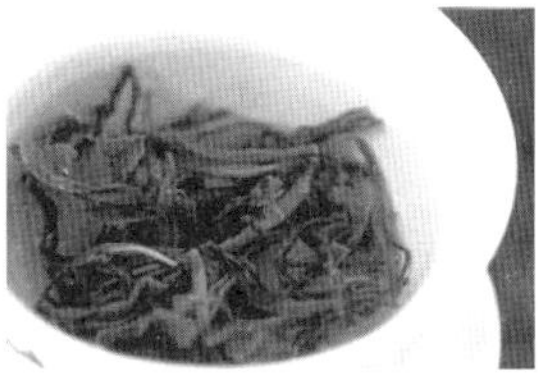

first bowls specifically for tea—the *temmoku*—were Chinese and when they did finally come to be manufactured in Japan, they were fanatically precise reproductions. *Namban* are those imported vessels (from Korea, the Philippines, or Ryukyus) often crude in appearance, dark and not enameled which are used in the way of tea as genuine ready-mades: found objects or objects recycled or misappropriated, through which Japanese society weaves a tapestry of references or allusions to elsewhere and other times—the *mitate*, a notion pertaining to poetry and the art of gardens. This heterogeneous tableware, brought from the most distant ovens—Seto, Mino, Iga, Bizen, Karatsu, Arita—is based on the dissymetry, irregularity and imperfection which the founders of the *chadô*—Shuko, Jôô, Rikyû—set up as an ethics, but also on the formal plasticity the infinite variations of which were displayed by later masters of tea—especially Furita Oribe (1544-1615).

Utensils in China

Kettle (clay, copper, iron); brazier (with flame burner); *zi sha hu* (purple clay teapot, in size between a walnut and a grapefruit, most often a mandarin) or *biao zhun hu* (standard in various sizes: two cup, three-four cup, five-six cup or eight cup); *chai hai* ("sea of tea"); *cha bei* (drinking cup, without handle, the size of a large thimble in varnished stoneware, porcelain or jade); *wen zian bei* (smelling cup); cup plate (saucer or little tray, made of tin, wood or china, for a set of two cups or five guests); bowl for used water; *cha guan* (tea box, in tin, wood or china); *cha ze* (measuring spoon in bamboo, silver or ivory); *cha chi* (cleaning stick, with one end bent to extract infused leaves from the teapot and the other end pointed to clean out the spout of the three pourers); *cha jin* (square of sponge-cloth); *cha chuan* (tea "boat" in china, round, oval or hexagonal); or tea tray (including hot water tap for water of various temperatures, provision for evacuation, aspiration and storage of used waters, drainage and storage compartments); or tea plate; cup steamer; pincers (to hold cups); porcupine quill on handle; measurer; funnel for leaves; ultrafine strainer; jewelers' scales; thermometer; seasoning soft brush; descaling hard brush; teapot rest (a sort of flower-holder, in polycarbonate, to raise a seasoned teapot out of the stagnant water of the "boat"); pair of pokers; fan (made of dried banana leaves, rattan or cane; it will be broken).

Utensils in Japan

Kakemono (scroll with calligraphy, poetry or ink drawing, hung in the *tokonoma* alcove); *han-ike* or *han-ire* (flower vase made of bamboo, china or metal, also in the *tokonoma*, in which will be placed the *chabana*, a sober floral arrangement differing from *ikebana*); *kama* or *kansu* (kettle, in cast iron, silver or gold); *mizusashi* (cold water jar in metal, ceramic or wood); *cha-ire* (tea box made of china for thick Koicha tea); or *natsume* (lacquer tea box for light Usucha tea); *shifuku* (silk case for the tea box); *chawan* (tea bowl in Chinese, Korean or Japanese ceramic), which if it

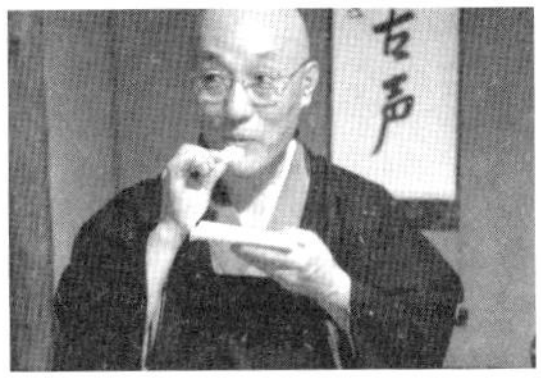

is a *temmoku,* is placed on a raised lacquer stand or saucer; *chashaku* (teaspoon made of bamboo, ivory or plum wood, pinewood or cedar); *futaoki* (tray for the kettle lid in bamboo, china or metal); *chasen* (tea whip, made of bamboo); *hishaku* (ladle of unpolished bamboo for pouring water); *mizutsugi* (covered pourer for filling the *mizusashi); kôro* (scent burner); *ro* (hearth cut in the ground of the tatami in winter where the kettle will stand on a metal tripod) or *furo* (portable brasier in cast iron, bronze or earthenware, in summer); *kôgô* (incense box made of ceramic, shell or ivory with *neri-kô* incense for winter and *byakudan* for summer); *kensui* (receptacle for receiving used water made of china, bronze or bamboo); *fukusa* (square of silk, for wiping the tea box, teaspoon and incense box); *chakin* (linen towel, to wipe the bowl); *gotoku* (tripod); *shikiita* (brasier stand); charcoal (the fineness, shape and price of this wood carbon distinguishes it from what it known by this name in the West); white spills (for lighting); kettle-holding rings; *hibashi* (pair of pokers, in mulberry wood, metal or bamboo); *habôki* (feather to clean the ashes); *haisaji* (ash spoon); *sumitori* (circular, square or five- or six-sided ash basket, lacquered or covered with paper soaked in black lacquer); *sumi* (ashes, which will be arranged in "Mount Fuji" shape); *haiki* (ash container); *hibachi* (vase to hold hot embers); basket for preparing hearth; *daisu* (display shelves for utensils); or *chabako* (box for transporting all the utensils); *handai* (meal tray); *hachi* (food bowls for *kaiseki*); *mukôzuke* (small receptacles for pickles); *kashibashi* (cake dishes made of ceramic, lacquer or basketwork); *komebitsu* (rice box); *wan* (bowls, with lids, for soup); *furosaki* (two-paneled screens); *robuchi* (frame for hearth); *shokuro* (meal trays and boxes); *jubako* or *fuchidaka* (meal boxes with superimposed trays); *meimeizara* (individual plates); *kuromoji* (cake slicing stick); *sensu* (fan); *fukusa-basami* (guest's silk wallet); *kaichi* (packet of cake papers); individual cake stick (*kashi-yôji*).

Utensils in Europe

Urn, hot water fountain; table kettle (copper, silver); cold water ewer; teapot—made of porcelain, stoneware or silver; tea cosy (to cover the teapot); tea box or bottle; teaspoon; tea measurer; tea strainer (separate or as part of the spout); saucer for strainer; small milk pot (mini pitcher or ewer); china tea cups, with handles; saucers; coffee spoon; butter dish; small pot of clotted cream; small butter knife or knife for clotted cream; jam dish (recipient with feet surrounded by set of spoons); sugar dish with lid or sugar sprinkler; sugar spoon; toast rack; cream pot; pot for strawberry jam; jam spoon; plate on stand; guéridon (higher than the previous item); dumb waiter (with superimposed dishes for petits fours or club sandwiches); tablecloth; table napkins; serving tray; shaking, trembling or surprise tumbler (with self-righting device); pocket cup or hunting cup (stirrup cup, with curved edges); *tasse à la reine* (truncated, with saucer and lid); tea mug.

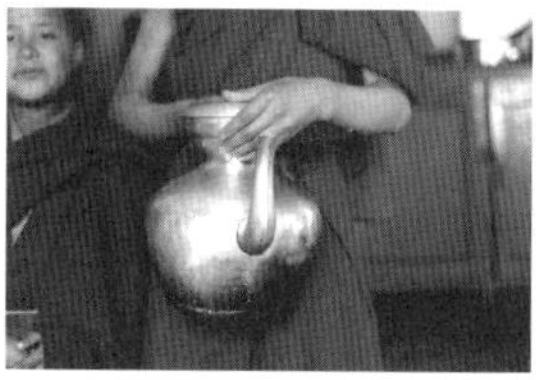

A Service Annexed

"It is an occasion for the richest to show off their splendor: cups, little pots and so on are always made in the most elegant shapes and always imitated from Etruscan or Antique models." (Faujas de Saint Fond, 1797). The first European teapots were modeled on Chinese receptacles that arrived before the importing of tea: ewers with spouts and lids, intended for water, wine or medicines, and teapots proper. Initially made of pottery, stoneware or porcelain; the oldest silver teapot dates from 1670 and only an inscription on it distinguishes it from a coffeepot. Pots from the Yixing region would long be imitated, before the classic shapes were fixed in the eighteenth century: the pear shape, topped by a domed lid; the globular shape; and the "Adam," firstly cylindrical, then oval and octagonal, with straight sides.

The addition of milk and sugar, which became general in Europe, developed the tea service in directions unknown in the East and led to the invention of various utensils: creamer or milk pot, adapted from the various "helmet-shaped" ewers or bowls intended for washing hands; the sugar bowl, an extension of the Chinese tea bowl; the jam dish, a smaller version of the large basin; scissors; tea pincers; strainer; tea measuring spoons; basket for petits fours; toast rack. The largest and most important receptacles are the teapot, which will increase steadily in size, and the kettle that can be more than sixty centimeters in heights; and, taller still, the urn or hot water boiler. While the last of these utensils has not survived the nineteenth century, the kettle has remained a dominant element on the table: "Since then, I have held open teatimes and everyone admires the kettle" (letter from Madame du Deffand to Walpole). Urn, kettle, teapot: the successive receptacles for water, heated water and infused water will be almost exclusively the province of metalworkers, contrary to what happens in China. The metal composition of these three main utensils made it easier to integrate them in the mechanism of the samovar.

Very early, the tea service, as it had been fixed in Europe, was manufactured in China. Thus the Middle Kingdom responded to orders for a type of tableware that it had never itself used, in order to prepare in "barbarian" fashion the tea which, moreover, it exported to the West. This chinaware, brought via the East India Company was called "Indian" even though the Subcontinent might only serve as a point of transit. Orders, detours, returns. Stencils expedited from Europe to Canton where they will decorate porcelain sent from Jingdezhen with a plain glaze. With his famous red stoneware, Wedgwood interpreted tea utensils made in China which were adapted from English silver pieces. Green, pink or blue and white porcelain. The long voyage—European firms, middlemen of the companies, hanist merchants—sometimes had unexpected consequences, such as the mistake on a vase where the Biblical motif bore the mark of "three mariners" instead of "three Marias."

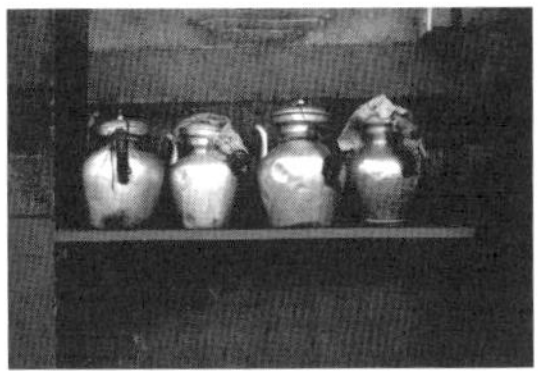

Tea Machine

The genealogy of the samovar is not widely known. The word, like *infusion* and *fermentation,* is supposed to derive from a word connected with boiling: either from the Turkish term *sanabar*, which means "kettle" or "cauldron" (*kessel*) or from the Tartar term *samuwar*. The object might be eastern in origin and related to all those recipients that serve to prepare dishes at the table. There are, for example, those covered pots for stews, such as *nabe* in Japan, China or Korea, which have a central tube that spreads the heat upwards from the brazier underneath. Some kettles for punch also have a similar heating tube that goes through the center of the container. The town of Tula, near Moscow, where Peter the Great set up the forges for his halberds and muskets had iron mines and stocks of wood for the foundry. It is here that tradition places the origin of the first samovar, dated precisely to 1778 and attributed to Ivan Lisitsyn. The industry developed rapidly because in less than twenty years, Tula increased by fifty factories and five thousand workers. A more ancient center of production was probably to be found between Russia, Siberia and China, in the Urals. The utensil was to be found in a great variety of shapes, sizes and materials—copper, brass, zinc, *tombak* alloy, silver and gold. It was less commonly manufactured in china, porcelain or crystal. From that point it became a mass-produced object.

The samovar consists of a central receptacle (*sheinik*) forming the main body of the object and supplied with a tap emerging from its lower part. It is placed on a brazier of burning coals or other forms of combustion: gas, spirits, electricity. It is surmounted by a little teapot in which has been prepared an extract of strong tea (*zavarka*). First the receptacle of the samovar is filled with cold water; then the charcoal is introduced into the central tube and when it reddens, the extension to the heating tube is raised to assure a continuous supply of oxygen. The water starts to boil in the reservoir and the charcoal is progressively consumed until no further smoke emerges from the extension. This is then removed and the teapot, with the tea liquor is placed on the opening of the samovar. Thermal isolation allows both the tea liquor and the simmering water (*kipyatok*) to be kept in its reservoir. When the tea is to be drunk, a little of the *zavarka* is poured into the cup, which is then filled up with hot water from the tap on the samovar.

The samovar permits one to maintain the heat, to boil the water, to prepare the concentrated infusion, to keep this liquor hot, to serve the hot water and to dilute the liquid in the cup. It has at once something of the teapot and the coffeepot. It is an extension of the teapot and a sort of percolator (or of cafetière using the drip method). It is more than an apparatus, it is a machine. Not entirely concretized, yet no longer entirely abstract, its system is a precise integration of its various parts. The outline of the object, like an oriental temple, reveals the superimposition of its domes or organs: the teapot over the kettle which itself rests on the base of the

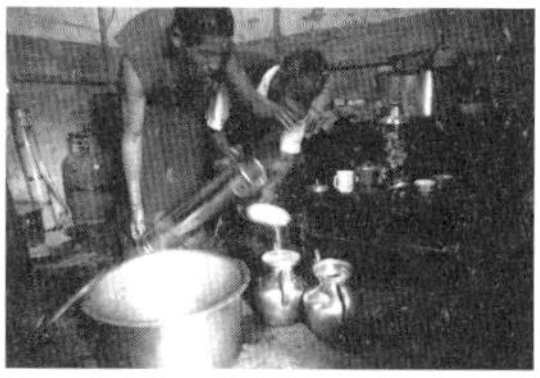

heater; and its accessories—the detachable extension, the tap of the *sheinik* and the drinking cup. The arrangement also places the preparation of tea *à la russe* somewhere between tea and coffee: tea is first made very strong—like "Turkish," as opposed to European coffee—then, later, it is diluted with water. It is as though tea were to pass as close as possible to coffee before becoming tea once again. This concentration of the liquor and this prolonged stay on the heating tube also raises doubt about its state: it is as much decoction as infusion. In this respect, "Russian" tea is halfway between the cooked tea of nomads and the strong infusion of the British, as though to confirm its geography and its economy. The crucial part of the samovar is the *sheinik*, which is to be found in stations, in the corridors of Russian trains and on each floor of a hotel (in charge of the *dezhurnaya*, or floor woman), that allows everyone to get hot water at any time. In this respect, it is less the traditional Chinese *feng cha*, those little tubs of tea waiting on pilgrim trails, than the present-day custom of supplying a thermos at places of work, which is general throughout Asian countries. And the samovar is also halfway between this electric thermos and the kettle on its stove, which accompanies *chanoyu, gongfucha* and *senchadô*. Though it has not entirely vanished—witness the electric element immersed in the water receptacle or even in recent models, identical with the bottom of the electrical kettle—the heating element is no longer visible as it was in the charcoal fire, whether portable or framed, of Chinese and Japanese preparation methods. The chimney for evacuating heat and smoke goes through the body of the liquid, and in this way the fire penetrates the water.

Coffee Machine

During the nineteenth century, in France alone, a thousand patents were entered for coffee-making machines. All the variations invented throughout the world come back to three basic types: the gravity cafetière (Kolschitzky, the "grandmother," the Neapolitan, the Melitta, the pump and the drip method); the air pressure cafetière (Cona, Moka and tip-up); and the steam pressure cafetière (espresso percolator) (cf. Michel Vanier). The first systems—that developed in Vienna by Kolschitzky in the eighteenth century, the one invented by the Frenchman Du Belloy or the "grandmother" method—completed the Turkish infused coffee by filtering the particles of ground coffee remaining in suspension, which allows one to clarify the liquid: an independent metal filter, an open compartment with a simple filter or a closed compartment between two perforated disks. Other devices offer variations on this filtration method: open conical filter (Melitta), paper filter, nylon filter and even gold filter (the best for avoiding intrusive odors), and a bain-marie to keep the infused and filtered coffee hot. In the piston cafetière, the filter, set on a handle, is slowly pushed down on to the grounds and the hot water which have been infused together for three minutes in a glass carafe, with the result that the liquid rises above the

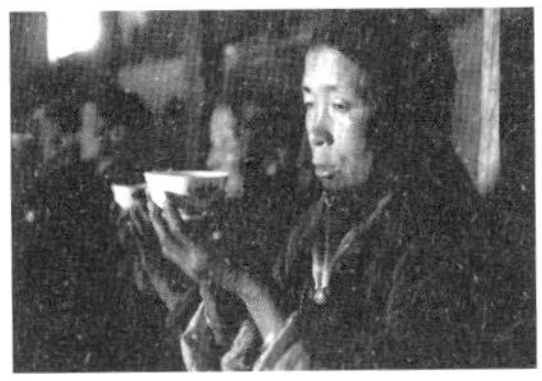

filter. In the widely used "drip" model, a pump sends the water to be heated in small amounts from a tank towards a pipe opening on the grounds which are placed in a conical filter, which is itself placed above a glass pot, heated by an electric element. Once it has been filled with water and ground coffee and set in motion, the machine will itself automatically maintain the temperature at 90 degrees, measure the small quantities of water, stop when the liquid is exhausted and keep the temperature even to ensure that the infusion is not spoiled. In the Neapolitan, invented by a Frenchman in 1819, a recipient for holding the grounds, with an inserted filter, fits above a second tank for the water. When the whole apparatus is turned over, the water impregnates the grounds; once the cafetière is turned back again, the liquid returns to the first compartment.

In the air pressure cafetière, the water that has been heated in a closed vessel is pushed by the expansion of the air trapped above it. The pressurized water arrives either from below (small percolator) or through a tube the end of which is at the bottom of the utensil and opens above the filter with the ground coffee (Cona type with spirit lamp). The source of heat is then extinguished, to lower the temperature of the air inside the bowl and create a vacuum. The coffee, no longer supported by pressure, goes through the filter and fills the bowl. In the moka cafetière, it is not the water, but the steam that is collected in the upper part, after passing through the intervening filter compartment containing the grounds.

In the steam pressure cafetière, the water does not pass slowly through the grounds as in other devices, but is forced through the mass of coffee by steam pressure. Unlike gravity cafetières, where the coffee forms a barrier against the water, the percolator requires the coffee to be more finely ground and this ground coffee to be pressed down (though not excessively), so that the water, under pressure, does not go through it too quickly. It also requires the use of a darker, more highly roasted coffee, to give color. While supporters of this system claim that the speed of its passage allows the water to pick up the essential flavors while leaving behind chemical elements that distort the taste, the conditions prevailing in the percolator—great heat, strong pressure and marked color—are better adapted to robusta or a common arabica. Whatever the system used, serving the coffee is entirely taken over by the machine, in a very precise system of industrialization, applying only one condition to the preparation, which is instantaneity. Indeed, from the water obtained from the town water supply and the preconditioned coffee—roasted, ground and shaped in filter measures for hydro-compression—to the cup, the apparatus brings together all the technical elements—the tip-up cafetière of the last century already signaled the successive integration of various automatic processes—so as to carry out the various stages of percolation in a few seconds. It does so after having fixed the effects of preparation and also of consumption, and somewhat like a camera, as

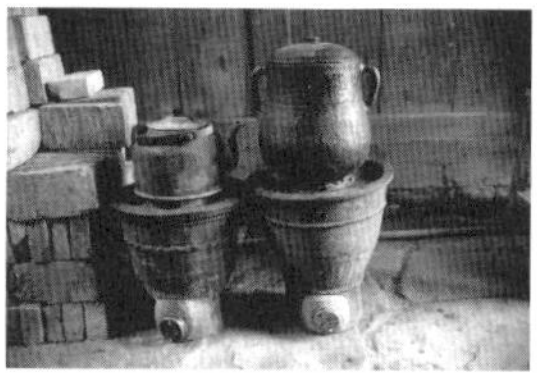

a result of pressure on a button. No doubt what still keeps the mediating and reified structure of the service still in an automatic machine is the need for coffee to be drunk hot and fresh. One can read evidence of how coffee consorts with machines on the front of an automatic drink distributor: where there is a single tea-with-sugar-and-lemon, we are offered at least fifteen types of coffee: expresso, long, moka, instant, cappuccino, with or without milk, with or without cream, with or without sugar, etc. The only variation permitted for tea is sugared or strongly sugared; the "non-sugared" button remains non-operational.

Tea, Water, Bowl

While the preparation of tea by infusion may approach in *gongfucha* or *senchadô* at some extremes of complexity, as much in the taxonomy of instruments as in the ordering of the ritual, it can also be reduced to a minimum of conditions: tea, water, bowl. This triad makes up the elementary ritual in the Middle Kingdom: the *gaibei*, a cup with a lid, made of china or enameled iron, is the instrument that every Chinese person takes with him or her, with a few leaves put in there in the morning which numberless pourings of hot water will exhaust as the day goes by. A recycled glass jar, with or without a lid, is often substituted, indicating greater poverty.
For this variant, the most exemplary vessel is the *zhong*: here, the tea service is reduced to a single porcelain utensil in which the preparation is carried out and which will afterwards be used to drink from. The *zhong* is a receptacle in three parts, entirely integrated with a typical outline of curves and counter-curves. The main element is a curved vessel without a handle, the size of a cup and often of a bowl (though this is not the ideal), surmounted by a lid and placed in a deep saucer. The lid may be lifted by a central protruding hollowed knob, in the shape of an open inverted cone—so as to insert the tip of a finger—, while the saucer, which is sometimes lobed, has a recess in its center where the cup stands; this system, close to that of the Arab *zarf* or the European tumbler, avoids the recipient accidentally tipping up and allows it to be held by its stand, so that one does not burn oneself. All that is needed now is the measure of tea and some hot water. The *zhong* is a summary instrument, yet one of immense possibilities. It provides the best means to examine the color of the leaves, to savor the most evanescent aromas of the tea; and it also allows one to control continuously the degree of infusion in order to derive the optimum taste. Its lid is simply placed on top, movable and capable of being tipped up; it is designed for non-fermented teas, which it does not stew, as a teapot would do. The *zhong* lid also serves as a receptacle for smelling, and as a spoon to homogenize the liquid or to moderate its temperature. The instrument permits the tea to exhale its lightest aromas and offers a full range of savors to be displayed. In this way, green tea can reach a degree of excellence otherwise unknown—which means however that the sample being tasted is subjected to a

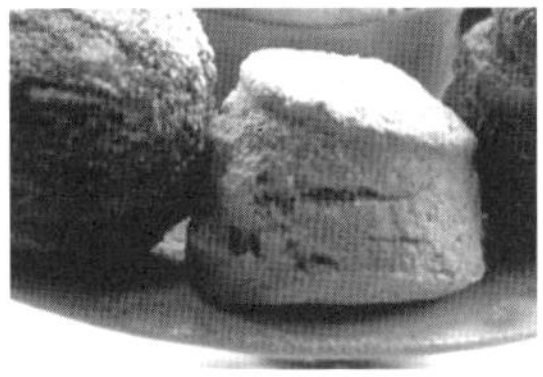

formidable test, bringing out both its qualities and any defects in freshness, manufacture or preservation, which might be moderated or suppressed by brewing in a teapot. While it does not allow one to get the best out of a Wulong or a black tea, it is still a tool for the Chinese master who wants to test the most prominent characteristics of these teas.

In another context, the wooden bowl, often trimmed with hammered silver, represents for Tibetans and Mongols the epitome of the tea service. This bowl, which is sometimes made of simple turned wood, crudely lacquered, or even in some impoverished lamaseries, of plastic, is held on the chest in the *ambag*, the single pocket formed by a fold in the monk's robe. Its essential nature, apart from the fact of being carried against the heart, is indicated by the fact that it is the last property of those who have given up everything else. The bowl, filled with churned tea, is held during the meal in the left hand while the right takes portions of rice or barley that have been served directly on to the monastic robe stretched between the knees. Sole possession, sole instrument, sole receptacle.

Zhong, Yixing, Large Teapot

Chinese connoisseurs use three preparations: the *zhong*, the *yixing* teapot and the large teapot. The choice is determined by the type of tea to be infused. The *zhong* is reserved for non-fermented teas—white, yellow or green—so as not to stew the infusion, which will be accomplished by pouring water (between 70 and 85 degrees, according to the type of tea) that has been allowed to cool or which will be preceded by a quarter of the volume in cold water, to avoid burning the leaves which are often fragile or covered in down. Preparation consists in placing the measure of tea (between one and two grams) at the bottom of the receptacle, and then pouring a first small quantity of water to rinse the leaves—which is then immediately thrown away—before filling the cup, for a period of infusion that will vary from two to three minutes. The leaves are infused until they sink to the bottom. The saucer is held in one hand while the leaves are kept inside the cup with the help of the lid that is held by the other hand; in this way, the tea is filtered before being drunk. Three pourings of water, still at the given temperature and on the same measure of tea, permit three successive infusions.

Preparation in a large teapot is the form that corresponds to the Western fashion; this is no accident, since black Anglo-Indian tea is manufactured like a Chinese red tea, which can withstand the least subtle form of infusion: an approximate measure of tea is placed in a large receptacle made of stoneware, china or sometimes even metal (iron, tin, silver) before being covered with boiling water.

Preparation in a *yixing* teapot, the most refined and most recent method, is necessary for tasting Chinese or Taiwanese Wulong teas and old Pu Er. After appreciating the quality of the dry leaves, take the kettle off the stove and pour a little boiling

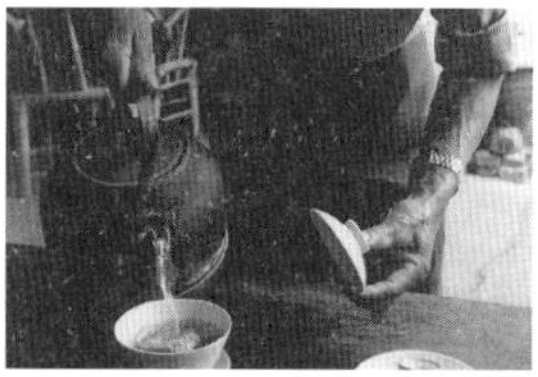

water to rinse out and heat the teapot (*yixing hu*) standing in a boat (*cha chuan*), on a plate or on a tray. Put back the lid, then empty the contents into the reserve teapot (*cha hai*, a pouring receptacle, open, in shape something like a milk jug). Take the necessary measure from the tea box (*cha guan*) with the teaspoon (*cha ze*), then put it into the *yixing hu*. Pour on a little hot water, to "wash the leaves"—or to "wake up the leaves" in the case of a Pu Er—, quickly put the lid back and immediately empty the contents into the *cha hai*; the operation must be performed quickly so that the leaves are hydrated without being infused. The *cha hai* is then emptied around the *yixing hu* in the *cha chuan*. The drinking cups (*cha bei*) and smelling cups (*wen xiang bei*) can also be dipped in the boat to heat them; before they are taken out and replaced on their common saucer, they must be turned into the liquid to heat them through. Fill the *yixing hu* with water to the top, to take off the froth, which makes the tea bitter; then cover. Pour hot water over the closed *yixing hu* to ensure homogeneous heating of the pot and the lid. Wait for the tea to infuse—from three to thirty seconds, according to type—take hold of the *yixing hu* and take the drips off the bottom against the edge of the *cha chuan* by a rotary movement—towards the body of the person who is serving. Pour the contents into the *cha hai*, allowing them to drain out completely, so that the leaves do not marinade in some dregs of water which would become astringent. Pour the *cha chuan* into the receptacle for wastewater (*cha yu*). Pour the liquid from the *cha hai* into the *wen xiang bei*, then lift it to the nose to enjoy the first bouquet. Pour the contents into the *cha bei*, in order to sniff the successive fragrances emanating from the empty *wen xiang bei*. Finally, raise the *cha bei* to the lips and taste the tea in small sips, to enjoy its various aromas. Using the same method, repeat the infusion several times on the same leaves before emptying the *yixing hu* and examining the infused leaves.

Abstraction & Concretization

The preparation of tea for tasting, as practiced in China, Hong Kong and Taiwan (and, to a lesser extent in Singapore, Thailand and Malaysia) is less a ritual or an art than a technique, in the sense that a spacing—a space and a time—is invented for and by utensils that involve a series of gestures. A whole range of variations still to be invented may be numbered between, on the one hand, the *gongfucha* preparation, with the thirty or so objects that it may involve and, on the other hand, tea drunk in the street, with a *zhong*, a pinch of leaves and a little hot water.

The *gongfucha* preparation is a rather abstract technical system ("abstract" in the sense used by Gilbert Simondon), to the extent that each of the objects has a precise function, which contributes to increase their number. Thus, in an exemplary fashion, the collection of the liquid is marked by considerable differentiation: the tea only stays for a few seconds in the stoneware teapot, before being poured into

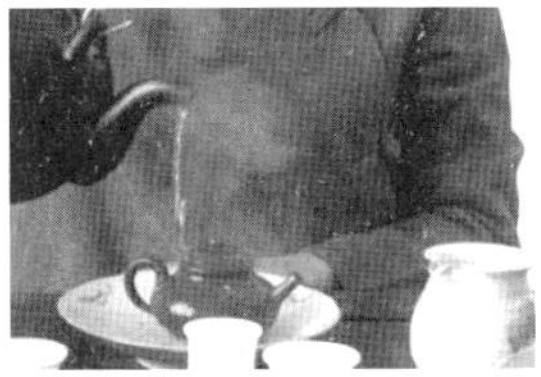

three successive receptacles. First of all into the *cha hai*, to obtain a precisely infused liquid; then in the *wen xiang bei*, a tiny tall and narrow china cup, the function of which is the olfactory appreciation of the aromas; and finally in the *cha bei*, of the same volume and made of the same material as the preceding object, but wider and less tall: this is a cup in the usual sense of the term, its usual function as a drinking cup being reinforced since it is distinguished from a "smelling cup" for the aromas. In the system of utensils, the *wen xiang bei*, the *cha ze* (the teaspoon) and the *cha chi* (wooden pike for clearing the spout of the teapot) are examples of hypertelic development: their existence is determined by a single or very limited function. On the other hand, certain instruments, such as the tea dish, the tea boat or the tea "mother" are already integrated objects which combine several distinct functions, either simultaneously, successively or in a complementary fashion: the dish that receives the tea spilled in pouring, acts as a base and heats the teapot and the cups; the "mother" of tea—*cha hai*, reserve teapot or decanter—serves as a storing place for the teapot's contents, while supporting it on its curved neck, at the same time allows control of the infusion. Many variations on the system have been suggested, especially in recent times when people like to singularize and occasionally to complicate the service, at the risk of superfluity. In technology, a machine that integrates its various components and combines them synergistically, tends towards performance, stability or closure. In the *gongfucha*, the tendency may combine two contrary logics: the integration of the utensils in a complete system and the infinite partition of functions in as many instruments. Thus, tea trays will display an elaborate machinery, with a tap for various temperatures of hot water, evacuation, aspiration and disposal of used water, strainer, storage compartments, multiplicity of materials... In this way, all sorts of utensils will arrive to take part in the performance, accessories in ever increasing numbers, and more and more accessory to the main action: the pincers to grasp and scald the cups without burning oneself, a porcupine quill mounted on a handle for unclogging, a teapot cleaner... And again measuring devices, funnels for the dry leaves, ultrafine strainers, jewelers' scales to weigh amounts to a tenth of a gram, thermometers and seasoning brushes.

At the opposite end of the scale, the *zhong* represents what Gilbert Simondon calls a "concretized" technical system, in that all the functions necessary to preparation, infusion and tasting are integrated. The curved bowl is everything together: pot for infusion, decanter and cup. The lid is at the same time the stopper for the infuser, a spoon and a filter. The saucer supports, stabilizes and allows the cup to be held. Because of its fine china, its size—a diameter of 7.5 centimeters to a height slightly less than that—and its brilliant white color, the instrument potentially brings together the optimal conditions for tasting. In the sequencing of gestures one may first observe the dry leaves being placed in the cup, then smelling the aroma of the

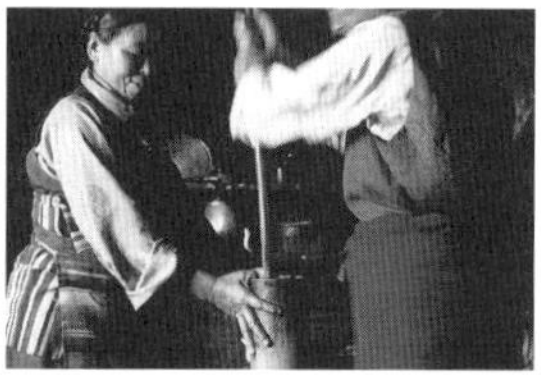

dry leaves, then after rinsing, smell the first bouquet of the rehydrated leaves out of the water, and afterwards, during infusion, see the tea slowly spreading into the liquid and smell how the scents develop, either above the surface, or in the concave part of the lid. In the course of the three successive pourings that will infuse the same measure of tea, the leaves will offer themselves for smelling and contemplation, alternatively floating in their liquid and at the bottom of the cup, out of the water. When the rim of the lid, slender and yet slightly blunt, is adjusted, it sits on the slightly convex inside of the cup, some three millimeters from the edge of the cup: positioned in this way, with no groove or relief to secure the lid, as there is on a teapot, it offers stability by fitting some three millimeters beneath the opening against the bell-shaped cup, but it also permits a swaying and pivoting in every direction, to stir the infusion, and to make it homogeneous or to cool it.

Tea Service, Chocolate Service, Coffee Service

In order to revive a culture that had completely disappeared, it was recently suggested in Korea that the Way of Tea was threefold: the Taiwanese art of tea, the Korean tea ritual and the Japanese tea ceremony (*senchadô*). These three possibilities, while not entirely inappropriate, are in reality all derived from the Chinese *gongfucha*. The objects of the service are very varied, but retain some common characteristics because of the gestural rites that accompany them, the most astonishing of which at first sight is smallness of size. At the end of the Ming Dynasty, the Portuguese brought these "red porcelains" to Europe and around 1680 the Dutch potter Ary de Milde began to imitate such objects, followed by the Englishman Elers, using red clay to satisfy the demand. But China quickly brought out models expressly intended for export, such as those bearing the mark *gongju* ("Tributary Office"), *tianqi gongju* or *shunzhi gongju*. These exports were still taking place in the nineteenth century to Japan, Mexico and other countries in Latin America. But the stoneware teapot and the china cups are so minute that foreigners long considered them merely as playthings or decorative miniatures; and by a curious process of induction, European pottery manufacturers gave their own kitsch versions of them, so pursuing the long deviation—or misunderstanding—which started with the fact that items from the tea service arrived in the West well before the drink for which they were intended, with the result that they were often adopted for other uses, such as coffee or chocolate.

The chocolate pot is undoubtedly the least used among the utensils for the three black drinks: drinking chocolate is only one of the possible ways of taking cocoa and the method of preparing it—by dilution of dry powder or melting of the block in water, milk or cream—does not absolutely demand an instrument: the use of a pot or open saucepan, with a spatula or a whisk often replaces the specific device of the chocolate pot, a pourer with an orifice in its lid through which one inserts the

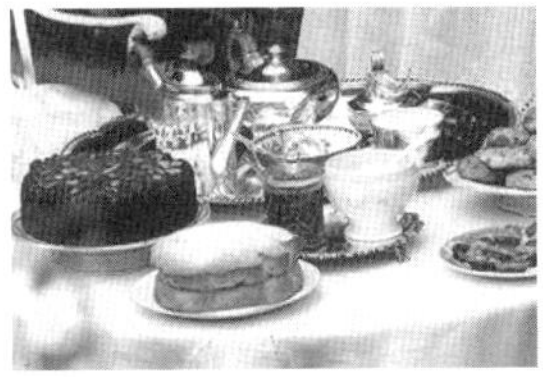

"frother"—a swivel with a fluted or openwork head. To serve the chocolate in the cup, one usually employs an adaptation of the teapot imported from China or a sort of pouring pot, like a milk jug.

For coffee, nowadays, a percolator usually takes over the process of infusion, filtration and pouring by delivering the black, hot liquid directly from a tap into the cup; most other devices exhibit a "pouring" recipient or compartment, more or less integrated to the whole: the glass "drip-method" carafe, the Cona bowl, or the "grandmother" earthenware jug. Before the appearance of these modern cafetières in the nineteenth century, in the original Turkish and Arab customs, coffee for a long time required at least two receptacles: the one that was placed on the fire for infusion or decoction, and a pourer for serving. In the various countries from the Maghreb to Iran, these two recipients were often multiplied by the successive addition of others of every size. This is why, at the start of the century, the method used by the Bedouin of the Arabian Peninsula and Jordan could be described as follows: "There are generally four pots. The largest is called *matbaha* or *kumkum*. For several successive days the coffee grounds are poured into this. A slave puts water on the grounds and places the pot near the fire. The three other pots are rinsed, *jesaneb,* the contents are emptied into the largest, they are cleaned with a camelhair cloth, then they are placed to the right of the fire where there is already a copper pot, *beriz,* as well as a *zedah,* a round receptacle about twenty centimeters in diameter by approximately ten centimeters in height, which serves as a glass... When the coffee has become a fine powder, *jelazzemha,* a slave pours it into his right hand, or directly into the medium-sized pot, in which he boils the coffee. This pot is called *masfa* or *ralaje.* The slave places the cloth with which he cleaned the pot on the handle and keeps it above the fire, preventing the coffee from boiling over. When the coffee is ready, *tbahat,* he places the pot beside the fire to rest. Then he puts a few seeds of cardamom and a pinch of saffron into the mortar, grinds it all together and pours the powder into the third pot, which has been washed and warmed. Then he pours in the coffee from the second pot. This third pot in which the coffee and spices are mixed is called *mabhara...* When the coffee with spices is ready, he pours a part of it into the fourth and smallest pot which is called *delle.*" (Robert Musil, *The Manners and Customs of the Rwala Bedouins,* 1928) The change in the name of the thing itself—rather like whisky in the course of manufacture—is enough to indicate the significance of the various receptacles through which the coffee passes.

Arabs, Persians, Egyptians

In the Arab world, there may be a proliferation of coffee pots: a large coffee pot, or kettle (*mefwâra*); a second pot for decoction or filtering (*mesfa*); a third pot for cooking (*metbaha*); a small pot, for pouring (*mosb*). Each recipient corresponds to a stage in the mixing: water, decoction, adding of cardamom, decanting of the

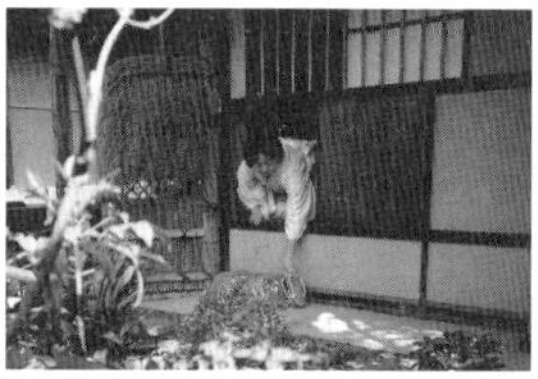

liquid; and each stage carries a different name: successively, the *sherble, kamir, mabhârah* and finally the *bikr*. The three main utensils—kettle, coffee pot, cup—are supplemented by others: the *zarf*, a stand for cups (comparable to the holders for Russian or Scandinavian tea glasses, or the *tasses trembleuses* in eighteenth-century France); the various trays; the serving cloths (*sitil ötürsü*) in velvet, silk or satin; the *sitil*, a stove suspended by three chains, perfected in the seventeenth century, with a cavity for hot coals and a tray pierced with holes, which included the coffee pot, the cups and an ewer for cleaning purposes. These objects, sometimes ordered from European manufacturers, were made by local craftsmen in metal—copper, gilded copper (*tombak*) or silver—simple, chased or worked with garland motifs. The cups, which first came from China, were made of porcelain, glazed earthenware or metal. If one includes all the variations from the Near East to the Levant, the list is still long. The archaic large red earthenware pot, unvarnished (*majûr*), and its communal bowl; the first full-bellied, slender-necked pots, with or without a spout for pouring, with or without a handle, made by local potters or sheet metal workers; the open broiler (*tawah*), the roasting spatula (*mihmâs*), the closed broilers (*kahve tavasi*), the burner for roasting, the distiller for orange-flower water to flavor the coffee.

Iranian utensils: *qahveh-jush* (coffee boiler), *qahveh-riz* (coffee pourer), *finjân* (cup), *gharâ-âftâbah* (black ewer, pot reserved for preparation), *qahveh-dân* (coffeepot reserved for serving), *sini* (serving tray), *piâlah* (coffee bowl), *qahveh-beryân-kon* (broiler).

Egyptian utensils: *bakradj, makradj, bakradj kabîr, saghîr, maghlî, batta, ghallâya, ghallâya tab', tabgh, balaî, talqîm, misabb, misfa, ibrîq, ibrîq baladî* (boilers, coffee pots and pourers), *tâsa, sahn, tbaq, tandjara* (receptacles), *findjân* (cup), *zarf, findjân muk'ab* (cup on foot), *siniyya* (tray), *kursî* (stand), *sukkariyya* (sugar vessel), *mîzan nuhhâs* (small copper scales), *hâwun bi-yad* (mortar with handle), *'amud hadîd* (iron pestle), *nasabat qânûn* (brick oven), *tâdjin hadîd* (iron grill), *munkhal* (sieve), *qas'a khashab* (wooden cooling jar), *sandûq* (box), *khazna, dûlâb* (cupboards), *lakan, sidriyya, disht* (copper basin for washing), *raff* (shelves for utensils). (From H. Desmet, M. Tuchscherer, A. Goushegir.)

"Turkish Style"

For preparing and serving coffee, the receptacles for decoction, transferal or pouring proliferate. However, the three main elements, as designated by the Ottomans, are: the *cezve*, the *ibrik* and the *fincân*. These indicate successively the little receptacle in metal, shaped like a sawn-off cone, with a long tail and a pouring spout, which serves as they say in Turkish to "cook the coffee"; the bowled receptacle, waisted and supplied with a spout, a lid and a handle used to serve the drink; and the little drinking cups, without handles, of Chinese origin. The *cezve (*or *rakwa)*,

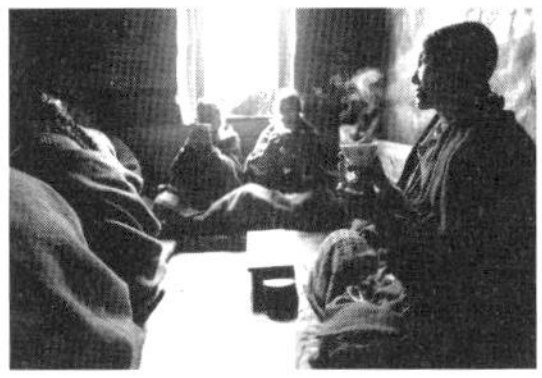

corresponding in size to a few cups, would allow the boiling liquid to be served at once. The *ibrik* referred to a pourer which could be used for all sorts of drinks; the coffeepot was called *kahve ibrigi* (in Egypt it was named *kanaka*). In the Maghreb countries, *bakraj* is more usually used to indicate a kettle, often for tea, while *barrâd* is the teapot itself.

"Roasting gives coffee all its properties, the brown color of the infusion, its taste and its aroma. Moreover, the powder, extract and decoction of green coffee has hardly ever been used except in Russia... in certain cases to replace quinquina." (*Grande Encyclopédie*, 1890) The late date of cultivation of coffee, in the fifteenth century by the Arabs, corresponds to the application of roasting and pulverization to the beans that the Abyssinians prepared by boiling then with their husks. The journey of the Sufi fraternities (which used it to keep awake through nights of prayer), from Aden and Mecca to Cairo, Damascus, Istanbul and Ispahan, came about because of the spread of the religion, but also through this new method of preparation. The Neolithic techniques of grinding in a mortar or dry grilling were optimized by means of objects that were quickly standardized and might have other uses (grill for chestnuts, mortar for flour, mill for salt or spices). While the preliminary stage of separation from the husk belongs to the sphere of agriculture, roasting and grinding are still linked to the phase of consumption, with an intermediary time, long considered essential: that of cooling, for which specific instruments were designed. A mortar and pestle, in stone or metal, pans for grilling coffee, soon replaced, supplemented or improved by tripods, detachable handles, large diameter cooking plates or copper mills which allowed one to roast larger amounts or to grind the measures for consumption more rapidly... Variations in all these objects would be dictated by technical considerations and they evolved less than the European coffee service: open or closed grill, in the form of a pan, a sphere or a drum on a turning axis, with a fastener, a slide fastener or a lever, with wire netting or perforated, and a wooden cooler, a mill with a drawer, in wood, iron or copper, whose the millstone will be replaced by a system of striated disks, fluted cylinders or rotating pallets.

The bean must not "be calcinated; it must be ground after being grilled and not crushed in a mill that will not produce a fine enough powder; above all, it must be grilled, ground and made on the same day." (Mure, 1778). "It is cooked in an oven and then by crushing it in a mortar, it is reduced to powder and boiled in water, then drunk while it is still steaming." (Jean Coppin, 1644). "The coffee was grilled, ground and prepared in some seven or eight minutes." (Edward Brown, 1674) To ensure the freshness of the aroma and the heat of the liquid, the three stages of preparation—grilling, grinding and decoction—took place just before serving, either in the same area of the tent among the Bedouin of Arabia or Syria, or in the

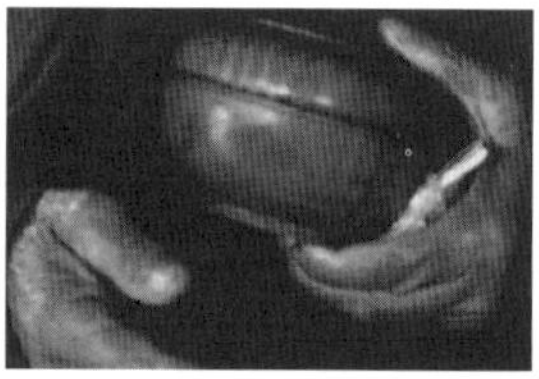

kitchen among the Turks and the Arabs. But the gap between the three preliminary stages—roasting, cooling, grinding—and those of the service—boiling, decoction, pouring—gradually widened. Nowadays, high quality coffee must be infused or "cooked" at the moment when it is served, but more rarely ground just before preparation—the coffee mill, either mechanical or even electrical, is a household object that is vanishing from the domestic sphere—and almost never to be grilled at the last minute—the best one can expect from one's supplier is a recently roasted coffee. While the merchandise known as "coffee" now arrives in the form of black powder, or at least as roasted beans, the coffee house—*qahvehâne* in Turkish, *bayt qahwa* in Egyptian—was long established close to a mill and an oven: a coffee grinder—*maddaqq al-bunn* in Egypt—combined the technologies of the miller and the baker. Rather than the occasional contemporary coffee roasters, this establishment anticipates the industry, which is nowadays responsible for preparing the final product.

The Three Teapots

The teapot differs from a coffeepot or a chocolate pot by the stability of its design: it is that broad receptacle, with a lid, a spout and an element serving as a handle. This stability has guaranteed the fact it would be used for other purposes: a coffee pot, a chocolate pot and a *tisanière* (for herbal teas) are nothing more than the adaptation of a pourer—Chinese in origin whose change of purpose was facilitated by the fact that the Portuguese, the Spanish and above all the Dutch imported ceramics, as well as silk and other special goods before they imported tea as a product: rhubarb, China root (*Smilax china*) and cassia.

In Europe, the teapot was known before tea itself and was to be (as it has remained) at once the place of infusion, the recipient for keeping the brewed tea and the pourer. This confusion of functions, with the increase in the capacity of the pourer and the cups, would lead to a more than inadequate use of those green teas and Wulong that were imported, and gradually establish an exclusive taste for red tea, the black Bree Tannic Tea. In China, however, especially in the regions of Fujian, Guangdong and later Taiwan, the serving of tea tended to separate the role of utensils, between three pourers or more which were successively used in preparing tea: the kettle, the teapot (for brewing) and the holding teapot (which is at once a reserve teapot and a pourer). A pot or ewer of cold water sometimes completed the early stages of service. A sort of watering-can with a very long curved spout (but no rose), may also be used by "tea doctors" in Chinese tea houses, for long-distance pouring or filling the *zhong* of each customer to renew the infusion, a feat of impressive precision. The earthenware, cast iron or copper kettle takes the water to bring it to the boil or to a simmer on a mobile or fixed stove. In present-day *gongfucha* services, this receptacle has a capacity of between half a liter and a liter and

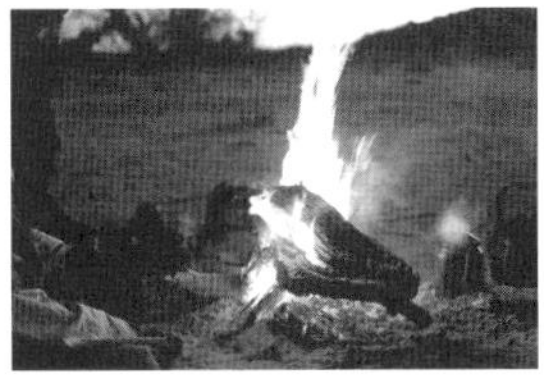

a half, so as not to heat too much liquid at a time which would "kill" it, making it flat or bringing out to excess whatever minerals it may contain in small quantities. Seen from the West, this kettle, the largest of the Chinese or Japanese receptacles, looks like a large teapot, with its pot-bellied form, its lid and its handle or holder. In formal *senchâdo* or *gongfucha* service, where the size of the kettle is still smaller, where it is exclusively made of unglazed earthenware, and placed high up on a vertical brazier, the ambiguity seems even greater. The confusion has been maintained, for the sake of marketing, by those Japanese cast-iron objects, made according to the ancient technique of *wazuku* and copying all the traditional forms and motifs, which are sold as teapots when in fact they are only kettles—*kama*—reduced in size—so reduced that the addition of a filter for the other use makes them unsuitable for either function. The enameled interior and the aluminum of the sieve confirm the anomaly of the situation, since the water cannot be heated in it without the risk of cracking the enamel, and the tea cannot be infused without ruining its aromas.

The other pourers are more exactly what one understands by a teapot, and particularly the *yixing hu*, which carries out the brewing so precisely that it serves only this purpose, and must necessarily be emptied at the end of the process; still, the time of brewing, especially in the case of Wulongs and Pu Ers, may be so brief that the role of the instrument, crucial as it is—a sort of alchemical test—is reduced to a period of time that is almost negligible. The *gongfucha* distinguishes or differentiates what is usually confused elsewhere: the period of infusion and the period of rest. The moment when the tea diffuses and the moment when the liquid is kept. The production area and the conservation area. The fact that in Chinese this other receptacle-pourer is called "sea of tea," *cha hai*, is surely not unconnected with this process in which the water that has been created must be preserved, safeguarded from its own course and from the spontaneous movement by which, if it were to continue, the tea would be ruined by excessive infusion. A repetition of the happy medium which takes place during the manufacture of tea, between fermentation and desiccation, between manipulation and heat. Preparation in this sense is only the necessary completion of manufacture, the continuation of the work.

Number of Infusions

When the leaves are placed in the *gaibei*, the considerable number of pourings of water that will infuse it will not be decided by the quality of the tea, which is often crude, but rather by the certainty that at the end of the day, the water will have lost all color and savor. During infusion, a good quality white, yellow or green tea will undergo an evolution of the same type as a wine, with its successive primary, secondary and tertiary bouquets. However, when a bottle has been uncorked, another

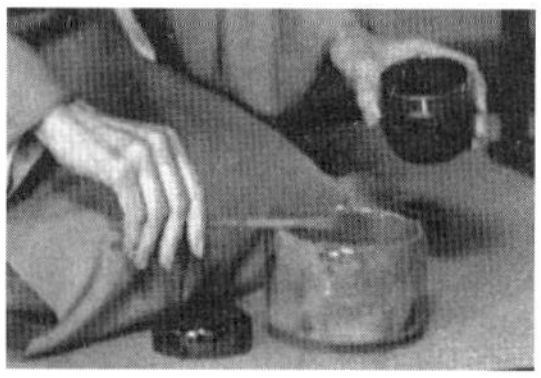

evolution takes place, not in the course of tasting, but in the lost balance of the wine, specifically by way of the acceleration of its exchanges with the air or by the mechanical movement necessary to serve it, which also affects it. Tea follows a similar course, but through various infusions, generally three: in the first one, the most flowery perfumes are diffused, then in the following liquor, the savor takes on its greatest fullness, and finally one sees the dominant character impose itself. This course will reveal even greater differences—more marked or more modulated—in Taiwanese Wulongs and in the huge blue-green family of Chinese teas, especially the Dan Congs or the "rock" teas, the aromatic complexity of which is sometimes even greater than that of wine. Considering that all the nuances of its most volatile aromas are obtained, the period of infusion is remarkably short, rarely as long as half a minute; so the quantity must also correspond to the amount that one will be able to drink before it goes cold; in this way the infusion brings out only a few of the possible qualities of the measure of tea, which must be diffused in later fillings of the teapot. A Wulong, prepared in the *gongfucha* manner, will thus allow between six and fifteen infusions taken from the same tea leaves. For some exceptional crops, these limits may even be exceeded... An old Pu Er is probably the tea in which the number of infusions will be taken furthest: one must say that the length of time for which the leaves are soaked is also, on a sort of compensatory principle, much shorter: the time for the measure of tea to be covered. The multiplication of "waters" on a black tea, only lengthening the amount of time that the leaves are soaked very slowly—by a few seconds at a time—might indeed carry on for several hours, or even days, if the climate is not too hot and if the tea has more than thirty or even ninety years of maturity.

"Rinsing water," Lu Yu said when speaking of bad teas. The phrase is literal if used to designate brewing as still practiced in the West, even in the most highly-regarded places, because it is indeed the first water that is consumed, the water which in China rehydrates the leaves and rinses off any dust. To confirm this general inversion of things, while one has not thrown away the first (washing) water, the leaves are left for too long in the infusion, annihilating any possible fragrances and spoiling the savors of the liquid, and the leaves are thrown away without being given the chance of another infusion. It is remarkable that the counterfeit versions of "British tea" in the nineteenth century, by recycling infused tea, paradoxically achieved what can be extracted from tea with a more precise economy of means.

Little and Often

"I shall not speak to you of the manner in which the Chinese prepare this drink, since no one in France is now ignorant of it, tea having become as much in fashion there as chocolate is in Spain. However, I have observed that, though the Chinese drink tea from morning to night (because it is rare for them to drink cold, pure

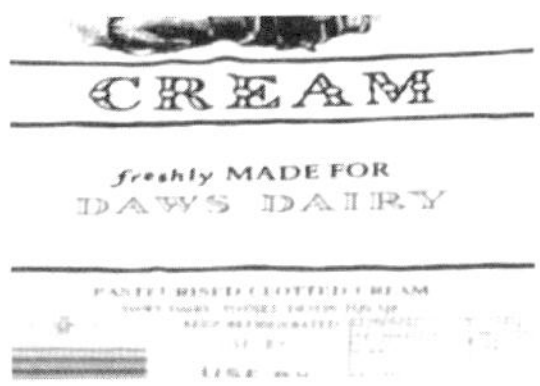

water), they only take a very small quantity at a time and in very small cups. They regard us as greedy and claim that this drink does not do us all the good that it would were we to take it in small quantities and often." (Giovanni Laureati, *Lettres édifiantes et curieuses,* 1843)

"As dusk draws to an end, at the first stars, these ladies arrive, with delightful curtsies [...] Around the room, on trays the shapes of which are elegantly varied, circulate candied fruits with spices. Then appear cups in transparent china, as large as half an eggshell and the ladies are offered some drops of tea without sugar out of dolls' house pots." (Pierre Loti, *Madame Chrysanthème*)

Vintage green tea in China, Wulong in Taiwan or Fujian, Sencha and above all Gyokuro in Japan, are drunk in small mouthfuls from cups barely larger than a thimble, and the teapot is minute. The teapot is as it were adjusted to the measure of tea and closes in around the tea: it is its narrow circumstance. The prototype of the teapot of the celebrated Su Dongpo was a very large teapot with a handle above the lid, but during the Ming Dynasty, pots grew steadily smaller. One may imagine that this pattern of teapot is derived from the ewer which served to pour the water for churned tea or medical preparations, wine pitchers with lids or even pourers to dampen the ink stone for calligraphy: the main development was a reduction in height, removing the neck and reducing the capacity. A Yixing teapot for serving three people is the size of a mandarin or even a walnut for one or two guests, and only rarely reaches the size of a grapefruit when up to seven people are being served. However, the art of tea does not recommend serving several guests: "If one person tastes for himself, he will reach the truth; if two share the tea, pleasure may be experienced; if three take tea together, only the taste of the tea will be appreciated; but if seven or eight are gathered for tea, the tea will merely be spoiled." The measure taken of an old Pu Er is like a pinch of pepper, while that of a Wulong, between six and fifteen grams, when the leaves are dry and rolled up—a Dong Ding or a Gao Shan Cha—occupies more than a third of the place where it is brewed. When the tea—a Wen Shan Bao Zhong or a Dan Cong—is not rolled but coiled, it is hard even to shut in its voluminous leaves. Once they have swollen up, unrolling and spreading, they will entirely occupy the interior of the teapot. The measure of tea, while it may vary according to the strength of infusion desired, is thus weighed out anticipating this expansion. The narrowness of the teapot is linked both to the short time needed for infusion and to the smallness of the cups, which allow the liquid to be drunk in three mouthfuls and at the right temperature. For the requirements and precision of tasting, when there are several guests—three is the ideal figure according to the *Classic of Tea*—the liquid must be divided carefully between all the cups, lined up side-by-side, pouring it out with a rotating, back-and-forth movement.

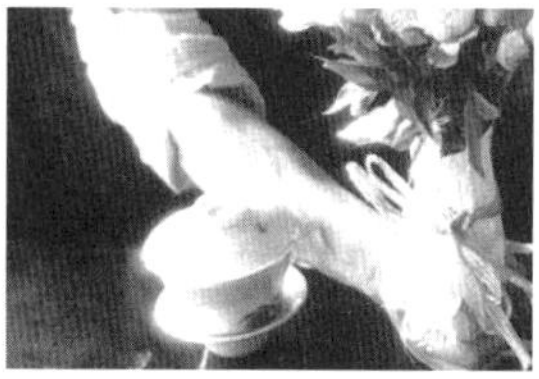

Refill

In the USA, in diners and coffee shops, the waitress or the barman will constantly come back to refill the customer's cup from a jug of "American-style" coffee. This, prepared in contrary manner to the Italian *ristretto* or Turkish coffee, is to be found in all countries of Northern Europe: a black liquid, much diluted yet quite strong in caffeine. It is however similar to English tea, where the broken leaves are infused to produce the greatest degree of blackness. Italians and French people are surprised by this practice of refilling as required, or even anticipating any request, which reduces the black beverage to a sort of water provided by the establishment. It is also a custom not without its dangers, encouraging the consumption of quite a powerful stimulant in large quantities. In a Chengdu tea house, the tea "doctor" is required to fill the *zhong* of his customers regularly with his watering can of hot water. These different waterings, like those that the connoisseur of Wulong pours one after another into his minute teapot, are not a simple extension of consumption, but the development of the infusion—the fullness of the tea appears particularly at the second pouring—or the progressive exhaustion of the leaves.

Lid & Saucer

The minute cups, which caused astonishment in China in the sixteenth century and again in Japan in the nineteenth century, were rapidly adapted for coffee in their import size, while they were enlarged for tea and chocolate. They were increased in capacity, but also by an addition, the handle, the absence of which is systematically remarked on in the descriptions of the first travelers in the East. In the opposite direction, the European beer mug, with its hinged tin lid, was reinterpreted in China as the *gaibei*, firstly in porcelain, then in enameled iron, with a little cord attaching the lid to the handle. The saucer would also be transformed from East to West, passing from the little raised stand of lacquered wood that religiously held up the tea bowl—of *tenmoku (tianmu)* type—to the reduced plate, more or less deep, in which the tea cup is placed in Western services. While the function of supporting without getting burned, is crucial for the under-cup of a *zhong*, which has no handle, and is reinforced by the central recess, in the European example, the saucer makes the handle of the cup redundant, yet offering a staging-post for the spoon, which stirred the infusion, and allowing one use which has become obsolete, though it is recalled in a few paintings: the pouring of part of the contents of the cup into the little plate to cool the liquid. In Russia, this under-cup is filled with *vareniya*—a liquid jam made from cherries, strawberries, raspberries, quinces or red currants— which is allowed to melt in the mouth while the strong, burning hot tea is swallowed.

Bowl & Cup

"A sort of vase in wood, clay, glazed earthenware, porcelain or metal that one uses to drink." (Richelet, 1728) The French word *tasse* derives from the Persian *Tâs*,

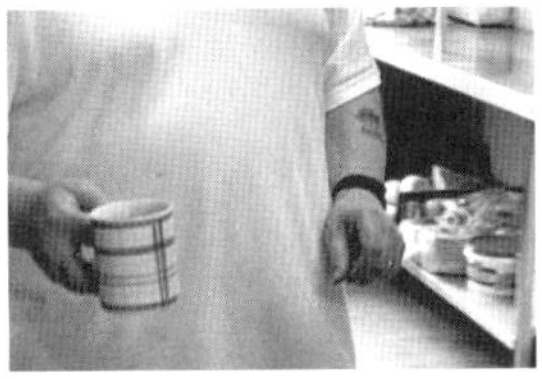

which was employed by the Arabs and Turks for any receptacle used to drink from, an open receptacle, the opening of which was wider than the base or the main body. The word appears in French in 1150, but was little used before the sixteenth century. The word came from the Middle East, where the object had arrived from the Far East. Admittedly, the form of a rounded, open receptacle, a bowl, is more or less universal, but the cup, a more specific receptacle, especially as it is used for coffee, has kept its Chinese associations: the cups without handles, coming from the Middle Kingdom—*pa-pei* (wine cup) or *cha-bei* (tea cup)—are named after the Persian term *finjân*.

The Chinese cup, which was rapidly hybridized, in size, and by the addition of a handle and saucer, is an intermediary format between the cup and the bowl which for the British, by its material and with all the other utensils of the great family of the table service, has retained the generic designation of "china."

In China, the cups that accompany the teapot, particularly in the gongfucha service are little bowls, because of their curved shape and lack of appendages, and in size sometimes approaching a thimble. They are of plain porcelain, white or pale green, sometimes in *yixing* stoneware with an interior glaze of magnesium white to show up the color of the infusion. Often lined up side by side on a ceramic, wood or metal cup tray, they form because of their number—six in China, five in Japan—an assembly, a little theatre promising a sharing-out: the time of tea.

Earth Tea

Tadzhiks, Kirghiks, Usbeks, Uigurs, Kazakhs, Mongols, Tibetans, Ladakhs, Sikkims, Kalmuks, Tartars, Afghans, Turks, Persians, Turkmens, Birmans, Thai, Tuaregs, Egyptians, Moroccans, Arabs, Syrians, Lebanese, Greeks, Russians, Azeris, Armenians, Georgians... The overland tradition of tea, which followed the caravan routes, the Khans and the *cha* vocalization, led to various forms of preparation in each of the countries crossed. Tea is however more often cooked here than infused and when it is infused, it is brewed for a long time. It is a green or black tea, compressed into bricks or cakes, less frequently loose (except in the Arab countries where it arrived later). Moreover it is always complemented by sugar or salt, milk, cream, buttermilk, butter (cow, yak, goat, ewe, mare or camel), lard (yak, beef, mutton, camel or horse), eggs, dried fish, spices (green cumin, saffron, curcuma, ginger, cinnamon or cardamom), aromatic herbs (coriander, peppermint, artemisia, mint—*na'nâ*—, basil, geranium, wormwood—*shîba*—, aniseed, sesame, lemon balm, marjoram or verbena), perfumes (orange flower water or rosewater), fruit peels (lemon, orange or other citrus fruits), cereals (barley, wheat, rye, millet, sorghum or rice), or even alcohol (vodka, rum or rice wines).

"The turn of tea arrived. I took off a small piece of the compressed brick, as hard as stone, made up of as much wood as leaves from the bush. This is slightly broken

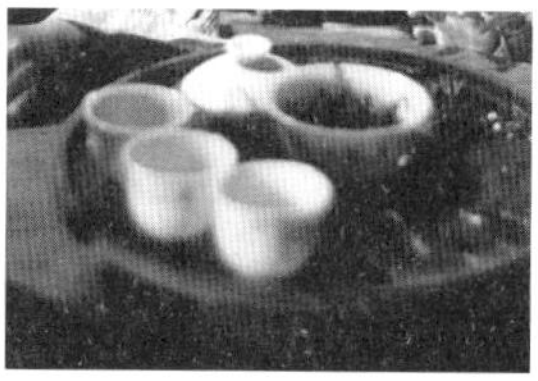

down in the hand then cast into the water: salt and butter are added after boiling for a short time. In fact, it is a second soup, all the more so since we add *tsampa* to our bowls." (Alexandra David-Neel)

Most of the people between China, Russia and India use compressed tea; they reduce it to powder or into larger fragments, throw it into a large receptacle of water which is either cold or already boiling, then proceed to a decoction. They add milk or butter supplied by domestic animals, and pieces of meat or animal fats. They dissolve a quantity of cereal or small balls made of cereals (*tsampa, momo* or dumplings). They complete this with local aromatic herbs, salt, bicarbonate of soda and more rarely sugar. According to the region and local custom, one ingredient or another is essential or not, and the proportions vary a great deal. The preparation can be churned, recooked or filtered... Tea will be the basis of the preparation or a basic ingredient, or otherwise a mere flavoring. Even its consistency will vary from the simple infusion of Ceylon dust in Egypt, prepared very strong and very heavily sugared, to the sort of thick soup, full of dumplings and pieces of meat, which makes up a meal in Ladakh.

The technical method of preparation may also induce considerable changes in the serving of tea: churning with a *gurguchaï* in Tibet; dry heating of the teapot in Georgia to produce a crackling and a scent of roses; the Russian samovar, also used in Afghanistan, Uzbekistan and Pakistan; the teapot place directly on the fire to reduce the liquid, in Morocco and in the desert, and pouring from a height.

The Crucible

Tea, like wine, was a perishable commodity that had to be sold as quickly as possible. Ships—as well as amphorae and barrels—were for a long time more important than cellars. "The lees and the air are the two blights of wine." (Abbé Pluche, 1744) Because of the action of *acetobacter aceti* and other microorganisms, which multiply in the presence of oxygen, wine soon turns to vinegar. The low temperature of a cold storage place and the large size of tuns which reduce the surface area in relation to the volume, slow down this undesirable fermentation of wine. However, it is the bottle, well corked and preserved in the constant, cold temperature of a cellar, that will, from the eighteenth century onwards, prevent uncontrolled modification of the savor and aromas, by only allowing a small amount of oxygen and carbonic anhydride and by preserving a balance among the five hundred different components and between acidity, tannins and sugar. Even wine that has rested on its lees, in cask and for months on end—between three and twenty-one—while being periodically shaken for it to become impregnated with the creamy savors of oak, should be stabilized. It is therefore "fined"—egg white is mixed in to retain all the particles in suspension—filtered and bottled. The bottle was not the invention of a wine-producing country, but of the land which, having been for a long time the greatest

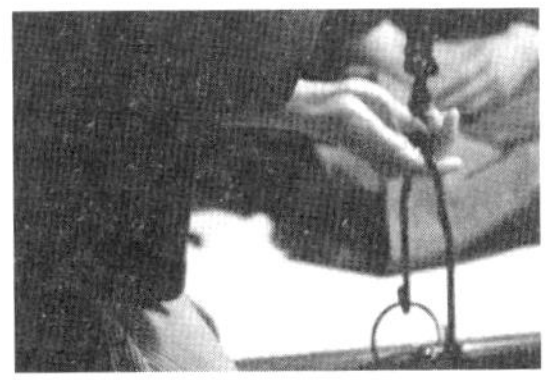

consumer of wine, was the one that shaped many of its characteristics: England (by Sir Kenelm Digby): "Of tubular shape, with a sloping shoulder and a fairly long neck supplied with a sort of ring for fastening the stopper." (Hugh Johnson) This receptacle, later completed by the cork, is the third essential site of wine after the fermenting vat and the wooden cask. When the glass flagon, hand-blown and fragile, was still too expensive, a container of Rhenish origin was used instead, a jug made of enameled stoneware whose glaze was obtained by hurling a handful of salt into the oven. This draped vitrification, of a gray-brown hue, ensured the protection and cleanliness of a liquid which up to then had made do with less perfect containers: bare stoneware, tin or even wood. Wine, already a liquid, has so little need of water that it represents the antithesis of it and must be contained, subject to conditions of impermeability and stability; and thus it depends on a fragile and transparent—though colored— container, and on the removal of the cork which disrupts a whole volume's balance.

After having drunk the spiced drink of cocoa, the Aztecs smoked the bitter herb, the divine herb *tabacco*—mixed with cactus, pimento or coca—in a large pipe of *acayelt* earthenware. The pipe is that hybrid container, between a bowl that one inhales and a hearth that one drinks. This duplication is moreover realized in nargiles and water pipes, which divert the inhaling and filter it through the liquid. The Yixing purple stoneware teapot—*zi sha hu*—is probably related as much to a bottle as to a pipe. The first Chinese utensils from which it derives were sorts of small flagons with narrow necks, serving to boil water and placed directly on the hearth. Its shape and size also make it the little hearth of an infusion which must be brought to a high temperature in order to unfold the rolled leaves in blue-green teas and extract the essence of what is often a thick leaf. It is these essential oils, diffused by the various waterings, that will also impregnate the matter of the teapot. This impregnation is not unconnected with that which occurs in barrels where wines are laid down to mature. Indeed, instead of being rapidly clarified and filtered like young wines, most wines must spend from three to twenty-four months in little barrels of new oak if they are to blossom. The quality of the wood—most often oak, or in Italy chestnut—is critical for wine: the oak trees of the Nivernais or the Limousin—less "spicy" than those of America or Slovenia, but more generous than the Baltic ones—are one of the important features of French wine production. Through its tiny pores, oak allows an essential and measured communication between air and wine. These pores also result in evaporation—the "angels' share" in the case of cognacs—and absorption by the wood, which require regular ullaging and decanting to keep the casks topped up. The Yixing teapot exhibits a similar porosity, which completes its lining. But oak, because it also gives tannin, scent—vanillin—and even empyreumatic aromas created by the burning of the curved

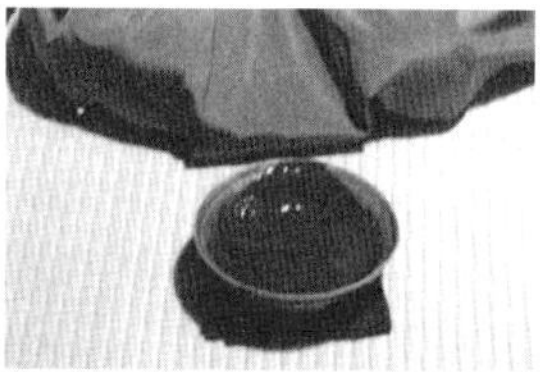

dowels, can only in general receive three wines. Like the teapot, the barrel is more than a receptacle; it is the crucible of a transmutation... However, the stoneware of the teapot does not "give" the tea anything that does not come from the leaf—unlike the cask, which adds its own tannins to those of the wine; it is the addition of the time—or times—of tea to the tea that is being drunk. From this point of view, the teapot is more like a pipe made of heather or meerschaum: it must be seasoned, that is to say, keep the sediment from earlier uses, the "burning" of its successive infusions.

Tea Earth

"When the sky and the earth were still without form, everything was merely outpourings and turbulence, darkness and mire. So this epoch was called the great beginning. At first, the *dao* changed into the immense void, then the void engendered space and time which in their turn gave birth to breaths. These breaths traveled in the network of channels. What was pure and clear evaporated to constitute the sky, what was heavy and murky coagulated to make the earth." This is the oldest Chinese cosmographic account, taken from the third volume of the *Huai-nanzi*, compiled in 180-122 BC. In Asia, the world is initially a soft mass, a mixture of water and earth. In the West, Adam's name comes from the red earth. In each case, clay.
However, clay, on the earth, is a remainder: the disintegration of the feldspar contained in rocks such as granite, a sedimentary deposit in which the amount of impurities varies proportionately to the amount of filtration and hence to the distance from the mother-rock. The earth thus appears in all sorts of states, from the purest, kaolin, indispensable for porcelain, to the most varied. Extracted from the soil, reduced to powder, sieved, cleaned, left to "rot," trampled, beaten, kneaded and shaped. It needs to be refined or recomposed, to have the air bubbles driven out or its porosity preserved, a proportion of mineral granulations to be eliminated or maintained; the balance of silica, feldspar and mica must be chosen and the types of vitrification, fusibility or plasticity selected. One must decide on the temperature for firing: earthenware is cooked at 1000 degrees, impermeable stoneware at 1200 degrees and vitrified porcelain at 1350. One must determine the temperature of the enamels: glazing by "small fire," covering by "large fire," unstable effects by firing with oxidation. Choose to remain below the threshold of maturation to obtain the "tea powder" effect, project salt for an aleatory glaze or wait for the fusion of the ashes for unpredictable runs in the glaze. Before the art of ceramics, clay is already this journey.
The material for a purple stoneware teapot is highly sought after for it combines properties of thermal conduction and measured porosity. The absorption rate of water by purple sandstone is 1.5 percent, with a distribution of air pores somewhere between porcelain and terracotta. This allows for rapid changes from cold to

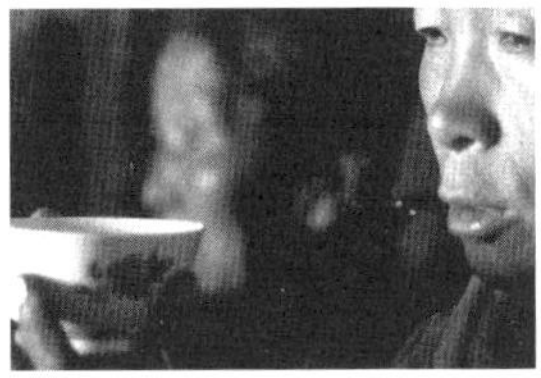

hot without risk of cracking and the maintenance of the high temperatures needed for Wulongs. Yixing sandstone also becomes progressively impregnated by the essential oils of tea, as it is nourished by the leaves' color and aromas. Without covering or enamel, this clay baked at more than one thousand two hundred degrees undergoes a hardening close to vitrification. It was only after the eighteenth century, and then only sporadically, that colored glazes were used, such as the opaque "robin's egg" enamel, or pale or black glaze. Other complements were added to the bare sandstone: a coating of red lacquer, a tin covering with jade handles, copper trimmings, on the spout, at the edge of the opening or on the lid. But these additions were seldom made because they contradict or disturb the interactions permitted by the very precise porosity of purple sandstone: exchanges of water, fire and vegetable matter. Because of these interactions, it is essential that an object which is modified at the molecular level should never be washed, particularly not with a detergent: it should be rinsed in hot water, brushed to prevent deposits and polished. It is filled up, impregnated and given a patina. Indeed, one must create and preserve the seasoning obtained by repeated infusions which leave an invisible deposit, nourishing the sandstone and permitting the infusion to release more and more subtle aromas. The injunction never to clean one's teapot, distantly derived from the Chinese art of tea, and which many European connoisseurs solemnly repeat to each other, is more than inadequate when applied to the materials which make most of their pots: porcelain, metal or glass. Never washing these impermeable receptacles can only ensure one thing: that the teapot becomes more and more dirty—perpetuating odors and moulds, and progressively adulterating infusions of already stunted teas... For a *chashi*, on the contrary, the teapot is "alive" and he is not content merely to care for it as a work of art, he waters it like a plant—so that it will give the flowers and the fruits of its infusions. In the "test" of an infusion, the crucible—the *têt* or *test* was the cupel of an alchemical experiment—does not remain intact; it is transformed, little by little, by what takes place in it and, by that very fact, becomes a better site for future operations.

Yixing Teapot

Made in the famous ovens of the Jiangsu region, with purple sandstone collected from quarries that have become rare and are strictly controlled, the Yixing teapot must harmonize with the most complex and delicate teas. The assigning of a teapot to its tea, the knowledge of clays and their very varied colors, and the appreciation of forms, masses and consistencies thus form part of a new field of experience, the complexity and long history of which have no equivalent in the West. What thus appears as a central aspect of "the tea of art" is a very specific piece of technical knowledge, such as a cellarer has of his pieces and his vats, combined with an expert knowledge of the history of ceramics. The ability to recognize a quality clay,

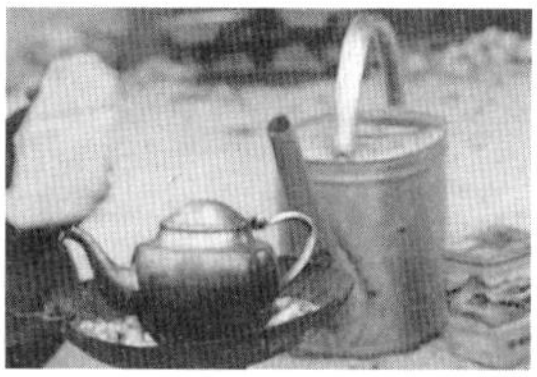

to appreciate the technical qualities of a teapot and to maintain it so that its qualities do not fade, form a whole branch of the practice of the *chashi.*

Chen Hongshou (1768-1822), nicknamed *Mansheng* and also known by the collective designation of the "Eight Masters of the Xiling School," was for three years the chief magistrate in Yixing and involved many scholars, calligraphers, poets, engravers of seals, officials and collectors in the creation of teapots with potters—Yang Pengnian, Yang Baonian and Yang Fengniang—either for the overall shape, but more often for the calligraphy, drawings or seals that were engraved on them.

From the Ming period onward, Yixing were collectors' items and the subject of discussion and of writings, among which the *Yingxian Minghuxi ("Chronology of the Teapots of Yangxian")* was the first monograph, featuring thirty famous Ming potters. Among tea amateurs and beyond, a whole world of connoisseurs started appearing several centuries ago around the Yixing teapot. The very large number of tourist-made versions available in China do not allow one to imagine the extravagant prices that sustain the true market: a good teapot for everyday use, still unseasoned, is worth between four hundred and one thousand dollars, while a collector's teapot can often exceed several tens of thousands of dollars. The last great Chinese master-potter, who died in June 1996, sold his final pieces for one hundred thousand dollars. In 1998, in Hong Kong, a small group of collector's teapots went for over a million.

In a tea house for well-informed amateurs in Taiwan, when a label hangs from a teapot, it is not attached to a teabag inside; this is the mark of a Yixing teapot "boarded out": as with a bottle of spirits kept aside in a *mamabar* in Japan, the purple stoneware teapot, often very valuable, is waiting for its owner when he comes in to drink a fine vintage in his favorite haunt. More than that: some Chinese scholars would always take their teapot with them, so that they could drink directly from the spout, with no other utensils—tea at the teat, so to speak.

Teapot Shapes

Some shards date the use of stoneware in China to the Song dynasty, but the oldest surviving Yixing pots mostly date back to the Wanli period (1573-1619). Unlike Jingdezhen, the other great center of Chinese ceramics which specializes in porcelain, Yixing—Jingxi or Yangxian—provides fewer points of historical reference for its objects: there are few varieties of use, few changes in shape over time, few indications in enameling or slipware, no mark indicating the reign and little reliability in the potters' seals. Indeed, while every type of object was manufactured at Yixing—flower pots, jars, vases, bowls, cups, tea bowls, tea mills, dishes, plates, boxes, stands, incense burners, perfume burners, ornamental fruit, wall brackets, snuff bottles, containers for locusts and various types of figurine—the teapot represents at once the most frequently produced object, the most typical and the one

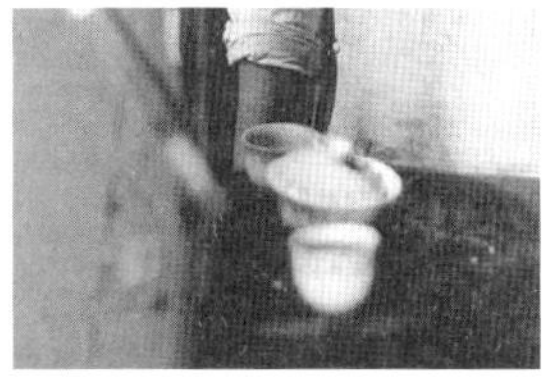

that makes the best use of its material—with flowerpots, also because of the porous nature of the stoneware. The renown of a name led to endless copies and a potter's descendants could carry on the style and signature of the founder over several generations (as in the case of Hui Mengchen in the seventeenth century). Thus, by a process accentuated in the present age, teapot manufacture involves a constant repetition of models, some of them classic, others related to famous prototypes. Unlike the Japanese practice which favors the risky surges of lathe-work or the irregular uniqueness of coil-work—reinforced by the baking of the *raku*—, the Chinese preferred techniques of slab-building, modeling and carving do not encourage a constant reinvention of shapes. The Yixing teapot, escaping from historicity, is the copy of a copy, and often bears superimposed marks: beside the copy of the original seal, that of the potter who made it and sometimes the seal of other intervening interpreters of the form.

While clay and porcelain are granular structures, the molecular structure of purple stoneware is "ladder-like." The plasticity and minimal degree of shrinkage in Yixing clay allows it to be finely modeled and not deformed in firing. These technical features, contradicting its status "outside history" and the predominance of its use as a vessel for brewing tea, make the versatility, ductility and polymorphous features of the pot. Indeed, though the Yixing teapot has varied very little as a device—being a container, with an opening, a spout and a handle—it offers a tireless and peculiar diversity of shapes, which seem to affect it in the same way as the morphing of a synthetic image. Outside Yixing and China, this polymorphy can still be observed in the kitsch of European teapots, which may not only be covered with all sorts of designs and painted scenes, but also adopt the most fantastic—but also the most stereotypical—shapes, like some kinds of porcelain piggy banks: houses, rabbits, trains, pumpkins, cabbages, elephants... One may note that in the early days of digital imaging, the design that was used by researchers in the fields of 3D and virtual reality, chosen for its simultaneous qualities of regularity and complexity, was a teapot. Like few other objects, apart perhaps from watches and cameras, the teapot has been displayed in simulation and dissimulation, adopting a whole register of shapes—geometrical, figurative or hybrid—with a kind of indifference, an endless interplay of disguises.

Hence at least three types may be distinguished among these teapots: I. Geometrical shapes, round, square, floral, nodular, egg-shaped, rectangular, triangular, hexagonal, octagonal, multifaceted, seal-like or cylindrical; II. Natural shapes derived from melons, fruits, flowers, plants, insects, fish or animals. Some forms are reproduced in their entirely: pine, bamboo, plum, colocynth, jujube, persimmon, lotus leaf, lotus seed, butterfly, bean, *ruyi* cloud, plum tree flower, begonia, chrysanthemum, lobed flower, morning glory or bamboo trunk. Others retain their

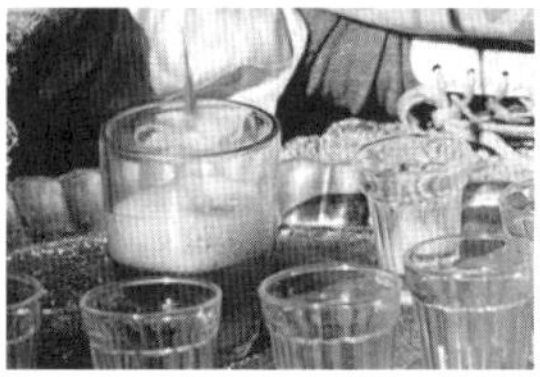

geometrical body with spouts, handles, lids or other appendages as figurative designs: bamboo trunk, squirrels, grapes; III. Shapes copied from other objects: the base of a column, a *dou* (unit of measure) square, tin pots, bronze cauldrons (*ding*), jade utensils, painted crockery, Qing dynasty bricks, Han dynasty tiles, bronze coins, or in the shape of a *sheng* (unit of measure), a knot, a pillow, a *ding* cauldron, bells, tripods or rings… Some examples make up riddles through a combination of shapes: sections of bamboo and pine, a pine trunk with a horse, a comb and a coin. When the teapot retains a non-figurative shape, it may be covered with a superimposed decoration: I. The application of animal, flower, fruit or bird motifs, first modeled then applied to the object; II. Paintings applied to biscuit ware with colors based on aluminum oxide, iron oxide or magnesium oxide; III. By incision and relief: calligraphy, drawings of figures or landscapes, seals…

Earth Colors

Like the porcelain clays of Jingdezhen and those of the Longquan kiln, purple clay—the Chinese word *ci* does not distinguish between techniques—is a composite of kaolin, quartz and, mica, but it contains a higher proportion of silica, iron and other metals. These last elements, their minute grains visible to the naked eye, determine several colors of stoneware. Sandstone also maintains a balance between kaolin that provides hardness and impermeability, and *petuntzi (baidunzi)* which supplies plasticity and fusibility. The first type of these sandstones, which gives its name generically to Yixing, is *zishani*—"purple clay"—dark red in color which on firing turns to various shades of brick, brown or violet. Another type is *lüni*—"green earth"—where the raw clay seems a whitish gray or gray-green, and which on firing becomes somewhere between light gray and yellowish gray. Finally, another variety, *hongni*—"red earth"—is reddish-brown and emerges from the oven gray-black. These three main deposits are situated in Huanglongshan in the prefecture of Dingshu, Yixing.

Less extensive deposits include other minerals that form a palette of nine colors, sometimes destined to be mixed together or tinted by the addition of other pigments. Yixing clay thus offers a quite wide range of color shades: begonia-red, cinnabar-purple, sunflower-yellow, green-black, sand-white, brown-black, aloe-white, emerald green, dull gold, bright gold, grape-red, pomegranate skin, pear skin, bean green, bronze green, jade green, etc. In the same way, by keeping, sifting or adding particles, all sorts of textures may be obtained: the "soft osmanthus" paste, glittering with golden shards, the "pear skin" with its sandy yellow grains on the surface, or others with rougher textures.

The clay of the pot is therefore touched by the same spectral virtuality as tea: passing from white to black, through yellow, green, blue-green and red. On one side, mineral composition, on the other, vegetable state; the effects of firing in the oven

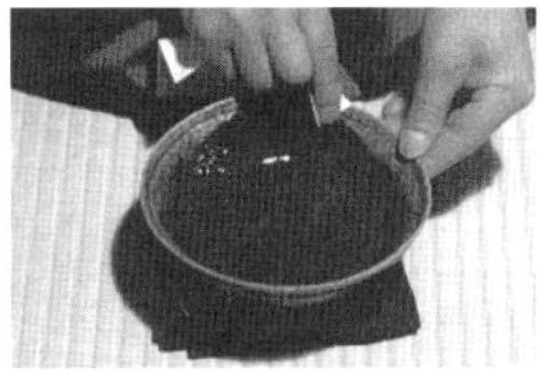

as much as the results of fermentation in the hands of the tea-grower—which is to say that, each time, and by reason of quite distinct physico-chemical reactions, heat—the potter's trial of fire or the heating of the tea—and oxidation—metallic or enzymatic—produce an alchemy in which transmutation is manifested as a rainbow. These virtualities, at once opened and covered together by the container and the content, create a world of shapes and colors, the vastness of which has still to be explored. Journeys in this space are those of the art of tea, of tea of the *gongfucha* art, when the *chashi* has to assign a teapot to its tea: judging the thickness of the sides, the consistency of the material and the harmony of shades, one must proceed to testing, with the constant risk of irretrievable mistakes.

Handle, Spout, Filter

The teapot—*kyusu*—arrived in Japan with Ingen, the Chinese monk who founded the Zen Obaku sect in 1651 at Uji and brought the infused preparation of Sencha. It is a tool—*dôgu*—which, after being imported, was regularly adapted or confronted with its provenance and then, in the nineteenth century, manufactured according to the methods of Yixing, especially in Tokoname, with red and purple sandstones. Even when the shapes are figurative, they are more sober and more usually turned on a wheel than modeled.

Japanese pourers have to adapt to the Japanese methods of tea treatment and the infusions that produce green tea is, unlike in China, brewed in a pot. The tea is of inferior grade to Chinese teas, in that the leaf, subjected to steaming, rarely remains whole. In recent years the fashion has been still further exaggerated—*fukamushi-sencha*—to obtain teas that give more taste and green color. Therefore the filter of the receptacle and the fineness of its mesh are important elements in the object. It may be integrated inside the body of the pot, at the base of the spout, in the form of a little perforated hemisphere made from the same clay. It may be of metal and fixed inside. It may also consist in simple grooves or serrations on the edge of teapots without handles. These appear like adaptations of the *zhong*, with a lid supported by a groove, and a simple notch in the edge acting as pourer.

The Japanese teapot varies the position of the different parts: a curved handle opposite the spout, a straight handle at right angles to the spout, an upper handle in wickerwork (for larger Bancha teapots). The spout can, as in China, be beveled, at right angles to the axis.

Risks of the Teapot

The history of every teapot is one of high risks. A teapot is first and foremost a ceramic utensil: it can be broken, chipped or scratched. It is in Japan that this aspect is noticed and made the most of: in a civilization of catastrophes—earthquakes, typhoons, tidal waves, fires, volcanoes and floods—the European idea of heritage does not exist—or, at least, does not affect buildings. The Shinto shrine of Ise is

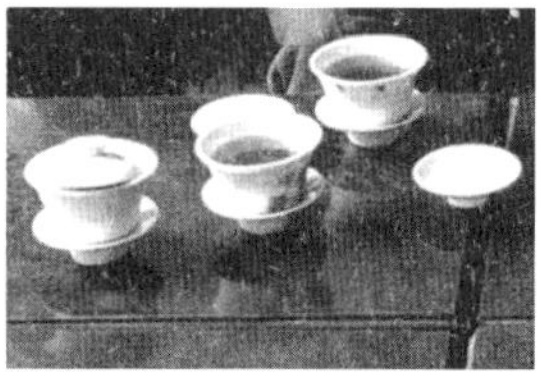

divided into two zones in each of which, alternatively every twenty years, the shelter for the emblems of the imperial goddess is reconstructed, while the other awaits its turn. This temple building in cypress wood is famous for reproducing centuries-old methods of construction, shifting the identity of the thing from the persistence of matter to its persistent renewal. While in fact one also finds in the Japanese archipelago the oldest buildings in the world in perishable materials—the Horyûji and the Todaiji—the model of Ise is still determinant for the Japanese view on matter. Here, the memory of things recedes in front of the transmission through the traditional arts, which are themselves placed under the responsibility of a school, ensured by the descent of a family and an authority, the *iemoto*. Tradition in Japan is always considered as preservation, the saving of a world that can at any moment vanish without trace. On the other hand, small things—bowls, incense boxes, calligraphy scrolls, ink stones, flower vases, bonsai, kimonos—are the object of formal conservation: all the instruments for tea, all the precious goods of the family and all sacred ritual vessels (whether Shinto or Zen) have thus been preserved in Japan in a way that has no parallel elsewhere in the world. Some of the oldest Chinese writings or the oldest Korean ceramics, brought by Buddhist monks or seized in military campaigns, are thus kept and venerated in the "treasuries" of Japanese temples, while others still change hands in the antique trade. *Chawan, cha-ire* or *chahaku*—the tea bowl, tea box and tea spoon of the *chanoyu*—are thus objects handed down with such precious care that each bears a name and the title of the work, and is accompanied both by the name of the artist who made them and the various "tea people" who have owned or used them. The Yixing teapots of *senchadô* and *gongfucha* are thus objects of care, conservation and collection. They are protected in cases of embroidered silk, paper padding and a light wood box, closed by a woven cord and wrapped in a cloth for transporting them—the *furoshiki* in Japan. This excessive protection, which wraps wrapper in wrapper, is so crucial that those close enough to the object itself are handed round for examination at the end of the tea service. It probably also contributed to the effective preservation of the utensils of the oldest masters of tea, which have gone through cataclysms, wars and the trials of inheritance. A purple sand teapot, when it has been seasoned, is at risk of other dangers apart from being physically damaged: it can "go out," "go to sleep" or "be ruined"; it can lose its patina or its aroma, or worse still attract some parasitic, alien smell. A slow preparation demands that before the first tasting, good teas be left to infuse, only to nourish the new stoneware; maintenance after every use consists in drying the pot, brushing off any deposit and making it shine. But the teapot demands that even at times when it is not being used, one should make sure, by occasionally filling it with boiling water, that it is not becoming moldy or shutting up.

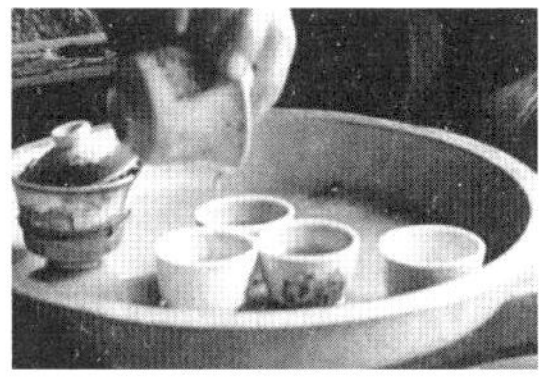

The Three Materials

According to Yamada Jôzan, the only master-potter of *shudei* pots alive in Japan, the pourer, the tea leaves and the water form a sort of trinity—*san mi itaï*. In China, the *gongfucha* would display the *wu xing*, the five Taoist categories of natural processes: kettle (metal), hearth (fire), infusion (water), tea leaves (wood), and teapot (earth); their combination—water, earth, fire—giving the teaplant as well as the pottery. The preference for the wheel-turned teapot in Japan is no doubt to be considered with the elements involved in the turn of the potter's wheel: set in motion by the turning plate driven by the foot and transmitted by the vertical axis, the lump of clay on the board is subject to the effects of centrifugal force: made of earth and water, it borders on the "pneumatic."

Whoever has been able to see the manual work—even applied to teas as different as a Long Jing in China, a Dong Ding Wulong in Taiwan or a Sencha in Japan—is struck by the recurrence of familiar gestures: the tea leaf is treated by hand as a paste that is kneaded, divided, brought together, stretched, packed down and rolled. These gestures, which are used on such dissimilar materials, are very similar to those of a potter—or, indeed, of a baker. And in reality, through the transformation that affects them, the materials of tea and clay—to which, in another sphere, one might add bread—stand in similar relations to the action of the hand, air and fire: kneading (or even stamping) of the earth / wilting of tea (plastic improvement of the material in a formless state); maturing / fermentation (plastic improvement of the form); turning the pot / rolling the leaf; molding of the clay / manipulation of the vegetable limb; desiccation / drying; baking in the oven / brewing in the teapot. (The analogy is even to be found in an additional detail: after firing, a technique is applied to Yixing sands that involves rubbing them with wax and polishing them: this protection for the pores will be removed before use; and, in order to improve the appearance of some green teas, they are occasionally placed in a machine to be polished with talcum and gypsum). This long parallel journey undoes the ancient opposition between the farmer and the artisan-potter, accused of sterilizing the earth with his fire.

The activity at the center of *gongfucha* takes place between the three necessary bodies of tea: the tea itself, the pot and the water. These three entities, by reason of their respective structures and materials—in particular when it involves a Wulong, a Yixing and spring water—share a fundamental quality which allows infusion to take place: that of capturing smells, tastes and colors in some profound manner. This quality of constantly endangering one's own character in order that one may be penetrated by another, of losing the signs of one's specificity in order to bear the appearances of foreign bodies, is what is at stake in tea. (One may recognize it, by contrast, in the use made of the remains of the infused tea. Tea leaves, emptied of their juice, may serve as fertilizer or as a filling for pillows, but above all to absorb

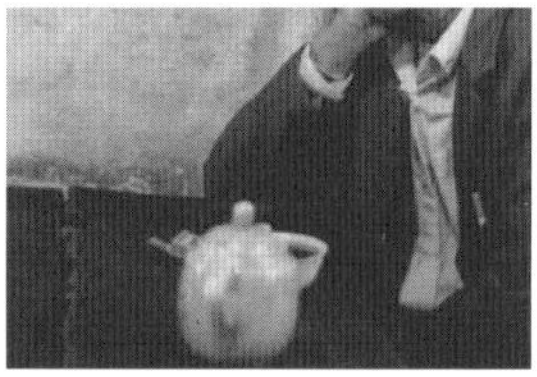

unpleasant smells; to deodorize a space, an object or the body; to drive away insects; to purify the air. One rubs infused leaves into one's hands; they are re-dried to fill sachets in a cupboard; they are dried and burned in a small dish like incense.) Spring water, which has been filtered for a long time by deep rocks, soft, vital, is the element which by its general circulation in the biosphere is defined as a liquid at once neutral and essential; its liquid state allows conduction, diffusion and dilution of everything that touches it much more certainly than air and earth, where bodies are liable to evaporate or collide. The art of tea—particularly of Wulongs, Dan Congs and "rock teas"—consists in finding varieties of shoots, cultivating them and extending gardens so that the plant may discover in its soil, climate and exposure, the unfolding of complex scents and savors: so that the tea leaf can absorb its mountain and its mist. The art of the teapot—especially the purple sand of Yixing—is to maintain a balance in the kneading of the clay, its maturing and its firing, between metallic impurities, air pores and kaolin, which will grant it that power of absorption, that margin of impregnation, that imperfection to slowly compensate, as well as a high degree of plasticity, efficient thermal conduction and undoubted impermeability. In the course of the *gongfucha*, the Yixing teapot is regularly watered with boiling water to keep it hot, to moisten it and to season it with tea, which subsequently helps it to bring out the taste, scent and color. The hot body of the teapot is also caressed with a soft brush moistened with the spillings of tea left in the plate or tea "boat." The container as much as the contents, the teapot as much as the infused liquid, are thus the sites of a subtle diffusion between leaf, water and heat. The stoneware of the teapot is nourished by the excellence of the tea, which leaves its essential juices on it, while the tea emerges all the better when the earth in which it unfolds has an historic patina of delectable infusions. A time of epiphany and the epiphany of time.

URBANITIES

Some Other Manners of Using Tea

"This herb is employed in various ways. Firstly, in substance when, being dry, a whole half-drachma is given in a glass of warm water. Secondly, as a decoction: as much as a drachma and a half is given, adding sugar so that it may be taken with greater pleasure, and it is drunk hot. Thirdly, by distilling it in a bain-marie, with the appropriate waters. Fourthly, one puts it to infuse up to one ounce and a half in some cordial water or a good, delicate wine, of which one takes up to three or four spoonfuls, adding a little sugar. Fifthly, one may make extracts of it, which are put in pills, the dose being up to ten grains. Sixthly, one makes of it scents in the same way as one uses Tobacco, in pipes, for cold sicknesses of the head or of the chest, or

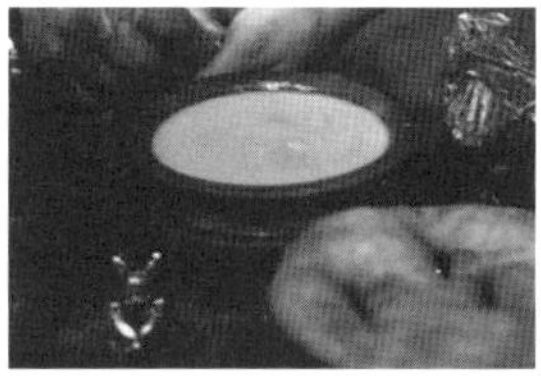

for the fluxion that descends on the nostrils." (Professor Tencke, quoted by Philippe Sylvestre Dufour).

Digestion, Cooking, Customs

"Dietary regimes, good manners, utensils for the table or for hygiene: all these means of mediation thus fulfill a double function. As James George Frazer realized, they no doubt play the role of isolators or transformers, relieve or lower the tension between poles where the respective charges were abnormally high. But they also serve as standards of measurement. In this case, their function becomes positive, instead of negative, as it was previously. Their compulsory character assigns a reasonable duration to each physiological process and each social gesture; because, in the end, good manners demand that what must be done is done, but that nothing should be done too fast. Thus, despite the routine roles that they have come to occupy in everyday life, objects that are apparently as insignificant as a comb, a hat, gloves, a fork or the straw through which we suck a drink, remain mediators between extremes: filled with an inertia that was once deliberate and calculated, they moderate our exchanges with the world and impose a calm, peaceful and domestic rhythm on them." (Claude Lévi-Strauss, *Mythologiques*, vol. III)
There is a sort of postponement that goes from the time of digestion, passing through the time of preparation, up to the time of manners of serving. These three moments correspond to specific places and different modalities, which involve microorganisms, technical utensils and instruments demanded by etiquette. "An organic, anticipatory model of culture," digestion is that temporary retention of food in order to assimilate and eliminate it in an elaborate form, just as cooking, with its recipes, is a suspension of the natural process that leads to putrefaction, and as table manners are a mediation added to consumption.
There are probably few other human products that have developed the three stages of this process to the same point as tea. If one considers it from the opposite point of view, the consumption of the Chinese leaf is one of the last around the world which is practiced as a ritual, its forms being very diverse and three of them in particular—*gongfucha, chanoyu* and teatime—reach degrees of technical complexity, esthetic metonymization or social formalism such that it would be hard to find any equivalent for another type of goods. Recipes for preparing it—Tibetan tea with butter, Japanese Macha, infusion in a *zhong*—are also very numerous, especially given the limitations on ways in which it is taken: it is not smoked or eaten, only drunk. Finally, at the level of the first—natural—stage of mediation, which is absorption-elimination by the biological body, tea stands as an emblem of the whole process: indeed, from its most ancient uses in the Chinese pharmacopoeia to its most recent chemical analyses, *Camelia sinensis* has been considered a plant which favors digestion, disintoxication and purgation. The manner—the time of

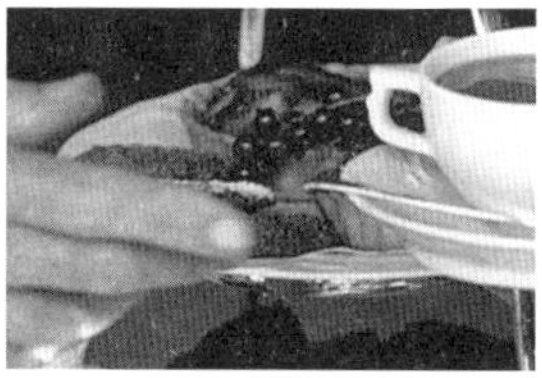

tea—which provides the circumstances of tea, is the effect of its matter: the time of tea is the temporalization of a general digestion; the time of tea is the postponement of a relationship with the world.

Manner, Matter, Time

"The aristocratic society of the court adds coffee to its repertoire of ostentatory signs and the use of this drink becomes a fashion on the same level as chinoiserie or the Moorish page boys whom people owned among their servants as though they were little hunting dogs. In reality, what matters to these privileged folk, is not the drink itself, but the forms in which it can be consumed and the opportunities that it offers to demonstrate one's elegance, grace and preciosity." (Wolfgang Schivelbusch) The instruments of coffee and the etiquette surrounding its service are essential to absolutism: the manners—the courtly ceremonial—the container—the porcelain tableware—are the very forms through which it manifests itself. For the bourgeois society of the seventeenth century, coffee was rather prized for "the thing, its properties and the physiological effects that were attributed to it," especially for two qualities which recur in the praise of it as a panacea: "temperance and sobriety." "It has been proved that coffee makes peoples sober. Whereas formerly artisans and clerks would take ale, beer and wine in the morning, becoming in consequence apathetic and incapable of serious industry, they are now accustomed to this middle-class drink that keeps them awake." (James Howell, 1660). Or, two centuries later, Jules Michelet: "The cabaret has been dethroned—the base cabaret in which, under Louis XIV, youth staggered from the barrel to the wench. Fewer drunken songs by night, fewer noble lords in the gutter [...] Coffee, the sober liquor, powerful in its effects on the brain, which—contrary to spirits—increases precision and lucidity, coffee which suppresses the vague, heavy poetry of the mists of the imagination, which makes the spark and lightning shaft of truth spring from clearly-perceived reality." This is the drink of the rising, rationalist bourgeoisie, which does less physical work and works less outside, and of the absolutist, bureaucratic state: "Coffee now acts as a drug of historical significance. It infiltrates itself into the body and operates chemically and pharmacologically what rationalism and the Protestant ethic operate in an ideological and ethical manner. With coffee, the rationalist principle gains access to the human physiology and transforms it in line with its requirements. The result is a body that functions according to new demands, a rationalist and bourgeois-progressive body." (Wolfgang Schivelbusch)

"Thus [coffee] may be considered as expedient for those to whom it is more important to save time than their lives and health, and who are obliged to work late into the night." Carl von Linné (Linneus) lists the elements at stake in a new economy—time, work, health—and the means by which coffee, apart from its price, became

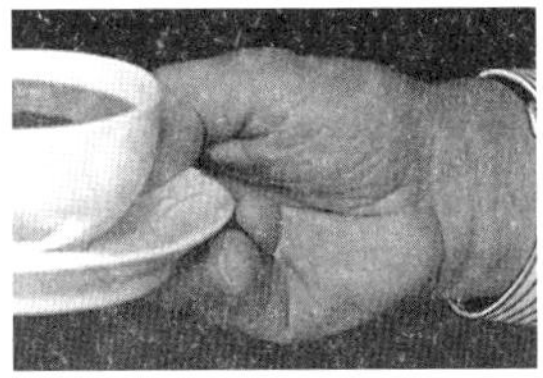

increasingly the dominant drink for European capitalism. Catholic chocolate was not to spread in the same way until it had been rectified by Protestantism: definitively dissociated by the Dutch method (cocoa / chocolate, powder / butter, drink / confectionery) or diluted with milk by the Swiss method. Chocolate, tea or even sorbets will always be subject to the caffeine drink, the paradigm of which is always displayed on the fascia of their outlets: "Café." But while "coffee-houses" or "chocolate-houses" in England, like the *kaffeehaus* in Germany or Austria, cafés or *caffe*, in France and Italy kept their privilege, tea also gave rise to places in which it was designed to be consumed: tearooms or *salons de thé* in Europe, but also tea houses—*çay xaneh*— in the Near East, which are distinct from coffee houses—*qahveh-xâneh*. This specific place for tea, this space for its species, reminds us (in however small a way) that tea invents a new time.

Ostentatious Prodigality

"After a brief discussion, [the Agha of Damiette] demanded that they should bring him the sorbet and the qahvé. I saw four servants arrive clothed in Dolimans of fine white linen, with belts of red satin brocaded in gold. They had velvet bonnets trimmed with cotton cloth, very fine, & their hoses, made of linen, which went down to the feet, was scarlet with very pointed shoes in yellow morocco. Two among them handed silk napkins to their Master & me, putting one knee on the ground & the two others served us liquors in porcelain with the same genuflections." (Jean Coppin, 1644)

In the etiquette of the Ottoman seraglio, the preparation and serving of coffee were carried out, under the authority of a superintendent (*kahveci basi* or *kahveci usta*), by three servants: while one carried the hanging tray with the coffee pot, and another held the tray of cups, the third served the coffee. A simpler service, with fewer staff and less precious objects took place outside the palace. A code determined the hierarchy of service, a definite number of female or male servants, and a fixed order of distribution among the guests. Clothing, carpets and materials, furniture, scents and incense might harmonize in the distribution of coffee. However, no piece of furniture apart from multi-functional ones (occasional tables) and no specific place was set aside for coffee, but simply decided by the proximity of the place of preparation to that of consumption. The participants were only subject to general obligations: decent dress and behavior, clean hands (ensured by an ewer for washing) and praise of the service... The personnel, wearing a "dark purple, lilac or brown" color, were expected to combine skill and grace, reserve and a smiling face, silence and coordination. This "coffee ceremony" was part of a collection of signs through which the gestures of everyday life in Ottoman society displayed "ostentatious prodigality."

In modern Turkish society, coffee is marked by contradictory tendencies. A simplification of the service, and an increase in the number of utensils: alcohol stove,

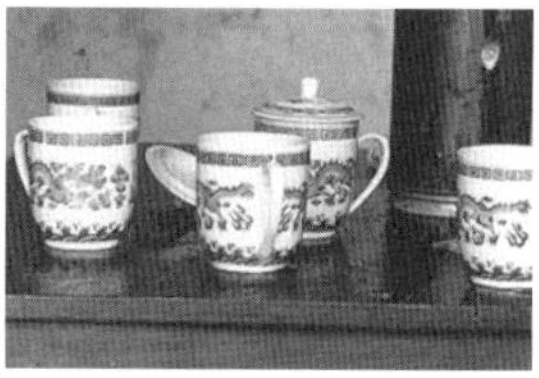

little portable cupboard for all the equipment, sugar basin, coffee pot, cups made in Turkey (ordinary crockery from Canakkale, or porcelain of Yidi or Incirli). The artificial survival of ancient forms of a ritual of hospitality without imaginary bases has reduced its instruments to simple accessories. And the caffeine drink, widely and commonly drunk in Turkey—street vendors, coffee houses, hammams—was finally to be dominated by tea.

Automaton, Service, Ceremony

The guarantee of the quality of a wine—the *appellation d'origine contrôlée*—is its name, which is to say its label, defining its "origin" within the progressively more restrictive limits of a region, a district, a château or a *clos*. The guarantee of a beer is also to be found on the bottle, but extends to a "brand," a firm or the name of an industry—in this, it is little different from a cola or other soft drink. You can "photograph [these bottles] as they were, not drink them." (Guy Debord) In this relationship, some receptacle or other—a glass or mug—, the gesture of pouring and that of opening the container are the only elements that stand between the commodity and the mouth that consumes it.

Unlike wine, the matter of which, a liquid, is already conditioned; unlike chocolate, the mass of which is entirely taken in charge and delivered by the industry; unlike coffee, the preparation and serving of which are taken over by the machine-apparatus, tea cannot be reduced to a manufactured product. When it is taken over by the industry, it is nothing. Tea is only produced through a process of preparation, the period of infusion, which takes place at the moment of consumption. Serving is an essential attribute of tea. Tea, as offered in a French café-bar, shows a clear symptom or sign of repression concerning its service: indeed, while this drink is more expensive than coffee—while it is undeniably more bland than it—this is not solely because it is not taxed, but because it must always be served in a teapot. This, however, is superfluous more often than not for infusing the usual presentation of tea, the tea bag. Adding further to the redundancy of the useless pourer is the supplementary pot of hot water. As well as making additional work for the person serving, this probably represents a theatre of signs, the thread of which has been lost: the ritual, void of meaning but still necessary, sad or laughable, of a *chanson de geste* without gestures.

With European tea, the preparation and the gestures that accompany it have been abolished by the machine for infusion or the industrial apparatus: the samovar that integrates the various sites of tea, the automatic distributor, the can. "Teatime" already devalued the ritual and its operation: "tea service" only refers to the objects for preparation. The English hostess, if she infuses the tea herself, does so in the kitchen, while it is usually a member of the domestic staff who carries out the serving. Each time, the work demanded by the time of tea is glossed over, hushed up or

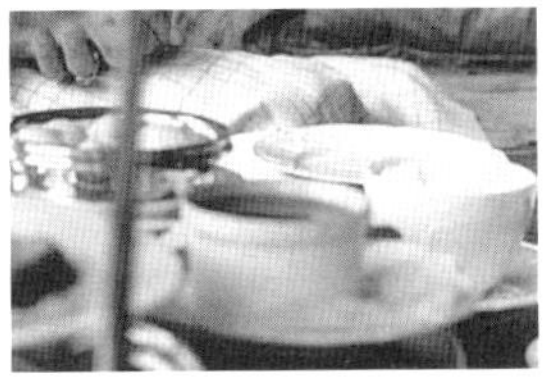

saved. Finally, in the ceremonial of tea at a reception, it is the decoration, by covering the instruments, and the richness of the materials, by ensuring ostentation and opulence, that blocks out the objects, instruments or receptacles by a symbolic or sumptuary demonstration.

The Tea Bag

"Sachet for one cup. Net weight: 2 grams. Preparation: Use one bag per cup. Bring to the boil pure, fresh water (preferably mineral water). As soon as it is boiling, pour the water on the bag. Let it brew for two to three minutes according to taste." (Twining, Merchants of Tea and Coffee, London)

Tea in sachets or bags, as it continues to be used by the majority of consumers around the world, as well as "instant tea" and "iced tea," are said to be American inventions—though in the two latter cases, Japan offers similar but more ancient practices. In Song Dynasty China, tea was parceled out into silk gauze sachets several centuries before Thomas Sullivan offered it in cotton muslin ones. After World War II, long-fiber paper became customary and, with its breaks and added colorings—identical to those of Coca-Cola—brought a deep color tint into the cup, the teapot and the sink. In the 1990s, the paper bag—with its chlorinated decolorant and the glue that seals it—was once again replaced by the individual muslin infusor, which rapidly gave way to the "crystal" sachet—first in nylon and later in polypropylene—, allowing one to observe the leaves of a less finely chopped tea, because the first synthetic material gave off carcinogenic substances at high temperatures. Recently, too, the Tetley bag known as "Drawstring Teabag" is a kind of apotheosis of the tea bag, allowing one to extract the last drop of liquid out of it: the label divides along a dotted line and there are two strings, so that one can squeeze the bag without using one's fingers.

In Edo society, "street culture"—*michi no bunka*—that of the "floating world"—*ukiyo*—or that of *kabuki* created or maintained, probably more than in Europe or China, all kinds of service and local trades. In addition to that, a great network laid down in the Meiji era, the structure of which survives in the modern economy, articulated and reticulated the country by chains of large department stores—*depatô*—which developed their own railway lines. It is in this context, that in the 1920s a private company was to start producing a service of meals-on-trays—*bento*—to be sold in stations and on trains, like those which used to be taken into the theatre. The tray was bought with a teapot specifically designed for it, made in bare stoneware and covered with advertising calligraphy, and with an integrated cup, placed upside-down under the wicker or metal handle and acting as a second lid for the pot. Mass-produced in the Shigaraki ovens, it was redesigned in the postwar period as a vertical model, quadrangular and fluted, on which the cup-lid rested as on a thermos flask. This version, which anticipated the tri-pack packaging, was later adapted in

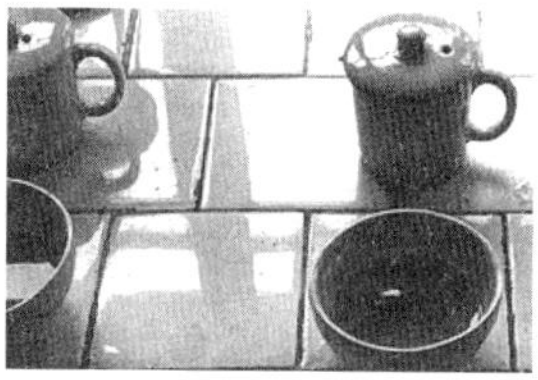

the same shape, but in plastic, including an integrated strainer and a screw-top cup. It was still being sold at the start of the 1990s in the Shinkansen train, with a cellophane wrapper and a sachet of broken tea leaves. Kept in a heatproof protector by the sushi seller, the translucid teapot contained hot water into which the contents of the sachet had to be poured directly and left to infuse, before the green tea was finally poured into the cup, the leaves being held back by the strainer. In 1995, this container-infusor was still being sold, hot, under a cellophane wrapper, but the metal sachet accompanying it contained… a paper tea bag. In other words, the preparation of fresh tea, which used to involve a teapot, a cup and some gestures—opening the hermetic wrapper, unscrewing the cup, opening and pouring the measure of tea, waiting for it to brew, screwing the lid back, lightly shaking the liquid, opening the receptacle and serving the tea, while straining it—which made this rather more than just a pastime in the high-speed train, suddenly became redundant. The little teapot, which, having gone from stoneware to vinyl polychlorate, and thus gained in transparency, doubtless heralded that loss of function in which it would become merely the manifestation of a ritual without foundation.

Teatime

"Teatime is an art of living. It implies knowing how to take one's time, looking after one's comfort, rising above the everyday and savoring the moment." (George Orwell, *A Nice Cup of Tea*)

"Surely everyone is aware of the divine pleasures which attend a wintry fireside: candles at four o'clock, warm hearthrugs, tea, a fair tea-maker, shutters closed, curtains flowing in ample draperies to the floor, whilst the wind and rain are raging audibly without." (Thomas de Quincey, *Confessions of an English Opium-Eater*)

"Under certain circumstances there are few hours in life more agreeable than the hour dedicated to the ceremony known as afternoon tea. […] From five o'clock to eight is on certain occasions a little eternity; but on such an occasion as this the interval could be only an eternity of pleasure." (Henry James, opening words of *The Portrait of a Lady*)

The "time of tea"—the teatime, the time of the tea—has been defined in its relation to the moment. Teatime is time to take tea, the time "for" tea. It's about time for tea. It's about teatime. Tea, it's about time. It is the moment for drinking tea. The time of tea is the imperative of tea. The imperative of the time of tea is time. But the time of tea is time without imperatives. Time as the present. The present as eternity. Eternity as outside time. The time of tea is time outside time. The time of tea is tea outside time. There lies all the pleasure.

Tea Break

The jasmine tea that accompanies the menu of Chinese restaurants in the West is only a form of exoticism, because in China tea is not drunk during the meal. In fact,

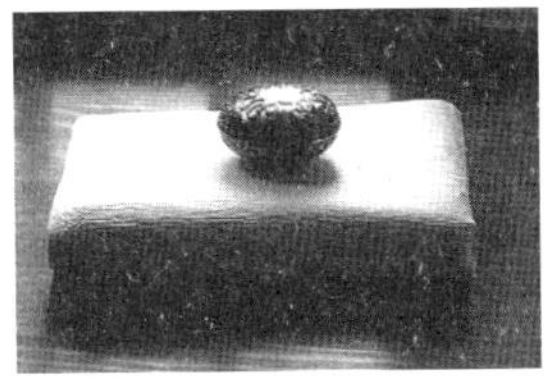

one never drinks while eating, except alcohol on great occasions. Between meals, however, and at any time, tea is drunk everywhere and in any container. In Northern Europe, Scandinavia and Russia, people drink quantities of tea as they might with beer. The handle of the tea cup, not found in China before the *gaibei*, is not unlike that of the beer mug. Henceforth it is in the Hanseatic states that the greater part of the tea market—which has deserted London—circulates for re-sale throughout the world.

Established custom among all classes in the United Kingdom is hard to alter: the soldier stops on the field of battle, the worker considers a "tea break" as one of the rights of employment, the aristocrat pursues teatime as a duty of his idleness. Repeated pauses that respect the rules of etiquette, or are taken informally in a mug. Moreover, Anglo-Indian tea, with its full-bodied insipidity, was designed to be drunk throughout the day. If the color of Bree Tannic Tea is very close to coffee, especially as prepared by the Anglo-Saxons, and if it represents a sort of extended coffee, the time of tea itself is an extension of the time of coffee. A pause, a halt in life's rhythm and a renewed vigour… In Japan, The time of tea is also a stasis, a specified time, whose ritual also exists under a formal mode—the meeting around Macha—and an ordinary mode—the Bancha Hojicha served at home or in the office—and even an intermediary mode: the way of Sencha, with its "informal" formalization.

In Morocco and among the Tuaregs, tea is drunk at a special time reserved for it, no doubt because of the time needed for pouring it from one container into another and for decoction, and because it is served during the pause of the mehari or when receiving guests. Tea in Tibet or Sikkim also shares this time of tea, with a wait for the churn and the occasions for consuming it—during prayer or a meal, or to welcome someone. The economy of this pause, that of the Tea Route, is linked to the time needed for preparation, in each case singularized in the location—mint tea, tea with butter—and because it is an essential commodity, expensive and imported from China—Zhucha, Gunpowder or Mi Zhuang, bricks of black tea—which does not consume it, but manufactures it specially.

Time for Tea

Teatime is the time for tea. In Japan and in England, the times for tea are formalized. The traces are to be found in present-day counters that dispense tea by a minimal therapeutic prescription, according to the moment of the day for which a tea would be most appropriate. There is a time for tea, and a tea for every time. In China, among the Tuaregs and in Tibet—but also in England and Japan, for ordinary tea—there is no time for tea since it is drunk throughout the day: it is therefore the tea of all times. There is no time for tea, but a tea of time.

Tea is thus always linked to a precise time, to time cut up, to time marked by the clock: Early Morning Tea, Breakfast Tea, Lunch Tea, Afternoon Tea, High Tea, Late

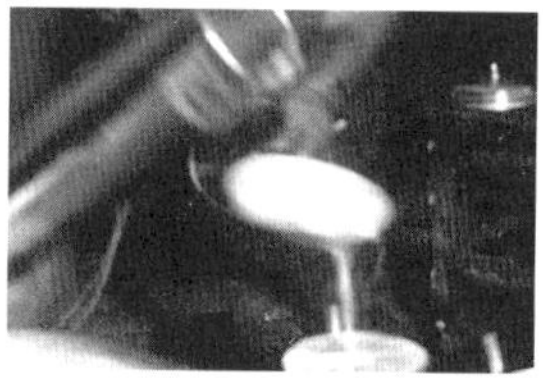

Tea. Before being subjected to formal etiquette by Edward VII and becoming a social obligation with its own dresses—"tea gowns"—its music, its gardens—"tea gardens"—five o'clock tea seems to have been taken up in the 1840s by Anna, Seventh Duchess of Bedford, as an interlude, to keep her guests occupied between the two main meals. It was the time at which tea was taken that would decide the type—informal tea, formal tea, reception tea—and the nature of the accompanying food—the food that accompanies it rather than the other way about, since tea, from the name of the meal or the snack, has become the subject of the matter: indeed, in country areas, and among the working—and middle-class, tea from the outset replaced soup to constitute the meal. This is especially the case with "high tea," still taken in Scotland and the North of England, which started in the Industrial Revolution as a hearty, filling, nourishing repast for workers in mills, mines and factories. All other attributes of tea—cream tea, man's club tea, tango tea, tea morality, nursery tea, tea dance—merely add a social or culinary detail to the main event.

The European time of tea is not the "service" of tea, but the "consumption" of tea—and the spending of time. This time only involves the drinking of tea, while even if the hostess takes charge of it herself, preparation is always relegated to the kitchen and usually carried out by domestic staff. In the Japanese *chanoyu* or the Chinese *gongfucha*, the preparation is not disconnected from the time of tea. In the Japanese archipelago, the social content, the interplay between host and guests, as well as the reinterpretation of the symbolic order of a culture continue to determine the posture of the bodies, the circulation of objects and the exchange of views. The Japanese service is that extremely complex and complete whole of minute events and insignificant things which are taken into account to make up the circumstances of the business of tea: from the wood charcoal to the tree leaf abandoned on the moss of the path, through the extent of rotation of the tea bowl, *chawan*, in the hand. Everything is considered, everything considerable; everything, around tea, is related to tea. In *gongfucha*, it is impossible to dissociate the service of tea and the taking of tea, like *yin* and *yang*, the two aspects of the movement of the world: the time of tea is the time of infusion, it is the moment when the leaf of tea abandons itself in its water, when its juices, which have been retained and developed, will let themselves go as a hot, scented and delicious liquid. Preparation, both by reason of its nature—the vegetable leaf whose fragility only abandons itself at the last moment—, of its technique—the pouring out of cool, bright water, heating it, infusing it—and of its function—welcoming, sharing, hospitality—must be carried out in the time of tea itself. The time of tea of the Bree Tannic Tea is the time of *served* tea. The time of tea of the Narrow Tea is time *around* tea. The time of tea of the Middle Tea is the tea *of* time.

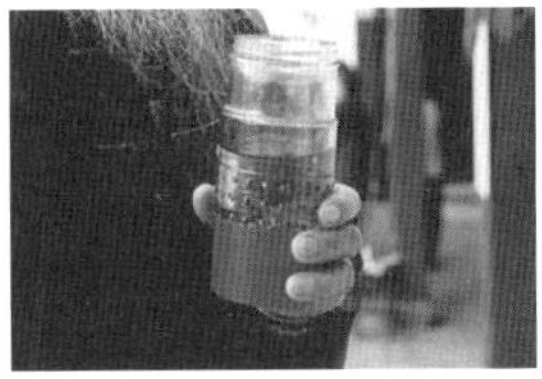

Meeting with Tea

"One time, an encounter," *(ichigo ichie)* is the subtitle of the Japanese time of tea; this moment is thus strongly ruled by the occasion that constitutes it: the meeting of a few people around tea. The participants in the meeting—*teishu*—are the master, the chief guest, and the other guests, who have been given at least three days' notice of the time when the ceremony will take place, of the occasion being marked by it and of the appropriate degree of formality (*shin, gyô, sô*). Ikkyaku Isshu calls the meeting: "One Host, One Guest." The usual number [of guests] is five, the most proper is three." (Alfred Sadler). Some count the Seven Times, others the Five Times, and one can equally well point to the three moments of the day: "morning tea" (*asacha* or *akatsuki*: "dawn tea" for the earliest risers); "midday tea" (the most common) and "evening tea" (*yôbanashi*, also sometimes known as "dusk tea"). Even exceptions can be designated: "tea of unusual moments" (*toki-hazure*), "tea after tea" (*atomi*) when guests arrive unexpectedly after a first gathering and the same utensils will be reused, and "rustic tea" (*yagake* or *fusube*), an informal tea taken out of doors, with the kettle hanging from the branches of a pine tree.

The variations on *gongfucha* are infinite and infinitesimal, to adapt to each tea and each time: according to climate, duration, ambiance, utensils, the provenance of the vintage, the material of the teapot, the quality of the water and the modalities of *fengshui*. For instance, a tea may "sleep" at certain times of the year or when the weather is too cold: one must wait for it to wake up before one can once again draw out its deepest scents. The technique and time of *gongfucha* consist in adapting the mode of preparation to these various circumstances: for the rare practitioners of this "art of tea," the gestures are subject to a degree of precision, attention, even intuition, that distinguish it radically from a ritual, because of the non-programmatic necessity that governs it.

Senchadô reflects these variations in a great diversity of accomplishments not know to *chadô*, where the ways remained more imperative and limited (above all, the three *senke* schools); each prefecture supplies its own school of *senchadô*, with its local instruments and arts, just as Japanese history has seen a proliferation of sects—at present, one hundred and eighty thousand!—through the schism of one Buddhist or Shinto disciple. However, *senchadô* has allowed this freedom through a formalization and infinite divisibility of form: this is not a matter, as in *gongfucha*, of exploring natural and cultural virtualities—the deep aromas of a tea, its effects on the organism or the techniques involved—but of working through all the possibilities of a system. While the gathering of Sencha is less ceremonious than that around the Macha, and while it is more "informal," this term must be understood in the sense in which it is used to designate the more cursive form of calligraphy. "Wild grass" writing is in reality one of the hardest to achieve.

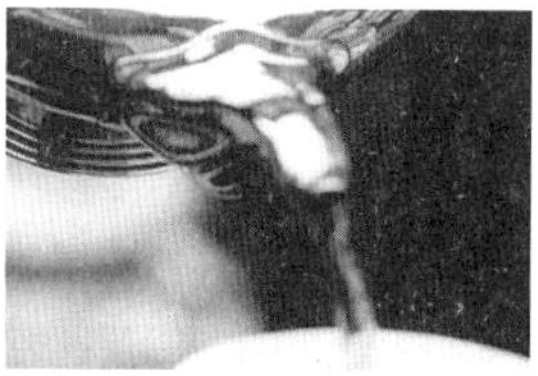

Tea Ritual

Preparation, service and clearing away. Cleaning the utensils and storing them. One might see the Japanese *chanoyu*, the tea ceremony, so often spoken about, so little known, as an obsessive extension of the simple gesture of drinking into an endless act of serving and a mad over-politeness; and even the demonstrative version, highly simplified and abbreviated—the *yose no chakai* performed in public places (major hotels, cultural centers, monasteries), sometimes for hundreds of participants, and consisting in preparing a light tea (*usucha*) and offering a sweet—, reserved for foreigners and tourists, still holds amazement and fascination. Yet what all Japanese treatises on tea claim that their way amounts to, contrary to the pressing evidence, is this simple gesture of drinking; and they quote and requote the famous poem of the founding master, Sen no Rikyû: "Never forget/ That the way of Tea/ Is no more than/ To pour out water/ To make tea and drink." At the very least this pronouncement, which is quoted in European texts as though it went without saying in relation to a séance that lasts for four-and-a-half hours and as though it summed up Japanese tea and its Zen serenity, is an antiphrasis, doubtless full of humor, certainly paradoxical, all the savor of which consists precisely in its description of one of the most formalized and complex rituals ever recorded in any culture. In Japan, tea may be as it were overtaken by the serving of tea, reframed to such an extent by its presentation—the bowl, the tea house, the garden, the opulence, the solemnity, the liturgy—that one forgets the drink that is at the center of all this—the "empty center," in the phrase Roland Barthes used to describe this Japanese topography of the exemption of meaning. This extreme archipelago indicates that, of all great drinks, it is tea that, in every circumstance, preserves or carries its circumstance. Even though it may be a matter, in its most widely used mode—from the Chinese *gaibei* to English mug, via the teabag—of a rudimentary preparation—the infusion of a dried leaf in some hot water—tea is open to all sorts of etiquette and every manner of ritual. Tea may exhibit, in the most acute and at the same time the most trivial manner what, in our world, is called consumption, in which many different factors come into play: I. The consumer society, as a "society of spectacle," the object of consumption being a commodity as spectacle and a spectacle as commodity. II. The ritual of consumption, in the sense that a raw material is transformed, consumed and incorporated in an act of mediation (divinatory or propitiatory) or transmission—and it is known that the *Li Ji* (treatises on rituals), compiled in the Han Dynasty, remained part of the foundation of China; III. The price list of drinks, through which one indexes, in the last location of the *socius*—public places for eating and drinking—the emblem or metonymy of all commodity and all laws, in this daily ritual of absorption of a drink: the taking of a liquid nourishment-stimulant, through which the human already displays the signs of a culture—for example, not lapping it up.

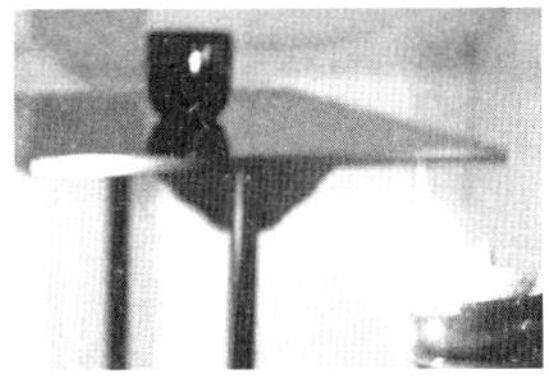

Ritual Tea

In our parts, one either savors something (*dégustation*) or one consumes it (*consommation*). However, tea seems to escape this alternative: it creates its own time and technique. The invention of the ritual is edification of the *templum*, in the sense of a circumscribed place and a sliced period of time (*temenos*). Unlike Japan, China did not sanctify the use of tea in a veritable ceremony, but it none the less established a rite: that of offering a bowl of tea to one's guest as a sign of welcome. In fact, from Japan to the Near East, the welcoming cup or glass that is offered to the visitor without caring whether he wants it, is an established custom. Tea is always linked to hospitality and this is the common denominator of all the tea rituals in the world (Asia, Arabia or Europe).
In the Qing period, the custom was sometimes to serve tea to visitors at the start of an audience: when the mandarin raised his cup for the second time, the visitor was supposed to understand the allusion and leave, and the servants hastened to bring "the means of transport without bothering to find out if the polite dismissal had been accepted." In the Qing code, there could be no third cup.
In Tibet, a distinction is made between "particular" and "general" tea, the latter being a rite of offering of tea by pilgrims to the lamas. In this way, the ritual of hospitality is inverted to become a pious offering.

Tea of Time

In Fujian and Taiwan, everyday tea, the one that is constantly drunk, in all situations, in the *gaibei*, is the *jie ke cha*, that is to say: "tea for thirst."
Throughout the long period in the twentieth century when, apart from a few gardens in Chengdu, tea houses almost entirely disappeared from China, some Taiwanese senior citizens gathered near temples and along river banks to drink tea in little cups, brewing it in Yixing teapots; this was called *lao ren cha*, "Old Men's Tea." It is still taken in Sungloping, near Nantou, in a region where many tea gardens are scattered among the palm trees and giant bamboo.
It is through this local custom that the method of *gongfucha*, "art tea," "tea of time and technique" or again "tea for when one has the time," was precariously handed down. Even in the gadgetized versions, *gongfucha* remains an open spacing, probably because of the gestures that must be performed, and it cannot be reduced to the closure of the expresso percolator, the automat or the vending machine. Nor can it be fixed in the formalized liturgy of a ceremony, as in *chanoyu* or in the Edwardian etiquette of teatime. However, all the objects make up a whole that requires a great number of operations to bring them into play...

Tea Ceremony

The translation "tea ceremony" has enjoyed worldwide success, with the result that it has been applied to all kinds of practices quite unconnected with religion or the liturgy, and traced back to a fictitious source in China or Korea—where, because

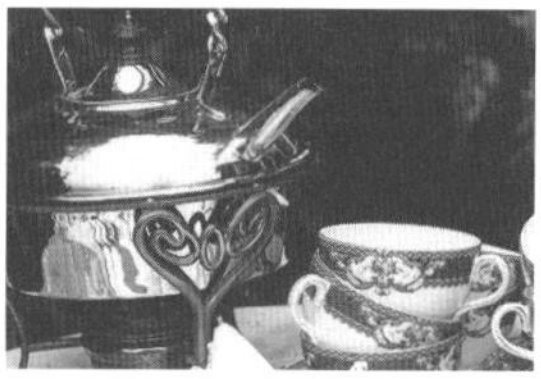

Japan got tea from these two countries, people insist on reconstructing formal observances which were never part of tradition. This generalization of the tea ceremony has even led Turkish writers to claim that they have found the equivalent of *chanoyu* in relation to coffee, in a "ceremony of serving coffee"—*kahve ikrami töreni*—referring to a ritual that existed in the court of the Ottoman rulers. The paradox of these historically incorrect deductions is that beyond national ideology or analogical degradation, they miss what founds of the precision of tea in Japan—*chanoyu*: "hot water of tea"—and what has been its movement in history. The *sadô* or *chadô*—the "way of tea"—consisted precisely in withdrawing from its ritual or liturgical basis in the narrow sense of the term. Indeed, at the start of the Kamakura period (1185-1333), tea belonged to a tea-offering ritual to the Buddha, the *obukucha*, acted out by the priests. Three hundred years later, the Higashiyama culture brought tea consumption from the hall of the monastery to the drawing room—*kaisho*, later *shoin*—where etiquette governed a form of behavior around the *daisu*, a free-standing piece of furniture on the shelves of which were displayed Chinese art objets. Murata Shukô (1422-1502) was the first to suggest an esthetic of *hiekareru*—cold and faded—with common utensils, and to reserve a room for tea: the *dôjinsai* in the *ginkakuji*. The latter would constitute the prototype of the separate tea pavilion—*chashitsu*—and the emblem of the *sôan* style, as defined by Takeno Jôô (1504-1555) and Sen no Rikyû (1522-1591), to accord with the *wabi sabi*, the culture of rusticity, frugality and restraint, defining the *chanoyu*. From the *ôchamori*, Buddhist gatherings around tea, through *tocha* tournaments at the imperial court, to *chaji*, the "matter of tea," as it has been practiced for more than four hundred fifty years now, a whole paradoxical history has formalized the ritual at the same time as it was secularized—if *chadô* is one of the ways of Zen, like Zen itself it is moving away from its Buddhist religious foundation.

Synthesis of Tea

So *chanoyu* has been interpreted through the doubtful Western translation of "tea ceremony," which removes the element of Taoist Zen triviality to make it closer to a liturgy. In the same way, *cha-jin*, which means "tea people," "tea practitioner," "tea man," has been translated by the authoritarian "Master of Tea," which does indeed take account of the place accorded in the *iemoto* system to the one who is heir to tradition, but suddenly displaces the symbolic field. The Japanese have allowed these very distorted translations to be repeated, both out of a sense of diplomacy, in order to preserve their *ura* (hidden face) and to make this cultural—and fossilized—fetish out of it. In the Japanese archipelago, this activity indicates a lucrative industry, at once elitist and touristic. And, in reality, the three schools of Ura Senke, Omote Senke and Mushanokoji Senke (but also the few others apart from these) each present themselves in three ways: as the manifest continuation of Zen,

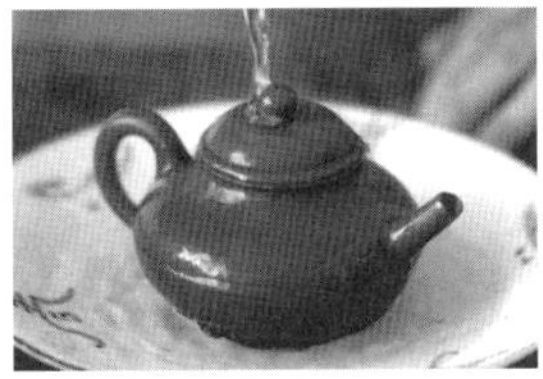

as a symbol of communal identity and as the keepers of a history not based on monuments. *Chadô*, a synthesis of "religion, morality, esthetics, philosophy, discipline and social relations" (Sen Sôshitsu, 15th *iemoto* of Urasenke) is also an ecumenical site in which all the arts, traditions and crafts of the Japanese archipelago are brought together: ceramics, calligraphy, architecture, landscape art, flower arranging, poetry, lacquer, basketry, bamboo, woodwork, bronze, casting, wattle, thatching, weaving, silk painting, stencil, brocade, metalwork, ivory, painting, arboriculture, physical culture, cooking, patisserie, household arts and Zen.

The *chanoyu* can be carried out in the characterless surroundings of a well-known hotel, museum or temple; it can also be learned, slowly, over a long period ("As tradition demands, I started to take lessons in tea at the age of six, on the sixth day of the sixth month." Sôshitsu) and with much patience, in order to complete one's education, in a school with exorbitant fees; and finally one can attend it as the privileged guest of the head of a big company, thus enjoying the legitimacy of tradition. It is slightly stupefying to consider how tea was first of all imported from China with a whole culture—Buddhist, Taoist and Confucian—adopted by noblemen, monks and samurai in a sort of ostentatious ritualization—with all kinds of china, silverware and silks from the continent—and then how it became, through the "Way of Tea," the site of this improbable Japanese synthesis in which religious morality, military code and artistic discipline are crystallized in Zen, and a simple non-alcoholic drink, plain dishes and a thatched hut sum it all; and finally how the invention of *chanoyu* in the *wabi-sabi* manner with all its inherent simplicity, poverty and humility, led through codification, formalization and estheticization, to the return of luxury, order and power in subsequent periods.

Form Without Limits

The utensils of *chanoyu* are all listed, codified and fixed. They are the subject of permanent exaggeration: works of art, precious treasures and even adored divinities; names and titles, like those of works of art, indicate their status;[3] they are the subject of endless treatises, analyses and histories. Rikyû had paper templates cut out so that he could classify the different kinds of bowl, tea box and kettle. Later writers would expand and fix these lists of possible configuration according to various criteria: function (bowl, spoon, receptacle); model (*temmoku, ido, raku*), form (*kaki* or "persimmon," *netsume* or "jujube," *nasubi* or "aubergine"), mode (formal, standard, informal), provenance (China, Korea, Japan), oven (Hagi, Karatsu, Bizen, Shigaraki, Iga, Seto, Mino, Arita, Kyoyaki), materials (china, lacquer, bamboo), season (winter or summer) and type of tea (*koicha* or *usucha*).

The ceremony (or, rather, the gathering, meeting or session) may take place according to three states of mind, ambiences or modes—inspired by the three main styles of calligraphy—which, in some cases, may follow on from one another: formal

3 – In the course of the *o-chaji* with Master Iwasaki, appearing in the photographic section, the main bowl is a Korean Irabo-Yaki, three hundred years old; the tea box is called *sennen no enishi* ("thousand year friendship"); the tea spoon is *jimok- shinde* ("ear-eye-heart-communication"). In Iwasaki Sama's private pavilion in spring 1998, the cold-water Kiyomizu recipient, from the ovens of called shirodanuki ("white raccoon") and the bamboo spoon, hototogisu ("cuckoo").

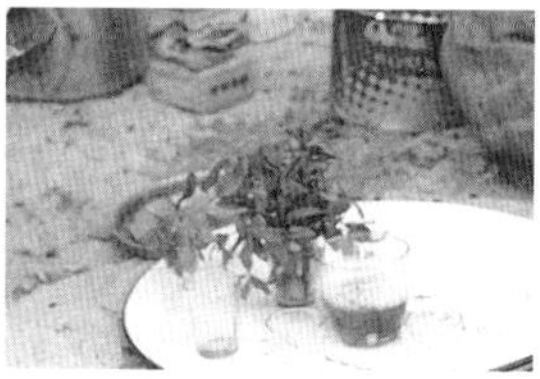

(*chin*), semi-formal (*gyô*) and informal (*sô*). In the garden (*rôji*), the same progression is indicated by the surrounding trees and the arrangement of stones, lanterns and ponds. In the same way, many *chanoyu* utensils are classed according to these three modes—such as the *chashaku*, which is formal if it is in ivory or carved from a piece of bamboo without a knot, standard if the knot in the bamboo is at the far end of the handle and informal if the knot is in the middle of the handle.

Compared to the first Japanese tea customs, which were part of religious life or court entertainments, the establishment of *chanoyu* in the milieu of the merchant bourgeoisie of the port of Sakai and the warrior class that was to establish national unity, was based on an esthetic that took account of object of daily use, and local or foreign tradition; this valorization and these changes in function brought into play notions which may even suggest the modern terms "rustic," "craft" and "folklore." The objects brought over from continental China—the tea mill, ewer and *temmoku* bowl—were replaced or completed by objects manufactured and taken over for the purpose in Japan, which were soon to be specially designed by *chajin*, or "tea people." These utensils, made according to the design, specific pattern or general indications given by a Master of Tea, were called *iemoto-gonomi*. A large number of highly applied arts was to be set up as a tradition around the tea ceremony, most often by several generations of the same family. A host of ultra-specialized craftsmen was soon to be set up to create, reproduce or reinterpret the various utensils and accessories necessary for the accomplishment of the ritual: from the *raku* tea bowl to the woven cord that fastens the box in which this bowl is kept, via the wooden box itself; from the wood charcoal to the bamboo basket that contains it and the feather to brush away the dust; from the powdered tea to its lacquer box, through the latter's protective case. Arts of ceramics, woodwork, iron casting, cabinet making, veneering, weaving, tin making, plaiting and basketwork. In each case, the work is divided according to the materials or their treatment: for example, arts of woodworking vary according to the tree and its species—cryptomeria, mulberry, cherry-tree bark, cedar, paulownia, bamboo; according to techniques—turned, curved, assembled; or according to covering—bare, varnished, transparent lacquer (*fuku-urushi*). But there are further criteria still: incrustation of metal alloys, hollowed wood (*kurimono*), veins cut out and incrusted (*moku zôgan*), mixed lacquers (green, red, black), dry empty lacquer (*dakkanshitsu*), gold motifs on black ground (*maki-e*). Incrustation with mother-of-pearl (*rade, aogai*), eggshell (*rankaku*), incision filled with gold powder or leaf (*chinkin*), metallic leaves set in layers of lacquer (*hyômon*).

Teasing Circumstance

There is no end to the tease of drinking teas.

From the spot where the bowl is placed, which is determined by counting the lines

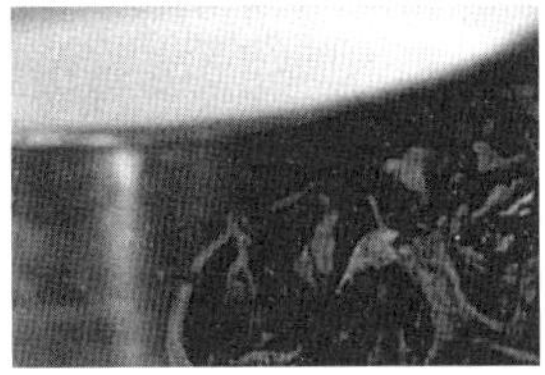

of woven straw in the *tatami* to the type of sandal that one wears in the *roji,* and including the place of the hands on the ladle; from the moments when one may speak to the number of mouthfuls to drink the tea, and including the moments when one may relax; from the manner of appreciating a box of incense to the manner of bending down, and including the succession of gestures for opening a door. This codification is somewhere between feudal etiquette, hierarchical military discipline and the daily rule of monastic life. The possible is thus proscribable or prescribable, to the point where discussing *chanoyu* closes any attempt to interpret it and at the same time opens an infinite number of ways to describe it.

This infinity is signaled again by the endless interlocking to which the object is subjected. One knows the care taken with wrapping in Japan—parcels, presents—which is an art of its own; but in the context of *chaseki,* there are no limits to the protection, to the formalization of that protection or to consideration of the formalization of that protection. At the end of the encounter, the tea box is inspected, then the case for the tea box, then again the signed wooden box into which the tea box, once wrapped in its case, is stored; and since this carries, on the front and back of the lid, as well as on its walls, some words painted by the craftsman, the master of tea or the owner, and since obviously it is subject to wear as a result of successive handling, it offers the possibility of being looked at, and of being provided with a supplementary protection and rise in value.

The manner in which an object which might appear as simple, archetypal and universal as a bowl—the *chawan*—can be deconstructed in texts on the ceramics of tea, is almost impossible to describe. Some fifteen names describe the various parts—points, places—in a shape whose figure—the *Gestalt,* totality— we would consider impossible to differentiate. The place where the lips rest and which is wiped between the thumb and index finger after sipping the tea is called *chakin-zuri,* the part in contact with the *tatami* is *tatami-mitsuki,* the bottom of the bowl in which a trace of green foam remains is *mikomi.* And so on. In the same way, no less than six names are applied to the various parts of the little stick of carved, round and curved bamboo used as a spoon for tea, the *chashaku.*

Tea Gestures

Among drinkers of Bree Tannic tea, tea is treated like coffee or chocolate: the spoon is turned in the cup to stir in the sugar or the milk. This implement—especially since it is metal—would be altogether inappropriate in China where it would disturb the process of infusion and risk oxidization. In the West, it belongs to a whole repertoire of gestures governed by etiquette: the picking up of the cup and saucer, respectively, the discreet movement of the spoon, the manner and place where it is put down. English handbooks on etiquette are very precise: "Those who take sugar in their tea are advised to propel the spoon with the minimum of effort and to

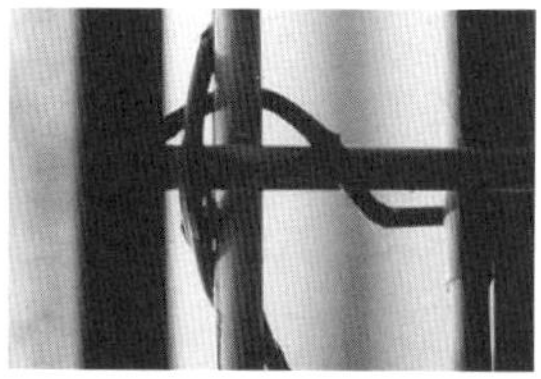

remove it without fail before raising the cup." The *chasen*, the Japanese whip used to obtain a "jade froth," or the pestle of the Tibetan *gugurtchaï* are, each in their own preparation, other blunt instruments which, in the liquid tea and beyond their mechanical effects, exhibit to the touch and to the eye the space of an intervention, a ritual.

Urbanity, Civility, Domesticity

"It is also customary for the youngest young lady or lady of the house to make the tea." (de Saint-Fond) The rituals of British tea parties suggest a stiff, bourgeois atmosphere, because one's manner of picking up the cup, or of stirring the spoon in it while skillfully maintaining the balance of the saucer, is designed not to express a spiritual state or the experience of a pleasure, but one's social origin, education and a set hierarchy.

Victorian and Edwardian society had many things in common with that of the Edo period in Japan, which helped the adoption of the European industrial revolution in the course of the Meiji Restoration. England in the nineteenth century and Japan between the sixteenth and nineteenth centuries laid down—that is to say, reinvented—the models of the gentleman and the samurai. "The three syllables of the word *gentleman*, so much used on the other side of the Channel, sum up the history of English society." (Hippolyte Taine) And, as the *Oxford English Dictionary* states, *gentleman* has shifted over the past century from indicating a man who possesses a chivalrous instinct to one who is not engaged in any trade and who is able to manage without earning a living. In the same way, in Japan, Tokugawa society imposed its state capitalism by a military regime, in which the warriors were disarmed, "without masters" and did not take part in any wars. *Bushido*, the Japanese martial code, is only a late version with an ethical function. The empire of His or Her Gracious Majesty and that of the Rising Sun base the conformism of their societies on a code of conduct that rests on a similar paradigm: the time of tea. In Japan, schools of tea are still deliberately used for educating the young.

A whole literature in Europe on the arts of living, etiquette and manners developed rapidly in the nineteenth century, deriving from Baltazare Castiglione's *Il Cortegiano*, Erasmus' *De Civilitate* and *Il Galateo* of Della Casa. At this time, Tokyo and London were experiencing a demographic expansion that made them the largest cities in the world and broke down the old class barriers. English society was henceforth seen as a confrontation between three elements: the aristocratic, the democratic and the plutocratic (T. H. S. Escott, 1885); so there was an attempt to give civility, that model of behavior deriving from the urban context of the sixteenth century, a new definition in the form of simple politeness or good manners. Beyond education—breeding —the manual of etiquette claims to offer a theory of propriety, conformity and representation. What had been a question of fine art reverted to

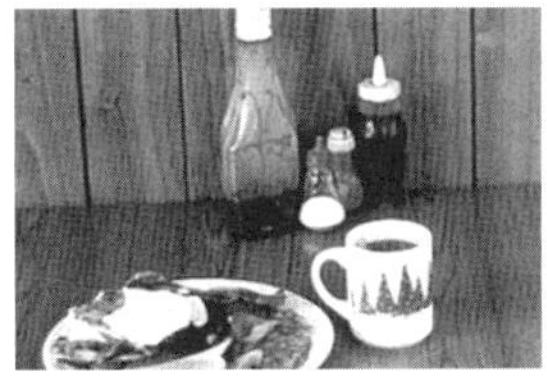

a matter of behavior. "The English, more than any other people, not only act but feel according to rule." (John Stuart Mill, 1869) Victorian society was indeed built on a basis of pre-established norms—cognitive, social, sexual—while at the same time it continually redefined them. An obsession with fine detail in the field of social manners constantly obliged the élite, which wished to distinguish itself from social climbers, to revise its code of etiquette. In this sense, the site of English tea, both ethically and esthetically, meets that of Japanese tea with its "unlimited circumstance." They are comparable, too, in their common support for domesticity, of which the royal family is the national representation and the teakettle the daily emblem.

Tea & Manners

A modern treatise of etiquette lays down the rules for English tea, starting with a reminder that, except for tea parties, receptions during the day have become rare. A tea party is no longer the great British reception for tea of yesteryear, but a friendly occasion for eating, drinking and talking... A modern tea party for three or four friends has one important thing in common with its Edwardian counterpart: the chief aim in both cases is to create favorable conditions for conversation. The activities of serving, eating and drinking should interrupt the flow of words as little as possible and all preparations should be made with that idea in mind. (*Debrett's Etiquette and Modern Manners*, 1981)

According to the same source, the food should be light, carefully prepared and, above all, easy to eat. The sandwich fillings should not run out or soak into the bread and the cakes should not be "chunky, over-crumbly or squashy." The traditional tea menu includes toasted tea cakes (if the weather is cold), thin slices of buttered bread, cucumber sandwiches, scones, cut in half and buttered, petits fours, biscuits and slices of cake... Each guest will need a cup, a saucer (with teaspoon), a small plate and a small knife. No forks: if a cake or patisserie is too difficult to eat with the fingers alone, it ought not to be served. When all the guests have arrived, custom requires the hostess to leave the room for a short time to make tea... The hostess should always be attentive to the cups of her guests and offer them more tea when the cup is empty.

Rules about pouring and, more particularly, about the refilling of the cup have continued to vary from one period to another, as well as from one country to another. Minute details, combined in an infinite variety of ways, govern the placing of the instruments and the gestures that link them. In the seventeenth century, when a lady had sipped enough tea, she placed her spoon across the top of her cup, or she gently tapped the cup with the spoon, or else she turned her cup over on the saucer. A gentleman would be expected to remove it. This language of objects might remain untranslatable to the extent of causing some embarrassment, as in the case

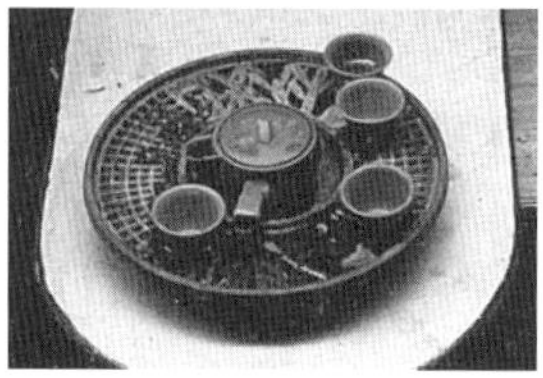

of the Frenchman who, not knowing the rule of the spoon, had to admit defeat after fifteen cups of tea: "Oh, Madame! Excuse me, I can take no more..." In Scotland, leaving the spoon in the cup, instead of placing it in the saucer, was the proper way. In the United States, a lady who had been invited to a tea party arrived with her own cup, saucer and teaspoon.

Tea Outside the Rules

In England, in a few highway pull-ins, there are still some refreshment vans which serve tea. Long awaited by truck drivers, these buffets stand at the side of the road, like *chaya* in the Japan of Hiroshige, Hokusai and Utamaro. They are generally called "greasy spoons" because of the surroundings that they offer: waxed cloths, faded lino and towels which are never washed to wipe the huge Thermos bottle. They serve huge round bacon sandwiches, sometimes supplied from an improvised pigsty in the neighboring field. On the Southampton docks, where the containers stand after the ships have discharged them, the buffet becomes a tea diner, housed in an Algeco and also reserved for truck drivers. It serves "bubble and squeak," mashed potato with broccoli; black pudding; and baked beans. The trio to accompany the tea is no longer made up of the club sandwiches, scones and patisserie of an Edwardian teatime, but of sausage, bacon and eggs. The portions are considerably more generous and range from "six wheels" to the formidable "36 wheels."
On each occasion, the tea—with milk and strongly sugared, brewed from a bag of PG Tips—is served in a mug which will be refilled as many times as required. The state of this tea is humorously described by regular customers: it should be prepared so that "the spoon will stand up in it." A mug of tea is called a "cuppa cha," a Cockney expression brought home by English soldiers and sailors who had traveled as far as China. These roadside tea-buffets are now relics threatened with abolition as a result of European Community regulations. The new laws have already virtually restricted the consumption of clotted cream to Cornwall alone; this preparation, in color and consistency perfectly situated on the margin between yellow butter and white *crème fraîche*, is nonetheless indispensable to the traditional cream tea; but, being more isolated than French cheese, clotted cream cannot defend itself and, imperiling its peculiar flavors, must either be pasteurized or become illegal.

Rules of Tea

Curiously, it is in France, and quite late, that the five golden rules for the preparation of Bree Tannic Tea have been stated: *I.* Heat the teapot, by pouring boiling water into it, which is then emptied out. The aim is to free the aromas of the leaves to come. When a filter is being used (in aluminum, polyamine or non-chlorated cotton), it should be put in place beforehand; *II.* Put a small spoonful of tea (almost three grams) per cup, plus "one for the pot," in the filter or otherwise in the infuser or teaspoon. Allow the steam to soften the leaves; *III.* Pour water that has started to

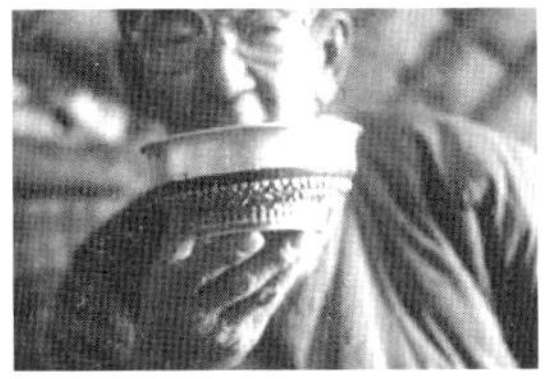

bubble, at 95 degrees Celsius—in other words, just below boiling—over the tea, being careful to impregnate it well; *IV.* Let it infuse for around three minutes, or slightly less for broken leaves and slightly more for whole leaves; *V.* Take out the infuser, stir with a regular motion, and serve after a short pause. Obviously, the sixth rule, which the British cannot forget, is to add the indispensable sugar and milk—or lemon. These rules for tea, thoughtlessly repeated in ordinary writing about tea, can only be applied to red Indian tea; because even a Chinese tea, and even a red one, would become unbearable at the prescribed quantity. But, beyond this limited use, there is nothing universal about these golden rules.

The Mariage Paradox

Mariage Frères represents the French art of tea, a weak local tradition, and, in its catalogue of four hundred fifty types, proclaims the universal declaration of the tea lover by assembling all the countries (China, Formosa, India, Ceylon, Japan, Siam, Korea, Indonesia, Bangladesh, Bhutan, Malaysia, Nepal, Sikkim, Vietnam, Russia, Persia, Turkey, Argentina, Brazil, Ecuador, Cameroon, Kenya, Mauritius, Mozambique, Malawi, Uganda, Rwanda, Tanzania, Zimbabwe, South Africa, Australia and Papua) where the plant is grown. Each citizen thus has the right to all the teas of the world, provided that such teas will submit to the same republican constitution: the same method of preparation.

And so tea is everywhere—in boxes, in jellies, in cakes, chocolates, alcoholic cocktails, museum display cases—and even plastered on the walls, but not in the teapot! This disappearance—let us call it "The Mariage Paradox"—is our guarantee that every tea is infused for its recommended time (three minutes for a broken tea, almost six minutes for a leaf tea and one minute and a half for a Japanese tea), by the waiter in white linen who, in front of his board of shelved jars, takes out the quantity of leaves of the desired kind, douses them with a jet of simmering water and, at the appropriate moment, removes the cotton infuser. But this rule, while trying to respect differences, reduces all teas to the same preparation in the felt-coated, metal-lined, china teapot—in which the infusion, at its height of excellence, is maintained at the correct temperature,—to the same service of porcelain cups marked MFs and to the same quantities of liquid. Only three teas are exempted from this legislation: the ceremonial Japanese Macha, a powdered green tea which has to be beaten in a wide, thick bowl using a bamboo whip; Gyokuro, another Japanese tea, which has to be prepared in a tiny earthenware pot, in order to extract several successive infusions and accompanied by a pourer to cool the water; and yellow tea, served in a glass teapot to show its "silver pins" standing vertically upright and dancing as they go up and down. These teas are the most expensive in the catalogue and by virtue of this fact, one had to exhibit their leaves, instead of throwing them away after having extracted their aroma, one could not serve them

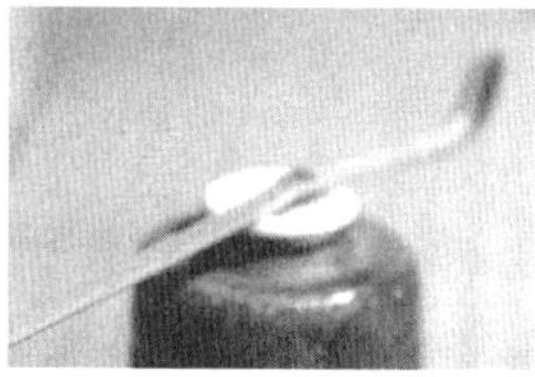

in the house china and one could not offer them in the usual quantity. In the Mariage Paradox, these three highly sought varieties, bringing their Oriental ritual with them, act as the return of the repressed, as a resistance to the general rule not so much of the *res publica*, the "public thing," as of what has been lost in more than three hundred years of import into the West. If one still imagines infusions of green tea in a teapot or made with simmering water, one can enumerate three further paradoxes in the serving of tea: the leaves have vanished from the pot; the tea has killed the water; the water has killed the tea.

Supplement for Tea

Bree Tannic Tea has been stunted, reduced and diminished. With no particular savor, no aroma at all, no precise color—gray, brown, dark. The method of fabrication favored, which comes from China, is that of red tea, where fermentation is completed rapidly. Otherwise, only smoked China tea is known. The story of how the immensity of a culture and the whole spectrum of aromas was restricted to almost a single tea, remains to be told. Meanwhile, the Chinese greens and Wulong, or the Japanese greens that were imported from the sixteenth to the nineteenth century will have fallen from Western memory, as it were, by the middle of the twentieth. While the names of the teas imported by the India Companies—Bohea, Twankey, Hyson, Congou, Souchong, Pekoe, Chunmee, Chucha and Oolong—leave no doubt about the teas that they indicate, the conditions of their importation—the length of the sea voyage, the humidity and heat of storage—which might last almost a whole year, or even longer, imply disastrous consequences for the state of the tea on its arrival, something which is not unconnected with smuggling at an international level and adulteration on an industrial scale. The time of tea for Europe would be very precisely determined by the time taken to transport it from China: going from green—or red—to black. But the tea developed in India and Ceylon, first of all by the choice of varieties of Assam type, then by advanced methods of mechanization, would only be "sculpted" to receive sugar, milk and possibly lemon. Tea tastings for Indian and Singhalese teas in the tea markets are always done with milk: lactose is an indispensable basis for decomposing the subtlest notes in the aromas and savors of the teas. Obviously, this practice would appear ridiculous to a Chinese amateur.
In the sixteenth century, Castela noted that the Egyptians mixed a decoction of coffee with drugs. It was also perfumed, according to Lane, with cardamom seeds or ambergris. In Yemen, ginger and other spices were put in coffee, to which in Ethiopia was added butter. At the start of the eighteenth century, in North America, the Quakers drank their tea bitter with butter and salt. And most Americans—one-third of the population drank more than one cup a day—preferred "Chinese green tea, perfumed with saffron, iris root or gardenia petals." "The Russians sometimes add champagne to their tea, the Germans beer, the Irish whiskey, the New Yorkers

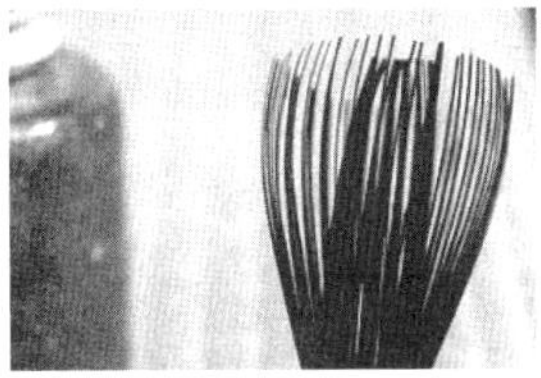

iced cream, the English oysters and shellfish, in season, real Bostonians rose petals and the Italians and Spanish, onion and garlic." (Arthur Gray) "Overland tea," along the silk route, runs the full gamut of all possible additions in preparing tea: salt, sugar, dairy products, animal fats, various condiments and cereal preparations.

Differences Over Tea

"I was recently a guest of Baron Rothschild in his palace at Seamore Place. Early in the morning, a liveried servant came into my room pushing a huge trolley. "Would you like tea or a peach, sir?" I chose tea, and immediately the second question was: "China, India or Ceylon, sir?" I chose Indian tea, and he asked: "With lemon, cream or milk, sir?" I chose milk, but he still wanted to know what breed the cow should be: "Jersey, Hereford or Shorthorn, sir?" I have never had such good tea." (Cecil Roth)

In his first advertisement, Thomas Garraway said that, "being prepared and drunk with milk and water tea strengthens the inward parts." Samuel, the ninth descendant of the tea merchants R. Twining and Co points out that sugar spoils the flavor, "and isn't very good for you, either," adding that no Twining has ever put sugar in his tea. According to Edward Bramah, "England has a cold climate and tea is refreshing, while milk gives energy." Milk is also supposed to take away bitterness and astringency, by neutralizing the tannins in tea. But these arguments, like all those which try to support this one side in the dispute about tea, can be countered. Concern about sugar is a recent fashion, their effect on energy levels is the same as that of the milk product and they have an equally ruinous effect on the flavor of tea. Moreover, when a plumber or roof-mender calls, the mistress of the house does not fail to add "three spoonfuls of sugar" as proof of her hospitality.

This matter of what should be added to tea is the site of a debate in which the replies are constantly discussed: with or without sugar, milk or lemon, milk before or after the tea... These alternatives are always repeated to the customer by a waiter in a café or bar, in response to an order for tea. The British world is divided over these choices—both absolute and irreconcilable—, in which a whole culture is at stake. Thus a minority supports lemon. Others prefer the milk poured into the cup before the tea. Yet another will choose to pour the tea in first so that the milk will spread through it like a cloud. The results, respectively are: that the tea provides the neutralized basis for hot lemonade; that the tea and milk merge into an opaque, gray beverage (brown if the leaves are not too broken up); and, finally, that the milk, stirring up the tea, creates a sort of nuclear fission in the cup.

Milk in First

The order of pouring milk and tea into the cup secretly divides the British Isles: "a very delicate question." Every writing about tea or etiquette has to take sides on the issue, often with no explanation, since it is necessarily a sophistry. In point of fact,

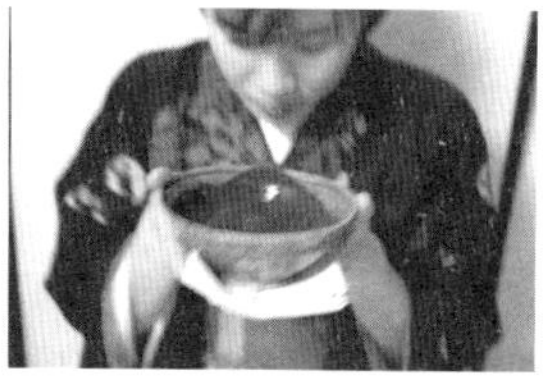

milk poured into tea produces a turbulence that coagulates the casein, while the opposite produces a dilution of a rich, fatty matter with hot water. Recently, a sociological theory suggested that milk before tea is a working-class habit, while tea before milk is upper class. Indeed, milk already poured out in the kitchen, particularly in a mug, avoids the need for a milk jug. But "milk in first" is also a preventive measure to reduce the thermal endangering of fine china, or even according to an explanation by no less a person than Sam Twining, a means of protecting less resistant English porcelain and pretending that it comes from China. A further question specifies the initial one and concerns temperature, though it seems less important than for coffee—*café au lait, café crème, noisette*: tea adapts better to cold milk.

Sugar With Tea

"These countries have given us such an abundance of sugar that all our kitchens are full of it, where it is devoured most excessively for gluttony's sake, when formerly sugar was only available in the shops of apothecaries, who kept it for sick persons alone, as it were, in such a way that what once served us as medicine serves now as sustenance." (Ortelius, 1572) Since the time of Henry VIII, the sugar bowl has been part of the English table, between the spice bowl and the sweetmeats, serving in particular to sweeten wine. "The vulgar populace alone take beer and ale in great quantities, while the gentry enjoy wines which they mix with sugar more than in any other kingdom," Morgson observed in 1617 about the British. English taste favored those wines with added sugar—rum, sherry, tokay, muscat, port, malmsey—which aided conservation. The association of a rare tea with a no less luxurious sugar was part of ostentatious hospitality, the elegant fashion being to keep a piece of crystal candy in the mouth while sipping tea. "Bite-and-stir" boxes included a place for a sugar bowl.

Towards the middle of the nineteenth century, free trade brought down the price of sugar and new forms took over from those that had been current among the ruling classes—light brown sugar, royal, demi-royal, brown, red and white sugar candy, barley sugar, sweets. Liquid sweeteners—molasses diluted to a clear syrup—are used, with colorings and taste enhancers, in the manufacture of jellies and jams made with very little fruit pulp or vegetables. These new foodstuffs would become popular in the working class, to be spread on bread that was their staple food. "An increase in income goes with a paradoxical impoverishment of diet. [...]. Porridge and vegetable soup are no longer made, but people eat more bread," with jam, and drink tea (Sydney Mintz). England, taking advantage of its colonies, deliberately transformed sugar into a national product, as it would finally do with the Chinese leaf.

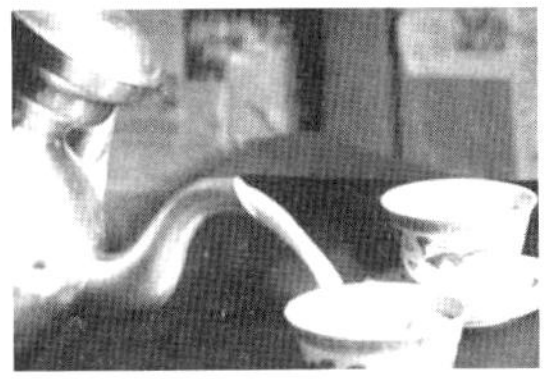

Scone, Clotted Cream, Strawberry Jam

British teatime is above all a collation—afternoon tea—or even a complete meal: high tea. There is a succession of dishes: sandwiches, scones, and cakes.

Six club sandwiches: on brown bread (with thin slices of cucumber, cream cheese and herbs or smoked salmon with a salmon mousse); on white bread (thin slices of ham, egg mayonnaise with mustard and cress or finely grated cheddar cheese). Variants: sardine, tomato or banana sandwiches.

Scones (small cakes with buttermilk), either plain or with currants, eaten with cream and jam. Variants: buttered toast; crumpets, with holes to absorb the butter; pikelets, smaller than crumpets and with fewer holes (a specialty of Derbyshire and Yorkshire); English muffins; drop scones; scotch pancakes.

Cakes for tea: Madeira cake, seed cake (with caraway or poppy seeds), marbled cake, sponge cake, brandy snaps, fruit cake, foreign cakes: madeleines, macaroons, meringues, florentines, brownies, panforte, devil's food cake, *tuiles*, choux pastry, sponge cakes with *crème Chantilly*, sugar frosting, millefeuilles, puff pastry, chocolate éclairs, strawberry tart, biscuits, flapjacks, Eccles cakes, trifle, shortbreads, Dundee cake and gingerbread.

For high tea, one would also prepare savories: smoked ham, egg and bacon pie, tomato salad, cress salad, prawns, scrambled eggs, welsh rarebit, oyster vol-au-vent, pieces of chicken.

It should be noted, however, that the great invention that, in itself, justifies the transformation of China tea into Bree Tannic Tea, is the triad that makes up a cream tea: scone, clotted cream, and strawberry jam. This tradition, originating in Devon and Cornwall, resides first of all on a little cake made with buttermilk, always cooked in the oven at the last minute and served cut in half. The scone is the emblem of a whole culture, which took over but would never have dared to create the over-extravagant gâteaux of France or the over-rich ones of America. A sort of little brioche with heavy pastry, the scone's austerity does not prevent it being the perfect vehicle for jam and cream. Clotted cream added to the rusticity of this vehicle, because of its intermediary state, not homogeneous, in short, "turned" cream. It is being replaced nowadays with double cream, thick cream or whipped cream. Jam, which is neither what the French mean by *confiture,* nor jelly, nor compote, but "marmalade," still exhibits that median state, which may sometimes be accentuated by components without pulp: rose petals, lemon juice (lemon curd), damsons, strawberries, raspberries, blackberries. Do we need to point out that this essential trinity of the British genius can only now be appreciated on rare occasions in the British Isles themselves, because of the threat to its impure cream from international regulations, which few of the natives seem to care about?

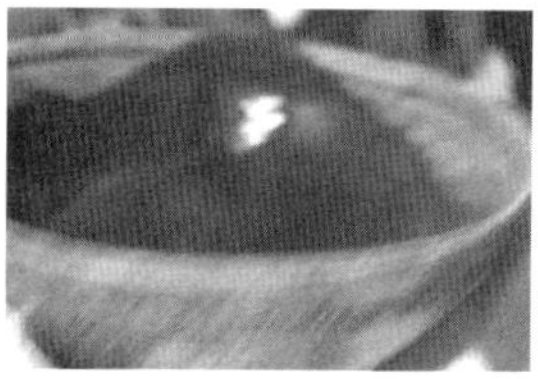

Cucumber Sandwich Among the half dozen club sandwiches whose filling is constant, the cucumber sandwich is the one that has become the emblem of the art of tea: cool, gracious, impeccable.

Peel a cucumber and cut it into thin slices. Sprinkle these transparent disks with a little salt and vinegar. After half an hour, drain off the excessive moisture in a sieve. Cover a slice of brown bread—"as thick as a leaf"—lightly buttered, with two layers of cucumber and cover with another slice of bread. Apply firm but gentle pressure with the palm of the hand. Cut off the crusts and divide into three rectangles. Pile them carefully on a china serving plate and cover with a damp cloth until tea is served.

Another choice arises over cucumber sandwiches: should the cucumber be peeled or not? If not, the preparation will have a narrow green border, which, disguised in the brown bread, will only appear when the sandwich is sliced: a delicate line that brings out the original color of a dish that has been worked and served in such a way as to tone down all colors. The cucumber sandwich, to which a whole literature has been devoted, is indeed the "aristocrat of teatime" (Jane Pettigrew), which makes the vegetable diaphanous and bread like paper.

Coffee House In a few decades at the start of the twentieth century, the tea house disappeared. From China, Japan and Taiwan. On a tiny handful of houses, patronized by old customers, survived on the continent, in Hangzhou and Chengdu, their decrepitude and pathos speaking of the end of a world. In an equally unique reservation in Sungloping, some other old people kept alive the Taiwanese tea of art and time. In reality, the "house" of these outlets has almost vanished, since in Hangzhou the place consists in a few chairs scattered in the bamboo grove beside the river that runs through the town, where people have their ears cleaned, get a massage or talk endlessly; while in Taiwan, the "tea house" itself had no structure anymore: for "old people's tea"—*lao ren cha*—one brings one's utensils and improvises a table, so that only the time of the meeting defines the site—just as old black men in New York gather on University Place for a game of chess.

The tea house, which was until the nineteenth century a central institution in the life of Shanghai, Canton or Kyoto, disappeared in historical contexts that are quite dissimilar, but for similar reasons: the establishment maintained a balance between the social life of a café or tavern and the organization of a brothel, with its concubines or geishas. The puritanical modernization of Meiji and the Communist regime of Mao Zedong could not tolerate these areas, both because of the new moral principles that they proclaimed and for a reason which has continued to treat cafés with suspicion, from Ottoman Istanbul to Europe in the Enlightenment: vizirs and ulemas have chronically threatened it with interdiction and royal edicts pre-

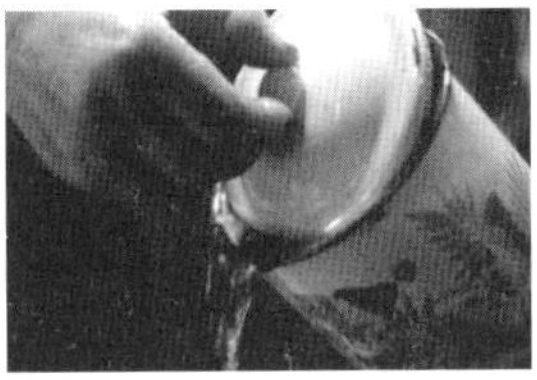

scribed the hours and amounts of consumption—just as, at around 1750 BC, Hammurabi's code of laws regulated outlets for beer and date wine which did not denounce rioters in Babylon. Indeed, while the medieval alehouse, reserved for pilgrims, students and wandering players, incited all sorts of criminal behavior, the coffee house or tea house, in which urban citizens gathered, produced another kind of threat: information was exchanged, politics discussed and art was happening. From this point of view, the only tea houses that managed to survive are those of the "middle of the route," in regions known in the seventeenth century as Xatâ (Mongolia, Turkestan, Tartary), as far as Turkey, Arabia and Iran: like the *çay-evi* in Erzurum, the *chaihane* which replaced the Turkish *kafube* in the 1950s, or the Afghan *tchaïkhana* which serves green tea, *tchaï sabz*, to quench the thirst, and black tea, *tchaï siyah*, to warm the drinker. It is remarkable that these regions, which made tea known in the West (through the first mentions by Arab travelers), contain a large number of variants when it comes to preparing it—concentrated infusion of black tea, decoction of green tea, mixture of compressed tea—and have often submitted to the contradictory effects of external policies. Egypt, Pakistan and Saudi Arabia consume black tea from India and Ceylon, while Morocco and Afghanistan import Chinese green tea, through the state monopoly company or by contraband. In Niger, Mali and the Sahara, the tea drunk by the Tuaregs according to the ritual of three successive teas—firstly bitter ("like death"), then milder ("like life") and finally highly sweetened ("like love")—is also a decoction of Chinese Gunpowder tea, with an aromatic herb added. For a long time, this tea was delivered by Muscovy, which had first received it, itself as a gift from the Mongol khan Altyn in 1638 to tsar Mikhail Fedorovitch, and which would sign an agreement for delivery by Tartary in 1679. The use of the samovar in Afghanistan, Pakistan or Iran is explained in this way, especially after the Iranian-Russian wars of 1802; tea followed the caravans of Central Asia, but also the other important route passing via the central Urals and the plains of western Siberia along the Tura River towards the town of Tjumén. Tea, cultivated in Georgia to supply internal demand, would also be exported southwards. When, in the nineteenth century, England made a major switch from coffee to tea, as a result of the efforts of temperance organizations, reductions in taxes and publicity for black Indian tea, many countries of the former Ottoman Empire, after the Crimean War, would take the Chinese tea in which the British continued to trade, but no longer consumed. This tea, when green, fitted better the Islamic prohibition on what is fermented, but above all it would arrive in less random or scant quantities than that which had previously come with the caravans. Later, India and Ceylon would export their own. And so, there is a sort of coming and going between wine—forbidden, but consumed—coffee—invented, then passed on to Europe—and tea—recognized, forgotten, then re-adopted. Tea had in

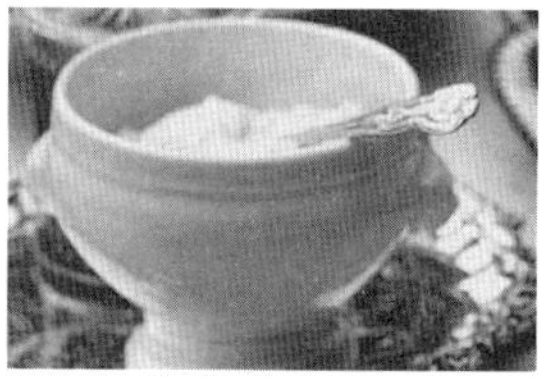

fact been introduced into Iran and Arabia as early as the thirteenth century by the Mongol conquerors, but had not caught on. This halfway situation was clearly evident in the proximity of the coffee house and the tea house, as nowhere else. According to the account of Oléarius, in Isphahan in 1635 at the same time as coffee grinders, there were a few Chinese tea houses—*tzai chattai xâne*. Later, *kahvekane* and *tchaikane* would coexist. This indicates something that distance and exoticism prevent people from seeing in each of their respective spheres: that the tea house in china—*cha kuan*, literally a studio for tea—and the coffee house in the West—*khâne, house, haus*—had comparable roles in business, ideas and literature. Theatre, music and opera—that of Peking in 1790—started in China is tea houses, just as literary and artistic life in Europe would be profoundly transformed by cafés—somewhere between theatre and drawing room. Family or commercial conflicts of interest were always decided in the *cha kuan*, while the Stock Exchange came into being in the City, at Garraway's, Lloyd's or the Golden Lyon. As for the circulation of rumors, just like the first newspapers—the *Tatler* founded at the Grecian—their very possibility of existing were identified with outlets for beverages.

Tea Salon

In England, after 1650, the coffee house and even the chocolate house take their place beside the ale house and the wine house—like the *kaffee hause* in Germany, the *koffiehuis* in Holland, the *cabaret à caffé* in France and the *bottega da caffè* in Italy. The "tea room" would only appear late and in small numbers after the closing of the coffee houses at the end of the eighteenth century, leaving the way free for pubs and clubs, and when tea gardens had lost their importance with the expansion of London in the middle of the nineteenth century. It was only in 1884, when there was no place left to take tea, that a chain of bakers, the Aerated Bread Company, opened the first tea room (or tea shop) in London, to be followed by other companies: the Express Dairies, J. Lyons (where the "nippies" waited on customers) and Kardonah. In Japan, the *kissaten*, which replaces the *chaya*—these were no doubt the first tea shops—imitated the model of the European café to the point of excluding from its menu the green tea that was drunk everywhere else, even though its name designated it as a "shop for tea [*sa*]." Before this, at the moment of the massive urbanization of Edo, Osaka, and Kyoto, the *chaya* were specialized as houses of "water," "restaurant," "erotic," "theatre" and "sumo." In France, the *salon de thé* seems close to the German or Austrian *kaffeehaus*, a place in which it has become customary to take cakes, in a more relaxed atmosphere, while it is also symmetrically comparable to the Japanese *kissaten*, its outlines being drawn clearly in opposition to the omnipresent bar-café: this contrastive definition has individualized it to such an extent that that the title *salon de thé* is posted on any window—café-bar, brasserie, ice cream shop, fast-food restaurant, cafeteria, hotel—as a necessary, but

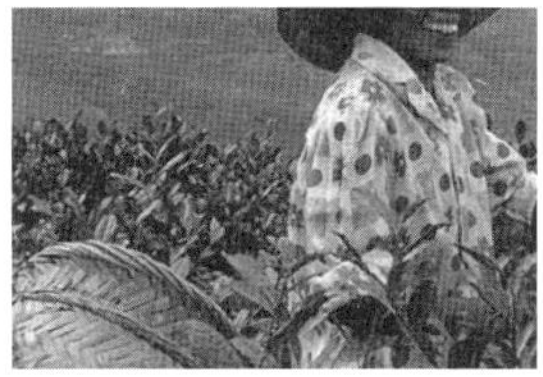

superfluous addition. Does this insistent mention on the front of the shop indicate some vague aristocratic prestige, does it imply a use for the tables, next to the counter, other than at meal times, or is it an attempt to attract senior citizens?

Tea House

In Taipei today, prostitution is officially prohibited, but has curiously come to disguise itself beneath a less reprehensible activity, the sale of *pin lang*, the betel nut. Along the strips, those repetitive bypass roads that run backwards and forwards across the Taiwanese metropolis, neon fans or rows of beacons confirm that the seller of the most common stimulant in Asia, seated on her stool or in her glass booth, may offer you still more complete stimulation. So, after the vine and the tea plant, a third green leaf has been plucked to take the place of the legendary fig leaf. In the north of Thailand one still meets with the Chinese custom of eating or chewing tea, which is like betel: *mi-en* consists in taking a tea leaf—of the woodland indonesia variety whose great crumpled limb is fermented in a tank—folding it around some salt or sugar and chewing it after a meal or while smoking a cigarette. While betel, henceforth more often associated with sodium monoglutamate than with lime to reinforce its taste and its effects, indicates the shop where bodies are for sale, tea has found another pleasure house. Indeed, in order to escape from the congested, stifling and humid megalopolis, the Taiwanese go at the weekend or in the evening after work to a new type of tea house which has recently sprung up; on some of the mountains sporadically colonized by suburban condominiums (Nankang, Mucha, Yang and Ming), dozens of terraces overlooking some tea gardens offer the reconstructed atmosphere of a time that will never return. A little to the north, one village even witnessed in less than a decade the appearance of souvenir stands, markets for culinary specialties and completely reconstructed tea houses, after the director Hou Hsia Hsien chose it as the location for a nostalgic movie. In fact, these places are created with the help of antiques, chinoiseries or japaneseries, like cinema sets. In these rather glitzy places, one can appreciate the imagination of the landlords—pools, winter gardens, screens, private rooms, free flying birds, fish, musicians, mahjong, calligraphies—while paying a high price for the escape from work and tasting teas that do not entirely deserve the compunction that tourists devote to them to appear amateurs. In Shanghai, Beijing and Canton, slightly less elaborate, but equally touristy tea houses have been—not reconstructed, since the original site was entirely abandoned—but entirely recreated, as though their space was not the stage, but the set of a theatre that was played out in the stalls. Indeed, even though, recalling past times, musical or acrobatic displays are put on, it is the consumers of tea who are the real spectacle: is not the first such establishment in Peking called Lao Che, after the author of the play *The Tea House?*

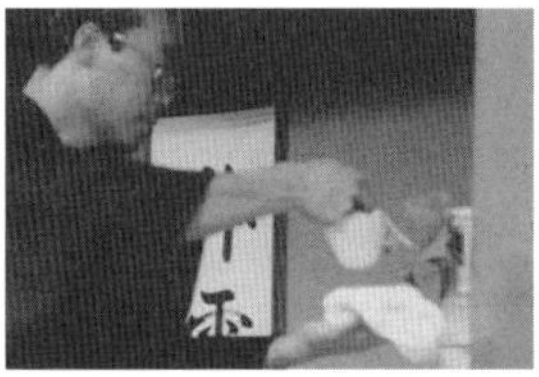

Tea Gardens

The word "tea" in a Chinese, Japanese or English dictionary is readily linked to make some new idea or designate some hitherto unknown object—the British "tea things" is surely the indispensable discovery in the field—or to modify the import of some common term. Thus, "garden" is three times associated with "tea" to indicate very different items. Tea gardens, in China and Taiwan, in India and Sri Lanka, in Japan and Vietnam, are a particular species of space. They are places where tea plants are grown. Though the most recent developments after its introduction in Africa, South America or Australia, have been carried out by intensive agricultural methods coupled with CTC treatment, in its traditional home countries, tea is a garden plant. Because of the upkeep it requires, the hand picking which is so uneconomical, and the contingency of its relations to the soil and to neighboring plants, the tea plant does not take to the open field. In Taiwan, without sparing himself, a planter can maintain a minute holding with a yield of not more than three kilograms. In Fujian and Guangdong, the "garden" might be reduced to a single tree. Another manner of understanding the term "tea garden" was that of the English pleasure garden: Vauxhall, Edgware, Ranelagh, Cuper's Garden, Marylebone, Hampstead (White Conduit Tea Garden). While only men frequented coffee houses, where tea was served with other black drinks, families of all classes crowded to these gardens. They were patronized by the royal family, and opened three days a week, from April to September. The entry price for the garden often included tea, bread and butter. Every kind of entertainment took place here: concerts, horse races, promenades, boat trips, illuminations, bets, games of bowls, ballrooms with orchestras, masked carnivals and fireworks. "Tea and wine, / Here you may have, and also dine. / But as you through the garden rove / Beware, fond youths, the darts of love." Similar gardens, using the London names, were opened in New York. In Japan, the first to use the term, the tea garden—*chaniwa*—is the minute leftover space surrounding the tea hut, which is discreetly enfolded in the urban space and of which the central axis—serpentine rather than rectilinear—is the "dew path"—*roji.* At the same time forming part of an historical development of Japanese gardens—paradise gardens around a pond, stone and moss gardens, walking gardens—the tea garden is a very precise yet paradoxical version of these, since the idea behind it produced an image the opposite of the one usually attributed to it: this Zen garden is not a dry *karesansui* landscape, but on the contrary has the deep, humid, green atmosphere of a mountain forest. The English tea garden, arising from the picturesque tradition, is a particular instance of landscape gardening that simulates nature in the center of town by reproducing the undulations of the natural forest and wooded countryside. The Japanese tea garden brings together the whole experience of Chinese Taoist miniature gardens, of "trees on a pedestal"—*bonsai*—and "jar gardens" which appeared on the patios of raised-up houses. At

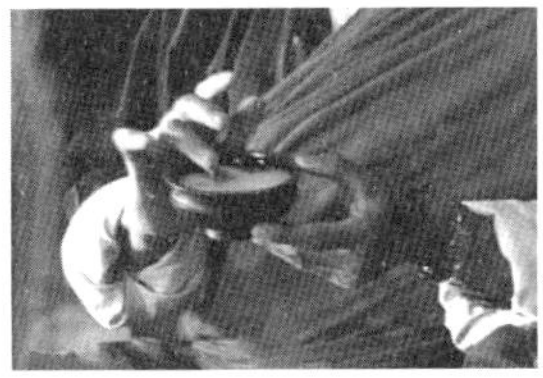

one and the same time, this garden appears the most wild and most artificial of Japanese landscapes—it is a décor with strict, written rules: flowers are avoided, as is any symmetry; the positions of the stones are all laid down and their wet appearance is displayed; the leaves fallen from the tree are selected; and certain species, such as the tea plant, are forbidden.

The *tchaïkana*, the tea house in Afghanistan, is often set up in the open air, and attracts craft workers, camel drivers and chauffeurs. In the Turkish and Arab traditions, the gardens of great palaces—*saray,* or seraglio—had a little wooden building called a *kieushk*: "These kiosks are quite appropriate to sustain the dreamy mood of the Turks: they settle down inside them on a sofa or platform with a pipe of tobacco and some *fingan* or cups of coffee and remain there sometimes for two or three hours in company..." (Grelot, *Relation nouvelle d'un voyage de Constantinople*) In the eighteenth century, German gardens would include a Chinese pagoda, a rococo reinterpretation of the pavilions around which the Chinese art of landscape was articulated, as well as those constructed by retired emperors in Japan to observe the full moon or enjoy a tea tournament. In China, the tea house is like a summerhouse; and it has been preserved as a holiday home. In the province of Sichuan, around Chengdu, tea houses are built near springs, ponds or streams. In the mountains of Yang Ming, north of Taipei, rustic tea houses, with the drink, become restaurants for citizens who come here after work to bathe in the warm water springs. The tea house is broken down into a group of kiosks, pavilions or belvederes scattered around an aquatic garden. In old Shanghai, the "pagoda in the middle of the lake"—*Hu Xing Ting*—is in the midst of the flowered and scented Yu Yuan garden; one reaches it across a swaying bridge which zigzags above a large pond. Along the river of Hangzhou or near Lake Xihou, the tea houses are barely protected by bamboo fences.

Fountains and hothouse plants make up the décor of the most elaborate houses in Taipei; but the gardens and lakes of the new tea houses are, in point of fact, video games, karaoke telescreens and the screens of cybernauts.

Outlets, Outpourings, Outset

According to Joris-Karl Huysmans, "certain beverages have this peculiarity: that they lose their taste, their *raison d'être*, when they are drunk anywhere except in a café... Such are apéritifs." The European bourgeoisie discovered exotic beverages in public places, most of all cafés; they would not penetrate the domestic sphere until several decades later. The aristocracy had encountered them in that place somewhere between private and public that is the royal court, where etiquette, fashion and society govern relationships and trivial pursuits. When they became the drinks of breakfast and the afternoon, tea, coffee and chocolate were no longer the emblem of public life, business and the arts, but marks of domestic comfort. Coffee, in

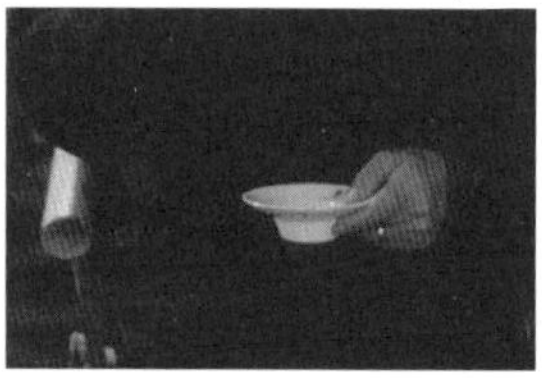

particular—in the outlet of its outset where it encouraged outpourings of ideas—"acted as an energetic instrument of change that created a new reality. When it reached the bourgeois household..., it became passive, suggesting something idyllic." Wolfgang Schivelbusch points out that this movement affects the history of inventions, in which a heroic phase precedes a conformist one: the coffee-place before the coffee-drink, railways before motor cars, cinema before television. "Each time the nature of things recedes." This reduction is made possible by technical and administrative elements—the brand of coffee, the road network, the television channel—which are more or less visible, though their size greatly exceeds the infrastructure of the outset.

Urbanity, Leisure, Hospitality

The present-day outlet—café, bar or *tabac*—finds it hard to maintain its function of urbanity. The efficiency and low cost of the toxic substances consumed there persist, but the city itself has changed in shape. The expression "Café du Commerce" describes, with its pleonasm, the general sociability which took place there and from which emerged a whole civilization and an art (Daniel Defoe, Laurence Sterne, Denis Diderot): meeting, negotiation, conversation. In the seventeenth century, the Iranian Qazvani noted that the café was a place for encounters, conversation and leisure. The proclamation of King Charles II in 1675 ordering the closure of these new places in which coffee, chocolate, sorbets or tea were consumed and where "numerous false, malicious and scandalous rumors are born" made it clear who was being attacked: idlers and malcontents. In 1822, William Cobbett claimed that the habit of drinking tea makes the organism feeble, unsuited for hard work or bad weather, and that it resulted in "all the characteristics of idleness." The drinking-place, as well as being a threat to the public order (delinquency, dissidence and decadence), opens a space for time. In the hierarchical societies of the Turkish and Arab world, the poles of public and religious life—mosque, madrasa, palace, fortress, hammam, bazaar—were all strongly controlled; cafés and tea houses represented intermediate spaces: both the use of time and the occupation of the space were freed. One was liberated from daily constraints: inadequate housing, urban congestion, family hierarchies, social obligations, religious duties and customs. The café is an interval, a space, an outlet, which is exhibited in its architectural plasticity, the terrace. This overflowing into the street or a patio marks the interpenetration of activities in the café, where one relaxes while doing business, where one takes refuge as well as showing oneself in public, where life becomes concrete as much as being a spectacle that one observes in silence. In Istanbul, in the district of Takhtacalah in 1554, where cafés appeared, rich people, janissaries on furlough or social outcasts could "be entertained and enjoy themselves at little cost." Drink, smoke, play, talk, exchange information, read. A supplement to the everyday. Thus

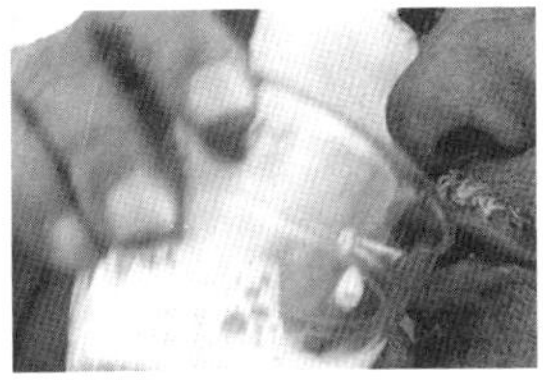

the breach created by coffee as drink in the time of Sufi prayer was extended to the coffee house as place. The same breach is to be found in the tea of lamas in Tibet or Sikkim: the hot drink is the only exception in a life where the invocative litany is not only vocalized, but walked, printed and turned—the (the 3 or 108) turns round the monastery by pilgrims, printed sutras and prayer wheels. Tea with butter, before it is consumed, may interrupt the religious address through a little ritual gesture that every bonze or the lama carries out: he dips the middle finger of his right hand in the liquid and spreads it around him in a gesture of blessing. This gesture is, as it were, magnified in Mongolia, where at the start of the day, before drinking, people throw a ladle of tea across the threshold of the yurt.

Coffee is not a foodstuff, but it does revivify the physical body and the body of the community: the austere equivalent of the festive banquets in a secular context. A liquid, bitter and burning stimulant, it allows one to proceed to another time, as do wine, tobacco or the powerful hallucinogens of South America. Cafés from the Near East or Europe, in all their avatars, have accommodated these stimulants, or even drugs, and extended another time outside religious rituals. An "empty" time (in Turkish: *bos vakit*; in Arabic, *faraj* or *fadaya*; in Persian, *vakt âzâd*), free time, dead time. Which may be taken literally: in 1810, in the Rue de la Corderie, near the Temple in Paris, a man called Montier took on board the effects of alcohol without the heroism of its bouts of intoxication: "This friendly poisoner had set up a special room for drunkards in the back of his shop; there was straw to serve as a bed, the stone floor as a pillow. This room was called The Morgue." (Charles Virmaître) The place must have resembled some Chinese opium dens, next door to or within the tea house: the tea allowed the smokers to rehydrate themselves. In the Near East, tea also accompanies tobacco or opium; the latter no longer eaten in jam—coffee was also consumed in this way—but smoked, is considered "cold" and counterbalanced by highly sugared tea—"hot." Thus tea plays a complementary role in these spaces. It is distinguished from its companions on the menu: the time of the chocolate drink is almost exclusively attached to breaktime, breakfast and childhood; the time of coffee is not determined by the moment in the day, but is reduced to a pause—in French, *pause-café*—and a resumption of work; only the time of tea has preserved a space for idleness, "empty" time, time for doing nothing. In tea-growing regions, Sichuan or Nantou, tea terraces—*cha kuan, lao ren cha*—are still occupied by people who no longer have any occupation: the old, the elders, the retired. Though it was possible, as in Western cafés, to spend whole days in the tea house, for more or less imperative reasons, possibly sustained by attractions at the expense of the establishment, these ultimate amateurs no longer supply an alibi for the time of tea. Beside the river or the pool, one walks one's caged bird and hangs it from the branches, and one listens to the storyteller among the bamboos, a tradition linked

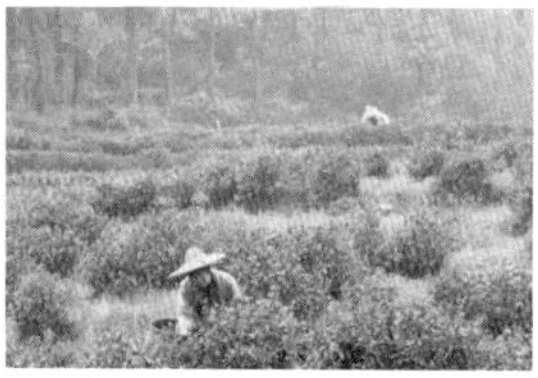

to the time of tea, since it is called *shu cha*—the " book tea." One can play cards or get news of friends, but most of all one wastes time, passes time, kills time. Here, too, tea gives rhythm to life, infuses it; it is the *xian cha*, "the tea of the time when one does nothing."

"After drinking what she [the old lady] served us, Sing-Hoo, turning to one of the porters, asked what we owed. The man replied: "one sapec (half a cent) per cup; tea is not expensive in this country." We counted out the money and offered it to the old lady. She refused, telling us that her house was not a shop where they served tea, and that if it ever were to become one, which would probably not be soon, then she could take our money. That was the first time I ever saw a Chinese refuse money." (Robert Fortune) In China, the tea house was the only place where one paid for tea, which is also why its sign soon came to indicate a place for rendez-vous. In England, tea bars have appeared recently, like chains of teashops at the end of the nineteenth century, while tearooms are rare in the provinces and reserved for the halls of some large hotels. In present-day Japan, the few remaining *kissaten* serve only imported foreign drinks, while only a few traditional patisseries add tables to their sales counter to make a salon. In its three empires, tea is served to guests in the home, in the office and behind office counters, but the public places for consuming it were only a period in its history. The tea house has only taken on a new life in countries, like France, where the drink has remained exceptional or, like Taiwan, where its tradition is recent and complex: the culture of tea, if it forms part of continental history, has taken advantage as much of English fashion and trade as of Japanese esthetics and techniques. And so, at the present time, countries where tea necessitates a house are those in which the drink is not essential to hospitality. As at the time of the first cafés, these houses insist on the thing being consumed and surround it with an esthetic—the tasting of great vintages—or a technique—*gongfucha*. Elsewhere, from the Near to the Far via the Middle East, tea is the first sign of hospitality: it is offered to the new arrival, whether an intimate or a stranger—an exchange that is drunk. For the Tuareg, the Tibetan and the nomad, it is the first thing prepared: it allows one to set up house, to warm oneself in front of the hearth and boiling water—fire and place that are drunk. For the Chinese, the Japanese, and the English it is the permanent social binder between people, between one and the place where one happens to be—word and link that are drunk. In the course of the *chanoyu*, the same bowl of thick tea, the *koicha*, is shared by three people—circulating like the *bombilla* of maté or the pipe of Indian tobacco. A Chinese word, *chashui*, associates water—as *shanshui* does the landscape or *fengshui*, geomancy—to tea: a sort of pleonasm that indicates "tea," the "hot water" or the "infusion." The term reveals the substances in infusion: not fusion, but diffusion of one in the other. Dissymetrical, the relationship is the first brush of the ipse

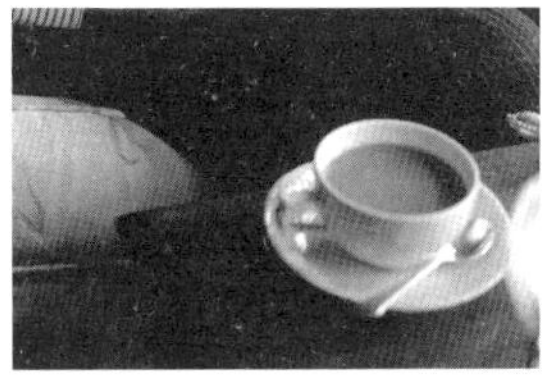

against the other, whether close or foreign. However, among hospitality drinks or infusions, tea occupies a remarkable place: the Chinese leaf does not abuse the hospitality of the water, nor does it act as a parasite, but makes a gift of its subtle presence, by knowing how to step aside and give precedence to its hostess. The infusion of tea, " water tea "—*chashui,* tea, *tee*—thus plays out at the most intimate level of its elementary chemistry the function to which a great part of humanity has dedicated it: welcoming others.

Disappointments, Disgusts, Disasters

Beside the main categories (FOP, GFOP, TGFOP, SFTGFOP, OP, P, FP, PS, S, GFBOP, GBOP, TGBOP, TGFBOP, FBOP, BOP, BP, BPS), to which the number 1 is sometimes added to show their superior quality, the most broken (fannings) and dusty teas are subject to a finer categorization imposed by the logic of industrial refinement by dissociating tea from all its potentialities: Orange Fannings (OF), Broken Orange Pekoe Fannings (BOPF), Pekoe Fannings (PF), Broken Pekoe Fannings (BPF), Pekoe Dust (PD), Red Dust (RD), Fine Dust (FD), Golden Dust (GD), Super Red Dust (SRD), Super Fine Dust (SFD), Broken Mixed Fannings (BMF). Minute discrimination taken to absurdity: what can a tea still signify at the state of "fannings of broken tips," or "powdered tips" or "broken mixed fannings"?
Bree Tannic Tea is sometimes called "Anglo-Indian" tea: the composite word reveals what is irreconcilable: a growth implanted by a nation in a different environment. And, though the import is recent and consumption long remained small in India, the identification continues. This tea, so English or European in its mode and fashion, only grows in India and Ceylon, which are the two greatest world exporters, with an income (from tea) reaching half the GNP in the case of the second of these countries. This tea, made obligatory though there is no local tradition, is no longer controlled by the British market, but preserves traces of it. The tea mania after 1860 moved Nepalese and sub-Himalayan tribes to the gardens of Darjeeling, coolies from Bihar, Chota Nagpur and Benares to the plantations of Assam, and later Tamils to the tea trees of Ceylon. The long journeys, concentration camps, forced labor by an inexperienced workforce, epidemics of malaria, malnutrition and ill-treatment had tragic consequences at the time: a third of these migrants died across India; there were 30,000 dead in Assam alone between 1863 and 1866. At a political level, these migrations, like those started by the Ottomans in the Balkans, had effects that persist a century later: the "violent disturbances" in Bengal, Sri Lanka and Brahmaputra. At an agricultural level, the standardization of production subjects these regions to a risk similar to that whereby Singhalese coffee, once a rival to that of Brazil, entirely disappeared from the island because of the effects of "rust" (*Hemeleia vastatrix*). "White blister" (*Exobasidium vexans*) represents as serious a threat, but to tea plants. There is no lack of other diseases: fungi that attack the

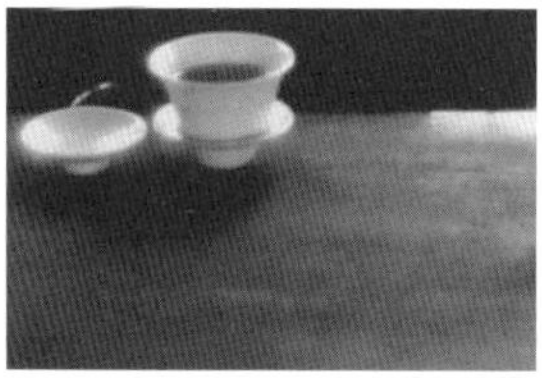

roots (*Armillariella mellea*, agarics, *Rosellinia arcuata, Rosellinia bunodes, Phellinus lamaensis, Leptoporus lignosus, Poria hypolateritia, Ustulina deusta, Sphaerostilbe repens*); leaf parasites (*Colletotrichum camelliae, Pestallozia theae, Corticium invisum, Calonectria theae*); sickness of the branches (*Corticium salmonicolor, Macrophoma theicola, Aglaospora aculeata, Poria hypobrunnea, Nectria theae, Phomopsis theae*); insects on the leaves (*Hopmona coffearia*, urticating caterpillars—*Macroplecta nararia, Parasa lepida, Thosea recta, Narosa conspersa, Scopelodes sp.*—, *Helopeltis sp., Lygus sp.*, aphids, *Toxoptera auranthii,* coccides, *Thrips,* acridians—*Brachytrypes achatinus*); insects on the branches (*Xyleborus fornicatus*, psychides, *Zeuxera coffeae*); termites (neotermes, glyptotermes, coptotermes); burrowing larvae (*Melanagromyza sp.*), white worms (*Holotrichia, Leucophilis, Anomala*), ants, nematodes, acarians (*Oligonichus coffeae, Brevipalpus sp., Calcarus sp., Acaphylla theae, Hemitarsonemus sp.*).

"It was the treat we were told in Yedo: the tea is fresh and very fine ground. A certain quantity is placed in a pot that is stirred with a stick, much like chocolate; after being well stirred it is poured into cups. It must be drunk at once or else the powder would sink to the bottom." In the eighteenth century, the Swedish botanist Charles P. Thunberg described the ceremonial Japanese beverage, as Portuguese Jesuits had already described it and as it can still be drunk today. The powdery fineness of Macha demands that its storage cases should be very tightly sealed, but that its serving containers—the lacquer *natsume* or the ceramic *cha-ire* which reuses Chinese medical flasks—should have a lid—in lacquer or ivory—that is simply placed on top so that the tea does not explode in a fluorescent cloud when opened, which might upset the tea master. This very fine grind, this very intense greenness and this taste close to cocoa are entirely Japanese inventions, but—while other types of consumption preceded it—whipped powdered tea is the oldest "form" of Chinese tea. In the island of Shikoku, Japan preserves a far less well-known method, which allows a less refined glimpse of ancient Chinese preparations: this is *koishicha*, which consists in steaming the tea leaves, fermenting them *en masse* and drying them in the sun in little cubes; this compressed tea will afterwards be broken down to make a broth—*dashi*—in which rice will be put to cook. More or less symmetrical to these two Japanese methods, which break down the Tang preparation described in the *Chajing*, is the Bree Tannic Tea, which has imposed itself on the greater part of world production and combined two successive methods, in this case the treatment of the leaf of beaten tea with the preparation of infused tea. Clearly, it is a matter of accentuating the color and strength, but also of eliminating diversity of flavors. Deciding to do this makes necessary all sorts of instruments for preparing the drink: sieve or strainer (with a handle, English-style with ears, exterior, integrated, movable, in bamboo, metal or nylon), tea ball (with clip, rotating or

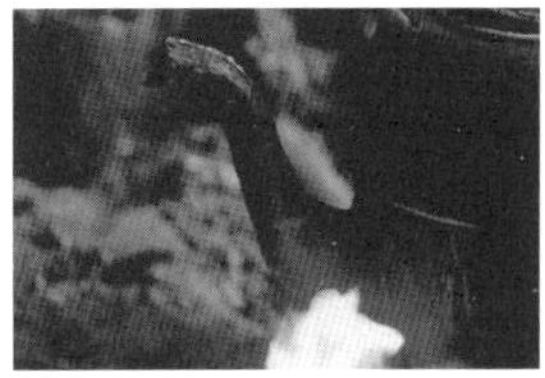

turning hinge, in stainless steel, silver or china), a soft "infuser" or filter (cotton, muslin or paper filter). Indeed, while whole leaf tea demands a filter—apart for the *zhong,* tea-tasting mug with teeth, or certain Japanese variants on these—, this filter, often constructed behind the spout of the teapot, is only a simple arrangement of orifices. The Bree Tannic Teas should be carefully filtered, either confined to an infuser, a receptacle—to which, as though making apologies for it, all sorts of shapes will be given: little house, egg, teapot—or an enclosed filter, which some eighteenth century Yixing teapots already offered a model—more judicious, it is true, since it involved a wide compartment of the same material as the receptacle, instead of those aluminum or PVC sieves which are now placed under the lid. Essentially, this was the achievement, from industrial manufacture to preparation, of a will to apply to the time of tea a very old idea that became a slogan: "to insure promptness." The *tip*—TIP marked on the collecting box at the entrance to coffee houses—is still used to indicate the supplement that the customer slipped into the slot to activate the staff by the sound of a falling coin. The French *pourboire*, the Russian *na tchaï* (literally, "for tea," which also describes a racket, a bribe or the price of silence), and the English "tip" thus allow a sort of paradoxical denial: mechanized harvesting, the result of a society that has tried to reduce the time of tea, ensures that another "tip"—the bud or pekoe—has disappeared. But this enterprise has none the less left its trace in the society that tried to achieve it: like a penance—a ritual—that everyone ought to practice every day at home: teatime. Indeed, TIP was a foretaste of the new economy that was to govern and accelerate the world: the equation between time and money, also known as TIM—"time is money"—while the East India Company, the first of all our world companies, will have led to another equation, TIM: "tea is money." Resistance in the very country that dragged the world into this race, emerged as a third term of the preceding equations: TIT: "tea is time."

Tea Testing & Taste-Vin

The general analysis of tea corresponds to that of wine: an examination of the color, the nose and in the mouth. The prescribed method, identical with that of coffee, consists in taking a little tea—always with milk added—in a spoon, swilling it around in one's mouth and immediately spitting it out. In a single session, as many as three hundred teas may be tasted, comparing the three successive states of infusion: the loose tea, the liquid from the infusion and the infused leaves. The toothed mugs with lids have been poured into a cup without a handle, between the small dish of dry tea and that of wet tea. The eye takes in the basic color of the infusion, that of the mass, that of the disk (its contact with the wall of the cup), and the nuance of colors, as well as brightness, intensity, limpidity or turbidity, viscosity or lightness—just as a wine taster will note *larmes, jambe* or *cuisse* in the glass.

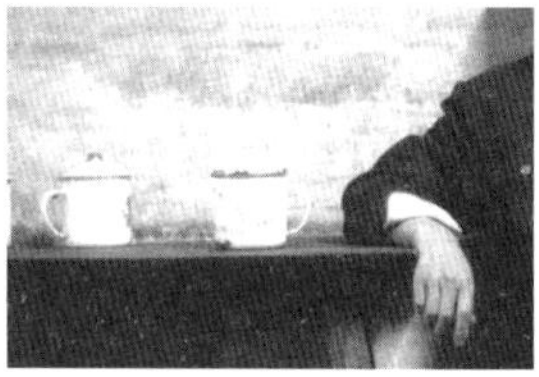

Compared with that of wine, the visual analysis is divided into three successive stages, here laid out along an axis perpendicular to the "horizontal" tasting—before and after infusion; the work of shaping or rolling, the color of the leaves, their shape, their brilliance or their "frosted" look, the uniformity of the picking, its season, the type of blade, the sharpness of the cut, the thickness of the lamina, the parchment or creased appearance of the vegetable surfaces... By contrast, in a tasting by a master or expert from one of the great Chinese or Taiwanese gardens, tea shows the same triplicity of olfactory appreciation as wine: the "smelling cup"—full, hardly tipped or emptied some time previously—allows an appreciation equivalent to the three "nose tests" of the wine taster, the first of which, leaving the wine motionless, brings out the most volatile aromas, which depend on the vine; the second, swilling the wine around in the glass, gives information about the winemaking process; while the third, shaking the glass hard and breaking the surface of the wine, brings out the heaviest aromas which develop with keeping. With tea, the order of aromas may be reversed: while a green tea or a Wulong will exhibit their lightest scents above their liquid and only briefly in the first infusion, old teas or roasted teas first of all show their age or treatment, before their nature. Moreover, tasting a single exceptional vintage—not the simple test of an expert trader—will extend over a period of more than three hours, during which the infusions will follow one another to bring out new aromas each time or to transform these scents. It is possible to remain over an empty cup for more than half an hour to follow the development of fragrances and to perceive "notes," even long after the cup has cooled. A heady scent of coconut or pineapple, hitherto imperceptible, may appear after scents of magnolia, lilac or orchid, having itself emerged behind a smell of fresh butter and biscuit. In the mouth, the taste—*papilliae* or buds on the tongue—is always somewhere between the sense of smell—olfactive nasal epithelium and retro-nasal bulb—and the sense of touch—the free extremities of the trigeminal nerve. Similarly, the passage across the tongue, retro-olfaction and the passage down the throat control taste, complexity of aromas and "length" in the mouth. The subtlety of Chinese tea-tasting is no less than that which has developed in enology, to analyze everything that with a wine pertains to the mash or the "sap," everything that depends on somesthetic, kinesthetic or even auditive sensibilities and which forms the stereognostic space: from these characteristics at the limit of taste—astringent, pungent, metallic—of texture—smooth, melting, granular—and of articulatory movements—tender, crunchy, crisp. The three poles of enological tasting (acidity, mellowness, tannic strength) are closely approximated in tea tasting (though acidity must be replaced by vivacity and greenness: what the tea taster calls "pungency"). Attention must be more sustained with tea because tasting it comes into a broad framework that has been divided up by the West, for example

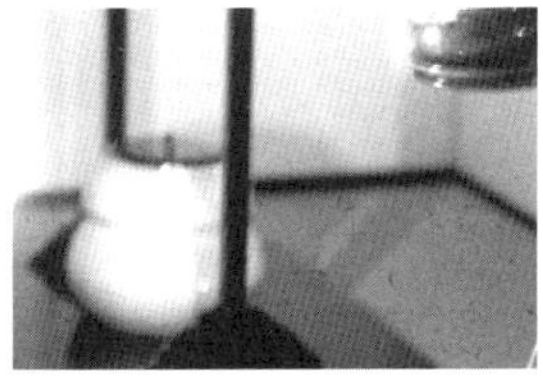

between esthetics and therapeutics. Indeed, beyond the aromatic or structural "length in the mouth"—the "peacock's tail" of old yellow wines—, the "return in the mouth," beyond the "body," the "weft," the "framework" and all the aspects that may describe it—flat, soft, nervous, green, supple, suave, liquorous, heavy, tender, light, lively—one also devotes all one's attention to the effects produced: how a white tea cools or a black tea warms the internal organs, how a green tea stimulates, how a tea can produce saliva. How an old tea can make one "put down the *qi*"—the energy-breath. The way it attacks the tongue, the way it impregnates the mouth—some teas swirl, others vaporize, others melt—and the way it spreads through the body. And, contrary to wine which progressively anesthetizes, because of the alcohol, and contrary to coffee and chocolate which inexorably coat the palate, tea is not subject to the usual paradox, that those who taste can only approximate. While professional tea tasters, like those of wine or coffee, must immediately spit out their tea with milk (which is, in reality, advisable both because of the mainly mediocre qualities that are submitted to them and because of the rather indigestible effects of the mixture), a quality tea can be drunk again and again, admittedly creating a sense of prolonged euphoria, but taking advantage of a property of xanthic bases—caffeine, theophylline, theobromine—which is to enhance the perception of tastes. In the course of a tasting of a great tea, the attention that is brought to bear on the aromas allows increased discrimination but, reinforced by absorption of theine, is sustained by senses that are all the sharper.

The Japanese language very early separated tea amateurs into three degrees: the "tea drinker"—*cha-nomi*—the "tea swallower"—*cha-kurai*—and the "refined tea amateur"—*cha-suki.* One can certainly recognize the first types, but few places make the great tea "vintages" available for tasting. The tea tasting carried out by brokers and mixers is only a tea testing, and the vocabulary established in the West for this assessment shows its deficiencies. Terms to describes the dry leaf: attractive, black, bloom, bold, brown, chesty, chunky, clean, cut, even, flaky, golden tip, grainy, gray (too much sieving or sifting), gritty (CTC leaf, too hard), heavy (leaf well rolled, thick tea), large, light (leaf too open, badly rolled), make (a tea which has "make" is well made), milled, mixed, neat, open (a hardly rolled tea losing its taste qualities), ragged (irregular and coarse), reddish (end of season or CTC clone), shotty, small, stalky, stylish, tippy, twist (whole leaf, well-rolled), uneven, well-made (uniform in color and size), wiry (twisted around the central vein), whiskery. Terms to describe the infused leaf: bright, coppery, dull (tea picked in the rainy season), even, green (first plucking), mixed/uneven (several colors), moldy (badly kept), musty, old, pungent, strong, sweaty (the undesirable taste of a tea that has been kept too long), thin (lack of body, too much wilting or bad fermenting), wild (end of season). Terms describing the liquor: altered, aroma, astringent, autumnal, bakey (too

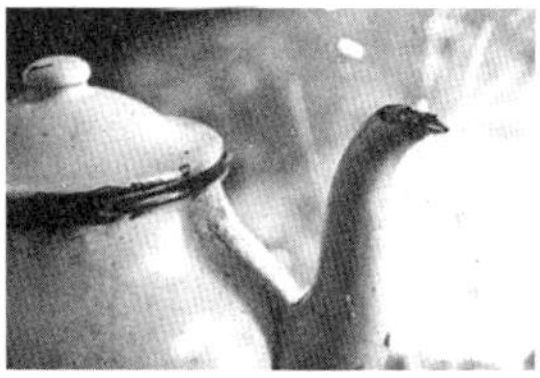

long dried), bitter, body, bright, brisk, burn, burnt, character, chesty (taste of wood, of the packing case), coarse (rough, low grown), colored, creamy (slightly cloudy), dry, dull (without character, monsoon tea), flat, flavory, fresh, full, grassy (too young or insufficiently fermented), harsh (not ripe), malted, plain (opposite of flavory), pungent (a biting but not bitter taste), spicy, strong, sweet, tasty, thick, thin (lacking in body). The vocabulary of this tasting is mainly negative and, while it does include a large number of terms, it is much less rich and metaphorical than that of wine-tasting. Hence it accompanies the industry towards an absence of sense of taste or smell that is destined to be our definitive state of being.

Of Tastes, of Colors, of Scents

Colors of wine: *I.* White wines: clear yellow, straw yellow, greenish yellow, lemon, straw, golden, buttercup, old gold, honey yellow, amber, bronze, copper; *II.* Rosé wines: stained white, peony, raspberry, vermilion, pink, old pink, gray, strawberry, cherry, smoked salmon, onion peel, brick, brown; *III.* Red wines: violet, purple, ruby, cherry, garnet, fawn, orange, brick, tile, rust, mahogany.

Flavors of wine: bitter, sharp, astringent, scented, fermented, heady, plump, well-built, common, complete, full-bodied, smooth, short, colorless, distinguished, hard, balanced, well-rounded, skimpy, fine, fresh, frank, *friant,* fruity, generous, lively (*gouleyant*), ropy, light, *mâche*, thin (*maigre*), mellow, soft, flat, young, powerful, *racé,* rough, color, rounded, dry, supple, silky, region, *tuilé*, worn, velvety, green, lively (*vif*), *vineux* (heady, high in alcohol).

Aromas of wine: vegetable series (grass, box, broom, heather, blackcurrant bud, green pepper, hay, tobacco, mushrooms, undergrowth); floral series (rose, faded rose, dog rose, honeysuckle, lime blossom, verbena, hawthorn, violet, peony, iris, acacia, pink); fruit series: fresh fruits (grape, redcurrant, quince, pear, apple, banana, pineapple, raspberry, strawberry, blackcurrant, blueberry, exotic fruits); dry fruits (prune, almond, walnut, raisin, dried fig, dried apricot); fruit with pits (plum, mirabelle, apricot, mango, peach); citrus (lemon, grapefruit, orange, citron); cooked fruits (compote, jam from the preceding fruits); series of spices and aromatic plants (pepper, liquorice, parsley, chervil, coriander, cinnamon, clove, nutmeg, garlic, onion); empyreumatic series (burned, smoked, soot, tar, coffee, cocoa, toast, tobacco); animal series (leather, fur, musk, fresh meat, venison, game, smoked meat, hare's belly); mineral series (hydrocarbons, gas, naphtha, flint, graphite, chalk); confectionery series (honey, caramel, vanilla, chocolate, fresh butter, milk, yogurt, praline, marzipan, fruit drop, gingerbread); abnormal series (rancid, putrid, madeira, cooked apple, jam, hatched egg).

Aromas Without References

A great number of the aromas used as references for classifying wine, spirits or perfumes, are found among amateurs of outstanding vintages to define tea: muscat,

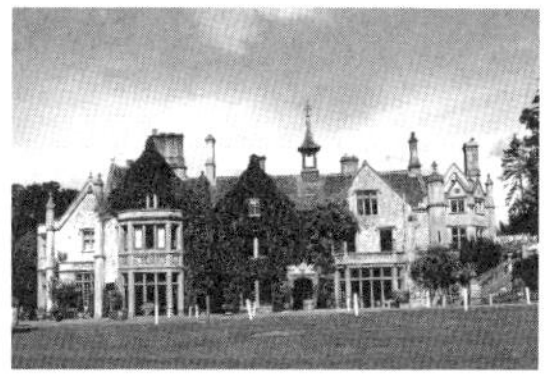

chocolate, white peach, strawberry, woodland berries, grapefruit, dry fruit, cooked fruit, straw, stable, leather, paper, milk, butter, toast, honey, molasses, humus, damp soil, undergrowth. Other tea scents may be added to the recognized classes for wines: chestnut, grilled chestnut, aniseed, absinthe (wormwood), green olive, beeswax. Just as the colors of the infused tea extend towards the greens—especially in Japanese and Korean teas—and not towards the pinks, purples and violets, so the aromas of tea do not extend far into the mineral or red floral ranges, but on the contrary exhibit series that are little known with wine, where references are often lacking: those of white flowers (lilac, jasmine, magnolia, osmanthus, orchid, lily, lotus, camellia, lily of the valley), exotic fruit (pineapple, lychee, coconut, passion fruit, custard-apple, arbutus), and oriental woods (aloe, sandalwood, cinnamon tree, young camphor, old camphor).

A chemical analysis of the components of tea has discovered many vitamins (C, B1, B2, B3, B5, B11, E, A, U), twenty-seven minerals (phosphorus, potassium, sulfur, magnesium, manganese, fluoride—the highest concentration in any plant—aluminum, calcium, sodium, iron, arsenic, copper, nickel, silicium, zinc, boron, molybdenum, lead, cadmium, cobalt, selenium, bromine, iodine, chrome, titanium, cesium, vanadium), and nearly six hundred volatile substances (alcohols, aldehydes, ketones, acids, esters, lactones, phenols, furans, thiophenes, pyrrholes, pyridines, pyrazins, hydrocarbons, amines, nitrogenous compounds and sulfuric compounds), the synthesis of which is produced in the course of enzymatic oxidization and the combinations of which produce all the nuances of scent and aroma. The glucides and sopicides are responsible, respectively, for the sensations of sweetness and freshness, especially in green teas, the experience of which has few equivalents in wine or coffee. In 1988, a Japanese biochemist succeeded in extracting from a top quality Wulong a chemical compound with a scent of jasmine four times as powerful as that extracted from jasmine flowers.

The description of tastes is limited, possessing only a few specific words, which are those that the analysis of the chemical senses (smell and taste) locates in different areas on the tongue: salty, sweet, bitter, acid, our four basic flavors to which the Chinese add astringency, and even the gummy and spicy—while in the West these three qualities are connected with somesthesia. As we know, many flavors fall outside the four basic ones: what is the taste of onion? Is liquorice sweet or salty? In China, a sweetness that is not sugary, often present in black teas of Pu Er type, is called *kan*, which describes the flavor of liquorice. The Japanese add *umami* (*wei jing* in Chinese) to Western flavors; the chemical formula is sodium monoglutamate and its over-use as a flavor enhancer and texturizer, is responsible for CRS—the "Chinese Restaurant Syndrome"; this very specific taste, which appears in celery, olives, tomato, parmesan and anchovy, is sometimes added to certain Japanese

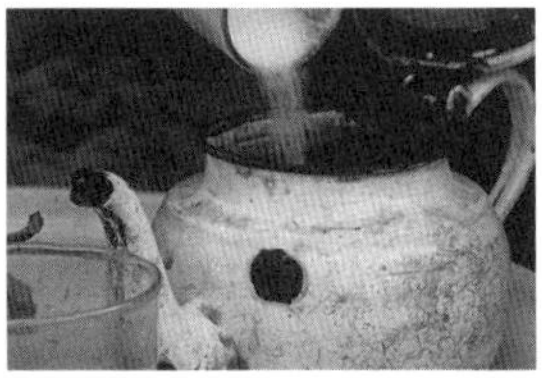

green teas, in cans, and even to some Taiwanese Wulongs to give a sweet aftertaste behind the "greenness." Roland Barthes wrote that "the scent of violet or the taste of tea, both apparently so special, so inimitable, so indescribable, are broken down into a few elements and subtly combined to produce the whole identity of the substance." In perfumery or gastronomy one does however posit certain aromas as references, like blank words that allow one to define others: such indeed are the smell of violet, the taste of liquorice, the smell and savor of hazelnut—the last being necessary to characterize bread, avocado or olive oil. The Bi Luo Chun, for instance, contains such a note of grilled hazelnut. The vocabulary of smell is even more summary than that of taste: no word belongs to it "in itself," it is entirely metaphorical, utterly caught up in a game of references. The aromatic lists that used for wine and the equivalents of which are found in the language of tea masters, may at first sight appear to be of the same order as chromatic scales of colors or musical notes, but with this difference, that they consist entirely of references to other odors. It appears somewhat like a dictionary in which all definitions were reduced to another word; or rather like a dictionary of synonyms; it would be useless to look in it for the slightest definition, there are only equivalents. In the minute cilia of the pseudostratified epithelium, the three types of cell—receptor, basal and support—allow the odiferous molecules to be caught as they arrive in solution in the mucus through thermal agitation. At the level of the taste buds, the proteins of microvillosities recognize the molecules linked to the central atom of the complex. In the nasal cavity and on the mucus of the mouth, perception takes place in three stages: reception by the papillae, transduction of the chemical signals into hyperlow electric and action potential, and coding into a "sensory image" of the same type as those of sight or hearing. Taste and smell are however distinguished by peripheral cells which are renewed every three months—which raises the question of the consistency of their receptive qualities, especially for senses which are not subject to aging. Distributed in a random manner and individually quite crude, the cells of the systems for taste and smell constitute an expert system that is shaped through life and possesses a memory: learning by analogy, contingency and classification. In this sense, the language of perfumes precisely interprets the bank of data and the interplay of correspondence or evocation through which biochemistry articulates them. When amateurs of Wulong pause over their smelling cup or their drinking cup, when a rare vintage extends beyond a dozen infusions, when the centered intoxication of tea intensifies, a tasting can open the way to endless exploration of these correspondences. This world, unfolding the phylogenetic virtualities of a sense of smell that, in a maritime environment, was limited to the duality of one signal for food and another—fecal—for danger, is crucial. It keeps us distanced from an economy that reduces our relationship to the world by regulating it in three

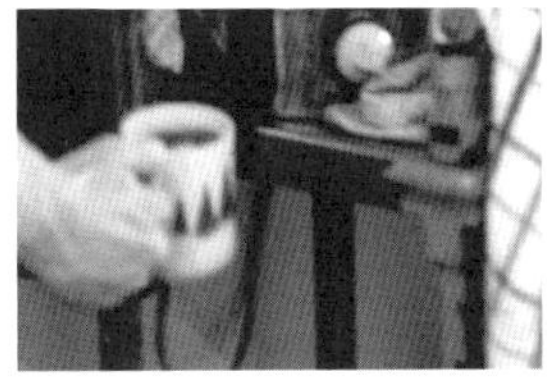

positions: *I.* Natural aromas and aromatic substances; *II.* Aromatic substances identical to natural ones; *III.* Artificial aromatic substances. This world which does not know the objectivity of musical language or the exposition of color theories, is carried by the art of *gongfucha* which, with that of enologists or "noses" in perfumery, attempts to base a body of knowledge on an experience that is usually not shared—and whose emotion Proust conveyed.

Tea Words

"*Cha*" is found in many everyday Chinese and Japanese phrases, from which tea is absent as such. When flirting one always suggests going to "drink tea." Okakura recalls that "having too much tea" or "lacking in tea," in Japanese, indicate a lively or indifferent temperament. Most restaurants and a great number of beverages or liquid medicines include the character for "tea." It also survives in some rites of passage: *chi cha*, which literally means "eating tea," is a phrase denoting an engagement to be married, where tea is one of the presents to mark fidelity—since a good tea plant does not leave its place of growth. Gifts which cannot be taken or given back are called *cha li* and gifts in kind *cha jin*. In Mongolia and Turkey, the moment of an engagement is also that in which the future bride's ability to prepare tea is tested: *demlikaçay.* In China, in the province of Sichuan, *cha jian cha* consists in settling a business or family quarrel amicably at a tea house through the intercession of the proprietor. The term indicates the "general round" by which a calmly reached arrangement should conclude, to be paid for by the person who has been acknowledged as being at fault.

After bringing the *chawan*, the tea bowl that the host has prepared, the guest at the Japanese tea encounter sits down, places the recipient between himself and the chief guest and says: "*Oshôban itashimasu*" ("I am going to join you"); then he places it between himself and the next guest, bows and says: "*Osaki ni chôdai itashimasu*" ("Forgive me for coming before you"); and finally he places it in front of himself, bows and says to the host: *"Otemae chôdai itashimasu"* ("Thank you for the tea"). After these three addresses, he can finally drink the tea, down to the last drop, which he will conclude in proof of it with a final audible intake of breath. These words of tea sum up the whole of what is involved, the whole ritual, as the final expression makes clear: the master of tea is thanked not for the tea, which does not appear here, but for the *o-temae*, that is to say for the "procedure," the "ceremonial," the "carrying out" of tea.

Words of Tea

"One can forgive a murder, but a breach of etiquette over tea—never." (Chinese proverb). During both English and Japanese tea meetings, it is expressly recommended that conversation should be kept "light," though without being gossipy or frivolous. What should be avoided are political, religious or business matters—

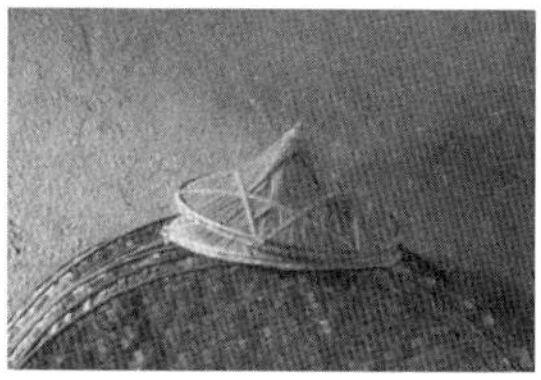

even though these were for a long time the main topic of conversation in coffeehouses and in the gentlemen's clubs that succeeded them. In the same way, in Japan, from the advisors, or *dôbôshû*—Noâmi, Geiami, Sôami—ancestors of the way of tea, down to the great masters who drew up the rules for it—Sen no Rikyû, Furita Oribe, Kobôri Enshû—all, sometimes at the risk of their lives, played a role in the service of retired princes or warlords. In Japan from the fifteenth century onwards and in the eighteenth century in England, politics—especially democracy—revolved around tea. The "voluntary" suicides—*seppuku*—of Rikyû and Oribe, as well as the transformation of the port of Boston into a teapot, may have marked the climax of this. However, English essays on etiquette and the rules for the Japanese matter—increasingly addressed to women—are very explicit in defining topics of conversation: public affairs and intimate private matters must be avoided. No sociology or psychology. Meteorology—the weather—the occasion for the meeting and the season—passing time—and the scene, with its objects that the guests are sharing—the time of tea—are the three favored themes for discussion. The aim is to achieve a kind of indifference.

Color-Odor-Savor

The history behind our hierarchy of the senses has been as little described as it is well-established: sight, hearing, smell, taste, and touch are favored in that descending order, as language—few escape it—constantly confirms by the metonyms that it weaves (theory, speculation, reflection), or—by contrast—by the gaps that it leaves (the poverty of vocabulary with respect to scents or savors). In a tasting by Chinese connoisseurs—as is also the case in a tea tasting by experts at the time of an auction—what arrives is decomposed in an order that can not really be reversed: the color of the dry leaves, then the color of their infusion, the scents of the liquor, then its taste; and, the subject of no less close attention, its consistency. In *gongfucha*, the utensils, especially the scenting cup, have been designed to follow the infusion along the course of its duration, while allowing for periods of pause and a sharing of coenesthesia. This is the experiment by which value is ascribed, along a scale between taste and distaste.

Sound of Tea

It is surely not surprising that the sense which does not appear in the rules of tea tasting is the one which all Chinese poetry and all the literature attached to the Japanese tea ceremony make the inevitably underlined aspect of tea: its sound. The rubbing of tea being broken (see above, Li Yi Chan), but also the ritualization of certain sounds of *chanoyu*: the "snap" of the cleaning towel as it is offered, the "click" of the bamboo spoon on the bowl, the forced breath at the end of drinking the Macha—but above all the hissing or rumbling of the kettle. The shape of the samovar is even "designed so that the water, as it boils, will rumble in the space

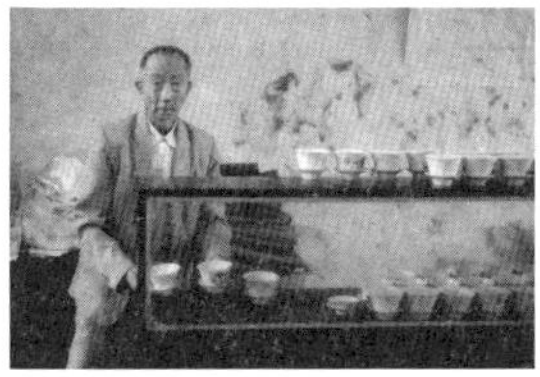

between the level of water and the top of the lid" (S. Yi), marking the three stages of boiling: firstly, it "sings," then it "sounds," and finally it "roars like a tempest." In fact, a metaphor, taken from Chinese literature, was settled on by the Japanese as the catachresis of the drink: the kettle hisses "like the wind in the pine trees."

In French, *gargote* designates a place where poor food is served and comes from *gargoter*, which described the sound of boiling. Levi-Strauss pointed out the incompatibility between cooking and noise—"noise," from *nausea* shows the traces of this: "The mediating action of the cooking fire between the sun (sky, heaven) and earth demands silence." When tea is taken in Sikkim and Tibet, the churning instrument is operated in the kitchen so that its violence and its noise are logically confined there, while women and junior monks will take a large pourer to serve the tea. On the contrary, among the Tuaregs, in Taiwan and Japan, the tea is prepared in front of the guests and the sounds of tea play a part: purring of the kettle, extended pouring from a height, little clinks on the table or the cups to express thanks. However, all these sounds are as it were specified, staged, and "cut out." They are surrounded by a halo of silence; or, rather, these sounds are there to highlight the silence. Much as the words of tea point to the suspension of meaning and the taste of tea to the taste of water.

"One drinks tea to forget the noise of the world." (Tien Yiheng)

TEA, ALL & NOTHING

The Times of Tea

Tea gives time; tea is only taken when one takes time; time is indicated by tea; tea quenches the thirst that recalls time; time passes while drinking tea; tea is time that is drunk.

Considering tea in its three empires, time must be variable: *I.* The time of tea among the Tannic Brits, is the time of tea served; *II.* The time of Narrow Tea is the time of the circumstance; *III.* The time of Middle Tea is the tea of time.

The time of tea is the time for tea. The time of tea is the meteorology of tea. The time of tea is the process of tea.

Tea Space

Considered in its three regions of Asia, tea extends over various spaces: *I.* Chinese tea is the Middle Kingdom which reorganizes the world around itself: the history of the drink began in China and continues there, apparently doing without elsewhere, or accepting it not as a possible partner in trade, but as an exclusive site of consumption. A tea was manufactured especially for export: compressed bricks for the surrounding nomads, red or smoked tea for more distant foreigners. The Middle Tea is therefore the middle (natural center of growing) of tea; *II.* Japanese tea, the

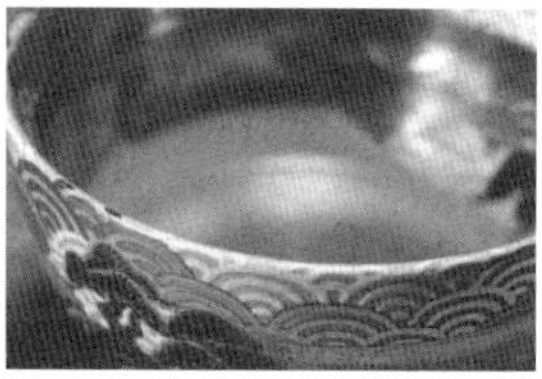

height of formalism, seems to set no limit to etiquette and rules of behavior. The simple act of drinking tea extends through a space that progressively absorbs the slightest aspects, events or things involved in it. Narrow Tea is the ultimate storeroom of the natural in the center of proliferating artificiality; *III.* Taiwanese tea, like Japanese tea, is concentrated in a limited area—Ryôkucha there and Wulong here—but, like Chinese tea, it extends across the spectrum, covering all grades of fermentation. A concentration on a type of tea from China—the semi-fermented teas—allows the accentuation of the power of discrimination: spatial complexity of aromas, extension of taste over time, return of an after-taste, synesthesia, coenesthesis, organoleptic scale. On Wulong Island, culture becomes nature.
From another point of view, the space of Chinese tea is closed in English tea, concentrated in Japanese tea and re-opened in Taiwanese tea.
"Nine is the number of difficulties concerning tea. One: work. Two: selection. Three: implements. Four: fuel. Five: water. Six: roasting. Seven: pulverization. Eight: preparation. Nine: tasting." (*Chajing*, III, 6)

Forms, Rituals, Functions

Three is the number of forms of tea: teatime, *chanoyu, gongfucha*, in other words, respectively, the most trivial, the most formal, the most expert.
Three is the number of rituals around tea: *chanoyu,* teatime, *tchaï*: the most liturgical, the most secular, the most necessary.
Three is the number of functions attributed to tea: *I.* It is a nutritional need, from Morocco to Tibet, via the whole of the Middle East and Central Asia; *II.* It is a cultural product, in the Far East, like wine in Europe, with a world of connoisseurs and experts, with its own esthetics, its hedonism and its demands; *III.* It is a drink, everywhere.

Welcome, Tax, Flow

"They pluck these leaves... using them almost always for drinking, not only at table, but whenever a guest comes to visit a friend. Because as he converses, he is invited to partake of this potion, and again a second and third time, if he should linger only a little." (Matteo Ricci). Among the first visitors, the Jesuits did not fail to appreciate the importance of the time of tea in the East. And even if, in its most expert forms, the Chinese art of tea managed without ceremony, the drink has always been linked to a ritual, not in the sense of a formal set of rules, but in the demand that puts each person under an obligation to the other.
In all civilizations where it has been adopted—from China, six thousand years ago, to Morocco, less than a century ago—: *I.* Tea is always a signifier of welcome, of meeting, of greeting; *II.* Tea is the repository of value: taxes, gift, exchange, one of those commodities like salt, iron or gold, which come to represent the rest; *III.* Tea is the fundamental drink, like water, a hot water enriched—purified, therapeutic, stimulating.

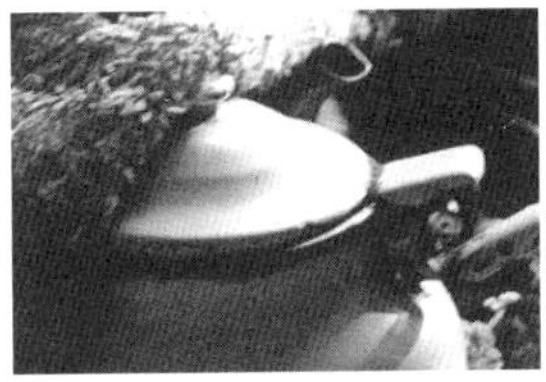

More than a signifier, more than a symbol, tea is the flow itself, the object of circulation, the subtle fluid, at once a full value and an empty one: a general equivalent. It is also in this sense that one must understand the fact which, despite being a statistic, is hard to confirm, yet is recalled at the start of every text devoted to it: after water, and perhaps milk, tea is the most widely consumed drink on the planet.

The Tea of Art

In the decorum of teatime, tea keeps its place as a stimulant and a food, as in Tibetan tea, but its function is detached from its form: mixed with milk and sugar, it could be replaced by coffee, and it remains unaffected by the design of the china or the fashionable intercourse at the moment when it is being consumed. With *chanoyu*, tea has taken on board its function—as an auxiliary to Zen meditation—in a pure form: from being an expedient, it has become the emphasis of concentration, which has not happened without risk to its truth, its meaning and its presence. With *gongfucha*, form and function can be distinguished, but are not separable or confounded or subject one to another. In Chinese tea, pleasure is obtained by circulation, delocalization, the interplay between a matter and its manner. Hence: tea of art.

Tea is Nothing and Everything

"Tea is tea." This was the only reply of the tea master to the questions directed at her. In these "teas," the being returns to a state of Being.

"Tea is nothing." This may be another position for this negative *tea-ology*: tea is nothing outside the circumstance, the rules and the context in which it is consumed. *I.* "Hot water"—a diluted coffee—served in a Western café-bar, is a neutralized, nothingized, gray beverage, without color, odor or taste (Lipton would oddly advertise his tea as: "The perfect tea to suit the water of your town."); *II.* In the course of the Japanese tea matter, the Macha, whose very dense green is covered by a "jade froth," a sort of protection, lightening or crystalline transparency, is an "empty center": the extreme attention devoted to every object, gesture or elaboration remarkably ignores the tea itself—its taste, aroma or vintage—a subject not to be broached; *III.* In the "welcome glass," known throughout the East, the tea is a degree zero of drink, a sort of water, a water that is charmed or scented, the liquid that is to create the bond of hospitality: it is neither neutral or void, but it is the undistinguished basis on which the relation to the other—the *hospis*, which means "guest" as well as "enemy"—becomes possible.

"Tea is everything." In the same movement, this is the kind of *panteaism* that would affect the civilizations—each one an empire—under the empire of tea. *I.* In the United Kingdom—the empire of the Bree Tannic Tea—it is time and money; it was the most importance trade at the height of the colonial days and has remained an emblem of the nation; *II.* In Japan—the empire of Narrow Tea—*chanoyu* is a gathering together, a metonymy and a résumé of all Japanese culture: its ethics—from

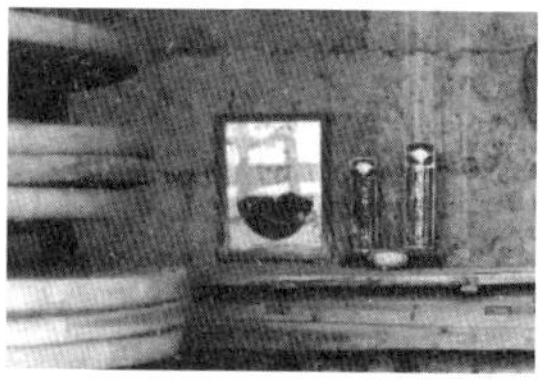

the bearing of the body, *zazen*, to an attitude of reserve—as well as its esthetics—all the arts: ceramics, gardening, architecture...; *III.* In China—the Middle Kingdom—tea is drunk in all its states, following all manners, to inspire all sorts of feelings: the nomad's food, a Taoist medicine, a Buddhist stimulant, a Confucian ritual, a connoisseur's tasting, the drink of each and every one, nine thousand vintages, six colors, originating in most Chinese regions.

Test of Tou

Speaking of tea leads one to speak about sugar (the energy drink), coffee (stimulant, supplement to alcohol, home), chocolate (entertainment, emulsion, froth), wine (drunkenness, vintages, cultivation), spirits (color, spirit, *eau-de-vie*), tobacco (smoke, pipe, time inhaled), tisanes (infused water), betel-qat-coca (green leaves), salt (barter). This diffraction of tea into all kinds of other substances or kinds is not reversible: one may speak of wine, cigarettes or sugar without mentioning the Chinese leaf. Doubtless, the specificity of tea resides in this genericity or totality.
Serving tea opens a space for water (for the infusion), air (in manufacture and tasting), fire (manufacture and preparation), earth (in the serving vessels), iron (contain in the china and in certain utensils) and wood (in the tea and the instruments six elements where the cosmogonies of East and West meet and complement one another.
While *tou* (*du* in pinyin) is the name of the bitter herb, the character for which, with one stroke difference, was the first sign for tea, it remains the "tout" of drink, food and medicine. From the very earliest Chinese collection of medical wisdom, *tou*—tea—is the model of the *pharmakon*: placed in boiling water—the prophylactic of fire—it becomes an infusion, allowing the liquid element to conduct its active substance, through which it remains a toxic/curative.

Empty, Insipid, Diaphanous

"Drinks that one drinks throughout one's life without liking them: tea, whisky. Flat drinks, drinks for effect and not for taste. The search for an ideal drink, which would be very empty in metonymies of every sort." (Roland Barthes) "Tea was a great help to me, for becoming bored in a calm way. Clouds after rain like snails in their grass, the sky." (Jacques Roubaud) "When it passes through our mouth /The Tao is insipid and tasteless: / It cannot be perceived, / It cannot be heard, / But it is inexhaustible." (Laozi)
While wine and tea are comparable because of the methods of cultivation, the techniques and the activities that create them, their modalities in Christianity and Zen Buddhism are very different: wine is symbolically loaded as a substance—and therefore still structures the liturgy; in communion at the center of the mass—while tea is abstracted in its function, it is a conducting body, a fluid, the play in a technique. Neither coffee, nor chocolate, nor alcohol have produced so many rituals

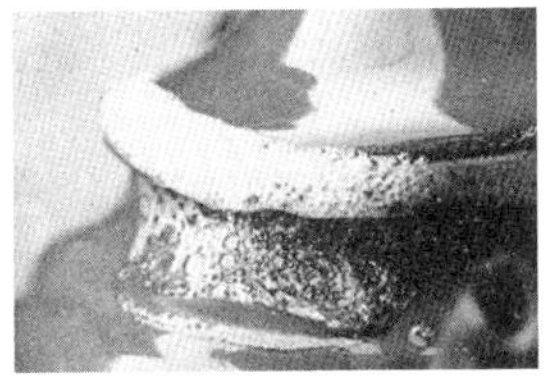

around them and objects to instrument them. Probably because tea does not have their "character," their strongly marked "identity"; hardly more than water, tea is almost nothing. Like a cigarette. In its curling smoke, time is killed and life burned away for the smoker, who is gratified in appropriating the world around him. The sacrificial ritual of the cigarette makes the solid vanish into gas. The smoke is the scattered body of time spent doing nothing. Tea, for its part, is caught up in the cycle of fluids: deep waters, vegetable sap, infused liquor. Its other states are the mist that shrouds its bushes, the steam above the kettle, the cloud in which it will end.

Honoré de Balzac starts his *Traité des excitants modernes* (1838) with the question of the effects and excesses of five substances on the "human economy": 1° spirits; 2° sugar; 3° tea; 4° coffee; 5° tobacco. Only the first and the last two of these have a whole chapter devoted to them. But, in the third part of the introduction, Balzac reports an experiment on human guinea pigs, the truth of which has been "guaranteed… by a scientist and a politician." "The English government allowed three condemned prisoners to have a choice between being hanged according to the usual custom of the country, or living exclusively, one on tea, the other on coffee and the third on chocolate, without adding to this any type of food whatsoever or drinking any other liquids. The poor devils accepted. Perhaps any condemned man would have done the same. As each foodstuff offered more or less chance of life, they chose by drawing lots. The man who lived on chocolate died after eight months. The man who lived on coffee lasted two years. The man who lived on tea did not succumb for three years. I suspect the East India Company of having requested this experiment in the interests of its trade. The chocolate man died in a ghastly state of decay, eaten by worms. His members fell off one by one, like those of the Spanish monarchy. The coffee man died in flames, as though the fire of Gomorrâh had devoured him. He could have been made into lime. This was suggested, but the experiment was considered inimical to the immortality of the soul. The tea man grew thin and almost transparent. He died of consumption, lantern-like: you could see right through his body; a philanthropist was able to read the *Times* by a light placed behind the man's body. English decency did not allow any more original test."

Thus the test of the three substances gives the literal effect of a radical tea-ology: to make, by tea, one's being transparent for the *Times.*

Test of Nothing

In 1905, three writers who did not know one another (*I.* A Japanese returning to his country to replace a foreigner enamoured of the archipelago in a professorship of English; *II.* A Japanese writing a monograph for his country in English; and *III.* A Portuguese, who, like the famous foreigner, would find exile in this country to write) wrote three peculiar small books in which tea shows its taste: "Ordinary

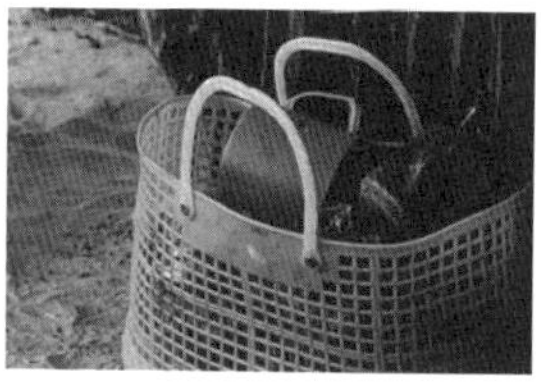

people believe that tea is for drinking, but this is a mistake. When the drop settles on the tip of the tongue and the pure element disperses in every direction, there is practically no liquid that can go down the throat. It is merely a delicious perfume that travels towards the stomach through the oesophagus." (Natsume Sôseki, *Grass on the Wayside*) "There is a subtle charm in the taste of tea that makes it irresistible and suitable to be idealized." (Okakura Kazuko, *The Book of Tea*) "Gyokurô, for example, which is the most highly prized tea of Uji and of all Japan, contains such balsamic subtleties in its savor, that it is more like a perfume; one would think that a marvellous alchemy has managed to liquify the aromas of flowers—garden flowers, woodland flowers—transmuting the pleasure of smell to that of taste." (Wenceslau de Moraes, *O culto da chà*)

From a delicate Yin Zhen, cultivated in a few dozen kilos a year, to a rare Pu Er that has aged for tens of years, via a Gyokuro, tea can extend from one form of vapidity to another. White tea at one extremity, black tea at the other, with dull green tea in the middle, each tends in its own precise manner towards such subtlety of tastes and aromas, that they are recognized by the singularity of their consistency: a certain way of unfolding, melting or vaporizing in the mouth and spreading through the body. To approach such rare teas, which often disappoint at first, is to discover an absence of taste; or, more precisely, the possibility of all tastes. As the sky is the possibility of all images. "Neither asceticism, nor privation, nor negative theology." (François Jullien) A time of detachment.

In coming into being, from its soil and climate, to the cup in which its liquor sums up its essence, tea is water, earth, fire, wood and air. But in its dry state, transformed and conditioned, it is fragile—more so than exotic commodities: it cannot stand humidity or heat or the presence of other aromatic goods. Not a bad companion, but an over-sensitive one. In France, the main distributors of loose tea are coffee roasters or chocolate shops; in either case the product is totally dominated and cannot struggle against the powerful, warm and heady aromas of other black powders. Patisserie and confectionery have long profited by the coffee-cocoa alliance, just as the "little espresso" can easily slip down after a meal between puffs of a cigarette. But the tea house must exclude smokers and the tasting of a great Chinese vintage must be made far from any invasive odor.

Between a Japanese green tea, an Anglo-Indian black tea and a Chinese Wulong, there is little to show in what sense they come from the same plant, still considered as a single variety. What is the taste of tea, whose bush takes its aromas from the depths of the earth, whose treatment creates a synthesis of flavors and whose preparation risks awakening it through an alliance with water and earth?

03.03.99 - 11.08.99 - (01.05.00)

ACKNOWLEDGEMENTS

Bruno Suet — Serge François, Ministère des Affaires étrangères, Catherine Schidlovsky, Jane Pettigrew, Jillie Faraday, Geneviève Sieffert, A. Gouti, Algerian National Tourist Office, Air Algérie, M. Benfarès, Indian National Tourist Office, G. Koujilal, Air India, Sikkim National Tourist Office, Teedy Dorjee Lachungpa, Darjeeling Planters Club, Goodricke Group (Darjeeling and Calcutta), Olivier Rames, Maïté Hangzhou, Katrin Rougeventre, Xiamen Tea Institute.
For Caroline, my parents… To Lila.

Dominique T. Pasqualini — Iwasaki Makoto and all the members of his school, Tseng Yu Hui, the monk Maeda, Doi Hideaki, Yamada Jozan, Fujita Kojiro, Sekiguchi Eriko, Ito Yukiko, Kazuichi Yoshida, Nagahiro Yasumori of the firm Horaido, Toshifumi Simon, Catharina Van Eetvelde. Chika Matsutani, Eric Cez, Fabien Maïolino, Abigail S. Lang.
For my parents, my three brothers… To Abi.

Yves-Marie Marchand — Publimod'Photo, Didier Jumeau-Lafond, the Marval-Vilo Team.
For my mother… To Marie.

FILMSETTING BY SELE OFFSET, TURIN
PRINTED BY GRAFICHE ZANINI, BOLOGNA, MAY 2000

Object Relations Theory and Practice: An Introduction edited by David E. Scharff

Object Relations Couple Therapy by David E. Scharff and Jill Savege Scharff

The Autonomous Self: The Work of John D. Sutherland edited by Jill Savege Scharff

From Instinct to Self, Volumes I & II: Selected Papers of W.R.D. Fairbairn edited by David E. Scharff and Ellinor Fairbairn Birtles

Refinding the Object and Reclaiming the Self by David E. Scharff

Projective and Introjective Identification and the Use of the Therapist's Self by Jill Savege Scharff

Object Relations Family Therapy by David E. Scharff and Jill Savege Scharff